COLD WAR PATRIOT
AND
STATESMAN

Recent Titles in
Contributions in Political Science

The Brazilian Legislature and Political System
Abdo I. Baaklini

Self-Determination in Western Democracies: Aboriginal Politics in a Comparative
Perspective
Guntram F.A. Werther

United States Electoral Systems: Their Impact on Women and Minorities
Wilma Rule and Joseph F. Zimmerman, editors

Comparative Judicial Review and Public Policy
Donald W. Jackson and C. Neal Tate, editors

American Ambassadors in a Troubled World: Interviews with Senior Diplomats
Dayton Mak and Charles Stuart Kennedy

Moving the Earth: Cooperative Federalism and Implementation of the Surface Mining
Act
Uday Desai, editor

Assessing Governmental Performance: An Analytical Framework
Eugene J. Meehan

Principled Diplomacy: Security and Rights in U.S. Foreign Policy
Cathal J. Nolan

Presidential Influence and Environmental Policy
Robert A. Shanley

Professional Developments in Policy Studies
Stuart Nagel

County Governments in an Era of Change
David R. Berman, editor

First World Interest Groups: A Comparative Perspective
Clive S. Thomas

Cold War Patriot
and
Statesman

RICHARD M. NIXON

EDITED BY
Leon Friedman
AND
William F. Levantrosser

Prepared under the auspices of
Hofstra University

Contributions in Political Science,
Number 312

GREENWOOD PRESS
Westport, Connecticut • London

Library of Congress Cataloging-in-Publication Data

Cold war patriot and statesman : Richard M. Nixon / edited by Leon
  Friedman and William F. Levantrosser ; prepared under the auspices
  of Hofstra University
       p.   cm.—(Contributions in political science, ISSN 0147–1066 ;
  no. 312)
    Includes bibliographical references and index.
    ISBN 0–313–28787–2 (alk. paper)
    1. Nixon, Richard M. (Richard Milhous), 1913–   —Congresses.
  2. United States—Politics and government—1969–1974—Congresses.
  3. United States—Foreign relations—1969–1974—Congresses.
  I. Friedman, Leon.   II. Levantrosser, William F.   III. Hofstra
  University.   IV. Series.
  E856.C64   1993
  973.924′092—dc20   92–30011

British Library Cataloguing in Publication Data is available.

Library of Congress Catalog Card Number: 92–30011
ISBN: 0–313–28787–2
ISSN: 0147–1066

First published in 1993

Greenwood Press, 88 Post Road West, Westport, CT 06881
An imprint of Greenwood Publishing Group, Inc.

Printed in the United States of America

The paper used in this book complies with the
Permanent Paper Standard issued by the National
Information Standards Organization (Z39.48–1984).

10 9 8 7 6 5 4 3 2 1

Copyright Acknowledgment

The publisher, editors, and contributors are grateful to the following for granting use of their
material:

Excerpts from *The Palace File* by Nguyen Tien Hung and Jerrold L. Schecter. Copyright © 1986
by Nguyen Tien Hung and Jerrold L. Schecter. Reprinted by permission of HarperCollins
Publishers.

Contents

DISCUSSANTS

Preface

Any attempt to analyze and interpret the presidency of Richard Nixon faces major obstacles at the same time that significant insight may be achieved. In Hofstra University's sixth conference on the modern American presidency held on November 19–21, 1987, we sought to gain greater understanding of the Nixon Presidency through new insight from a conference of scholars, journalists, and administration officials through an exchange of views thirteen years after President Nixon left the White House. Recording these interactions is perhaps the unique contribution this volume of the conference proceedings makes toward gaining a better understanding of the Nixon Presidency.

Richard Nixon may well turn out to be the most influential figure of the second half of the second century of the American government under the Constitution. He pervades so many aspects of the political scene that we may eventually refer to this period as the Nixon era. After three days of intensive discussion in November of 1987, the complex nature of the man and the provocative actions of his tenure as the thirty-seventh president were more clearly evident. At that time, even as during his time in office, discussions of his presidency aroused extremes of reaction ranging from enthusiastic approval to strong antagonism. Our efforts to organize the conference were directed at providing balance in the discussions so that all points of view could be revealed. Your evaluation of this volume will determine how successful we have been in that effort.

This was the first time that a Hofstra presidential conference had focused on the presidency of a man who was still alive. There were some concerns that participants would somehow restrain their views or formulate those views differently, were this not the case. Fortunately, these concerns did not turn out to

be justified. Perhaps Mr. Nixon's presence would have overshadowed a free
exchange of views at the conference, although he would have been welcome,
and we would have been willing to take that chance.

We found that the Nixon persona and the Nixon Presidency meant many things
to many people, all of whom had experienced the same phenomena. Nixon was
both objective and biased. He was vindictive and ruthless, yet gracious. He was
uncomfortable with people but extremely loyal and thoughtful to close friends.
He was involved in the nuts and bolts of the presidency, and yet he was aloof.
He was a man of loftly vision, yet he got caught up in petty intrigue. His
intellectual grasp was perhaps unequaled, but he found it difficult to express
simple emotions. He was a consummate political strategist, but he could self-
destruct by committing clumsy tactical errors. He had a driving ambition, but
he lacked inner tranquility. There are witnesses in this volume to support all
these contentions, but none claims to know the man thoroughly.

In planning the conference, we sought both papers and discussants who would
examine these contrasting impressions. They are either scholars, journalists, or
people who served in the Nixon Administration. We wanted to make the panels
as comprehensive in scope and as extensive in depth as possible in order to
create the optimum environment for the exchange of ideas. In a few instances
we realized that a comfortable time frame would not afford the opportunity to
balance views on one panel, so another panel devoted exclusively to opposing
views was established. When papers were presented, discussants had already
read them; as a result, they were able to evaluate them and add their own
observations. The discussions have been edited to make them compatible with
a written format, but the flow of thought has been preserved as much as possible.
Audiocassettes were made of all panels for distribution to those who desired to
purchase them, and C-Span televised about half the panels nationally.

This volume would not have been possible without the assistance of many
people. We would like to thank all those who prepared papers and those who
served as discussants. A special word of thanks goes to Frank Zarb, Hofstra
alumnus and chairman of the Board of Trustees at the time of the conference,
for his help in recruiting many of the participants who had worked in the Nixon
Administration. We are grateful to James Hastings and his staff at the National
Archives for acquainting us with the documents of the Nixon Presidency and
the researchers using them. We also thank the staff of the Hofstra University
Cultural Center, which is capably directed by Natalie Datlof and Alexej Ugrinsky,
for coordinating many of the details and arrangements of the conference, along
with Athelene A. Collins, Marilyn Seidman, and Laura J. Tringone. We are
especially grateful to Jessica Richter for the various tasks connected with shep-
herding the pages of the manuscript to the publisher. Finally a word of thanks
to Linda Merklin of Special Secretarial Services and David Klein of the Academic
Computer Center for their assistance at Hofstra University in preparing the final
copy of the figures and tables.

_____ Part I _____

Foreign Policy Initiatives

The only apparent consensus about the Nixon Presidency is that his accomplishments in the foreign policy arena far outshadowed those in the domestic arena and that the advances for which he was responsible—in particular, the opening to China—brought the most significant improvement in foreign relations among the great powers in decades. As Henry Kissinger explained in his speech to the Hofstra Conference, the Nixon era corresponded to a period when American power had lost its preeminent position in world affairs, and it could achieve its objectives only through diplomacy, realism, planning, and the setting of priorities. Aided by a skillful group of advisers, Nixon was able to lay the foundation for a more realistic foreign policy that took into account the lack of U.S. resources to accomplish all its aims, the changes in the Communist world, the emergence of Third World resistance to great power hegemony, and the growing economic power of Western Europe and Japan.

The Nixon diplomacy worked while many of his domestic programs failed. This was true because there was more of a sense of realism and caution in his dealings with foreign governments and a willingness to compromise and accommodate their interests—a tolerance he lacked in the domestic area.

This volume outlines the main components of the Nixon foreign policy, beginning with the significant effort to bring China into the world community. We see here the manner in which the Vietnam War ended and the evolution of American policy in the Middle East. The efforts at détente are also detailed. In addition, the diplomatic and foreign policy process is also described.

It is impossible to discuss the Nixon record in world affairs without putting China at the head of the list of accomplishments and without acknowledging the importance of Henry Kissinger as the major architect and administrator of the policy. Dr. Kissinger attended the Hofstra Conference and gave a detailed overview of the Nixon foreign policy initiatives. His speech also serves as an important guide to the detailed discussions of the end of the Vietnam War, of détente and relations with the Soviet Union, and of the Middle East.

OVERALL ASSESSMENT

1

The Nixon Foreign Policy

THE HONORABLE HENRY A. KISSINGER, INTRODUCED BY THE HONORABLE HAN XU

INTRODUCTION

Mr. President, Mr. Chairman, conference guests and participants, members of the Hofstra University community, ladies and gentlemen: It is my distinct honor and pleasure to introduce to you Dr. Henry Kissinger, the keynote speaker at this evening's plenary session. Yet, I am not so sure whether this introduction is necessary. It is certainly not in China. If you stop anyone on the street and ask about the living American he knows of, the answer would not be Bill Cosby or Michael Jackson. Most probably, it would be either President Nixon or Dr. Kissinger, and for good reason.

Committed to Sino-U.S. friendship, Dr. Kissinger is held in high regard by both the Chinese leaders and people. He has made fourteen trips to China and played a key role in executing the Nixon initiative that helped bring about the normalization and consequent development of relations between our two great countries in the early 1970s. Dr. Kissinger is now co-chairman of the U.S.-China Society, an influential organization set up last March with three former presidents as its honorary chairmen. We in China admire Dr. Kissinger for what he has done to help bring our two countries together and hope that he will make continued contributions to growing ties of China-U.S. friendship.

I also speak from my personal experience. My friendship with Dr. Kissinger goes back sixteen years ago when he made his first secret trip to China. As our acquaintance grows closer through numerous contacts, he has won my increasing respect and admiration for displaying a profound sense of political foresight, realism, understanding, and flexibility in approaching complex issues. In these qualities, Dr. Kissinger truly stands unique. Once a friend asked me what secret weapon President Nixon used to open the door of China. My answer was that the secret weapon was Dr. Kissinger himself. For if someone less capable and intelligent than Dr. Kissinger had been sent, the result might have been totally different.

I think it is perfectly fitting that Dr. Kissinger has been asked to deliver the keynote speech. After all, who was more intimately involved in President Nixon's foreign policy initiatives than Dr. Kissinger? And who is more qualified to offer insights into the Nixon Presidency than Dr. Kissinger who worked closely with President Nixon during his presidency?

Although Dr. Kissinger has left office for a number of years, he has remained active in public life. More than once, his cool-headed and penetrating analysis of the intricate and changing international developments has been valuable to us in gaining a thorough understanding of the major global issues that affect the future of the world.

I believe, and I am sure the belief is shared by the audience, that we can expect an equally enlightening and thought-provoking presentation from Dr. Kissinger this evening.

As I am as eager as all of you to benefit from Dr. Kissinger's keynote speech, I think that the best way to proceed with my introduction is to stop it right now and let Dr. Kissinger take the platform.

Now, Dr. Kissinger.

DR. KISSINGER

Mr. President, Mr. Zarb, ladies and gentlemen: It means a lot to me to be introduced by my old friend the Chinese ambassador, who greeted me when I arrived in China, and knew a lot more about me than I knew about China. I was induced to come here by my old friend, Frank Zarb, who asked me to come to Hofstra to give a little speech on President Nixon. He did not reveal to me that it was part of a three-day conference, attended by many former colleagues, the media, and some individuals whose admiration for me does not quite equal that of my mother. In any event, to talk about the foreign policy of President Nixon, which is the subject I'm most knowledgeable about, is a rather complex undertaking.

Let me begin by stating a few propositions. I had the privilege of working intimately with President Nixon for five and a half years. He appointed me to positions from which I could make a contribution to our country and maybe to world peace, despite all my previous experience supporting Governor Rockefeller who was not known for his unquestioning affection for Richard Nixon. I had never really met President Nixon before he appointed me. I saw him once for five minutes at a cocktail party, and cocktail party conversation was not a subject for which he will go down in history.

I am proud of having had the privilege of working with President Nixon; I think he presided over the most significant period in American foreign policy.

I was his associate and his subordinate, and I make this point so that we can avoid the question of who did what. President Nixon had the responsibility, and he has an extraordinary knowledge of foreign policy. It is a fruitless exercise to try to segment decisions to see who contributed what to a particular decision.

You should also keep in mind that it is next to impossible to do justice to contemporary history. When I, as a Ph.D. student, enrolled in courses on 19th century history, I studied a period when ambassadors were three weeks away from their governments, communications were handwritten, and the only instructions that could be given were conceptual. Therefore, it was fairly easy to determine from the records what various people were thinking. In the modern period, with modern communications, instructions are not conceptual, and governments instruct precisely what the various individuals are supposed to do. The British Foreign Office in the middle of the 19th century had 40 permanent officials. The State Department today has 15,000 permanent officials, and the Defense Department has more. They have typewriters and xerox machines which produce an unbelievable quantity of material, most of which is never seen by decision makers and is therefore not of prime importance. I should warn you about investigative reporters who proffer documents bearing top secret stamps in order to draw conclusions. The only documents that matter are those that actually went across the desk of the Secretary of State, the President, and the Security Advisor. It is very hard to determine which documents of the mass of information were actually seen by the decision makers.

It is particularly difficult to do an objective historical analysis of President Nixon because he was and is one of the most complex human beings that one is likely to encounter. I am sure that all of us in this room who worked with him will be able to give a truthful account of quite different facets of his personality. I mention this to make clear that it is quite possible to have conflicting views.

I will talk about Richard Nixon, the foreign policy president. I think the key element was that, while he considered domestic politics a necessary prerequisite to being in office, he considered foreign policy as involving the fundamental national interest and the ultimate responsibility to his country and to world peace. I cannot think of one decision that was made in the foreign policy field in which the motive was principally or even importantly domestic politics. In foreign policy, Richard Nixon attempted to determine the fundamental national interest, the long-term objective, and sometimes in intricate extended conversations, to work out a strategy to achieve it. Indeed, I would say the most important contribution that he intended to make to American foreign policy was not in the initiatives that were taken but in articulating an approach to foreign policy which could avoid the endless American oscillation between optimism and despair. Instead of our obsession with personalities or abstract moral judgments, he tried to define something for which there is little historical experience and very little precedent, namely, a permanent involvement of the United States in international affairs.

I have brought with me excerpts from the annual reports to Congress on foreign policy which President Nixon submitted, the only president ever to have done so. These were reports on which we had spent many weeks of endless work, only to find that the only subject of them ever reported on in the press was Vietnam. That illustrates one of the dilemmas of the Nixon foreign policy presidency. He wanted to construct a new international order, but he inherited a war from which those who had involved us in it had walked away. There were also passions which he had not originated, which by temperament he was not perhaps ideally suited to deal with, and which often obscured, while he was in office, the larger design he was creating. The constellation of that larger design is emerging more and more clearly in the sense that no subsequent president has been able to get away from the categories that were established and from the basic premises of the Nixon period.

What were some of his premises? I will draw from the annual reports to avoid the impression that this is an ex post facto analysis invented to suit contemporary conditions: We in the Nixon Administration were convinced that by the end of the 1960s a phase of American policy had ended. The '40s and '50s witnessed American involvement in world affairs but from a posture that was more comparable to the conduct of domestic politics than of foreign policy. As late as 1950 the United States produced 52% of all the goods and services in the world. We had an atomic monopoly. Therefore, the question of security to be defined, analogous to the experience in World War II, was aggression across clearly defined borders anywhere around the world. The problem of political stability could be defined as economic recovery, and we had enough resources to take care of both of these requirements. By the late 1960s, with or without Vietnam but brought home sharply by the war, it became clear that American resources were no longer adequate for so global a role and that the United States would have to conduct foreign policy as other nations had to through their history, by setting priorities and by defining a national interest. This ran totally counter to the American experience.

In 1936 when the Nazis occupied the Sudetenland, President Roosevelt asked the Secretary of State what the meaning of this was. The answer was that it violated an agreement with France and maybe an agreement with Britain, but it violated no agreement with the United States. There was not one word of analysis that it had changed the strategic situation in Europe, or that it made a mockery of the French system of alliances. What President Nixon attempted was to base his policy on the following analysis, which I draw from the annual reports: In the '40s and '50s we were the only great power whose society and great economy had escaped World War II. In the '70s this would no longer be the case, and we were living in a world that was no longer bipolar but multipolar. New nations were being born of turmoil and uncertainty that were also key factors in international relations. In the '40s and '50s we were facing a communist world that to us, at least, appeared monolithic. It was the perception of the Nixon presidency that the nature of that world had changed and that we no longer faced a monolithic world in communism. This, I must say, was written in 1969 before we had the slightest contact with the People's Republic of China. We pointed out that the nature of military technology had changed in that we had to adapt to a period of nuclear parity. Therefore, the basic principles were put forward that our objective was to define our interests precisely, and the more that policy was based on a realistic assessment of our own and others' interest, the more effective our role in the world would be. We were not involved in the world because we had commitments, the first report claimed, but rather we had commitments because we were involved. Our interests must shape our commitments rather than the other way around.

This was the basic thrust of the Nixon foreign policy, and it led to a situation in which his Administration was attacked by both liberals, who believed there was too much emphasis on power, and conservatives, who argued there was not enough emphasis on ideological conflict. After a while, a strange coalition emerged between conservatives, who hated communists, and liberals, who hated Nixon and who felt that if Nixon was for peace perhaps a little confrontation would not do any harm. This coincided with Watergate and made the second term more complex than it should have been.

With this background let me talk about the Nixon approach to the Soviet Union, the People's Republic of China, the Middle East, Europe, and to some extent Vietnam. I read in the papers occasionally, especially in the more conservative ones, about how President Nixon was mesmerized by détente and how he tried to envelop the Soviet Union in a web of relationships in which they would not notice that they were being tied down, and that in the process he made great concessions. To those of us in this room who worked with President Nixon, the argument that he was taken in by the Russians strains credulity. Rather, his approach to the Soviets was expressed in the first annual report as follows:

We are under no illusions; we know there are enduring ideological differences; we are aware of the difficulty of moderating tensions which have arisen from the clash of national interests. These differences will not be dissipated by changes of atmosphere or dissolved in cordial personal relationships between statesmen. They involve strong convictions and contrary philosophies. The United States has interests of its own and will defend those interests. But any nation today must define its interests with special concern for the interests of others. If some nations define their security in a manner that means insecurity for other nations, then peace is threatened and the security of all is diminished. This obligation is particularly great for the nuclear superpowers on whose decisions the survival of mankind may well depend.

The fundamental objective of the Nixon Administration was to attempt to define those actions which would in fact threaten fundamental national interests. It, therefore, placed less emphasis on ideological controversy and great emphasis on actual conduct. It resisted any attempt to expand the Soviets' sphere or to violate what we perceived to be an existing balance of power. It was prepared to respect Soviet interests within its national borders.

As early as 1969, for example, at a time when we had no relationship with the People's Republic of China and when we didn't even know how to make contact with Beijing, we feared that the Soviet Union was considering an attack on China. We may or may not have been correct in this judgment and I'll be glad in the question period to tell you why we thought so. But it was our conviction. We were prepared to do our utmost to prevent this and to give the maximum diplomatic and other support to the People's Republic with whom we had no relationship whatsoever, because we thought that such a move would so threaten the balance of power and therefore so fundamentally affect American interests that it had to be resisted, whatever the state of our relations with China. At the same time the Nixon Administration was prepared to make agreements with the Soviet Union on specific subjects. It attempted at the beginning to link political and arms control negotiations on the theory that almost every war you can identify has been caused by political tensions and not simply by the development of arms. That effort floundered on the resistance of bureaucracy, which was ideologically committed to arms control as an end in itself. Therefore, those two policies tended to go on somewhat different tracks. Nevertheless, in all areas in which President Nixon had discretion, and in the end there were many, he never lost sight of the fact that unless one could achieve some restraint in the national conduct of the Soviet Union, no arms control agreements could possibly last.

A lot of discussion has taken place about the so-called principles of conduct that we signed with the Soviets. We never believed that simply signing these agreements would lead to restrained conduct. We thought it was the beginning of negotiations that, over a period of time, could be used to test whether the Soviet Union was prepared to keep its military power inside its borders rather than insist on finding its security in the physical domination of neighboring territories. The various arms control agreements that were signed in that period have become highly controversial, and there is no point in debating that today. Perhaps the students here will not remember a period in which there were, almost monthly, massive demonstrations in our streets, in which the Congress was reducing the military budget by significant percentages each year, and in which the President had to fight for the most elementary sinews of national strength against heavy media and Congressional opposition. It is very easy now to speak about the Anti-Ballistic Missile Treaty of 1972. You should remember that President Nixon managed to achieve approval of ABM defense in 1969 by exactly one vote, that the system that was then developed was based on twelve defensive sites, and that every year thereafter the Congress reduced the number of sites so that by 1972 we were down to two, to defend the entire United States. The only question was whether we could get anything for it before the Congress gave it away unilaterally. All of those who are now speaking about how tough they would have been never put the issue in the context of that period.

With all of this, President Nixon in my view put relations with the Soviet Union on a more realistic basis than they were before or since. Precisely because he was insisting on a cool analysis of the national interest, we spoke a language that Soviet leaders understood. There is no possibility that a Soviet leader can return from a meeting with an American president and tell his colleagues that he has just met the most charming American and that therefore they should make concessions that they had not previously thought of. Nobody proclaims that President Nixon at any point in his career relied on personal charm to have his way. Since he dealt with the Soviet leaders without illusion, there developed a relationship of mutual respect that led to a series of fundamental agreements that are still being observed, have been observed in every administration, and have been carried out by every critic that subsequently took office.

Let me turn to the People's Republic of China. President Nixon entered office convinced that one could not conduct a serious foreign policy that excluded a quarter of the human race. He came to that view before he ever met me and therefore that should settle the argument of who thought of it first. I had come to the same conclusion independently. There's no question that he was dedicated to improving relations with Beijing on the basis that China was and had always been throughout its history a key factor in Asia. It had a long border with the Soviet Union and borders with Southeast Asia and all major Asian countries. The problem we had was that we didn't know how to approach the Chinese. At first, we tried various communist countries without any success, partly I suspect because leaders in Beijing thought other communist countries were too closely allied with Moscow for them to entrust sensitive messages relating to our commitment to improving our relations. We made it clear in our very first annual report to Congress that we would avoid dramatic gestures which might produce dramatic rebuffs, but we would take specific steps that would not require Chinese agreement at first but which would underline our willingness to have a more normal and constructive relationship. In due course, answers from the Chinese leadership were received through the Pakistani channel.

There started a relationship that remains of the greatest importance, almost the only major American relationship that has remained free of partisan controversy in subsequent years through four administrations of both parties. It was a complex relationship because at first the United States did not even recognize the government in Beijing with which it was dealing. The ambassador knows the agonies we went through to find a formula in our first communique that reflected the fact that we accepted the proposition that there was only one China. We finally came up with the formula that Chinese on both sides of the Taiwan Straits affirmed that there was only one China and that the United States did not contest that proposition.

The interesting thing about the relationship between the United States and the People's Republic, especially in the Nixon period, was that we had very little actual diplomatic business to conduct with each other. On the other hand, the only detailed interest we had was a common concern to prevent what we call 'hegemony,' which meant the domination of the world by one country or a group of countries. Most of the discussion was spent on careful explanation by each side to the other about how it viewed international relations. The Chinese never asked anything from us, and I don't remember that we ever asked anything of the Chinese of a concrete nature. Gradually some specific things developed, but they were of secondary importance in the first five or six years. By working through a series of remarkable leaders on both sides on the common conception of international affairs, what developed was not only a confidence but a certain parallelism, especially on the overriding issue of maintaining the international balance.

In the Middle East, we faced a situation in which Israel after the 1967 war occupied a large territory in Egypt, the West Bank and on the Golan Heights and in which the Arabs did not recognize Israel; some 20,000 Soviet troops were ultimately located in Egypt. President Nixon received a great deal of advice to get negotiations started. He believed that it was, above all, important to make clear that the United States could not be blackmailed into pressuring friendly countries by the presence of Soviet troops. We had to evolve a very complex diplomacy whose first objective was to show to the moderate Arabs that, while the Soviets could deliver weapons, only America could bring progress toward peace. I can think of no area in which personal convictions of the top leaders were of more crucial importance. In 1973 when there was a war, President Nixon was determined that the opportunity be used to make a breakthrough toward peace. From the first day of the war we conducted ourselves in this manner, so that while we would prevent the defeat of Israel, we would also try to lay the basis for a negotiated peace. Many of the breakthroughs in Middle East diplomacy date to that period.

I don't want to go through every aspect of the Nixon foreign policy, but I must say a few words about Vietnam. President Nixon's greatest ambition, as I said earlier, was to create a new structure of international relations. In that light, his relations with Europe were of cardinal importance. However, much of the first term was taken up with ending the war in Vietnam. When he came into office there were 525,000 Americans in Vietnam and the number was still increasing under the timetable established in the previous administration. The Democratic Party, which had engaged us in that war, had been deeply divided on it, leading to the extraordinary demonstrations in the streets of Chicago at the time. What is generally not recognized is that President Nixon in fact carried out the minority plank of the Democratic Party, which was not accepted by the then administration, within six months of coming into office. I mention this because so often the issue is defined in terms of prolonging the war or of not being willing to end the war. Nobody who inherited such a tragedy could have any other desire but ending the war. I had come from Harvard University, and I was closely tied emotionally both to my students and to my colleagues; but what the people who claimed a monopoly on the desire for peace would never face is that what the North Vietnamese wanted was not a compromise but victory.

We proposed in a personal message to the North Vietnamese even before President Nixon entered office to separate the military and political discussions. We wanted to have a cease-fire and mutual withdrawal to leave the political issues to the Vietnamese parties. This was not only rejected, but within three weeks of coming into office we faced an offensive that killed over 1,000 Americans every month. Two-thirds of the casualties of the Nixon Administration, it is generally not recognized, were suffered in the first year of his presidency, and of those casualties, in turn, two-thirds—or over 6,000 in the first six months of the war—occurred before any policy was carried out and could have any effect.

The fundamental problem faced by the Nixon Administration was that the Vietnamese were asking us to withdraw unconditionally, to overthrow on the way out all those who had associated with us, and to leave the subsequent evolution to their tender mercies, which we have now seen end violently by both peoples in the mass killings in Cambodia. There were never any other terms. All the people who now say that we could have had in 1969 the terms that we finally settled for in 1972 are playing games with the honor of the American people and with their sentiments. We said from the beginning that we were prepared to withdraw provided there was a political process in place in which we were not asked to turn over the millions that had relied on us to their enemies. That condition was not met until October 8, 1972. The terms which we then accepted had been proposed secretly in May 1971, publicly in January 1972, and repeated publicly in May 1972. These terms had always been attacked by our critics as being far too stringent and would never be accepted. The question was whether America would end the war which the Nixon Administration had not started by abandoning all the people who in reliance on our word had committed themselves to the political process that we had put forward.

President Nixon had nothing to gain personally from such a course. He also felt that a president had no right to turn off a major policy as if he were switching a television channel and it was presumptuous of so many outsiders to try to prevent that as if they had a monopoly on virtue and to suggest that those of us who had to conduct a war which we had inherited under unbelievable harassment were doing it because there was some psychological push in that direction.

I have spent this much time on the Vietnam war because it explains why the ultimate design could not be carried out in the Nixon Administration. There were at least three problems. The first is that President Nixon was not emotionally the best leader for the kind of civil war that was being conducted on the issue of Vietnam and sometimes, on the pretext of Vietnam, on the fundamental institutions of America. It touched too many insecurities in him and brought out too many defensive attitudes. Secondly, he was too solitary a personality to be a great educator of the American people, to move them from their moralistic and legalistic traditions to a perception of a permanent involvement in international affairs based on an analysis of the national interest. Thirdly, it was so ambitious an undertaking that in the end he was attacked by both liberals and conservatives because he was operating against preconceived perceptions and fundamental nostalgias. Yet when all was said and done, none of his successors has been able to avoid the basic categories of our public discourse which we've established on the Middle East, on East-West relations, on U.S.-China relations and on Europe. Thus he will have left a major legacy.

Let me end by reading to you from the conclusion of the first volume of my memoirs, because it sums up my assessment of President Nixon, when he called from the Lincoln sitting room where he was alone:

He was wondering whether the press was appreciating what had been done; probably not. But that was not really what he had on his mind. He knew that every success brings a terrific letdown, he said. I should not let it get to me. I should not be discouraged. There were many battles left to fight; I should not weaken. In fact, I was neither discouraged, nor did I feel let down. Listening to him I could picture the scene: Nixon would be sitting solitary and withdrawn, deep in his brown stuffed chair with his legs on the settee in front of him, a small reading light breaking the darkness, and a wood fire throwing shadows on the wall of the room. The loudspeakers would be playing romantic classical music, probably Tchaikovsky. He was talking to me, but he was really addressing himself. What extraordinary vehicles destiny selects to accomplish its designs. This man, so lonely in his hour of triumph, so ungenerous in some of his motivations, had navigated our nation through one of the most anguishing periods in its history. Not by nature courageous, he had steeled himself to conspicuous acts of extraordinary courage. Not normally outgoing, he had forced himself to rally his people to its challenge. He had striven for a revolution in American foreign policy so that it would overcome the disastrous oscillations between overcommitment and isolation. Despised by the establishment, ambiguous in his human perceptions, he had yet held fast to a sense of national honor and responsibility, determined to prove that the strongest free country had no right to abdicate. What would have happened had the establishment, about which he was so ambivalent, shown him some love? Would he have withdrawn deeper into the wilderness of his resentments, or would an act of grace have liberated him? By now it no longer mattered. Enveloped in an intractable solitude, at the end of a period of bitter division, he nevertheless saw before him a vista of promise to which few statesmen have been blessed to aspire. He could envisage a new national order that would reduce lingering enmities, strengthen friendships, and give new hope to emerging nations. It was a worthy goal for America and mankind. He was alone in his moment of triumph on a pinnacle that was soon to turn into a precipice. And yet with all his insecurities he had brought us by a tremendous act of will to an extraordinary moment when dreams and possibilities conjoined.

Two nights before his resignation, we were discussing his role in history and he was deeply despondent. I said to him, "history will treat you more kindly than your contemporaries." And I believe that this conference is proof that this process is well under way. Thank you.

THE OPENING TO CHINA

2

President Nixon and Sino-U.S. Relations

THE HONORABLE HAN XU

Ladies and gentlemen: It is a great pleasure for me to attend this conference on President Nixon at a time when China and the United States have just commemorated the fifteenth anniversary of the issuance of the Shanghai Communique. I wish to thank our hosts for their kind hospitality. To the man on the street in China, the name of Richard Nixon is inseparably linked with the opening of Sino-U.S. relations.

Together, we Chinese and Americans have come a long way. When President Nixon paid his historic visit to China in 1972, the more than two decades old gulf between China and the United States was yet to be closed, and our two nations and their leaders had to do the initial job of getting to know each other. Today, frequent contacts and exchanges of visits between our leaders and peoples have become routine, and Sino-U.S. mutual understanding and friendship are ever deepening.

In 1972 there was almost no bilateral trade, let alone scientific-technological cooperation. Today, our annual bilateral trade is over $7 billion. Our economic joint ventures and scientific-technological cooperative projects number in the hundreds.

In 1972 educational and cultural exchanges were nonexistent. Today, twenty thousand Chinese students and scholars study in the United States. Thousands of Americans go to China on various courses. Across the Pacific, cultural groups travel back and forth. What is more, each year a quarter of a million American tourists go to China.

Although no individual can take total credit for the above dramatic progress, the role played by President Nixon was extremely important. After all, in 1972 it was Chairman Mao Zedong and Premier Zhou Enlai on the Chinese side and President Nixon on the U.S. side who made the historic first move. I am not here to talk about the details of the opening of Sino-U.S. relations, nor about its specific implications. I thought it might be more relevant to share with you my views on President Nixon's leadership qualities in the opening of Sino-U.S. relations. Three major points come to my mind.

First, leaders should have the courage and foresight to seize opportunities to promote national and world interests. Arriving in Beijing in 1972, President Nixon said to Chinese leaders that he came for American interests. Chinese leaders appreciated his candor. They, too, acted in their own national interests. On the other hand, both President Nixon and Chinese leaders had world peace and stability in mind. A simple fact was that, if China and the United States could be friends again, the world would be a much safer place. Toward the end of the 1960s and the beginning of the 1970s, the international balance of force underwent important changes. President Nixon saw the necessity and possibility of rapprochement between China and the United States.

Yet, in view of the prolonged animosity between the two countries and the then existing political climate in the United States, one must give President Nixon credit for showing courage and vision in taking the initiative to open Sino-U.S. relations. "Great risks existed for both U.S. and Chinese leaders at the time," recalled President Nixon at a reception given by the Chinese Embassy to mark the fifteenth anniversary of the Shanghai Communique on February 27 in 1987. However, he stressed, and I quote: "One must take risks in order to succeed. We must not allow apprehension that taking risk will fail to deter us from taking risk for peace in the future." "We must not stand still," he urged. President Nixon pointed out that "the lessons of the reopening of our relations is a great risk taken and a great goal achieved." These are words of foresight that all of us should remember. Great changes have taken place in our relations since then, but the leadership quality shown by Chinese and American leaders in 1972 is still very much needed today and will be in the future to ensure that Sino-U.S. relations stay on the right track and move forward steadily. Just as fifteen years ago, a willingness to take risk for the sake of peace is still needed to ensure that world peace and stability are maintained.

Second, in dealing with international relations, leaders should face the reality and go along with the general trend of development. The Shanghai Communique issued during President Nixon's 1972 China trip is a case in point. It is a unique document in that each side stated its own set of views on a host of international issues, views that were very different from those of the other side. On the other hand, both sides expressed their commitment to the five principles of mutual respect for sovereignty and territorial integrity, mutual nonaggression, noninterference in each other's internal affairs, equality and mutual benefit, and peaceful coexistence. The important principle of one China and Taiwan being a part of China was accepted by the American side. The basic principles jointly established by our two countries in the Shanghai Communique not only laid down a solid foundation for the formal establishment of diplomatic relations between the two countries in 1979, but are also of great practical significance in guiding the development of Sino-U.S. relations today. Unfortunately, the Taiwan issue has not been solved. Although the United States recognizes the government of the People's Republic of China as the sole legal government of China, it continues to sell large amounts of arms to the Taiwan authorities. Moreover, the Taiwan Relations Act passed by the U.S. Congress in 1979 treats Taiwan as a separate political entity. It is the deep aspiration of the entire Chinese people to bring about Taiwan's return to the motherland so as to realize national reunification. The Chinese government holds that the formula of "one country, two systems" offers the best solution. As a first step in that direction, the Chinese government advocates the exchange of mail, trade, shipping, and air services between the mainland and Taiwan. Here again the U.S. government is confronted with a choice, namely, going along with the general trend of development by adopting a positive attitude toward the Chinese government's above proposal or letting the Taiwan issue linger on. Bearing in mind the critical link between the solution of the Taiwan issue and the steady development of Sino-U.S. relations, one hopes that the U.S. government will come to the right decision.

Third, leaders can play a very constructive and important role even out of office. President Nixon's contribution to Sino-U.S. relations did not end with his presidency. All along he has been working for better Sino-U.S. relations. In recent years, he has made a number of visits to China and has exchanged views with Chinese leaders on various issues. It is particularly noteworthy that he has shown creative thinking in many different ways.

Whenever any undercurrent threatens the development of Sino-U.S. relations, President Nixon comes out reiterating the importance of these relations. In a recent interview with NBC's "Today" show, he stressed that as the United States and China have different political systems, cultures, and history, it is not wise to impose one's own culture and value on the other. These words have strong relevance for today. Experiences have shown that mutual respect and understanding are vital in ensuring the steady growth of Sino-U.S. relations. Whenever this principle is violated, our relations suffer. Therefore, it is important that all of those who commit themselves to promoting Sino-U.S. ties will heed what President Nixon has said.

President Nixon was also among the first to stress the importance of Sino-U.S. economic ties in cementing the overall bilateral relations. He pointed out the complementary nature of Chinese and American economies—hence the great potential of economic cooperation—and he called on American businessmen to benefit fully from China's open policy. Facts have testified to the validity of his point of view.

In the same interview, President Nixon said "U.S.-China economic cooperation will hold together the two nations. Let's keep this in perspective." Indeed, the burgeoning economic ties between the United States and China is an important outgrowth of the diplomatic initiatives undertaken by President Nixon and Chinese leaders fifteen years ago.

Unexpected even by President Nixon himself, the rapidly developing Sino-U.S. economic ties have become a powerful force underlying the growth of our bilateral relations. China is the largest developing country in the world, which is engaged in an unprecedented modernization drive. It has opened its door wide open to the outside world to absorb advanced technology and capital. The just concluded National Congress of the Communist party of China will greatly speed up China's modernization drive. As the largest developed country in the world, the United States is well placed to meet China's tremendous needs for capital and technology. In turn, it will gain a firm share of China's market and obtain more orders for American businesses. It is a two-way traffic that benefits both parties. As the economic cooperation between China and the United States intensifies, it will give both countries a greater stake in developing their overall relations.

Yet, the importance of normalization of our relations is by no means confined to the economic field. The most important ramification of the 1972 Nixon-Mao Zedong initiative is that the normalized relations between China and the United States has contributed significantly to maintaining peace and stability in the world at large and in Asia and Pacific in particular.

We have moved away from animosity to mutual understanding, and hostility between us has been replaced by friendship. Fifteen years ago, we opened the door of Sino-U.S. relations with the conviction that the reconciliation between our two great countries would contribute to world peace and stability. Experiences over the years have more than borne this out. When our two countries work for peace and prosperity instead of facing each other with suspicion and distrust, it benefits not only ourselves but others as well. I think all those who are not biased will agree that, with Sino-American rapprochement, the Asia-Pacific is certainly safer than it used to be. With the passage of time, the importance of our relations to the maintenance of world peace and stability will become increasingly evident and better appreciated. This gives us all the more the reason to carefully nurture Sino-U.S. relations and prevent them from being undermined. We must work to ensure that the process set in motion by President Nixon and Chinese leaders will provide continued impetus to the enduring growth of the friendly bonds between our two countries.

Ladies and Gentlemen, although I am not in a position to pass judgment on the entire Nixon Presidency, I dare say that his contribution to our bilateral relations is exceedingly important and will long be remembered in China as well as in the United States. We in China have a saying: "When you drink water from the well, don't forget those who dug it." We will not forget all those people, both Chinese and Americans, both present here and elsewhere, who have made their contributions to the forging of China-U.S. friendship. In particular, we will not forget President Nixon. We will not forget his political courage and vision. And history will certainly not forget him for facing the reality and taking the daring initiative that changed the world.

Thank you.

3

The Asian Balance and Sino-American Rapprochement During the Nixon Administration

ROBERT G. SUTTER

INTRODUCTION

The secret diplomatic opening to China conducted by President Richard Nixon and his national security adviser Henry Kissinger was a bold and successful stroke that transformed, to American advantage, the Asian balance. In retrospect, it seems to have been a natural step. But this view ignores the three less recognized perspectives that emphasize the risks, the gambles, and the vision of the administration's action:

- First, the tenuous position of those in China with whom President Nixon and Henry Kissinger were negotiating;
- second, the long history of American unwillingness to recognize and take advantage of the potential for an important convergence of interests of the Chinese Communist movement and the United States in the Asian balance of power; and
- third, the dangers and pitfalls of using secret diplomacy to transform key features of American foreign policy.

This paper looks first at the conventional view of the events of the late 1960s and early 1970s which, in retrospect, makes the rapprochement of 1971–72 now seem such a natural outgrowth of both Chinese and U.S. interests. It then discusses the three other perspectives—internal Chinese political dynamics, the culture of U.S. Asian policy, and the character of American policy-making—which made the rapprochement such a bold, innovative, and skilled diplomatic venture.

THE ASIAN BALANCE AND SINO-AMERICAN RAPPROCHEMENT[1]

One of the marks of great statesmen is the capacity to seize opportunities created by changing and seemingly adverse circumstances. Such boldness characterized President Richard Nixon, Henry Kissinger, and Chinese leaders Mao Zedong and Zhou Enlai, when they broke through decades of hostility and distrust to establish a Sino-American understanding in the mutual interests of their countries. The historical record shows that the leaders were not motivated in this endeavor by romantic fascination, ideology, or perceived commercial advantage. Rather, it was their clear view of changing international circumstances, relating particularly to the balance of power in Asia, that persuaded Chinese and U.S. leaders that their nations' well-being and their own political standing would be best served by improved Sino-American understanding.

China's Interests

The rapprochement with the United States achieved during President Richard M. Nixon's February 1972 visit marks China's most important success in realigning the Asian balance of power in modern times. In the late 1960s, Chinese leaders became increasingly aware of China's vulnerable strategic position.[2] That vulnerability stemmed in part from disruptions of China's military preparedness during the Cultural Revolution, and it was enhanced by significantly greater Soviet military power deployed along the Chinese frontier. But at its heart lay Beijing's strident opposition to both superpowers.

The August 1968 Soviet incursion into Czechoslovakia and Moscow's concurrent formulation of the so-called Brezhnev Doctrine of limited sovereignty demonstrated to the Chinese that Moscow might be prepared to use overwhelming military superiority in order to pressure, and even to invade, the People's Republic of China (PRC). The Sino-Soviet border clashes of 1969 increased Beijing's concern over the Soviet threat.[3] In response, Chinese officials—under the leadership of Mao Zedong and Zhou Enlai—began a major effort in 1969 to broaden Beijing's leverage against the Soviet Union by ending China's international isolation. In this pursuit, they utilized conventional diplomacy and played down the ideological shrillness characteristic of Chinese foreign policy during the earlier stages of the Cultural Revolution.

Because of Moscow's massive power, Beijing realized that improving diplomatic and other relations with most foreign nations would be of relatively minor significance in helping China with its pressing need to offset the USSR. In East Asia, only the other superpower, the United States, seemed to have sufficient strength to serve as an effective deterrent to Soviet pressure. In the past Moscow had shown uneasiness over signs of possible reconciliation between China and the United States. Thus, the Chinese leaders were aware that they held an important option: they could move closer to the United States in order to readjust Sino-Soviet relations and form a new balance of power in East Asia more favorable to Chinese interests.

Although the Chinese faced increasingly heavy Soviet pressure in 1969, the newly installed Nixon Administration was beginning policy initiatives designed to pull back American military forces from Asia and to reduce U.S. commitments along the periphery of China. It was soon apparent that the policy of gradual troop withdrawal, part of the later-named Nixon Doctrine, was perceived favorably by Beijing. The Chinese leaders saw the American pullback as solid evidence of the Nixon Administration's avowed interest in improved relations with China. They also viewed it as a major opportunity for China to free itself from the burdensome task of maintaining an extensive defense network along China's southern and eastern borders against possible U.S.-backed armed incursions. Beijing now saw greater opportunity for China to spread its own influence in neighboring East Asian areas as the United States gradually retreated.

Primarily on the basis of these two factors—a need to use Sino-American rapprochement to offset Soviet pressure on China and a desire to take advantage of prospects opening for the PRC under terms of the Nixon Doctrine in Asia— Beijing agreed to receive President Nixon and to begin the process of normalizing Sino-American relations. Although the joint communique signed by Nixon and Zhou Enlai in Shanghai in February 1972 acknowledged major differences between the two sides over ideology, Taiwan, and several foreign policy issues, it showed that they had reached an important agreement on what principles should govern the future international order in East Asia. In particular, both sides agreed that they would not seek hegemony in the Asia-Pacific region and would oppose efforts by any other country to establish hegemony there.[4]

This accord served China's interests well. For the previous two decades, Beijing had existed within a generally hostile East Asia environment and had periodically faced threats to its national security. The Sino-American rapprochement presented Beijing with an opportunity for a more relaxed stance on its eastern and southern flanks. It also provided major support for China against Soviet pressure. Support from the United States for the so-called antihegemony clause in the Shanghai Communique represented for China an important strategic statement. It put Washington on record as opposing any effort by Moscow to dominate China, and it made it possible for Beijing to relax its vigilance on the eastern and southern flanks and concentrate on the north.

U.S. Interests

The Chinese-American agreement also conformed with U.S. strategic interests. By the late 1960s, the cost and futility of massive U.S. military involvement in Vietnam had vividly demonstrated the limitations of the American use of force to counter what Washington had previously viewed as the strategic threat of international communism. The experience forced Washington to reassess the prevailing international order in light of its newly perceived weakness. Over the previous decade, while the United States had become increasingly involved in Vietnam, the Soviet Union had drawn abreast of the United States in strategic weapons. During the previous twenty years, the United States had enjoyed strategic superiority and commensurate international influence, allowing it to pursue an ideological campaign against international communism and to support the free world. Washington now realized that it could no longer afford such a policy. In particular, it saw that the United States could no longer, on its own, sustain the balance of forces on continental Asia.

Thus, the United States, under the Nixon Administration, began to put aside past, undifferentiated prejudice against communist regimes in general and to actively capitalize on nationalist divergencies in Asia, hoping thereby to achieve a more favorable strategic balance. The major divergence Washington chose to exploit was that between Moscow and Beijing. The United States realized that, by withdrawing from forward military positions along China's periphery—a move that would conserve American resources for use in support of more important interests against Moscow—it could reach agreement with Beijing and possibly establish a more favorable equilibrium in the area.

At the same time, the president and his advisers were anxious to use perceived international leverage derived from the opening of China in order to elicit greater accommodations from the Soviet Union over pressing international and arms control issues; and from Communist Vietnam over conditions for a peace settlement. The president was also motivated by the prospect of personal political benefits from success in improving U.S. relations, on generally favorable terms, with a heretofore hostile China.

RISKS ASSOCIATED WITH THE SINO-U.S. OPENING

Since the benefits of Sino-U.S. rapprochement now seem so clear, it is reasonable to ask why U.S. and Chinese leaders did not act earlier. This clarity of hindsight, however, greatly underplays the bold accomplishments of U.S. and Chinese leaders.

Such an assessment ignores the substantial risk of failure the leaders on both sides took in their efforts to improve relations. Ideological and systematic differences, domestic politics, and differences in international strategy made the Sino-American policy an extremely sensitive topic in both capitals. Thus, President Nixon had to take careful account of the legacy of past emotional and partisan debates on U.S.-China policy; the need to preserve unity within his own conservative political constituency; and the imperatives of confidentiality in delicate interaction with a heretofore hostile adversary. Although the president made clear his desire for better relations with China and took some public steps designed to ease tensions and improve ties, he felt compelled to keep secret his efforts aimed at a breakthrough until Henry Kissinger completed his secret trip to Beijing in July 1971.

Analysts of Chinese affairs point out that the stakes in the policy debate in

China at this time were even higher. Moves by Zhou Enlai and his associates to improve relations with the United States during 1968–71 had produced vigorous criticism from Zhou's rivals. Such internal opposition, for example, had forced Zhou and his associates to drop, just before a scheduled Warsaw meeting, an initiative to explore the new Nixon Administration's intentions in February 1969.[5]

This was a period of intense leadership conflict in the PRC. It subsided only with the death of Defense Minister Lin Piao and his family in September 1971 and the arrest and detention of the main leaders of the Chinese Military High Command.[6] These events came just two months after Kissinger's secret visit to Beijing.

Officials associated with Lin, through speeches and commentary in the Chinese media, had made known their opposition to the opening to the United States. The success of Zhou's opening to the United States presumably was an important factor in his ability and that of his followers to win the life and death struggle for power with Lin Piao and his associates then underway in Beijing. Had the opening to the United States failed, it is safe to conclude, Zhou's fate and that of his followers might have been quite different.[7]

THE HISTORICAL CONTEXT

The risks of failure that Chinese and U.S. leaders ran in the late 1960s and early 1970s were all the more apparent when viewed against the background of thirty years of mutual hostility that preceded Kissinger's secret trip. They were also cast in sharp relief by previous aborted attempts by leaders of one side or the other to reach accommodation during this thirty-year period.

Chinese Policy

Thus, the rise of the Chinese Communist party (CCP) at the head of a growing political and military organization in China during World War II had coincided with Washington's emergence as one of the dominant powers in East Asia. The early postwar years found them on opposite sides during the Chinese civil war and the Korean conflict. Subsequently, the two sides maintained an armed confrontation along China's periphery over the next two decades. Chinese Communist efforts to seek accommodation with the United States date back, however, to the early days of this conflict. During World War II, for example, the Mao-Zhou leadership encouraged the United States to establish a military mission at the Communists' headquarters in northwestern China and offer close cooperation with the United States during negotiations with American envoy Patrick Hurley. The Mao-Zhou leadership also sought closer contacts with the United States at other times, notably during the 1955–57 Sino-American negotiations in Geneva.

As in Beijing's move toward the United States during the Nixon Administration, the prime factors motivating the CCP leaders to seek a *modus vivendi* with the United States on these earlier occasions centered on the evolving balance of power in China and East Asia.[8] They failed because American policymakers failed to recognize that the interests of the United States and the Chinese Communists in East Asia could be compatible. They chose to emphasize American ideological, strategic, and other differences with the Communists, over the common interests of the two sides in the balance of power in Asia which could have served as a basis of accommodation.

This pragmatic openness to accommodation with apparent adversaries had firm roots in CCP experience. Even before World War II, Mao, Zhou, and their colleagues in the CCP had proven themselves adroit practitioners of balance-of-power politics. Their experiences as leaders of a hunted minority group in China since the 1920s had taught them to be keenly aware of the balance of power around them. The CCP leaders had to consider first of all their ability to survive and expand in a hostile environment. They had to understand how to manipulate the power balance in China in order to offset the superior strategic power of their chief enemy, the Chinese Nationalist (Kuomintang) forces under Chiang Kai-shek. The Communists, of course, had ideological plans and programs with which to remake the ancient Chinese society into one that would stand as a unique model in the modern world. But they realized that all these plans would come to naught if they failed to survive and develop vis-à-vis their adversaries in China.

Thus, the Communists usually viewed the establishment and maintenance of a favorable balance of power as critically important in protecting the interests of their movement. The most important CCP interest was to ensure its own survival and security so that other goals could be attained. A major communist concern was to complete the revolution begun in the 1920s, which would entail dismantling the rival Chiang government and asserting CCP authority over all Chinese territory. The Communists were anxious to develop China into a strong, modern state, free from intimidation and pressure from adjacent powers.

Soon after the founding of the Communist party in the early 1920s, the Communists realized how slim were their chances of survival alone in warlord-ruled China. They compromised ideological principles and joined forces with the more powerful Kuomintang under Sun Yat-sen. Following the Xian incident of 1936, the Communists agreed to join in a united front with Chiang Kai-shek in order to end the nationalists' extermination campaigns, which were threatening to snuff out the Communist resistance.

The American entrance into the war against Japan on the side of Chiang Kai-shek in December 1941 resulted in another major shift in the balance of power affecting CCP interests, which in turn prompted the CCP's first major effort at accommodation with the United States.

The United States rapidly became the predominant power in East Asia, and in China it brought its power, influence, and aid to bear solely on the side of Chiang Kai-shek's nationalists. For the CCP leaders, there was a serious likelihood that the United States, because of growing association with Chiang Kai-shek, might use its enormous power against the CCP during an anticipated Chinese civil war following Japan's defeat. To counter this prospect, the Communists had the option of looking to their Soviet ally for support. But Moscow at that time was showing little interest in defending CCP interests against a challenge by U.S.-backed, nationalist forces.

The Communists saw that only at great risk could they ignore the change that had taken place. Hoping that the United States would not become closely associated with Chiang Kai-shek against CCP interests, the Communists decided to take steps on their own to ensure that Washington would adopt a more even-handed position. They strove to put aside historical difficulties with the United States, and they soft-pedaled ideological positions that might alienate Washington in order to arrive at a power arrangement that would better serve CCP interests in China.

The United States chose to rebuff the Communist initiatives, an action that resulted in a period during which the Communists faced the likelihood of a CCP confrontation against a strong, U.S.-backed Chinese Nationalist Army at the end of the Pacific War. Fortunately for the CCP, Moscow gradually built its strength in East Asia during the final months of the war and the period following Japan's defeat, and the United States rapidly withdrew its forces from East Asia at the war's end, shifting the balance of power in a direction less unfavorable to the Communists. Later in the 1940s, the Communists obtained more support from Moscow. For a time they appeared uncertain as to how closely to align with the USSR against the United States.[9] After prolonged negotiations, Mao and Stalin finally solidified bilateral ties in the February 1950 Sino-Soviet alliance. On this basis, the Chinese leaders judged that their national security in the face of U.S.-backed power in Asia was more secure. Beijing was accordingly more confident of China's continued national survival when it chose to confront rather than appease the American forces that were threatening Chinese frontiers in the first months of the Korean War.

After the Korean armistice, the Chinese were still prepared to confront the United States, not only to protect PRC frontiers but also to obtain other CCP interests concerning Taiwan. Since China's security was guaranteed by the Sino-Soviet alliance, Beijing now strove to attain such goals as the dismantling of the Chiang Kai-shek regime, the reunification of all Chinese territory under the PRC, and the establishment of an independent Chinese international position free from outside pressure. While Beijing seemed prepared to keep pushing against U.S.-backed positions in East Asia that blocked its objectives, Moscow, in the wake of Stalin's death, showed decidedly less interest in supporting such Chinese moves.

This reduced Soviet support, combined with increased American military-political containment efforts against Chinese interests following the Korean War, marked another shift in the power balance against PRC interests. It prompted another effort by the Communists to achieve a *modus vivendi* with the United States. Although China's security did not appear threatened, and the Sino-Soviet alliance remained in force, Beijing realized that any progress toward completing the Chinese civil war and establishing an independent foreign policy would be seriously impeded by the developing East Asian balance in the mid–1950s. Moscow's unwillingness to back PRC confrontation with the United States ruled out Chinese use of force to achieve the objectives. Beijing instead tried to establish a more favorable balance by compromising with the United States during the ambassadorial talks of 1955–57 held in Geneva. Beijing hoped that accommodation with the United States in the talks would lead to a relaxation of American containment in East Asia and a loosening of Washington's stance on Taiwan. Despite the attractiveness of the Communist initiatives, the United States chose to rebuff Beijing once again.[10]

U.S. Policy

As in the case of the Chinese leadership, American policymakers also have long been affected by the shifting balance of power in East Asia.[11] Ever since the release of the Open Door notes at the turn of the century, and perhaps earlier, the United States has endeavored to respond to shifts in the East Asian balance in a way that would maintain an equilibrium favorable to American interests. In particular, Washington has historically followed policies designed to prevent any individual state from dominating the area. In China, Washington supported British efforts in the nineteenth and early twentieth centuries to ensure that no power gained the dominant position. It refrained from recognizing Japan's territorial acquisitions in China in the 1930s, and it determined to resist Tokyo in the Pacific War, in part because it judged that Japan's hegemony over China and East Asia ultimately would seriously threaten American national interests.

Since the United States became actively involved in Pacific affairs in the late nineteenth century, Washington has seen some basic U.S. security interests tied in with the East Asian power balance. In particular, the United States has judged that any power that is able to dominate East Asia would soon pose a serious security threat to American territorial interests in the Pacific islands, including Hawaii. It has also held that such a power would gravely endanger longstanding U.S. trade, business, missionary, and other activities in the region. Thus, Washington has striven to ensure that a balance of power favorable to these interests is maintained.

In the period after the start of World War II, however, and especially following the divisive partisan debates in the late 1940s and early 1950s over China policy, the United States did not respond realistically to changes in the East Asian power equation affecting American interests. In particular, its dedication to ideology frequently led the United States into policies that, on balance, were detrimental to its own national interests.

Toward the end of World War II, for instance, the United States realized that the balance of power in East Asia would change drastically following Japan's defeat. Policy planners in Washington were especially concerned over future

Soviet dominance on the Asian mainland. At first, the United States hoped to foster a strong, Chiang Kai-shek–led China that would block Soviet expansion, but Chiang's weakness and poor administration scuttled the plan. Washington then settled on a policy designed to achieve a favorable balance through direct political arrangements with the USSR, culminating in the understanding on East Asia reached at the Yalta Conference of February 1945. Washington wrongly judged that such accords would guarantee a stable power equation in which China would maintain its independence without the need for continued U.S. military presence in the area.

In view of a traditional American ideological concern that the use of U.S. military power had to be justified on grounds higher than national interest, American planners judged that they could not support a continued U.S. military presence in Asia after Japan's defeat. American strategists—though they themselves were not necessarily moralists convinced of the ethical mission of U.S. foreign policy—were well aware that a pervasive moralism among the American people and their representatives in Congress regarding the conduct of U.S. foreign policy blocked Washington's use of military force to maintain the postwar East Asian balance of power. Use of such power in a time of peace was still seen as anathema to the American way. Because of such ideological considerations, Washington became wedded to an unrealistic policy, in effect relying heavily on Soviet goodwill to secure a favorable East Asian balance.

This policy was partly responsible for the American rejection of the CCP leaders' offers at this time to cooperate closely with the United States. Because of its reliance on Moscow, the United States was intent on maintaining a stable internal situation in China that would not complicate the Yalta arrangements worked out with the USSR. Rather than risk disrupting the Chinese situation by aligning with the CCP, the United States continued to back Chiang Kai-shek. It judged that undermining Chiang's leadership would have led to a civil war in which the American-Soviet agreements on the postwar situation might have become unraveled. As a result of its focus on Chiang, the United States rebuffed the Communists, who were demanding a greater role in Chinese internal affairs.

Although the emerging bipolar confrontation of the Cold War in the late 1940s prompted a briefly more realistic U.S. approach to East Asia, subsequent Chinese involvement in the Korean War served to solidify an ideologically based prejudice that was to dominate American China policy until the 1960s. Beijing's unexpected entry on the side of Pyongyang caused U.S. planners to consider the Sino-Soviet bloc as a monolith and to scrap earlier hopes that Beijing would eventually come into conflict with Moscow. The United States now judged that it would have to expand its containment policy to secure not only against Moscow but against Beijing as well.

This world-view caused Washington to fail to perceive the significance of CCP overtures in the mid–1950s. It was inconceivable to chief American strategists that China would follow a policy that was basically more in the interests of the United States than of the Soviet Union. Washington had lost sight of the fact that the interests of the Chinese state might lead Beijing to an independent posture vis-à-vis Moscow, which in turn might be compatible with American national interests in Asia. Washington did not completely put aside its ideolog- ically based view until the late 1960s, when fundamental shifts in the international and East Asian balance of forces constrained the U.S. leadership to reassess its policy in China, resulting in the Nixon Administration's initiatives toward the People's Republic of China.

The experience of the thirty years leading up to the Nixon opening to China demonstrated clearly that the evolving balance of power in East Asia played the crucial role in leading to the Sino-American rapprochement of the 1970s. Al- though the ideologies, historical experiences, and different cultures of the two sides tended to keep them apart, the developing East Asian balance forced them to put aside such negative factors and prompted both sides to see that their vital national interests in the area were compatible and provided the basis for mutual understanding. The achievement of President Nixon, Henry Kissinger, and their Chinese counterparts was to see clearly the compatibility of these interests and the basis for mutual understanding, despite the many important difficulties facing U.S.-PRC reconciliation at that time.

SOME IMPLICATIONS FOR FUTURE POLICY

One of the weaknesses of the Sino-U.S. rapprochement during the Nixon Administration was that it had a narrow base. That is, it depended heavily on the force that brought it about in the first place—mainly, the evolving balance of power in Asia. Thus, if the balance of power were to change substantially, it was probable that American and Chinese concerns would also change, leading to a shift in their bilateral relations. For example, fear of the Soviet Union was an important element motivating China to maintain close relations with the United States. If Moscow were significantly to moderate its policy toward China and reduce its military power along the Sino-Soviet border, Beijing might find less need for close ties with the United States as a hedge against the Soviet threat. Under these new circumstances, China would appear freer to adopt a more even- handed policy, playing one superpower off against the other.

Under the new Soviet leadership of Mikhail Gorbachev, the Soviet Union has significantly reduced pressure against China, notably by withdrawing some troops from China's northern border. China has reciprocated by improving Sino-Soviet economic, political, and border relations. But Sino-U.S. relations have not suf- fered as a consequence. In part, this results from the broadening of Sino-U.S. relations since the first openings in the 1970s. Especially following the reforms initiated after Mao's death, China has encouraged a range of economic, cultural, and intellectual contacts with the United States that have gone well beyond the expectations of most observers in the 1970s. China's more interdependent de- velopment and foreign policies have reinforced PRC interest in close ties with the United States. For its part, the U.S. government has moved well beyond the secret diplomacy of the 1970s and built firm understanding in the United States regarding the utility of a strong, independent China, and continued close U.S. relations with China. Thus, variations in Sino-Soviet relations have had less of an impact on such broadly based Sino-American ties than they likely would have had ten years ago.

Another legacy of the secret U.S. opening to China, seen especially in Dr. Kissinger's covert mission to Beijing in 1971, was its attractiveness as a model to later U.S. administrations as a means to carry out sensitive and important foreign policy initiatives or missions. Such secretive practices do not always mesh well with common values held in democratic societies like the United States. They implicitly challenge the powers of legitimate, established authorities in the administration and the Congress, who in turn represent the interests of the American people and are accountable to them.

It was fortunate for the coherence of the U.S. China policy that Nixon and Kissinger were able to obtain terms for reconciliation with China that did not alienate large segments of American opinion when the secret China opening came to light. It was also fortunate that the opening was successful. Contrasting experiences were seen in later years. Thus, President Carter's administration successfully held highly secret talks that led to the normalization of U.S.-PRC relations in December 1978. But the terms Carter accepted in secret alienated large segments of American opinion, including key leaders of his own party in Congress. Among the results was congressional toughening of the Taiwan Relations Act, with provisions that proponents of improved U.S.-PRC relations still see as major obstacles to future ties.

A more graphic example of the dangers of such secret policies and missions in a democracy like ours is seen, of course, in the outcome of the recent Iran/Contra affair. Not only did the policy offend large segments of American opinion, but it also failed to meet its stated objectives. I have no intention to link the malfeasance of later officials to the U.S. practice during the secret opening of China. My main point is to observe that the recent Iran/Contra scandal has almost certainly served as a warning to those who would use such secret diplomacy that they run great risks in the event the policy they are pursuing is seen as unpopular, unsuccessful, or unethical. It may prove to be as much a watershed in American foreign policy behavior as was the Nixon-Kissinger secret opening to China.

Indeed, the type of secret operation seen in Dr. Kissinger's trip to China in 1971 may prove increasingly difficult to carry out without fuller consultation with Congress—a process that risks possible disclosure that could abort such missions. Following the Iran/Contra affair, U.S. leaders are more sensitive to the possible negative consequences of using National Security Council staff on secret missions and in the conduct of other covert operations. In particular, Congress has focused significant legislative attention on possibly increasing congressional oversight in these areas.

Concern has been raised regarding the means by which the president and others in the Reagan Administration avoided notification to Congress of covert actions that would normally be reportable under section 662 of the Foreign Assistance Act (the Hughes-Ryan Amendment) or under section 501 of the National Security Act of 1947. Among other things, the CIA director, at the express order of the president, withheld from the Intelligence Committee of Congress a January 17, 1987, presidential "finding" authorizing Central Intelligence Agency (CIA) covert actions related to the arms sales to Iran. Furthermore, staff of the National Security Council used personnel and other CIA resources to facilitate arms sales to Iran in a manner that would avoid congressional scrutiny and awareness of these activities. The two congressional committees investigating the Iran/Contra affair have received testimony that the president does not recall approving at least one December 1985 "finding" needed to authorize CIA covert action in the sale of arms to Iran.

Consequently, Representative Louis Stokes, the chairman of the House Permanent Select Committee on Intelligence, and others have cosponsored legislation (H.R. 1013) to eliminate the perceived ambiguities in current law regarding prior notification of covert actions to Congress and thus help ensure that it can fulfill its responsibilities to oversee them. A key question Congress faces is whether or not it should amend existing law that governs notification to it of covert actions by the United States. Even if the law is not strengthened, it appears safe to conclude that U.S. officials, at least for a time, will be more careful in the use of secret operations for fear of prompting the kind of counterproductive reaction caused by the secret arms sale to Iran.

APPENDIX

TEXT OF U.S.-PEOPLE'S REPUBLIC OF CHINA COMMUNIQUE ISSUED AT SHANGHAI, FEBRUARY 27, 1972

President Richard Nixon of the United States of America visited the People's Republic of China at the invitation of Premier Chou En-lai of the People's Republic of China from February 21 to February 28, 1972. Accompanying the President were Mrs. Nixon, U.S. Secretary of State William Rogers, Assistant to the President Dr. Henry Kissinger, and other American officials.

President Nixon met with Chairman Mao Tse-tung of the Communist Party of China on February 21. The two leaders had a serious and frank exchange of views on Sino-U.S. relations and world affairs.

During the visit, extensive, earnest and frank discussions were held between President Nixon and Premier Chou En-lai on the normalization of relations between the United States of America and the People's Republic of China, as well as on other matters of interest to both sides. In addition, Secretary of State William Rogers and Foreign Minister Chi Peng-fei held talks in the same spirit.

President Nixon and his party visited Peking and viewed cultural, industrial and agricultural sites, and they also toured Hangchow and Shanghai where, continuing discussions with Chinese leaders, they viewed similar places of interest.

The leaders of the People's Republic of China and the United States of America found it beneficial to have this opportunity, after so many years without contact, to present candidly to one another their views on a variety of issues. They reviewed the international situation in which important changes and great upheavals are taking place and expounded their respective positions and attitudes.

The U.S. side stated: Peace in Asia and peace in the world requires efforts both to reduce immediate tensions and to eliminate the basic causes of conflict. The United States will work for a just and secure peace: just, because it fulfills the aspirations of peoples and nations for freedom and progress; secure, because it removes the danger of foreign aggression. The United States supports individual freedom and social progress for all the peoples of the world, free of outside pressure or intervention. The United States believes that the effort to reduce tensions is served by improving communication between countries that have different ideologies so as to lessen the risks of confrontation through accident, miscalculation or misunderstanding. Countries should treat each other with mutual respect and be willing to compete peacefully, letting performance be the ultimate judge. No country should claim infallibility and each country should be prepared to re-examine its own attitudes for the common good. The United States stressed that the peoples of Indochina should be allowed to determine their destiny without outside intervention; its constant primary objective has been a negotiated solution; the eight-point proposal put forward by the Republic of Vietnam and the United States on January 27, 1972 represents a basis for the attainment of that objective; in the absence of a negotiated settlement the United States envisages the ultimate withdrawal of all U.S. forces from the region consistent with the aim of self-determination for each country of Indochina. The United States will maintain its close ties with and support for the Republic of Korea; the United States will support efforts of the Republic of Korea to seek a relaxation of tension and increased communication in the Korean peninsula. The United States places the highest value on its friendly relations with Japan; it will continue to develop the existing close bonds. Consistent with the United Nations Security Council Resolution of December 21, 1971, the United States favors the continuation of the ceasefire between India and Pakistan and the withdrawal of all military forces to within their own territories and to their own sides of the ceasefire line in Jammu and Kashmir; the United States supports the right of the peoples of South Asia to shape their own future in peace, free of military threat, and without having the area become the subject of great power rivalry.

The Chinese side stated: Wherever there is oppression, there is resistance. Countries want independence, nations want liberation and the people want revolution—this has become the irresistible trend of history. All nations, big or small, should be equal; big nations should not bully the small and strong nations should not bully the weak. China will never be a superpower and it opposes hegemony and power politics of any kind. The Chinese side stated that it firmly supports the struggles of all the oppressed people and nations for freedom and liberation and that the people of all countries have the right to choose their social systems according to their own wishes and the right to safeguard the independence, sovereignty and territorial integrity of their own countries and oppose foreign aggression, interference, control and subversion. All foreign troops should be withdrawn to their own countries.

The Chinese side expressed its firm support to the peoples of Vietnam, Laos and Cambodia in their efforts for the attainment of their goal and its firm support to the seven-point proposal of the Provisional Revolutionary Government of the Republic of South Vietnam and the elaboration of February this year on the two key problems in the proposal, and to the Joint Declaration of the Summit Conference of the Indochinese Peoples. It firmly supports the eight-point program for the peaceful unification of Korea put forward by the Government of the Democratic People's Republic of Korea on April 12, 1971, and the stand for the abolition of the "U.N. Commission for the Unification and Rehabilitation of Korea." It firmly opposes the revival and outward expansion of Japanese militarism and firmly supports the Japanese people's desire to build an independent, democratic, peaceful and neutral Japan. If firmly maintains that India and Pakistan should, in accordance with the United Nations resolutions on the India-Pakistan question, immediately withdraw all their forces to their respective territories and to their own sides of the ceasefire line in Jammu and Kashmir and firmly supports the Pakistan Government and people in their struggle to preserve their independence and sovereignty and the people of Jammu and Kashmir in their struggle for the right of self-determination.

There are essential differences between China and the United States in their social systems and foreign policies. However, the two sides agreed that countries, regardless of their social systems, should conduct their relations on the principles of respect for the sovereignty and territorial integrity of all states, non-aggression against other states, non-interference in the internal affairs of other states, equality and mutual benefit, and peaceful coexistence. International disputes should be settled on this basis, without resorting to the use or threat of force. The United States and the People's Republic of China are prepared to apply these principles to their mutual relations.

With these principles of international relations in mind the two sides stated that

—progress toward the normalization of relations between China and the United States is in the interests of all countries;

—both wish to reduce the danger of international military conflict;

—neither should seek hegemony in the Asia-Pacific region and each is opposed to efforts by any other country or group of countries to establish such hegemony; and

—neither is prepared to negotiate on behalf of any third party or to enter into agreements or understandings with the other directed at other states.

Both sides are of the view that it would be against the interests of the peoples of the world for any major country to collude with another against other countries, or for major countries to divide up the world into spheres of interest.

The two sides reviewed the long-standing serious disputes between China and the United States. The Chinese side reaffirmed its position: The Taiwan question is the crucial question obstructing the normalization of relations between China and the United States; the Government of the People's Republic of China is the sole legal government of China; Taiwan is a province of China which has long been returned to the motherland; the liberation of Taiwan is China's internal affair in which no other country has the right to interfere; and all U.S. forces and military installations must be withdrawn from Taiwan. The Chinese Government firmly opposes any activities which aim at the creation of "one China, one Taiwan," "one China, two governments," "two Chinas," and "independent Taiwan" or advocate that "the status of Taiwan remains to be determined."

The U.S. side declared: The United States acknowledges that all Chinese on either side of the Taiwan Strait maintain there is but one China and that Taiwan is a part of China. The United States Government does not challenge that position. It reaffirms its interest in a peaceful settlement of the Taiwan question by the Chinese themselves. With this prospect in mind, it affirms the ultimate objective of the withdrawal of all U.S. forces and military installations from Taiwan. In the meantime, it will progressively reduce its forces and military installations on Taiwan as the tension in the area diminishes.

The two sides agreed that it is desirable to broaden the understanding between the two peoples. To this end, they discussed specific areas in such fields as science, technology, culture, sports and journalism, in which people-to-people contacts and exchanges would be mutually beneficial. Each side undertakes to facilitate the further development of such contacts and exchanges.

Both sides view bilateral trade as another area from which mutual benefit can be derived, and agreed that economic relations based on equality and mutual benefit are in the interest of the peoples of the two countries. They agree to facilitate the progressive development of trade between their two countries.

The two sides agreed that they will stay in contact through various channels, including the sending of a senior U.S. representative to Peking from time to time for concrete consultations to further the normalization of relations between the two countries and continue to exchange views on issues of common interest.

The two sides expressed the hope that the gains achieved during this visit would open up new prospects for the relations between the two countries. They believe that the normalization of relations between the two countries is not only in the interest of the Chinese and American peoples but also contributes to the relaxation of tension in Asia and the world.

President Nixon, Mrs. Nixon and the American party expressed their appreciation for the gracious hospitality shown them by the Government and people of the People's Republic of China.

NOTES

The views expressed in this paper are those of the author and not necessarily those of the Congressional Research Service, the Library of Congress.

1. This perspective relies heavily on my book, *China Watch: Toward Sino-American Reconciliation* (Baltimore: Johns Hopkins University Press, 1978), 155 p. The basic sources on U.S. policy during this time include, most notably, Henry Kissinger, *The White House Years* (Boston: Little, Brown, 1979), 1529 p. Several prominent specialists have examined Chinese and U.S. motives from different perspectives. See, for example, Michel Oksenberg, "A Decade of Sino-American Relations," *Foreign Affairs* 61, no. 1 (Fall 1982); A. Doak Barnett, *China and the Major Powers in East Asia* (Washington, D.C.: Brookings Institution, 1977); Richard Solomon, "The China Factor in America's Foreign Relations," in Richard Solomon, ed., *The China Factor* (Englewood Cliffs, N.J.: Prentice-Hall, 1981).

2. As seen from the discussion below, Chinese leaders reacted very differently in this changed situation, setting the stage for one of the most serious power struggles in the history of the PRC. For background, see notably Thomas Gottlieb, *Chinese Foreign Policy Factionalism and the Origins of the Strategic Triangle* (Santa Monica, Calif.: Rand Corporation, 1977).

3. There is debate among scholars as to just how concerned Chinese officials were about the Soviet threat. See, for instance, Richard Wich, *Sino-Soviet Crisis Politics: A Study of Political Change and Communication* (Cambridge, Mass.: Harvard University Press, 1980); Harold Rinton, *China's Turbulent Quest: An Analysis of China's Foreign Policy Since 1949* (New York: Macmillan, 1972); the Gottlieb study cited in note 2; and the Barnett book cited in note 1.

4. See appendix for the text of the communique, taken from U.S. Department of State, Selected Documents No. 9, U.S. Policy Toward China July 14, 1971–January 15, 1979.

5. Among other places, this is discussed in my book, *China Watch*, pp. 63–82.

6. These senior military leaders, who wielded great power during the late 1960s, were not seen again for ten years, until they appeared along with Mao's wife and other members of the so-called gang of four in a series of trials designed to legitimize their continued detention.

7. In this context, it appears more understandable that the first person to greet Dr. Kissinger on his arrival in Beijing in July 1971, and the leader at his side and responsible for his safety throughout his first stay in China, was Zhou's most senior and important associate in the People's Liberation Army, Marshall Ye Jianying. Ye's exact role in the leadership struggle leading up to Lin's death remains to be fully disclosed. But the rise in his stature following Lin Biao's demise and his identification with Zhou during the period of intense struggle with Lin Biao are matters of record.

8. See, for instance, James Reardon-Anderson, *Yenan and the Great Powers: The Origins of Chinese Communist Foreign Policy, 1944–1946* (New York: Columbia University Press, 1980).

9. See Dorothy Berg and Waldo Hendricks, eds., *Uncertain Years: Chinese American Relations, 1947–1950* (New York: Columbia University Press, 1980).

10. This view is based on research for my book, *China Watch*. A different and authoritative view is seen in Kenneth T. Young, *Negotiating with the Chinese Communists: The United States Experience, 1953–1967* (New York: McGraw-Hill, 1968). Young sees little sign of PRC flexibility toward the United States at this juncture.

11. For background, see John K. Fairbank, *The United States and China* (Cambridge, Mass.: Harvard University Press, 1983); Warren Cohen, *America's Response to China: An Interpretive History of Sino-American Relations* (New York: John Wiley, 1971); and Akira Iriye, *Across the Pacific: An Inner History of American-East Asian Relations* (New York: Harcourt, Brace & World, 1967).

Discussant: Jerome A. Cohen

It must be a source of great satisfaction to Ambassador Han, who has taken part in this whole process, today to have a chance to look back and also to look forward. Mr. Sutter has helped us to understand what Ambassador Han meant when he talked about the risks involved in this great move. Thinking about Mr. Sutter's drawing of future implications from this story, I just happen to think we're lucky that President Nixon did not entrust Colonel North with the mission to China. Now, I just want to give a couple of personal reflections on the background to this problem and talk about a couple of the international law problems that articulated the challenge. I also want to talk a moment about the choices made by the administration and the cost of the consequences.

First, some personal background: I think it's important for you to understand what the situation was like in the United States vis-à-vis the China policy. In 1960 there were four congressmen who voted for a resolution calling for what we called Communist China to come into the United Nations. In the autumn elections, three of them suffered defeat, and this was the salient issue. In January 1961 as President Eisenhower escorted President-elect Kennedy down Pennsylvania Avenue down the inauguration route, Ike said, "If Kennedy moved to recognize Communist China, that would bring Ike out of retirement to challenge him." It wasn't until the September 1966 Fulbright hearings that it was demonstrated that the country had great support for change in our China policy. Indeed, I remember a session shortly afterward when many of us in academic life criticized the State Department for being too passive. The defense made by one of the articulators in the State Department was that the department had to wait for the Fulbright hearings to show national support. I said, "I suppose you mean the function of the Congress is to lead foreign policy and the function of the executive branch is to follow it." That seemed to be implicit.

Of course, you remember Nixon's famous *Foreign Affairs* article in 1967 in which he hinted about the importance of moving towards a reconciliation with China. We shouldn't give Mr. Kissinger all the credit. Indeed, so far, I haven't heard much reference to Mr. Kissinger, but I want to make some. In 1968 Mr. Kissinger didn't know much about China, but as he was the first to say he's a quick study. He used the bee method: he went around like a bee to hundreds of little flowers, taking honey wherever he could. Many of these flowers were academic, and, knowing that academic flowers flourish when they hear flattery, he notoriously engaged in that, recognizing that psychic income is not taxable. He could look into your eyes with the greatest of sincerity and say, "You know, without your participation, we couldn't do this exchange in China policy." Of course, the common academic response was to say, "Henry, I bet you tell that to all the girls." But it worked, and he learned a lot.

Some of us at Harvard, together with Professor Pyle from MIT and Professor

Barnett from Columbia, gave Mr. Kissinger a report on November 6, 1968, whose first recommendation said, "You should seriously explore the possibility of arranging confidential, perhaps even deniable, conversations between Chinese Communist leaders and someone with whom you have confidence." Now this idea was articulated in this way because it was a memorandum to the president-elect, Mr. Nixon. The first draft said he should select the secretary of state, but then we thought about it for a while, and knowing that Mr. Kissinger would be a decisive influence here and that he wasn't going to be secretary of state, we thought we would cast it in a matter that might be more likely to attract him. So we simply said the president should select someone in whom he had confidence and indeed he did; the consequences have been highly beneficial, as you have already heard.

There was also a partisan aspect to this matter. In 1969 the Democrats were beating the drums for a new China policy. In March 1969 Senator Ted Kennedy made a nationally broadcast speech calling for a new China policy. Senator George McGovern, eager to run in 1972, was also very active in this regard. What the Kissinger-Nixon group did brilliantly was to take this issue away from the Democrats and make it a Republican issue. With this spectacular coverage that Nixon's week in China gave them, of course, it was a tremendous stepping stone to reelection. I was McGovern's policy adviser in 1972, and even I, when I witnessed the eleven o'clock commercials at night during the campaign, showing Nixon stepping down after arrival in Beijing from Air Force One, shaking hands with Zhou EnLai, to the tune of the Star Spangled Banner, playing in Beijing, it even brought me to tears, night after night. It was a fantastic performance, and I think richly deserved praise.

At first, there were many issues to handle, but essentially there were three. The United Nations question had to be resolved: the question of how we would handle the problem of Taiwan. Was Taiwan to be regarded as part of the territory of China? The United Nations question involved many obscure, difficult issues: was it a new entry by China as a new country into the United Nations, or was China merely resuming its rightful seat as the representative of a Chinese state that had already long been a member of the United Nations? This led to different consequences in the Security Council. Was it a procedural question or a substantive question in the General Assembly? Should it be a two-thirds vote or a majority vote? All of those questions were forgotten. I used to earn my livelihood by talking about them.

Now the stage was set for handling the two more difficult questions: recognition and the territorial status of Taiwan. We had quite a debate in the State Department at this time. Essentially there were two approaches. Some of us advocated biting the bullet, as I did in the *Foreign Affairs* article in 1971, recognizing the PRC as China's only legitimate government and trying to ease the shock on Taiwan and dealing with the territorial question later. The other approach was the opposite: we should first deal with the territorial question and then try to give both sides some assurance that we would not engage in a desperate policy vis-à-vis

Taiwan and gradually come to grips with recognition later. That was very well articulated in a book called *Remaking China Policy*, written by two students of China policy, Dick Morestein and Mort Abromowitz. (It had a red cover, and I used to call it the little red book of U.S. foreign policy toward China.) Nixon chose the second approach, and it worked brilliantly. It has enabled China to move ahead, even though it wasn't formally recognized as the government of China in 1972.

Lots of other problems remained to be handled, including the question of American prisoners in Chinese prisons. But again, the president and Kissinger handled this issue very cleverly. My former college classmate, Jack Downey, was languishing in a Chinese jail under a life sentence. Yet at a press conference in January 1973 the following question arose about prisoners of war in Vietnam: how would they be released in light of our withdrawal from the Vietnam War? It was also asked whether this meant the release of Downey and Richard Fecteau, another American [CIA agent sentenced to prison by the Chinese for violating Chinese airspace and promoting espionage]. The answer from the president was a very skillful "No." That was a different case, involving the CIA. Most people in America had no idea what it was all about. But that kind of recognition meant a great deal to the PRC because from 1952 until then, when these people were arrested in China, having been dropped in by a CIA airlift, the United States always denied that this was a CIA operation. Six weeks after the statement by President Nixon, who didn't say, like McGovern, "I'm willing to crawl all the way to Hanoi to get our boys out of jail," (Nixon's comment in constrast being a dignified factual reference, just saying that that case involved the CIA), Downey was out of prison, and that problem was behind us. I just want to use that as another example of how they handled China policy very skillfully.

There were costs to this policy, but they were not at all comparable to the benefits. One cost was our memorandum to President-elect Nixon: we had urged that the process of change be handled in a way not to upset our allies, especially Japan. Nevertheless, Nixon and Kissinger socked it very hard to Prime Minister Eisaku Sato. They were furious with him for failing to fulfill what they thought was a commitment—it's not clear that Sato made such a commitment—to handle the problem of Japanese exports to the United States. They didn't give him the advance warning that was needed. It was a terrible blow to U.S.-Japan relations, and we're still suffering from the mistrust it has sewn. There were also some costs in the right-wing support for Nixon in American politics, as Mr. Sutter has indicated. The right wing was very unhappy with the secret trip, specifically with the changing of policy, and that's how this memorandum that we gave to President-elect Nixon and Kissinger surfaced. It was released in the congressional records shortly after Kissinger's return from his secret trip, in an attempt to embarrass Kissinger and show he was the captive of his supposedly left-wing colleagues at Harvard. So the right wing wasn't happy, and Japan wasn't happy. But when those costs are weighed against the great benefits that Ambassador Han and Mr. Sutter have pointed out, we have to say they were quite right in asserting that this was not only a very bold move but also an enormously successful one. Moreover, I would say that it was the outstanding move of the Nixon Administration, in either the domestic or international arena.

In the next conference, which is scheduled to review the accomplishments of the Carter Administration, I hope that people will observe that Nixon nevertheless left the toughest problem to his successor. He didn't have to incur the domestic costs or the international costs of withdrawing recognition from Taiwan. That's what Carter had to do. Because Carter was weakened, not only because he did it through secret negotiations, as any of these would have to be, but because he already did it in December 1978—later in his administration he was already suffering—he never got the credit he deserved. Carter had come a long way from 1975 to 1979 on his China policy. When he first considered it, his view was, "why don't we just recognize both of them?" By December 1978, he was able to articulate the reasons why it made sense to recognize only the PRC: namely, it controlled the population of China; it had the real control over resources; and it represented the Chinese people. So we ought to give some credit to Carter, and I hope the next session looks into that question. Thank you very much.

ENDING THE VIETNAM WAR

4

The American Withdrawal from Vietnam: Some Military and Political Considerations

WILLIAM M. HAMMOND

President Richard M. Nixon's decision in 1969 to begin the American withdrawal from South Vietnam had its roots in years of suppressed American frustration. A few members of the American news media recognized the problem before many within the U.S. government were willing to admit it existed. An article by Ward Just in the November 6, 1966, edition of the *Washington Post* was typical of what those reporters had to say. Describing conditions in Quang Nam Province, where the city of Da Nang is located, Just observed that the province chief, who had received a Ph.D. in political science from Michigan State University, was honest and intelligent but also a native of North Vietnam who had little in common with the South Vietnamese he supposedly governed. After only six months on the job, he had taken a six-week sabbatical to lecture in the United States. As a result, important social reforms critical for the outcome of the war in the province had gone unattended. Just continued that the U.S. Marines, by default, had become the only functioning government in Quang Nam. They provided what security the people possessed; they trained the local forces; and they supplied the muscle and know-how that gave impetus to many government programs. The reason they had assumed so important a role in the life of the province, Just said, could be seen every Friday afternoon, when U.S. Marine units returned to their bases from the field "bone tired and dragging their butts," while freshly shaved and neatly dressed South Vietnamese junior officers went down the road the other way, toward the "bright lights" of Da Nang for the weekend. So pervasive had the Marines' influence become, the reporter concluded, and so weak was that of the South Vietnamese government, qualified

observers believed the province would revert to Communist control within two
weeks of the Americans' departure.[1]

Just's perceptions were controversial at the time but more than a little accurate.
Although Quang Nam was hardly representative of every province in South
Vietnam, the situation the reporter described—the lack of concern of high government officials, the indifference of the armed forces, and the impatient efficiency of the Marines—prevailed in many parts of the country. With time, its
results were also clear. Over the years, the United States poured men and money
into the country to insure its existence as an independent, non-Communist nation
and to avert any possibility that Red China might expand its influence in the
area. Yet during that time, rather than fade before the military might of the
United States, North Vietnam and the Viet Cong, with the help of China and
the Soviet Union, seemed always to come out ahead. In the process, despite
severe losses in South Vietnam and damaging American bombing campaigns in
the North, they managed to retain and even increase their capacity to make war.[2]

The administration of President Lyndon Johnson was at first unwilling to admit
that American efforts had resulted in at best a stalemate, but doubts lingered
beneath the surface of the official optimism it sought to convey to the outside
world. They emerged late in 1966 in intelligence reports but became public only
in 1967. During August, Secretary of Defense Robert S. McNamara testified in
secret before Congress that the United States' very expensive bombing campaign
against North Vietnam and its supply route into the South, the Ho Chi Minh
Trail, was incapable of cutting off the flow of oil, weapons, and ammunition
that the enemy needed to continue the war. McNamara's testimony was leaked
immediately to the press, where it caused a sensation.[3]

Similar uneasiness existed within the Defense Department's Office of Systems
Analysis. Even if military body counts were to be believed, researchers there
asserted, it appeared unlikely that the United States would ever be able to inflict
enough casualties on enemy forces to affect North Vietnam's will to continue
the war. The British during World War I had suffered much more, losing almost
an entire generation of young men. Yet they had managed to carry on the conflict
against Germany for years.[4]

The Communist Tet Offensive in February 1968 brought many of those mis-
givings into the open. Although the American military contended—with considerable justification—that they had won a significant victory, the enemy's
ability to mount a simultaneous, coordinated campaign against virtually all of
South Vietnam's cities and major towns threw into question earlier claims of
progress. The American commander in South Vietnam, General William C.
Westmoreland, for example, had stated during a speech in Washington just two
months before the offensive that his operations had rendered Communist forces
incapable of mounting large unit operations near South Vietnam's major population centers.

In the reappraisal that followed the offensive, high U.S. officials traveled to
South Vietnam to review the situation. They came away with a number of painful

observations. American and South Vietnamese forces seemed more than able to defend themselves, they asserted, but military victory still seemed elusive. To defeat the Communists, allied forces would have to destroy them in battle. Yet the enemy could find sanctuary at will across South Vietnam's border in Laos and Cambodia, in areas that for reasons of politics and diplomacy would probably always remain off limits to conventional military units. The United States thus seemed condemned to run a treadmill, winning battle after battle but lacking the ability to strike the sort of blow that would make the enemy seek some kind of reasonable peace agreement.[5]

The government of South Vietnam was also a problem. To many within the Johnson Administration, the South Vietnamese leadership seemed to lack any incentive either to wage an effective war on its own or to make the sort of concessions that might lead to a proper negotiated settlement. American forces bore the brunt of the fighting against the enemy's main forces, so the reasoning went, providing relatively complete security for the South Vietnamese people. Yet rather than free the country to fight the Viet Cong, the American presence seemed to have the opposite effect. Lacking any fear either that the United States would go away or that the Communists would triumph, the country's leaders had adopted a business as usual attitude that presupposed continuing, all-out American support. The flood of dollars that had accompanied the arrival of American troops complicated matters further. Corrupting South Vietnam's institutions, the presence of so much easy money made continuation of the war more profitable than peace for many of the country's politicians.[6]

Officers within the American military command in South Vietnam would have contested many of those conclusions. The South Vietnamese armed forces, they pointed out, though hardly the match of the U.S. Army, generally suffered more killed and wounded per year than their American allies, an indication that anti-Communist forces were more than willing to fight. Leadership was the problem, and with time that would improve. In the same way, if corruption seemed a way of life in South Vietnam, that was to be expected. The country had just emerged from a period of colonial misrule by the French. It thus lacked the political maturity of democracies such as the United States that had existed for hundreds of years. Time and additional seasoning would once more cure the problem.

High-ranking officers also questioned the political restrictions that determined how far they could go in meeting the enemy. Although respectful of civilian authority, General Westmoreland, for one, was convinced that the best way to defeat the Viet Cong in South Vietnam would be to send a combined American-South Vietnamese force into Laos to cut the Ho Chi Minh Trail permanently. The White House refused to consider so radical an escalation, but Westmoreland never completely abandoned the idea. He held on to the base at Khe Sanh, which was located near the Laotian border and would be essential for any operation to cut the trail, until well into 1968, long after it had ceased to be of any immediate use.[7]

The chairman of the Joint Chiefs of Staff during the final years of the war,

Admiral Thomas H. Moorer, remains convinced to this day that he knows what should have been done. At a recent U.S. Navy seminar, he stated that the United States could have won the war without difficulty "if we'd done the same thing to Hanoi in 1965 that we did in 1972." He was referring to the campaign that occurred toward the end of 1972 in which the United States sent B-52 bombers against North Vietnam's capital, Hanoi, and mined the waters of the country's main seaport, Haiphong.[8]

Whatever the validity of those assertions, the United States had considered all of those options at one time or another and had rejected them because they were either militarily impractical or politically inexpedient. To have cut off the Ho Chi Minh Trail, for example, might have tied down several American divisions in Laos for years. In the same way, as McNamara had pointed out in his August 1967 testimony before Congress, if the United States had mined the harbors of North Vietnam, the enemy would have had little difficulty bringing what he needed—a mere 540 tons of supplies per day—across the border from China.

Perhaps American policymakers should have been more daring, but there was one consideration that bore heavily on the Johnson Administration. The president could never continue the war without the backing of the American public and Congress, and neither had ever been more than lukewarm in support of the war. Indeed, by 1968 and the Tet Offensive, lacking demonstrable progress on the battlefield, both had begun to grow impatient.

American casualties were the key. As researcher John Mueller would later demonstrate, responses to the Gallup Poll question, "In view of developments since we entered the fighting in Vietnam, do you think the United States made a mistake sending troops to fight in Vietnam?" indicated that public dissatisfaction with the war grew by about 15 percentage points each time the number of American killed and wounded increased by a factor of ten. When total casualties from all causes, in other words, went from one thousand to ten thousand or from ten thousand to one hundred thousand, public opinion survey responses showed a corresponding growth in public disillusionment and regret of about 13 percent (see Figure 4.1). By August 1968, 53 percent of respondents to the poll said that the United States should never have become involved in the conflict.[9]

The effect hardly indicated that Americans were so concerned about casualties that they favored outright, ignominious withdrawal from Vietnam. As Mueller's logarithmic progression demonstrated, they became so inured to their losses as the war lengthened that it took more and more American injuries and deaths to activate their concerns. Yet if there was little support for the extreme alternatives of either total withdrawal or all-out war, other polls suggested that there was substantial support, as early as 1966, for a policy of holding military operations at an even level while seeking an honorable peace.[10]

Although formal studies such as the one by Mueller had yet to be made, President Johnson's advisers had more than enough political acumen to discern that public unhappiness with the war was increasing and that American casualties

Figure 4.1
Casualties and Public Opinion, 1965 to 1969*

War Not a Mistake

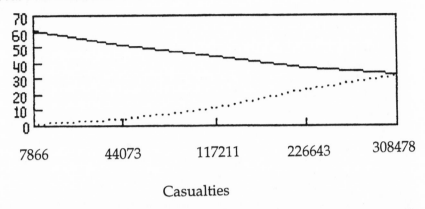

Casualties

*The casualty figures are from U.S. Department of Defense, *Southeast Asia Statistical Summary*, 1973, Copy Center of Military History files. The statistics on public opinion are taken from Hazel Erskine, "The Polls: Is War a Mistake," *Public Opinion Quarterly* 34 (Spring 1970): 134.

were at least partly to blame. The conclusion seemed obvious. As Secretary of Defense Clark Clifford put it in May 1968, since "more men, more bombs, and more killing" had done no good, it seemed time to try something else: to concentrate on the negotiations just beginning in Paris and to cut American losses by gradually turning the war over to the South Vietnamese.[11]

By the time Richard Nixon became president, few decisions were left to be made. Lyndon Johnson had already made the basic moves by agreeing to negotiations with the enemy and by very clearly turning the government of the United States against continuation of the war on the old terms. In the process, Johnson contributed to the sense of disillusionment surrounding the war by removing himself as the spokesman for those who favored military alternatives and by creating an atmosphere in which opposition to the war by disciplined Democrats in Congress was much more politically acceptable than in the past. After all, if the president, the leader of the party, recognized that military victory had become impossible and had begun to seek a way out, might not members of the party's rank and file, who had followed the president's lead on the war, break step as well and voice their own concerns?

In taking his new direction, Johnson gave no indication of a willingness to lose face by abandoning an ally or by allowing any appearance that American forces had somehow suffered defeat at the hands of North Vietnam. Yet, in the process of seeking an honorable peace, he created a dilemma that surely led in that direction. For how was the United States to negotiate a satisfactory peace agreement with North Vietnam while at the same time disengaging from the fighting and eliminating the base of military power in the field that made credible negotiating possible? With the Americans leaving, all the enemy had to do was wait. Once they were gone, he could settle with the South Vietnamese. He had little need to bargain.

Left to his own devices, the new president would probably have favored a more vigorous attack on North Vietnam, but his advisers, especially Secretary of Defense Melvin Laird, were quick to point out the harsh realities. Laird was convinced that the conflict had bled American strength around the world in places such as Europe, that were far more important for the security of the United States than South Vietnam. In that light, a lengthening, endless war would inevitably reduce the ability of the United States to defend itself. A former congressman who had cultivated a broad range of political contacts throughout the United States, Laird also had a strong sense of the nation's mood.[12] Recognizing that time was short, he told the president bluntly after his first trip to South Vietnam in 1969 that public support for the administration would begin to waver if the war continued too long. To keep that from happening, he said, Nixon would have to withdraw between fifty thousand and seventy thousand men by the end of the year—even though the South Vietnamese armed forces were unprepared to replace them.[13]

The U.S. ambassador to South Vietnam, Ellsworth Bunker, passed the president's concerns to the South Vietnamese. "There is no question," he told South Vietnamese President Nguyen Van Thieu, "but that as our casualties rise the Communists have an effect on American opinion. Our people show no interest in enemy casualties but they are very sensitive to ours. President Nixon regards this as one of his most difficult problems."[14]

The prospect of American withdrawal troubled U.S. commanders in South Vietnam. They believed that they had turned the enemy's Tet Offensive into an important American victory and that Communist forces were at a sore disadvantage. During October 1968, for example, while the Johnson Administration was turning away from the large unit war that had prevailed to that point, the chief of the U.S. Military Assistance Command in Vietnam, General Creighton W. Abrams, informed his superiors that the Communist logistical system in both North and South Vietnam was a shambles and that, as a result, the United States faced a moment of "supreme opportunity."[15]

Abrams later withdrew that assessment because he believed that Johnson's November 1968 bombing halt had reversed many of those gains, but he still remained confident.[16] During March 1969, when the enemy launched a fierce offensive in South Vietnam, coming close to equaling the number of battalion and larger sized attacks he had launched during the Tet Offensive, Abrams sent a powerful message to the Joint Chiefs of Staff advocating a blow against North Vietnam of "such proportions" that it would force the enemy to reassess his entire strategy. In addition to resuming air attacks against the southern portions of North Vietnam, he recommended air and ground attacks against the enemy's sanctuaries in Laos and Cambodia. Communist forces were seriously overextended in South Vietnam, he said, especially in the region around Saigon. In that area, the entire offensive seemed to depend for support on a limited number of bases in Cambodia and a single line of supply through the port of Sihanoukville. Enemy commanders would never have taken such large risks, Abrams concluded, unless they believed that the United States would be unable to respond for political reasons.[17]

The enemy's assumption proved correct. President Nixon lacked enough confidence in American public and congressional support for the war to launch the sort of attack Abrams advocated. Rather than move so dramatically, instead, after further provocations and several delays, he chose to begin bombing the enemy's Cambodian sanctuaries in secret—a move that he hoped would demonstrate his resolve to the Communists without stirring up more opposition than necessary at home.[18]

The enemy, of course, was counting heavily on what he called "the contradictions in the enemy camp" to achieve his goals.[19] To that end, between January and June 1969, he concentrated on surprise artillery, rocket, and sapper attacks designed to kill as many Americans and South Vietnamese as possible. In all of 1968, for example, the enemy had launched only 215 attacks of that sort against American positions while concentrating 494 on the South Vietnamese. During the first six months of 1969, he doubled the rate of his attacks on South Vietnamese installations to 424, while tripling it to 303 against American positions.[20]

Under the circumstances, the Nixon Administration had little choice but to attempt to cut American casualties while seeking to obtain more mileage from the South Vietnamese. As the chairman of the Joint Chiefs of Staff, General Earl G. Wheeler, observed in a message to Abrams, the subject of casualties "is being thrown at me at every juncture, in the press, by the Secretary of Defense, at the White House, and on the Hill." He was concerned, he said, that if the pressure continued, the president might have little choice but to seek a negotiated settlement at variance with U.S. objectives.[21]

General Abrams passed the word to his commanders, but he remained ill prepared for the cutbacks that accompanied Wheeler's declaration. First, he learned that the Defense Department was reducing the number of B-52 sorties in South Vietnam by 11 percent. Then word arrived that the Air Force was weighing cuts in the number of squadrons supporting the war, that Navy administrators had proposed reductions in the number of destroyer patrols along the coast of South Vietnam, and that the Army was considering a 2 percent cutback in the number of South Vietnamese civilians it employed. Stunned, the general protested that he saw nothing in the situation to warrant such drastic measures. He learned in return that the reductions had been prompted by the Department of the Treasury in order to cool down an overheating American economy.[22]

Abrams had known that a decision on American withdrawals was in the offing, but he was likewise astounded when Wheeler informed him that the first American departures would occur on about July 1 and involve at least twenty-five thousand men. Realizing that the coming drawdown would be larger and faster than anything anyone in the field had anticipated, he cabled Wheeler immediately to observe: "I have listened carefully to Ambassador Bunker and General Good-paster report on their meetings in Washington, and while I anticipated from this the pressures for U.S. troop reductions and Vietnamizing the war my impression was that it would be reasonably deliberate so that U.S. objectives here would have a reasonable chance of attainment." The date under consideration for the first departures, he said, implied "an acceleration of troop reductions not previously contemplated here in light of the enemy situation and the anticipated capabilities of the Vietnamese" who had yet to grasp "the realities of what they must do."[23]

Nevertheless, Abrams had little choice; the pressure for withdrawal was too great. In theory, the Defense Department might have gained time for him by dragging out implementation of the decision, but, as Wheeler observed, much of the force behind the push for early reductions was coming from the secretary of defense himself.[24] As a result, on July 8 the first contingent of returning troops landed in Seattle, Washington. By August 31, twenty-five thousand had departed. From then on, the president's announcement of new troop withdrawals became a regular feature of the war.

If the Nixon Administration was reducing the number of Americans exposed to enemy attack in South Vietnam, however, it still sought to achieve the United States' goals in Southeast Asia. The president had merely determined to approach the task from a different direction—one that promised to overcome American disenchantment with the war while demonstrating to the world that the United States could honor its commitments to an ally. To that end, the president adopted what became known as the Nixon Doctrine. Under that formulation the countries of Asia would handle their insurgency and subversion problems on their own, without any illusion that U.S. ground forces would respond to anything less than a large-scale external attack. As for South Vietnam, its armed forces would gradually take control of the war. A powerful contingent of Americans would remain to provide advice, logistical assistance, and technical support but, with time, U.S. forces would be less and less involved in the fighting.

The key to the arrangement was the South Vietnamese, but, as Abrams and his commanders had long perceived, they were unprepared for the task and might not be ready for years. Their army was an example. Poorly led, poorly paid, lacking basic necessities, and suffering from poor discipline and high desertion rates, it sometimes fought well but more often badly. The commander of the U.S. 9th Infantry Division, Major General Julian Ewell, described the situation in the heavily populated Mekong Delta region where his units operated. Hearing rumors that the 9th would be the first American division to depart, Ewell cabled Abrams to warn that the South Vietnamese forces in the region were unequal to the burden his men were carrying. Referring to a commonly held assumption that an accommodation existed between South Vietnamese units and the enemy in the Delta, he observed that if such was the case the arrangement was very simple: "The GVN [Government of Vietnam] holds the towns, the VC [Viet Cong] hold the people, and the GVN moves anywhere it wishes in battalion strength and even then gets racked up every few months."[25]

The government of South Vietnam was an equally uncertain quantity. President Thieu controlled it in theory, but his regime had little popular support. Thieu's government took its legitimacy from the country's military, who allowed it to exist because it had the support of the United States.[26] By itself, that would hardly have mattered. Many governments exist by some sort of military fiat and manage to perform at an acceptable level of competence. Yet South Vietnam was different. Its people staggered under a host of problems brought on by the war, from rapidly increasing inflation to the exactions of corrupt politicians. In addition, black marketeers leached, by conservative estimates, tens of millions of dollars from the country's economy every year—enough, according to Ambassador Bunker, if properly accounted for and taxed, to solve at least some of the country's fiscal problems.[27]

Possible solutions seemed simple and straightforward on the surface: expand the base of the government to include members of a loyal opposition; improve the military system by increasing pay and benefits and by promoting men of true ability to positions where their talents could have some effect on the war; and eliminate corruption by bringing black marketeers and their official allies to justice. Yet little was ever simple in Vietnam. As Clifford had perceived, the government had almost no incentive to change and every reason to stay the same.

Nguyen Van Thieu's situation is a case in point. Despite American remonstrances, he refused to incorporate members of his opposition into the government. He told Ambassador Bunker that he had offered positions to his critics, only to be refused because they wanted more prestigious jobs.[28] In fact, as the South Vietnamese Ambassador to the United States, Bui Diem, noted in a conversation at the State Department, Thieu trusted no one and, as a result, tended to become more and more politically isolated.[29] Lacking much of a popular following, he was too insecure to give political opponents any latitude. If one of them became too popular, he might attract the attention of the Americans and become a serious rival.

The same was true of Thieu's relationship with the military. He seems to have struck a rough balance with his officers because he was the clear choice of the United States, yet he left nothing to chance. If an individual disagreed with him, he won compliance through a crude form of blackmail. He kept dossiers on all of his officers and their corrupt dealings. When one or another proved recalcitrant, he had only to threaten to release the information to the country's prosecutors to reestablish control. Those who went along with him remained in their jobs, whatever their infractions, unless American pressure became too great. Then Thieu transferred them, often with promotions, to positions of equal responsibility elsewhere in the government.[30]

Thieu's system had serious effects. Unwilling to alienate any supporter, the president had little choice but to countenance practices that were detrimental to the efficiency of both his government and his armed forces. The wives of high-ranking officers, for example, were sometimes involved in the sale of choice military commands to the highest bidder. Thieu did little about it. The result sorely impeded the ability of the best officers to rise to ranks and positions where they could have some effect on the war. Obviously, some honest men managed to make their way to the top, but more would undoubtedly have been present if the system had been less corrupt.[31] In the same way, so many important political supporters of the regime were involved in the black market that very little was ever done to eliminate the system. The United States pointed out time and again areas that needed supervision, providing names, times, dates, and locations. The major figures of the government took copious notes, nodded their heads in approval, and did nothing.

In truth, of course, more was involved in South Vietnam's failure to come to terms with its circumstances than the venality and intransigence of the country's establishment. As a South Vietnamese officer told one American, American money had become so pervasive in South Vietnam that it was like opium. "Our people have become dependent on it and have let the Americans do what we ought to be doing for ourselves."[32]

Perhaps with time that might have changed, but as Laird had perceived, time was running out. Although the first troop withdrawals seemed to have a calming effect on antiwar protest in the United States, Laird told the president in September 1969, "I believe this may be an illusory phenomenon. The actual and potential antipathy for the war is, in my judgment, significant and increasing."[33]

As if to bear the secretary out, over the next two months the two largest antiwar demonstrations in the history of the American involvement in South Vietnam occurred in the United States. The October 15 Moratorium on Business as Usual spawned peaceful, middle-class demonstrations across the United States. The November 15 March on Washington, while marred by a few incidents of violence and much more radical in origin, attracted more than two hundred thousand largely peaceful demonstrators to the nation's capital. Indeed, by mid-November, President Nixon had announced a second troop withdrawal, and more withdrawals were clearly in the offing.

As the American drawdown proceeded, U.S. casualties became less and less an issue, but the withdrawal nevertheless took on a logic and momentum of its own. With field commanders under orders to reduce casualties, American military units that remained behind fell into routines that had little meaning for many of their members. No one wanted to be the last American to die in Vietnam. As morale declined, reported the U.S. commander of South Vietnam's northernmost region during 1970, Lieutenant General Arthur S. Collins, an "excessive number of accidental shootings" occurred—too many to be accidental. In addition, "the promiscuous throwing of grenades . . . lent new meaning to the expression 'fragging' " and left every officer "with an ill-at-ease feeling." A number of incidents also occurred along South Vietnam's roads, when Americans in a wide variety of speeding vehicles ran down unsuspecting civilians or fired on them in passing.[34]

Drug abuse also flourished. By 1971 Army investigators had found that almost 69 percent of the men departing the country had at least experimented with marijuana, while 45 percent freely admitted, under promises of immunity from prosecution, that they had used unauthorized narcotics, barbiturates, or amphetamines at least once during their tour of duty. Twenty-nine percent said they had used them regularly (more than ten times and more than weekly), and 20 percent reported that they had been addicted. Thirty-eight percent had tried opium, 34 percent heroin, 25 percent amphetamines, and 23 percent barbiturates.[35] Under the circumstances, with discipline falling and drug abuse spreading to American bases outside of South Vietnam, the government's only recourse was to cut off the source of the problem by proceeding with withdrawals as expeditiously as the situation would allow.

By 1972 the president had few options left. When the Hanoi regime dropped its objections at the Paris Peace Talks to continued American military aid to Saigon and agreed to cease the infiltration of troops into the South, Nixon endorsed the proposed treaty as the best he could get. South Vietnam's president, Thieu, objected that the arrangement left him naked to the enemy, but Nixon responded with assurances that "far more important than what we say in the agreement is what we do." If North Vietnam renewed its aggression, "it is my intention to take swift and severe retaliatory action." If Thieu, however, became "the obstacle to a peace which American public opinion universally desires, I would, with great reluctance, be forced to consider other [unilateral] alternatives."[36]

In a subsequent message to the U.S. ambassador to South Vietnam, Ellsworth Bunker, Nixon explained what was happening. Emphasizing his promise to "take massive action against North Vietnam in the event they break the agreement," he continued that Thieu would have to go along "or we have to go it alone." There were no alternatives. "Despite the mandate I personally received in the [1972 presidential] election," Congress would not continue support of the war in the light of Hanoi's offer. The main congressional supporters of administration policy on Vietnam were adamant. If Saigon was "the only roadblock for reaching agreement on this basis, they will personally lead the fight when the new Congress reconvenes on January 3 to cut off all military and economic assistance. . . . The door has been slammed shut hard and fast by the long time supporters of my policies in Vietnam in the House and Senate who control the purse strings." Nixon concluded that further delays by Thieu were dangerous to South Vietnam's well-being. "Tell him that the fat is in the fire," and "it is time to fish or cut bait."[37]

In the end, President Nixon might have succeeded in fulfilling his promise to Thieu. For although American forces indeed withdrew, powerful air contingents remained within striking distance of South Vietnam. Flying in support of South

Vietnamese troops on the ground, they were capable of providing the support those units needed to turn back the largest enemy attack. They proved it during the enemy's 1972 Easter Offensive, when North Vietnam stripped its defenses bare in a vain attempt to conquer the South.

Any attempt to use those forces in the face of rising opposition in Congress depended, however, on President Nixon's ability to rally public support to his policies. Nixon's involvement in the Watergate affair precluded that by forcing his resignation from office. Lacking the public following he had commanded, his successor, Gerald Ford, could do little. As a result, when the enemy attacked again in 1975, no American bombers arrived to help. South Vietnam fell, the victim of its own insufficiencies and those of its supposed protector.

In fact, the country might have fallen anyway. For its leaders, despite more than fifteen years of constant American advice on the matter, proved unable—even in the end—to wean themselves from the abuses that had done so much to undermine their government's ability to win the loyalty of their people and to combat the enemy. A meeting between Ambassador Bunker and President Thieu in June 1972 exemplified the problem. Bunker spent much time pointing out that the practice of relieving commanders because of corruption and assigning them to equal or more important posts not only destroyed the effectiveness of the attack on corruption, but also led to cynicism among the people. Thieu agreed, Bunker noted later, "but . . . I have discussed the problem of corruption with him on numerous occasions and while statements have been made condemning it, no forthright position or effective action has been taken by Thieu or the government." Perhaps the seriousness of the situation facing the country would lead to action, Bunker continued. Unless that happened, nothing would be accomplished: "Action—and results—are essential if the country is to survive in its struggle with a tough, disciplined, determined, and highly motivated foe."[38]

As for the American public, its intolerance for rising casualty rates may possibly have expressed something deeper than mere softness, moral laxity, lack of will, or an inability to face the necessary frustrations of a long war. Perhaps it was simple common sense. If more men, more bombs, and more killing had been to no avail, and if South Vietnam itself showed few of the traits necessary for survival, what was left? Maybe, as Richard Nixon had observed, it was indeed time to "cut bait."

NOTES

The views expressed in this essay are those of the author and do not represent the position of the Department of Defense.

1. Ward Just, "Pacifying a Province," *Washington Post*, November 6, 1966.

2. Unless otherwise indicated, this section is based on William M. Hammond, *Public Affairs: The Military and the Media, 1962–1968* (Washington, D.C.: U.S. Army Center of Military History, 1988).

3. See "Hill Report: We Have Not Achieved War Objectives," *Washington Post*, September 1, 1967.

4. Office of the Assistant Secretary of Defense for Systems Analysis, "Military Results and Initiative in Vietnam," October 17, 1967, Papers of Thomas Thayer, folder 38, Comparative Forces file, U.S. Army, Washington, D.C.: Center of Military History (CMH).

5. This section is based on George Christian, Handwritten note, July 19, 1968, Sub: Private conversation, Sharp's Office Between Rusk, Clifford, Rostow, Christian, Office Files of George Christian, box 12, 1 of 2, Open Collection, Lyndon Baines Johnson Library, Austin, Texas (LBJ Library).

6. Ibid.

7. William C. Westmoreland, *A Soldier Reports* (Garden City, N.Y.: Doubleday, 1976), p. 198.

8. "Seminar Report: Lessons Learned in the Air War Over Vietnam," *U.S. Naval Institute Proceedings* 113 (August 1987): 8.

9. The same relationship prevailed during the Korean War. See John Mueller, *War, Presidents, and Public Opinion* (New York: John Wiley, 1973); Mueller, "Trends in Popular Support for the Wars in Korea and Vietnam," *American Political Science Review* 65 (1971): 358.

10. These were the findings of a National Opinion Research Center poll conducted in early March 1966. The survey's findings are in Sheldon Appleton, ed., *United States Foreign Policy: An Introduction with Cases* (Boston: Little, Brown, 1968), p. 336. See also Nelson W. Polesby, "Political Science and the Press: Notes on Coverage of a Public Opinion Survey on the Vietnam War," *Western Political Quarterly* 22 (March 1969): 46.

11. "Poll Rates Nixon Best at Handling War," *New York Times*, August 25, 1968. See also Clark Clifford, "Notes for Meeting, 25 May 68," undated, Papers of Clark Clifford, box 1, Notes Taken at Meeting, Open Collection, LBJ Library.

12. Interview, author with Jerry Friedheim, Deputy Assistant Secretary of Defense for Public Affairs, 1969–1973, October 3, 1986. Friedheim met with Laird almost every day and knew his mind on many subjects.

13. Message, General Earl J. Wheeler, Chairman, Joint Chiefs of Staff, JCS 3218, to General Creighton W. Abrams, Commander, U.S. Military Assistance Command Vietnam, March 14, 1969, Abrams Papers, CMH.

14. Msg, Saigon 7462 to State, April 18, 1969, State Department files.

15. Msg, Abrams MAC 1340 to Admiral John McCain, Commander in Chief Pacific, October 13, 1968, Abrams Papers, CMH.

16. Msg, State 274394 to Moscow, November 17, 1968, relaying Msg, Abrams to JCS, November 17, 1968, State Department files.

17. Msg, Abrams MAC 2836 to JCS, March 5, 1969, Sub: Retaliatory Actions, Abrams Papers, CMH.

18. Henry A. Kissinger, *The White House Years* (Boston: Little, Brown, 1979), pp. 244ff.

19. Msg, Abrams MAC 4689 to All Commanders, April 13, 1969, Sub: Hanoi's Strategy, Abrams Papers, CMH.

20. Fact Sheet, Office of the Assistant Secretary of Defense for Systems Analysis, October 10, 1969, Sub: Indicators of Enemy Activity in South Vietnam, Papers of Thomas Thayer, folder 127, CMH.

21. Msg, Wheeler JCS 4092 to Abrams, April 3, 1969, Abrams Papers, CMH.

22. Msg, Wheeler JCS 3939 to McCain, Abrams, April 1, 1969, Abrams Papers, CMH.

23. Msg, Abrams MAC 4967 to Wheeler, April 19, 1969, Abrams Papers, CMH.

24. Msg, Wheeler JCS 5988 to McCain, Abrams, May 16, 1969, Abrams Papers, CMH.

25. Msg, Major General Julian Ewell MHU 292 to Abrams, March 29, 1969, Abrams Papers, CMH.

26. Memo, Melvin Laird for the President, April 4, 1970, Laird Papers, Washington National Records Center, Suitland, Maryland (WNRC).

27. Msg, Saigon 1514 to State, January 31, 1970, Sub: Discussion with President Thieu, State Department files.

28. Msg, Saigon 20975 to State, October 18, 1969, Sub: Meeting with President Thieu, October 17, Abrams Papers, CMH.

29. U.S. Department of State, Memo for the Record, December 11, 1969, Sub: Views of Ambassador Bui Diem on President Thieu and Vietnamization, Laird Papers, WNRC.

30. Memo, Richard Helms for Secretary Laird, September 22, 1969, Sub: Corruption with the Inspectorate, Laird Papers, WNRC.

31. State A-131, August 13, 1971, Sub: Some Aspects of Personal Relations Among Senior RVNAF Officers, Abrams Papers, CMH.

32. "State of the War: An Intelligence Report," U.S. News & World Report, October 27, 1969, p. 36.

33. Memo: Laird for the President, September 4, 1969, Sub: Vietnamizing the War, copy State Department files.

34. Senior Officer Debriefing Report, Debriefing Report by Lieutenant General Arthur S. Collins, RCS-CSFOR-74, January 7, 1971, Laird Papers, WNRC.

35. Lee N. Robbins, Ph.D., Executive Office of the President, Special Action Office for Drug Abuse Prevention, The Vietnam Drug User Returns (Washington, D.C.: U.S. Government Printing Office, 1973), pp. vii–ix.

36. Ltr, Nixon to Thieu, November 15, 1972, Bunker Papers, State Department files, quoted in Jeffrey J. Clarke, Advance and Support: The Final Years, 1965–1973 (Washington, D.C.: U.S. Army Center of Military History, 1988), p. 491.

37. Msg, Kissinger WHS 2257 to Bunker, November 26, 1972, repeating two memos from Nixon to Kissinger. Quoted in Clarke, Advice and Support, p. 492.

38. Msg, Saigon 8227, Bunker to the Secretary of State, June 3, 1972, Sub: Corruption, State Department files.

5

Secret Commitments in President Nixon's Foreign Policy: The National Security Council and Nixon's Letters to South Vietnam's President Nguyen Van Thieu

NGUYEN TIEN HUNG AND JERROLD L. SCHECTER

When Richard Nixon chose Henry Kissinger to be his assisant to the president for national security affairs in December 1968, he approved a major change in the role of the National Security Council system that extended its power far beyond the original intentions of its founders. Under Nixon, the threads of all major foreign policies were gathered in the White House and in the National Security Council staff led by Kissinger.[1]

A recent book by one of Kissinger's key aides and defenders, William Hyland, now the editor of *Foreign Affairs,* praises Kissinger for achieving "a new balance in world power." By exploiting Chinese and Soviet rivalries, Nixon and Kissinger opened communications with Beijing and created the basis for a new relationship with the Soviet Union, the policy of détente. It is this policy, says Hyland, which "helped to extricate the United States from Vietnam."[2]

What Hyland avoids saying is that in its efforts to withdraw from the Vietnam War the United States, under Nixon and Kissinger's leadership, betrayed South Vietnam while promoting the fallacious claim of having achieved "peace with honor." Nixon, Kissinger, and later President Ford, at Kissinger's behest, made a deliberate set of written promises to the government of the Republic of South Vietnam which were never kept. These secret commitments on behalf of the American government were withheld from the Congress, the American people, and members of the President's cabinet. Secretaries of defense who were responsible for enlisting congressional support for military and economic aid to South Vietnam were not told of the correspondence. In twenty-seven letters to President Nguyen Van Thieu, Nixon and Kissinger promised to continue economic and military aid and to retaliate with military force if and when the North Vietnamese violated the Paris Agreement.

Henry Kissinger was instrumental in conceiving and drafting Nixon's secret promises to South Vietnam. Kissinger dissembled with Congress and members of the cabinet. He refused to make public President Nixon's promises. Kissinger has written that he consulted fully with President Thieu and had his concurrence.[3] Thieu denies Kissinger's claims. He insists that he was never asked, but was only told what the Americans wanted him to hear, and that he never agreed to the terms Kissinger negotiated in Paris in October 1972.[4]

Kissinger used the National Security Council to bypass the State Department, the Congress, and even the president's cabinet. When Saigon fell on April 30, 1975, the secret promises made to President Thieu had never become part of the debate on whether and how to end the war. Kissinger continued to deny them. The sense of betrayal of the Republic of Vietnam has added to the confusion and malaise that have still to be overcome and assimilated in our national psyche. Why did the United States follow a no-win military policy while committing American troops to action and then negotiate away the peace?

In order to understand the Nixon-Kissinger diplomacy in Vietnam, it is essential to study Kissinger's secret negotiations with the North Vietnamese in Paris from 1969 to 1973. The secret letters are an integral part of the record.

THE SECRET VIETNAM NEGOTIATIONS

"Statesmen must act as if their intuition was already experience, as if their aspiration was truth," Henry Kissinger wrote in his study of Metternich.[5] It was to become his guiding principle when he became a statesman. Kissinger relished acting alone and excluding the bureaucracy. Nixon, for his own reasons—mostly because he detested the State Department and the style of its career diplomats—wanted foreign policy power centered in the White House. He gave Kissinger full rein, pulling him back only when Kissinger sought to claim credit ahead of the president. At the height of his power, the Italian journalist, Oriana Fallaci, asked Kissinger about his style, and he told her, in a controversial reply, which he later denied: "The main point arises from the fact that I've always acted alone." Then he explained that "Americans like the cowboy who leads the wagon train by riding ahead alone on his horse, the cowboy who rides all alone into the town, the village, with his horse and nothing else. Maybe even without a pistol since he doesn't shoot, he acts, that's all, by being in the right place at the right time. In short, a Western."[6]

Kissinger created his own Western in the Paris negotiations, operating in secret with the North Vietnamese, as he tried to lead the American wagon out of Vietnam. He operated in secret, agreeing to the North Vietnamese demand to leave their troops in the South in order to get an agreement.

In order to convince South Vietnamese President Nguyen Van Thieu to sign the Paris Accord ending the war in South Vietnam in 1973, President Nixon promised, in a series of secret letters, to continue military and economic aid to the Republic of Vietnam. The language of these private promises and assurances to the Republic of South Vietnam was more specific and detailed than statements President Nixon and his advisers made in public.[7] President Nixon and his successor, President Gerald Ford, wanted to continue supporting South Vietnam, despite strong and rising public sentiment against the war. In the thirty-one letters to President Nguyen Van Thieu from Presidents Nixon and Ford, there was specific language committing the United States to a military response against the Democratic Republic of Vietnam if the North Vietnamese violated the Paris Accords of January and June 1973.

On October 16, 1972, Nixon wrote to Thieu and told him,

As far as I am concerned, the most important provision of this agreement, aside from the military features, is that your government, its armed forces and its political institutions, will remain intact after the ceasefire has been observed. In the period following the cessation of hostilities you can be completely assured that we will continue to provide your Government with the fullest support, including continued economic aid and whatever military assistance is consistent with the ceasefire provisions of this agreement.

On November 14, 1972, Nixon told Thieu in a letter:

But far more important than what we say in the agreement on this issue is what we do in the event the enemy renews its aggression. You have my absolute assurance that if Hanoi fails to abide by the terms of this agreement it is my intention to take swift and severe retaliatory action.

On January 5, 1973, Nixon again urged Thieu to sign the Paris Accord:

As we enter the new round of talks, I hope that our countries will show a united front . . .

Should you decide, as I trust you will, to go with us, you have my assurance of continued assistance in the post-settlement period and that we will respond with full force should the settlement be violated by North Vietnam.

On January 17, 1973, Nixon repeated his assurance that

the freedom and independence of the Republic of Vietnam remain a paramount objective of American foreign policy. I have been dedicated to this goal all of my political life, and during the past four years I have risked many grave domestic and international consequences in its pursuit. It is precisely in order to safeguard our mutual objectives that I have decided irrevocably on my present course. . . . Let me state these assurances once again in this letter.

—First, we recognize your Government as the sole legitimate Government of South Vietnam.
—Secondly, we do not recognize the right of foreign troops to remain on South Vietnamese soil.
—Thirdly, the U.S. will react vigorously to violations of the Agreement.[8]

Five essential elements are related to these secret commitments. First, there was a clear pledge to continue to supply military and economic aid to South Vietnam at a level sufficient to sustain a defense against North Vietnam.

Second, the United States undertook to maintain the peace alone in Vietnam, a provision stated in the letters, and completely outside the framework of the Paris Accord which called for an elaborate international control mechanism to supervise the peace.

Three, President Nixon made solemn pledges to reintervene militarily in Vietnam should Hanoi launch an invasion of the South.

Fourth, the written pledges were backed by concrete actions and oral reaffirmations after the signing of the Paris Accord.

Fifth, a top secret military plan in operation maintained South Vietnam in a state of constant readiness for the resumption of American air activity against North Vietnam and North Vietnamese forces in the South.

These five points were never fulfilled, yet Kissinger claimed he was bringing "peace with honor." Kissinger failed to perceive the essential strategy of his adversary. It took him four years to achieve a peace agreement that was essentially the same one that the Communists had presented to him in 1969.[9] Those four years cost an additional 20,000 American lives and 131,000 wounded, as well as hundreds of thousands of Vietnamese casualties.

Upon entering the White House, Nixon and Kissinger decided to end the Vietnam War through negotiations. The United States adopted a two-track approach, which was Defense Secretary Melvin Laird's plan: negotiations and Vietnamization, Laird's program for troop withdrawals defused the rising public opposition to the war. Vietnamization, instead of being sustained with the necessary war materials, became the smoke screen to cover the American retreat. Kissinger's strategy focused on secret negotiations. The two strategies would eventually conflict and become mutually defeating.

At Midway in June 1969, Nixon met with South Vietnamese President Nguyen Van Thieu and told him that there would be private, secret contacts between the United States and North Vietnam. Thieu agreed to this plan providing he was kept constantly informed.

In July 1969 Nixon and Kissinger visited Thieu in Saigon. They did not tell Thieu that Kissinger would fly from Saigon to Paris to begin direct secret talks with Le Duc Tho. Kissinger never had a State or Defense Department representative on his negotiating team; it was all done by the National Security Council staff. He compartmentalized the work so that no one member of the staff, with the exception of Winston Lord, Kissinger's draftsman, knew how all the pieces of the puzzle fit together. Kissinger consulted only with Nixon, and gradually differences emerged between them. Nixon believed in the commitment to defend South Vietnam against a Communist takeover as part of the long-term American strategic interest. For Kissinger, Vietnam was an obstruction preventing improved great power relationships between the United States, China, and the

Soviet Union. Kissinger was prepared to sacrifice Vietnam on the altar of détente and normalization with China.

In the Paris negotiations, Kissinger's strategy was to separate two sets of problems. He sought to isolate the military from the political issues and concentrate on the key military issue, the mutual withdrawal of forces. This was a serious and deadly fault because he misjudged the North Vietnamese intentions not to withdraw their troops from the South. This policy led to an American failure, the loss of South Vietnamese morale, the routing of South Vietnamese forces, and full concessions to Hanoi.

The Nixon-Kissinger design had many flaws. The decision to seek a negotiated settlement as the only way to end the war generated an overriding need for a signed agreement. Domestic American political pressures for the 1972 election gave Hanoi the power to hold the United States hostage to its signature. In Saigon the belief that Kissinger had negotiated a "false peace with shame" gave the South Vietnamese their own ability to hold the United States hostage by withholding their signature from the Paris Accord.[10]

The decision to conduct negotiations in secrecy produced a need to justify all secrecy once the negotiations faltered. As secrecy was heightened and the inner working of the negotiations became more tightly controlled, there was no way for experts in the State, Defense Department, or the CIA to have input. Kissinger shut out the bureaucracy and retained control with Nixon's approval.

In the talks with the North Vietnamese Kissinger was an ardent advocate of replacing confrontation with negotiation. Initially, he was optimistic about applying this formula to the Vietnamese. "I had great hopes for negotiations— perhaps, as events turned out, more than was warranted," Kissinger concluded in his memoirs. "I even thought a tolerable outcome could be achieved within a year."[11] Casually commenting on his naivete, Kissinger failed to acknowledge the consequences of his strategy and his insistence on a monopoly of wisdom. He believed that a process of give and take could be applied to bring Washington and Hanoi to agreements. In the Western mind, incentive is a powerful force working in any negotiation. Kissinger viewed the policy of Vietnamization as an incentive. In his words: "We needed a strategy that made continuation of the war seem less attractive to Hanoi than a settlement."[12]

To the North Vietnamese, Vietnamization was clearly a cover for the American departure, characterized by the late columnist Stewart Alsop as "an elegant bugout."[13] Defense Secretary Melvin Laird pressed hard to increase American troop withdrawals while Kissinger sought to slow the pace to keep the North Vietnamese negotiating in good faith. The policies were contradictory and self-defeating. The faster American troops withdrew, the less interest the North Vietnamese had in negotiations.[14]

Fear is a more powerful factor in the Asian calculation than incentives. The leadership in Hanoi feared a permanent American presence in South Vietnam. As a result, the North Vietnamese, since the mid–1950s, were committed to a policy of complete and total American withdrawal without conditions. Ho Chi Minh's last will and testament decreed that "the American invaders will have to quit." American withdrawal was not negotiable to Hanoi.[15] There was no way the talks could have developed along the lines of Kissinger's "conceptual overview."

"Where do we go from here," Kissinger asked in his January 1969 article in *Foreign Affairs*, which appeared just as he entered the White House. He answered: "Paradoxical as it may seem, the best way to make progress where distrust is too deep and the issues so interrelated may be to seek agreement on ultimate goals first and to work back to the details to implement it."[16]

Kissinger and the North Vietnamese never agreed on ultimate goals. Step by step, the North Vietnamese forced him to reverse the order and work on the details before there was an overall structure. It took him from 1969 to 1971 to realize that the North Vietnamese were not going to engage in a give-and-take negotiation, nor were they going to define the framework in any but their own terms. Secrecy shielded Kissinger from public or even internal government scrutiny of his conduct. He enjoyed a high degree of immunity from serious questioning by the press and the Congress. The bureaucracy played no role in the secret negotiations and its expertise was not called upon. Even Secretary of State William Rogers was not told of the secret negotiations until "well into 1971"; Defense Secretary Melvin Laird was never formally told.[17] Laird and the Joint Chiefs were working with Thieu to sustain Saigon for a long-term peace while Kissinger negotiated with Le Duc Tho for a "decent interval." By keeping the negotiations in the National Security Council, Kissinger thought he was preventing the bureaucracy and the Congress from intervening in the peace process. But Kissinger was caught in a trap of his own making. Hanoi, aware of Kissinger's need to produce an agreement for the 1972 presidential election, stubbornly kept him at bay, refusing to sign until its demands were met. Within this context, we can understand why it took four years to reach a signed agreement and why it failed. Kissinger's confrontation with Thieu, the awesome Christmas bombing, Nixon's secret pledges, and the collapse of South Vietnam followed.

Kissinger and Nixon have written their own versions of how the negotiations unfolded. Kissinger devoted more than one-third of his memoirs (492 pages) to them. Yet, from all the available evidence their versions are far from complete.

The secret negotiations can be divided into three distinctive phases. The first phase, between 1969 and 1971, saw Kissinger insisting that the United States not become involved in the political settlement and concentrate primarily on the issue of mutual troop withdrawals from South Vietnam. Hanoi refused to budge on the withdrawal issue. Kissinger floundered on this issue for two years before capitulating in the summer of 1971 when he accepted the principle of unilateral American withdrawal. On August 17, 1971, Kissinger offered a timetable for American withdrawal to be completed in nine months. In October the offer was shortened to seven months; on January 26, 1972, to six months; on May 8 to four months, then finally on October 8, 1972, Kissinger accepted the North Vietnamese proposal for withdrawal in sixty days.

Hanoi had upheld its first commandment: oust the United States from Vietnam. On May 8, 1969, at the start of the Nixon Administration, the North Vietnamese Communists produced a ten-point program. Point two insisted that "the U.S. Government must withdraw from South Vietnam all U.S. troops, military personnel, arms and war material, and all troops, military personnel, arms and war material of the other foreign countries of the U.S. camp without posing any conditions whatsoever."

On January 27, 1973, the final signed Paris Agreement read: "Article 5. Within sixty days of the signing of this Agreement, there will be a total withdrawal from South Vietnam of troops, military advisors and military personnel, armaments, munitions and war materials of the U.S. and those of other foreign countries."

The only concession Hanoi made was to change the word "must" to "there will be" a withdrawal. The period of withdrawal was fixed at two months from the date of the cease-fire. For Hanoi it was an improvement over the original, which did not specify a timetable.

In the summer of 1971, the North Vietnamese demanded that Kissinger drop the two-track approach—the separation of the military from the political issues. Two years had passed, and during that time nearly eighteen thousand American soldiers and sixty-three thousand Vietnamese troops had been killed and hundreds of thousands wounded. More than $45 billion had been spent on the war. Kissinger returned to the drawing board, and the two-track policy merged into one: a comprehensive settlement as demanded by Hanoi. The United States could no longer avoid determining the political future of South Vietnam.

In the second phase, between the summer of 1971 and 1972, Hanoi pushed for a political settlement which included a coalition government. At the same time Hanoi pressed for the details of unilateral American withdrawal. Thieu believed that the combination of a coalition government and the unilateral withdrawal of American troops was death to South Vietnam. He could point to numerous historical precedents in which coalitions with Communist participation meant the extermination of all non-Communist political participants.

On August 16, 1971, Kissinger offered a new eight-point proposal in which the political process was translated into a political solution. The requirements were for total U.S. neutrality in the Vietnamese elections, U.S. acceptance of the outcome of the elections, and nonalignment for South Vietnam and the other countries of Indochina. The American concessions only made the North Vietnamese more intransigent. They demanded that Thieu must step down.

To this demand, Washington again conceded in a roundabout way, making it look as if Thieu himself had taken the initiative. On October 11, 1971, Nixon offered a new peace proposal, calling for presidential elections in South Vietnam. The plan called for President Thieu to step down one month before the election.

Then he would have to run for office again. Nixon's October 11 proposal also called for an independent body, including the Provisional Revolutionary Government (PRG), to conduct the election. Since this was only a short step from a coalition government, Hanoi pressed for its goal.

Kissinger has often claimed credit for saving President Thieu and the Saigon government through the Paris Agreement. Actually, if Hanoi had wanted to oust Thieu, it would have accepted the October 11, 1971, proposal. The real political goal of the Communists was a coalition government, not the replacement of one South Vietnamese leader with another who would continue to oppose them. The North Vietnamese wanted to gain recognition for the legitimacy of the Provisional Revolutionary Government as a step toward a Communist takeover. Hanoi's demand that Thieu step down was a phony issue used as a tactic in the bargaining to win legitimacy for the PRG. In October 1972 that goal was achieved when Kissinger and Le Duc Tho met in Gif-sur-Yvette outside Paris and agreed on a National Council of Reconciliation and Concord (NCRC), an interim form of coalition government.

In the Paris Accord, it was agreed that the National Council of Reconciliation and Concord would have these functions:

- promotion of the two South Vietnamese parties' implementation of the agreement;
- achievement of national reconciliation and concord and ensurance of democratic liberties; and
- organization of the free and democratic general elections . . . and decide the procedures and modalities . . . of such local elections.

This result was a mirror image of the North Vietnamese demand for a provisional coalition government made in May 1969. The initial proposal from the Communist side listed the coalition government's functions:

—To implement the agreements on the withdrawal of the troops of the United States and other foreign countries

—To achieve national concord

—To achieve broad democratic freedoms

—To hold free and democratic general elections in the whole of South Vietnam

Thieu was adamantly opposed to Kissinger's suggestion that Hanoi's proposal for a coalition government should be dealt with through a three-part National Council of Concord and Reconciliation. Kissinger saw this approach as burying the issue of a coalition, but Thieu saw it as legitimizing the Communist claim for the Provisional Revolutionary Government to participate in the government of the South on an equal basis. Kissinger understood that for Thieu

to accept the potential legitimacy of those seeking to subvert it [the South] was to undermine the psychological basis of his rule. Yet their acceptance in some form was inherent in even the attenuated compromise proposal. Thieu's domestic imperative imposed intransigence. We could sustain our support for him only by a show of conciliation. Our goal was honor; we could (as the phrase went) run a risk for peace. But Thieu's problem was survival; he and his people would be left indefinitely after we departed: he had no margin for error.[18]

THE FINAL OUTCOME

October 8, 1972, was a bright, beautiful day in Paris. To Henry Kissinger this was the most moving day of his career in public service. "For nearly four years we longed for this day, yet when it arrived it was less dramatic than we had ever imagined." On that day, according to Kissinger, the North Vietnamese made a concession of major proportions to arrive at an agreement with the United States. "After four years of implacable insistence that we dismantle the political structure of an ally and replace it with a coalition government, Hanoi had now essentially given up its political demands."[19] The "breakthrough" was achieved, Kissinger claimed, because "we stood on the threshold of what we had long sought, a peace compatible with our honor and our international responsibilities."

President Nixon set the tone when he told Congress on May 3, 1973, that

on October 8, 1972, the North Vietnamese presented a new plan in Paris accepting the basic principle of our position. It was the essential breakthrough toward a negotiated settlement. For the first time, Hanoi agreed, in effect, to separate military questions from the principal political issues. They spelled out specific solutions to the former while the latter were to follow later and were left basically up to the South Vietnamese. Moreover, they dropped their insistent demand for President Thieu's resignation and formation of a coalition government.[20]

Kissinger's memoirs adopt a similar line:

And so it was, Hanoi had finally separated the military and political questions, which I had urged nearly four years earlier as the best way to settle. It had accepted Nixon's May 8 proposal and conceded that the South Vietnamese government need not be overthrown as the price of a cease-fire. Having ignored our offer of a presidential election, Hanoi even removed the necessity of Thieu's temporary withdrawal before it. The demand for a coalition government was dropped; the political structure of South Vietnam was left to the Vietnamese to settle.[21]

For the South Vietnamese, October 8, 1972, was the darkest day in the history of the Republic of Vietnam, the day of betrayal by its closest ally, the United States. As the record demonstrates, the United States agreed to allow the North Vietnamese to retain their forces in the South while at the same time claiming peace with honor.

President Nguyen Van Thieu was not consulted in advance of Kissinger's concessions. Thieu found out about Kissinger's perfidy from captured North

Vietnamese documents.[22] Kissinger insists that Thieu agreed to the concessions to Hanoi. Thieu continues to deny that he was consulted in advance, and insists he never concurred.[23]

In the aftermath of Vietnam, both Kissinger and President Nixon selectively used the letters to President Thieu to make their case, but in fact the letters tell a different tale.

THREATS AND PROMISES

After making major concessions to Hanoi, Kissinger and Nixon turned on Saigon. In the climax of the negotiations, in the fall of 1972, the United States imposed on South Vietnam the agreement Kissinger negotiated in Paris. Nixon needed President Thieu's signature on the Paris Accord in order to conjure a defeat into a victory, what the South Vietnamese called "peace in the tomb."

In his letter of October 29, 1972, Nixon warned Thieu that unless South Vietnam signed the Paris Accord, there would be an end to U.S. support. Nixon wrote:

Just as our unity has been the essential aspect of the success we have enjoyed thus far in the conduct of hostilities, it will also be the best guarantee of future success in a situation where the struggle continues within a more political framework. If the evident drift toward disagreement between the two of us continues, however, the essential base for U.S. support for you and your Government will be destroyed.[24]

Nixon continued to use economic and military aid as a bludgeon, threatening Thieu in his November 23, 1972, letter that any further delay in signing "can only be interpreted as an effort to scuttle the agreement. This would have a disastrous effect on our ability to continue to support you and your Government."[25] As Thieu continued to resist signing, Nixon's tone grew sterner, and in a January 5, 1973, letter the president told Thieu: "I am firmly convinced that the alternative to signing the present Agreement is a total cutoff of funds to assist your country."

Thieu was also warned that he might be overthrown and eliminated if he continued to oppose the agreement Kissinger had created. In his memoirs, Nixon describes Thieu's reluctance to accept the agreement and General Alexander Haig's mission to Saigon to convince Thieu. Nixon wrote:

Haig flew to Saigon and assured Thieu that we would not rush headlong into an agreement. But he also described the difficult domestic situation we would face if the Communists made a reasonable offer and we refused to act upon it. Then they would be able to put the blame on Thieu for blocking peace.

Theiu was visibly shaken, he was suspicious of the motives behind the North Vietnamese proposals and unsettled by our willingness to accept them as even a basis for negotiations. He railed against Kissinger, who, he said, did not "deign" to consider Saigon's views in his negotiations. Haig tried to reassure him. Finally Thieu broke into tears.

> I sympathized with Thieu's position. . . . But I felt that if we could negotiate an agreement on our terms, those conditions could be met. I sent Thieu a personal message: "I give you my firm assurance that there will be no settlement arrived at, the provisions of which have not been discussed personally with you well beforehand." Knowing his penchant for headstrong action, however, I reminded him of the dangers inherent in stirring up his domestic situation as well as our own.[26]

Nixon's elegant phrasing of "dangers inherent in stirring up his domestic situation" was a not-too-veiled threat that Thieu might face forceful overthrow by his own generals. In a personal message to Thieu on October 6, 1972, Nixon wrote: "I would urge you to take every measure to avoid the development of an atmosphere which could lead to events similar to those which we abhorred in 1963 and which I personally opposed so vehemently in 1968."[27]

Nixon's reference to the 1963 "events" was an unmistakably clear reference to the overthrow and assassination of President Ngo Dinh Diem in which the United States was intimately involved. The 1968 events that Nixon opposed were rumors of a Johnson Administration effort to oust Thieu for refusing to negotiate with the North Vietnamese and Viet Cong in Paris before the election.[28]

When the threats failed, Nixon turned to promises. On January 5, 1973, Nixon urged Thieu to sign the Paris Accord:

> As we enter the new round of talks, I hope that our countries will show a united front. . . .
> Should you decide, as I trust you will, to go with us, you have my assurance of continued assistance in the post-settlement period and that we will respond with full force should the settlement be violated by North Vietnam.[29]

Was this a policy of wishful thinking, or at worst outright deception to keep South Vietnam in the war while struggling to stabilize the domestic situation following Watergate? In the spring of 1973 Thieu realized a longstanding promise of Nixon's and made a trip to the United States. He was welcomed at San Clemente instead of the White House because Nixon was preoccupied with the flood of Watergate. The White House believed it could better control the visit in California than in Washington.[30] At the Pacific White House, Nixon promised Thieu once more to continue economic and military aid, but he made no public commitment to the resumption of bombing or the use of force if the North Vietnamese violated the Paris Accord.

Kissinger insists that Watergate prevented President Nixon from fulfilling his promises in the letters to use full force against North Vietnamese violations of the Paris Accord. After Thieu returned to Saigon and the violations continued, Nixon considered bombing Hanoi and the Ho Chi Minh trails in the spring of 1973. But, as Kissinger explains in his memoirs, Nixon, hobbled by Watergate, never ordered the bombing.[31]

It was during this period that Congress was considering the military and economic aid bills. Both Nixon and Kissinger carefully concealed the existence of the secret letters to Thieu and their promises of continued aid.

Defense Secretary James Schlesinger, who had to urge Congress to continue support for Saigon, was never told of the letters, nor were his predecessors Melvin Laird and Eliot Richardson. Schlesinger found out about the letters in April 1975 when his trusted aide, Eric Von Marbod, then controller of the Pentagon, was sent to Saigon to assess the deteriorating situation and was given five letters from Nixon to Thieu by Thieu's special assistant, Nguyen Tien Hung.[32]

The late Senator Henry Jackson (D-Wash.), who was close to Schlesinger, was told of the existence of the letters. He charged publicly on April 8, 1975, that "secret agreements existed between the United States and the Republic of Vietnam," which had never been acknowledged, and about which President Ford had only recently been told.

The Ford Administration denied that there were any secret agreements. Ford's press secretary, Ron Nessen, was authorized to acknowledge that Nixon and Thieu had exchanged private letters, but said, "The public statements made at the time reflected the substance of those private communications."[33] Henry Kissinger maintains that the administration never made any promises in private that it did not make in public.

Now that the letters have been published, the differences between the private promises and the public record is clear. James Schlesinger said:

I believed Ford was being bamboozled on the letters. I found them quite shocking at the time. I was really disturbed by them, particularly because the administration was in a period of launching an attempt to blame the defeat of South Vietnam on the Congress, which, Lord knows, had its responsibilities. But it sure as hell wasn't going to help the country if we had a great stab-in-the back argument, particularly given the fact that the letters were floating around, which showed that, to say the least, the Congress had not been fully informed with regard to the nature of our commitments after the departure of our forces from South Vietnam. Congress knew nothing of these letters, when it started bugging out of Vietnam in the summer of 1973.[34]

It was in the summer of 1973 that Schlesinger was trying desperately to rally support in Congress for continued military aid to South Vietnam.

If I had known of the letters at that time I would have told the Congressional leaders about them and we would have taken those promises into account. Either we would have continued the aid or we would have had to go back to the South Vietnamese and tell them we couldn't keep the promises made by President Nixon.[35]

Kissinger, who was secretary of state when Jackson raised the question of secret agreements had the State Department spokesman say that the United States had no "legal commitment" to South Vietnam, but it had a "moral commitment." For the South Vietnamese, Nixon's letters were a commitment from the president of the United States in the name of the American people. For Vietnamese leaders with a Confucian cultural background, the letters from the head of state and government of the greatest superpower, were both a moral and legal commitment.

The Senate Foreign Relations Committee's request for copies of the Nixon-Thieu correspondence was rebuffed by President Ford. "I have reviewed the record of the private diplomatic communications," Ford wrote to the Committee. "Since the same policy and intentions contained in these exchanges were declared publicly, there was no secret from the Congress and the American people."[36]

In an interview at Rancho Mirage, California, on February 10, 1986, President Ford acknowledged that he had not read all of the Nixon letters to President Thieu. When he saw copies of his and Nixon's letters promising economic and military aid, Ford shook his head and said: "Well, there is no doubt these were very categorical commitments." Ford added, "I didn't personally review all the correspondence. I knew that there had been many exchanges of letters, but I did not personally go over each and every document."[37]

When he took office on August 10, 1974, President Ford wrote to President Thieu, promising him that "the existing commitments this nation has made in the past are still valid and will be fully honored in my administration." Ford added that "these reassurances are particularly relevant to the Republic of Vietnam." He assured Thieu that military and economic aid would be forthcoming. "Although it may take a little time, I do want to assure you of my confidence that in the end our support will be adequate on both counts."[38]

As a reader of the letters will see, and as President Ford himself admitted later, the letters were different from the public statements. The language was more explicit and categorical in terms of an American commitment.[39] How was such a deception possible?

KISSINGER'S LEGACY

The answer has important bearings on the recent congressional inquiry into the Iran/Contra affair and the role played by the National Security Council (NSC). National security adviser John Poindexter's NSC, supported by President Reagan, followed the organization and style of Kissinger's NSC. It cut off the cabinet secretaries from policies run by the White House. Under President Nixon, the power of the NSC was enhanced to the point where presidential commitments could be withheld from the Congress and the cabinet. This was the president's basic decision, but it was Henry Kissinger, then both secretary of state and national security adviser, who urged that the promises made by President Nixon be kept secret from the Congress and the cabinet. To understand how this was possible, we have to see the role Kissinger played and how Kissinger restructured the National Security Council with Nixon's approval.

It is instructive to look briefly at the history of the NSC, which was established under the National Security Act of 1947. The NSC was to be a policy advisory body to the president, with an executive secretary who brought its recommendations to the president. Members of the Council are the president, the vice president, secretary of state, and secretary of defense. The president can invite additional members of his cabinet or staff to sit in on the NSC meetings. This structure and practice continue.

Each president since 1947 has chosen to mold the NSC in an image that has suited his own needs and style. President Eisenhower had a strong cabinet system with a powerful secretary of state. He also strengthened the NSC by adding the staff system and the first assistant to the president for national security affairs, Robert Cutler, who became a direct adviser to the president. The NSC executive secretary remained in a staff coordinating role.

Under President Kennedy, the role of the NSC, headed by McGeorge Bundy, was further enhanced because of Kennedy's strong role in foreign policy and his distrust of the State Department. Under Lyndon Johnson, the NSC grew in power because the president dominated the Vietnam War from the White House. However, under LBJ the State Department, the Defense Department, and the CIA were still playing important roles and the war was being debated throughout the government.

When Nixon took office, the nature of policy-making changed abruptly. Kissinger proposed a reorganization of the NSC as soon as Nixon was elected. Henry Kissinger provided the blueprint for President Nixon's total control of foreign policy through the National Security Council staff. The plan, approved by Nixon, gave Kissinger the power to decide the agenda for National Security Council meetings and for policy review group meetings. The Policy Review group had previously been chaired by the secretary of state. Kissinger, as chairman of the review group, could call on the bureaucracy to prepare option papers. Previously, this had been a prerogative of the secretary of state. Kissinger instituted the system of National Security Study Memoranda, which organized policy decisions into a series of presidential options. The president's decisions were promulgated as National Security Decision Memoranda. From a staff role the NSC had become the originator and formulator of foreign policy. The State Department was left the role of implementing the president's policies.[40] As Roger Morris observed: "What had been in the Johnson regime, a shifting contest of several personalities, now became very much the rule of two minds in the White House."[41]

In retrospect, Nixon delegated too much power to the national security adviser. His new system streamlined the foreign policy-making process, but it also cut back on the democratic process because it reduced consultation with Congress, the cabinet, and the American people. Kissinger deliberately did not advise Congress of the letters and insisted that what had been said in public was said in private; he committed a serious breach of public trust.

Kissinger still clings to the myth that there were no private presidential promises to Thieu and that Thieu approved his concessions to Hanoi. He saw himself as a statesman with a high purpose: to remove the United States from an unpopular war at a time when there was domestic upheaval. He sacrificed an unpopular ally and weakened American credibility; the results continue to haunt us. Kissinger created a disproportionate role for the National Security Council that has grown and continued to abuse the checks and balances of a well-functioning executive bureaucracy.

In the final analysis, it is the president who is responsible for his National Security Council, but Nixon was gone and Kissinger, first as Nixon's secretary of state and then as Ford's, became the de facto president for American foreign policy. Kissinger wrote Nixon's letters to Thieu, and then Ford's, urging him to sign them without ever fully explaining to Ford the commitments he (Kissinger) and Nixon had made to Thieu to get him to sign the Paris Accords.

Kissinger's style and behavior became a campaign issue in the 1976 election, and as a reaction against Kissinger, a serious effort was made to limit the power of the national security adviser in the Carter Administration. Secret White House foreign policy initiatives were again conducted through the National Security Council in the Reagan Administration and have led to further abuses in the system. The basic Kissinger and Nixon reorganization of the NSC system made these abuses possible.

Kissinger's role at the NSC was unique. From September 1973 until November 1975, he was simultaneously secretary of state and assistant to the president for national security affairs. On Vietnam it is possible to chart Nixon's and Kissinger's differences in approach, timing, and personal motivations, but their relationship remains an incompletely told story.[42] Both President Nixon and Kissinger have downplayed the importance of the letters to President Thieu, yet there is an important lesson to be learned. The president must develop a consensus with Congress, beginning with a relationship of trust with key leaders. He cannot operate on his own over a sustained period of time without paying a heavy price in personal and national credibility.

In assessing the Nixon Presidency, the resolution of the Vietnam War stands not as a triumph of détente and great power diplomacy, but as a retreat from the traditional standards of foreign policy conduct. The betrayal of an ally remains part of the legacy that has still to be assimilated.

NOTES

1. William G. Hyland, *Mortal Rivals* (New York: Random House, 1987), p. 5.

2. Ibid.

3. Henry Kissinger, *White House Years* (Boston: Little, Brown, 1979), pp. 282, 1043, 1334.

4. Authors' interview with Nguyen Van Thieu, June 13, 1985. Thieu said: "The Americans did brief me on several occasions, but they only informed me of what they saw fit."

5. Henry A. Kissinger, *A World Restored* (New York: Grosset & Dunlap, 1961), p. 329.

6. Oriana Fallaci, *Interview with History* (Boston: Houghton Mifflin, 1976), p. 41.

7. Nguyen Tien Hung and Jerrold L. Schecter, *The Palace File* (New York: Harper & Row, 1986), pp. 1, 2 and Appendix A. See letters from Nixon to Thieu dated October 16, 1972, November 14, 1972, January 5, 1973, and January 17, 1973, in which Nixon was categorical in his promises and agreed to use "full force" against North Vietnam.

8. The letters are reprinted in full in *The Palace File*.

9. Ibid., pp. 446–448. Appendix F provides a detailed comparison of the North Vietnamese 1969 proposal and the final Paris Accord signed in January 1973.

10. Kissinger's peace plan was labeled "the death warrant" by the Vietnamese in Saigon. Thieu gained strong support from his government as he battled Kissinger; this helped him to resist signing until written American assurances were given in Nixon's letters.

11. Kissinger, *White House Years*, p. 262.

12. Ibid.

13. Hung and Schecter, *The Palace File*, p. 95.

14. Ibid., pp. 94–96, provides a more detailed discussion of how the debate emerged within the Nixon Administration.

15. Ho Chi Minh, *Selected Writings* (Hanoi: Foreign Languages Publishing House, 1973), pp. 356, 361.

16. Henry A. Kissinger, *American Foreign Policy* (New York: W. W. Norton, 1974), p. 128.

17. Kissinger, *White House Years*, p. 448.

18. Ibid., p. 1325.

19. Ibid., p. 1344.

20. Richard Nixon, *Foreign Policy in the 1970's: Shaping a Durable Peace: A Report to the Congress May 3, 1973* (Washington, D.C.: U.S. Government Printing Office), p. 52.

21. Kissinger, *White House Years*, p. 1345.

22. Hung and Schecter, *The Palace File*, pp. 83–85.

23. Ibid., pp. 16–17.

24. Ibid., pp. 379–380.

25. Ibid., p. 391.

26. Richard Nixon, *The Memoirs of Richard Nixon* (New York: Grosset & Dunlap, 1978), p. 690.

27. Hung and Schecter, *The Palace File*, p. 376.

28. Ibid., pp. 62–82, and Seymour Hersh, *The Price of Power* (New York: Summit Books, 1983), pp. 22–23.

29. Hung and Schecter, *The Palace File*, p. 392.

30. Ibid., pp. 159–171.

31. Henry Kissinger, *Years of Upheaval* (Boston: Little, Brown, 1982), pp. 315–317.

32. Hung and Schecter, *The Palace File*, pp. 296–298.

33. Ron Nessen, *It Sure Looks Different from the Inside* (Chicago: Playboy Press, 1978), p. 106.

34. Hung and Schecter, *The Palace File*, pp. 354–355.

35. Author's interview with James Schlesinger, November 27, 1985.

36. Hung and Schecter, *The Palace File*, p. 308; see also Nessen, *It Sure Looks Different from the Inside*, p. 106.

37. Author's interview with President Gerald Ford, February 10, 1986.

38. Hung and Schecter, *The Palace File*, p. 434.
39. For a comparison, see Kissinger, *Years of Upheaval*, n. 6, pp. 1236–1240.
40. Hersh, *The Price of Power*, pp. 25–36.
41. Roger Morris, *Uncertain Greatness* (New York: Harper & Row, 1977), p. 150.
42. Hung and Schecter, *The Palace File*, pp. 90–95.

Discussant: Frances FitzGerald

It's a little hard to know where to begin with this discussion because so many issues are involved. Mr. Hammond is absolutely correct when he says that there are a great number of mysteries left. One of them is certainly the kind of estimates that Nixon and Kissinger were making about the war in the period 1969–72. Did they think the war could be won—if winning meant the continued existence of a non-Communist South Vietnam that could sustain itself without the aid of American troops or American bombers? The underlying assumption of Mr. Schecter and Dr. Hung's paper seems to be that the war could have been won in this sense.

This is a large assumption, and in my view there is little evidence to support it. After all, even in 1970–71, after the United States had virtually defeated the Viet Cong in the South, the U.S. military command still had no strategy for winning the war. There was no strategy for defeating the North Vietnamese Army, any more than there was a strategy when Clark Clifford looked at the situation in 1968. It was that simple. The strategy Nixon and Kissinger adopted was to withdraw U.S. troops while continuing, and indeed increasing, the bombing. The strategy was politically acceptable in the United States, at least for some years, but it was not a winning strategy. Possibly—were it not for Watergate—they could have maintained the military stalemate long enough to pass the whole problem on to the next administration. But how could they have hoped for more than that, with or without negotiations? Kissinger himself said that if guerrillas do not lose, they win.

Maintain a stalemate and hope for a miracle—or pass the problem on. This is how the war was fought from the beginning—by the Eisenhower Administration, by the Kennedy and Johnson administrations. How could Nixon and Kissinger have hoped for anything more? Nixon, of course, made some very original efforts in this regard. One thing he did was to go to the Soviet Union and to ask the Soviets to sell out the Vietnamese. This was not politically possible for the Soviets, although they did sit by while Nixon escalated the war against North Vietnam. Another thing he did was to create the opening to China, but, of course, the Chinese could not abandon the North Vietnamese at that point. Nixon had nothing left to do but to fight a series of rear-guard military actions, including, while the American troops were still in the country, the bombing of the Cambodian sanctuaries and the incursion into Cambodia, and later the incursion into Laos.

These rear-guard actions proved fairly ineffective militarily. The incursion into Cambodia probably delayed the North Vietnamese prosecution of the war by about six months. That, at least, was the estimate of American commanders in the Delta at the time. By the beginning of 1972 the administration was still stuck between the same rock and the same hard place: the rock being the North

Vietnamese Army and the hard place being the fact that the American public would not support the return of U.S. troops to Vietnam. At bottom the problem was that, even with a million men under arms, the Saigon government had nothing to oppose to the North Vietnamese troops. This became quite clear in the spring of 1972, when the North Vietnamese launched their first major offensive since 1969, and when that offensive was stopped only by intensive American bombing, B–52 raids in central Vietnam. Nixon and Kissinger began serious negotiations only after that, with the Thieu government quite naturally resisting them all the way.

Of course, the United States and the Saigon government could not win through negotiations what they could not win on the battlefield. Nixon and Kissinger may have deluded themselves, but the most they could have hoped for was a "decent interval," or an agreement that would make it appear that the United States had not lost the war and that the United States had not "abandoned" its South Vietnamese ally. But the only weapon they had left was the threat of strategic bombing. For a time the negotiations had far less to do with North or South Vietnam than with the presidential election of 1972. For Kissinger to say that peace was at hand in October 1972, was clearly a tactical error in terms of the negotiations. He never made an error like that when he was negotiating with the Chinese or the Soviets. He may have misread the Vietnamese sides, but more likely he was simply concentrating on the problem of how to pull out a solution acceptable to the American public before the election. He failed. To punish the North, or to force concessions from it, the administration ordered what became known as the Christmas bombing of Hanoi. B–52s, by the way, make craters as large as this auditorium and sound like the end of the world. The Christmas bombing left 2,200 Vietnamese dead. The idea was to show that Nixon—just reelected by a landslide—could do anything he wanted without political constraints, even something that most people considered risky or irrational. The message to the North Vietnamese was that they could not expect the usual pressures to work on the administration.

But, of course, the usual pressures were still at work, and the negotiations recommenced. The agreement that Kissinger finally signed in January was not the best he could have hoped for. He might have done much better had he begun serious negotiations some years earlier. The agreement said, after all, that Vietnam was one country; it implied that the United States was there illegitimately and had to withdraw; it permitted North Vietnamese troops to remain in the South (because Vietnam was one country); and it gave the Thieu government only the status of another administration in the South, and not the status of a sovereign government. That was it. That was the end for Thieu. That was a concession of defeat, and what happened after that was merely a delay of the inevitable.

That was the end for the Thieu government because to have maintained its control over the South, that government would have had to carry out a revolution. And it was not capable of such a thing. This was not Thieu's fault. He could no more change the system and end the corruption around him than a fish can change the sea it lives in. I was in Vietnam at the time, and an Embassy official said of the Thieu government what the French used to say of the colonial regime— that it was held together by *la densité de la pourriture,* the very density of the rot. Indeed, when the 1975 offensive came along, it became clear that this was exactly the case, for the ARVN crumpled first in the central highlands, where there was no money, and therefore no corruption, left.

If there was ever a time to reconstruct South Vietnamese politics, it was in the late 1950s and early 1960s under the Ngos. After that, it was too late. The American presence in South Vietnam created a false, foreign economy; it disrupted the whole society, driving millions of people out of the countryside and into the cities, where they lived off the United States. It subordinated Vietnamese politics. On our side there was nothing left but people, grains of sand.

That the U.S. and the Saigon governments were not going to win the war was obvious in 1968. It's the prosecution of the war by the Nixon Administration that fills me with the greatest sense of outrage because it was done in that knowledge and because far more civilian lives were lost in Vietnam in those years than in all previous years. The Nixon Administration also managed to bring Cambodia into the war. The bombing and the massive generation of refugees—in a country so unused to war—is said to have given impetus to the Khmer Rouge. The holocaust followed and ended only with the Vietnamese invasion.

There are many "ifs" in the history we are dealing with. Could Kissinger have come to a better agreement with the North Vietnamese earlier on? What would Cambodia be like today if it had not been engulfed by war? What would Vietnam be like if the war had ended five or six years earlier by agreement? Possibly at least it would not have taken those who fought a war on their soil for thirty years so long to look toward their own economy and to make overtures to their neighbors in Southeast Asia.

Discussant: Guenter Lewy

Mr. Hammond's paper is excellent; I would urge you to read it in its entirety. His brief summary only gave you some of the highlights. My only reservation is the final paragraph which, intended or not, seems to suggest that the final disaster was practically inevitable. Yet it seems to me that at various points during this long war, options were available which might have brought about a different outcome. In the years 1954–75 the United States could have pursued policies different from those that were actually followed. What, for example, if instead of making a piecemeal commitment of military resources and adopting a policy of gradual use of these resources, America had pursued a strategy of surprise and massed strength at various decisive points? What if the mining of Vietnamese harbors had taken place in 1965 instead of 1972? What if the United States from the beginning had implemented a strategy of population security instead of fighting General Westmoreland's doomed war of attrition? What if Vietnamization had begun in 1965 rather than 1968–69? Although we cannot be sure that these different strategies, singularly or in combination, would necessarily have brought about a different outcome, neither can we take their failure for granted.

Relations with the South Vietnamese and Vietnamization also could have followed a different course. As a result of anticolonialist inhibitions and many other reasons, the United States refrained from pressing for a decisive reorganization of the South Vietnamese armed forces and for a combined command, as the United States had done so successfully in Korea under the mantle of a U.N. mandate. Similarly, in regard to pacification and matters of social policy generally, America sought to shore up a sovereign South Vietnamese government. Therefore, for the most part it limited itself to an advisory and supportive role, always mindful of the saying of Lawrence of Arabia, "Better they do it imperfectly than you do it pefectly, for it is their country, their war and your time is limited." Western aggressiveness and impatience for results, it was said, went counter to oriental ways of thinking and doing things and merely increased resistance to change and reform. But if the internal weaknesses in South Vietnamese society and the high level of corruption, described so well by Mr. Hammond in his paper, were indeed as important a factor in the final disaster as all the evidence seems to suggest, might a radically different approach perhaps have been indicated? Should the United States initially have accepted full responsiblity for both military and political affairs as suggested by experienced Vietnam hands like John Paul Vann, and should it only gradually have yielded control over the conduct of the war to a newly created core of capable military leaders and administrators? Should the United States have played the role of the good colonialist who in this way slowly prepares a new country for viable independence? At the very least, should the United States have exerted more systematic leverage over its South Vietnamese ally? The long record of American failure to move the government in Saigon in directions that in retrospect would have clearly been desirable for both the people of South Vietnam and America suggests that we would have had little to lose and much to gain by using more vigorously the power over that government that our contributions gave us. We became their prisoners, rather than they ours—falling into the classic trap into which great powers so often fall in their relationships with weak allies.

We will never know, of course, whether any of these different approaches would have yielded better results. However, I think these alternative policy options must be mentioned in order to prevent the acceptance of the idea of an inevitable collapse of South Vietnam.

The Hung-Schecter paper correctly describes the main chain of events, but the interpretations of these events in many places, I think, are wrong or at least highly misleading. The central argument is stated at the beginning of the paper where the authors write, "in its efforts to withdraw from the Vietnam War, the United States betrayed South Vietnam while promoting the fallacious claim of having achieved 'peace with honor.' " This, I think is an unsubstantiated assertion. Yes, the United States withdrew from Vietnam, but I don't think it betrayed Vietnam. Kissinger and Nixon sought more than a decent interval; they indeed hoped for a peace with honor, and they had reason to assume that such a peace could be achieved. Had Watergate not undermined the Nixon Presidency, the North Vietnamese, as we know from their own writings, would not have staged their final offensive. Had they staged this offensive, Nixon would have sent in the Air Force as he had done so successfully in stemming the Easter Offensive of 1972.

Let's briefly review Nixon's public pronouncements during this time. At a news conference on March 15, 1973, Nixon stated that, while truce violations by both sides were to be expected, the infiltration of men and equipment exceeding the replacement provisions of the Paris Agreement was a most serious matter. Using strong language, Nixon went on to say, "we have informed the North Vietnamese of our concern about this infiltration . . . and I would only suggest that based on my actions over the past four years, that the North Vietnamese should not lightly disregard such expressions of concern when they are made with regard to a violation." Weight was added to this threat by the resumption of American reconnaissance flights over North Vietnam. [On March 29, 1973, the last American prisoners were released in Hanoi, and the final installment of American troops left South Vietnam.] Also on that day, in a nationwide address, Nixon hailed the completion of the American withdrawal from Vietnam. Some problems, he said, such as continued infiltration remained, and he went on to warn that "we shall insist that North Vietnam comply with the agreement and the leaders of North Vietnam should have no doubt as to the consequences if they fail to comply with the agreement." Less than a month later, according to reliable sources, the president had just about decided to follow through on these threats and resume bombing of North Vietnam when the floodgates of Watergate opened up. Nixon learned that his counsel, John Dean, had begun to talk to the Watergate prosecutors. Realizing that Dean's testimony could tie him directly to the Watergate scandal and knowing that a resumption of the bombing would draw violent criticism, Nixon refrained from approving the raids.

This decision, coupled with the failure of the Congress during 1973–74 to approve enough aid to Saigon, was the beginning of the end. As General Van Tien Dung, the North Vietnamese commander put it in his account of the final offensive, President Thieu was forced to fight a poor man's war. Heavily out-gunned, the demoralized South Vietnamese collapsed in the spring of 1975. The responsibility for this collapse, I believe, is shared by many. It surely falls on the government of Thieu, which failed to build a political community for which the people of South Vietnam might have been willing to lay down their lives. The Thieu government failed to control corruption, and it failed to establish an effective military leadership.

The U.S. Congress must be faulted for reneging on the promises of aid that had been made. Last, but not least, there's the responsibility of the antiwar movement, which had delegimated the American war effort by charges of whole-sale atrocities and deliberate violations of the law of war in order to pressure the Congress to abandon South Vietnam. A typical example of these charges can be found in Frances FitzGerald's book, *Fire in the Lake*, where she accuses the United States of committing genocide. This charge is even more absurd than most others, for many reasons, not the least because, according to figures com-piled by the United Nations, the population of North and South Vietnam during the war period, despite all casualties, increased at twice the U.S. rate. All this contributed, then, to the final disaster. The Hung-Schecter formula is far too simple in explaining it. Vietnamization was surely more than a smoke screen. As I argued earlier, failure was not foreordained. The crucial role of Watergate is acknowledged by the authors of the paper when they write, "Watergate prevented President Nixon from fulfilling his promises . . . to use full force against North Vietnamese violations of the Paris Accord." But if that is conceded, then it seems to me that the entire argument of betrayal becomes irrelevant.

I would argue that the defeat of the United States in Vietnam has had serious ramifications, most of them negative, for U.S. foreign policy. The Vietnam trauma continues to afflict us today. Southeast Asia is a human disaster of major proportions. Millions have died since the collapse of Vietnam in Cambodia, and there prevails a peace that is no peace. What Frances FitzGerald in 1972 ad-miringly called "the discipline of the revolutionary community" had led to the horrors of Kampuchea, the Vietnamese gulag, the tragic flight of the boat people. With America staying the course, all this might have been prevented, but for many complex reasons this proved impossible. I see here a tragedy. To make Nixon and Kissinger scapegoats will prevent us from learning the necessary lessons. Thank you.

Discussant: Frances FitzGerald
(Response)

Mr. Lewy flatters me by saying that I helped to delegitimate the American war effort. This is to give the messenger credit and to miss the point. The American war effort was, first and foremost, delegitimated by failure. The U.S. command did not lose the war, but it never at any point had a workable strategy for winning it. From the time the U.S. forces arrived in Vietnam until the time they departed, the U.S. command had only one strategy, and that was attrition, or the attempt to kill more enemy soldiers than the enemy could replace. This did not work because "the enemy" turned out to be most Vietnamese. As a result, the strategy itself could not be morally legitimated. In *Fire in the Lake* I wrote: "No one in the American government consciously planned a policy of genocide. The American military commanders would have been shocked or angered by such a charge, but in fact their policy had no other military logic, and their course of action was indistinguishable from it."

On a tactical level, the American forces had a good deal of difficulty distinguishing enemy soldiers from other Vietnamese. It was not just Lieutenant Calley who failed to make the distinction, but, on a routine basis, the bombers and the artillery. And such was U.S. technological might that in 1969 Vietnam became the most heavily bombed and the most heavily shelled country *in history*. In his book, Mr. Lewy admits that a shocking number of civilian casualties resulted. But he tells us that in the Southeast at least the Viet Cong were to blame as they hid out in the villages and attracted U.S. bombers and artillery fire to them! Now he tells us there was no question of genocide because the U.S. "body counts" never matched the Vietnamese birth rate. Orwell would recognize this logic.

Discussant: Robert H. Miller

First, I feel obliged to state that the views I present are my own and not official.

I find much to agree with in both papers: The United States made plenty of mistakes in Vietnam. Despite all the shortcomings, all the legitimate frustrations in the White House, I think it was a mistake for White House staffs to ignore professional advice as much as it did. The latest manifestation of the dangers of doing so is the Iran/Contra affair. I also think it was a mistake for Henry Kissinger to become so personally involved in detailed Vietnam negotiations. When things got tough, he had nowhere to turn other than to the president—the last resort—and Hanoi exploited that vulnerability. I think, too, that the U.S. negotiating proposals were always too little and too late, thus giving the initiative to Hanoi and gaining our side nothing in the end. Finally, I think that our allies in Saigon had every reason to lack confidence in our staying power. Considering the ultimate outcome in Vietnam, a more realistic negotiating posture would have been far preferable to "too little and too late."

But the U.S. mistakes in Vietnam began long before Nixon and Kissinger came into office. In my own view there were four principal mistakes among many others:

1. It was a mistake for us to see Moscow, Beijing, and Hanoi as a monolith; we played to their strengths rather than to their weaknesses by our massive commitment of forces. In effect, we drove them together rather than apart.

2. We allowed the war to become more important to us than it was to the South Vietnamese. Mr. Hammond's paper amply describes this error.

3. Thieu and other South Vietnamese leaders before him were able to use our unstinting support as a substitute for dealing with their own internal political problems.

4. We misled ourselves with a short-term rationale for what turned out to be a long-term problem.

Nevertheless, the Hung-Schecter paper ignores the fact that Nixon and Kissinger inherited an unpopular war with 500,000 U.S. troops in Vietnam already committed to combat. The Hung-Schecter paper also ignores what I think is an indisputable fact—that no U.S. president representing the mainstream of the U.S. electorate sufficiently to get elected would or could have followed an essentially different course in Vietnam. Hung and Schecter detail Nixon and Kissinger's "betrayal" of Vietnam and their secret commitments to Thieu. Hindsight, of course, is always better than foresight, but I assume that we all agree that Nixon and Kissinger were faced with very tough problems when they came into office. The U.S. public and Congress would no longer support the war at the level Westmoreland had requested—another 125,000 troops. The war had to be terminated, and the United States had to be extricated in a manner commensurate with the sacrifices of thousands of young Americans. I don't think this is an idle judgment. Rather, it accurately reflects the temper of the people at the time, the people who elected Richard Nixon. Mr. Hammond details the manifold inadequacies of Vietnamese forces that led us to get involved with a deep commitment of forces.

The essential gordian knot in the negotiations was that both sides sought to achieve at the negotiating table what they had not been able to achieve on the battlefield. The U.S. and South Vietnamese governments sought North Vietnamese troop withdrawal before any political compromise was made on the South Vietnamese governing structure. Hanoi sought withdrawal of U.S. support for the Thieu regime, before agreeing to any troop withdrawal. Each side had a different approach to negotiations: The United States viewed the negotiations as a means to resolve conflict on acceptable terms, inevitably involving compromise; Hanoi viewed the negotiations as another way of achieving its goal, namely, taking over South Vietnam. The South Vietnamese government viewed the negotiations as a threat to its existence.

So the negotiations were unequal, as the Hung-Schecter paper points out. U.S. firepower was offset by an eroding public support in the United States for its use. Hanoi totally controlled the Viet Cong, whereas the United States did not control the South Vietnamese government. Each U.S. negotiating proposal strengthened the North Vietnamese and the Viet Cong, and weakened the South Vietnamese government. And, of course, Watergate became the final inequality in the negotiations for the United States—a wholly unnecessary U.S. vulnerability. Watergate made it impossible for Nixon and Kissinger to carry out any commitments to Thieu. None of the parties to the negotiations—Hanoi and Saigon included—covered themselves with glory in this affair.

But the two papers under discussion today ignore the broader context that is important to address for the future: Five administrations share the blame for Vietnam (Eisenhower, Kennedy, Johnson, Nixon, and Ford). Successive U.S. administrations underestimated Hanoi's unbending determination, as Hammond's paper supports. Successive U.S. administrations underestimated Sino-Soviet and Sino-Vietnamese tensions. Finally, successive administrations overestimated our own ability to succeed where the French had failed.

The two papers are unclear on alternative solutions. In condemning Nixon and Kissinger, the Hung-Schecter paper implies that there were better solutions, but they don't name any. As Mr. Hammond suggests, the war, in effect, had been lost in terms of U.S. domestic political support when Nixon and Kissinger came into office—Lyndon Johnson had been forced to withdraw his candidacy over the war. Should Nixon and Kissinger have continued, or even widened the war, despite the restrictions of the Geneva Accords and despite the growing unpopularity of the war in the United States and in fact throughout the world? Should they have withdrawn unilaterally, immediately, abandoning Thieu? Should they have negotiated unilateral U.S. troop withdrawals à la Mendes France in Geneva in 1954 or DeGaulle in Algeria a few years later, also abandoning Thieu? Should they have immediately negotiated a political solution with Hanoi which could only have been done by abandoning Thieu?

My own view is that the Nixon-Kissinger Administration faced no good choices on Vietnam and that they made no good choices. Their predecessors had put them in a position where the choices were unacceptable either to the American people or to Thieu. They managed to alienate both. In the final analysis, their responsibility was to the American people who elected Richard Nixon, not to Thieu. Their mistake once again, was, to underestimate Hanoi's determination and to assume that they could bring Hanoi to an agreement by a combination of continuing military pressure and world opinion. They would have been far better advised, with the benefit of hindsight, to negotiate a time-phase U.S. withdrawal under a cease-fire, leaving resolution of the internal political differences to the Vietnamese. In the long run, this approach would have been fairer to Thieu; certainly, it would have been fairer to the American people. The result would probably not have been different, but perhaps it would have been as a result of South Vietnamese rather than U.S. political failure.

Let me close with a few other thoughts. Vietnam was a tragedy for both the United States and Vietnam. Both countries continue to live with the consequences. The Hung-Schecter paper suggests that Thieu's tragedy was to lose power and that Nixon-Kissinger's machinations were responsible. Without in any way condoning or endorsing the Nixon-Kissinger record on Vietnam, I would suggest that LBJ's and Nixon's tragedies in losing office were equally great for the American public and that one could argue that Thieu's machinations and failures played their role in those tragedies as well.

Hanoi won its war but may have lost its peace. The last chapter of history is never written, but today Vietnam is almost totally absorbed with its internal problems and with its occupation of Cambodia. Wars of national liberation, Hanoi's banner in the 1960s, are no longer considered to be the wave of the future as they were when we went into Vietnam. The Association of Southeast Asian Nations (ASEAN) region is one of the strongest, most stable, dynamic, and cohesive regions in the world today. Moreover, the Nixon and Kissinger objective of extricating the United States from Vietnam by opening negotiations instead of widening the war paved the way for the strategic and historic opening to China. And the United States today remains strongly and constructively engaged in East Asia.

To sum up, could it have all been done differently? Could we have won the negotiations by earlier concessions or with stronger military pressure? Nixon and Kissinger were faced with a major war involving five hundred thousand U.S. troops, a major commitment to an ally that began with Eisenhower after the Geneva Conference of 1954 and continued with Kennedy and Johnson. Whatever the shortcomings of successive South Vietnamese leaders, extricating the United States from this situation in a way acceptable to the American people was an anguishing problem for the new administration. The North Vietnamese did not make the choices easier for us; they were determined to absorb South

Vietnam. After commitments by three presidents, it would have been irresponsible to walk away from South Vietnam. Plenty of mistakes were made, including mistakes by Nixon and Kissinger in my view, but my point is that the choices were all bad for those who had the responsibility of decision making. Had Nixon and Kissinger simply liquidated the war by declaring a unilateral cease-fire and withdrawing our forces, the uproar in this country would have been huge. The region would have been in bad shape. And the credibility of the United States in the region would have been zero.

Thank you very much.

DÉTENTE AND THE SOVIET UNION

6

The Rise and Stall of Détente, 1969–1974

ROBERT D. SCHULZINGER

From 1969 until 1974 an era of détente emerged in the relations between the United States and the Soviet Union. At the time it was described variously as a "structure of peace," or "an attempt to work out ground rules and agreed restraints in our relations with the Soviet Union that will lessen the danger of international war and international conflicts to which either party might become involved," or even "something that wasn't much of anything anyway." In retrospect, Raymond Garthoff, who has written the most comprehensive study of U.S.-Soviet relations in the 1960s and 1970s, concluded in 1985 that "[i]n practice, the development of detente was a gradual and uncertain process."[1]

During the Nixon Administration the United States and the Soviet Union explored détente through three summits between President Richard Nixon and Communist party Secretary Leonid Brezhnev and numerous meetings between National Security Adviser and later Secretary of State Henry Kissinger and various Soviet officials. The two countries restricted antiballistic missiles, promised progress on limiting strategic weapons, stipulated the basic principles regulating their relations, pledged to prevent nuclear war, promised to reduce the yield of their underground nuclear explosions, and opened new trade relations. Most of these agreements were reached between 1971 and 1973, generating wide but hardly universal approval in the United States and Europe.

In 1974 an administration discredited by Watergate and scrambling to cope with an oil crisis ignited by the Mideast War of October 1973, made no more progress toward détente. Indeed, during the last year of the Nixon Administration all the forces were at work which led to the eventual collapse of efforts at improving relations between the United States and the Soviet Union. Yet Watergate and Mideastern preoccupations were not the sole reasons for the stall of détente. The process itself was flawed from the beginning, as Nixon and Kissinger raised public expectations beyond what the actual new relationship with the Soviet Union would bear. As Garthoff puts it, the "discrepancy between . . . the realistic management of power and the promise of 'a new era' of 'durable peace' ultimately came to haunt détente and undercut popular support."[2] How détente arose and eventually failed to meet the high expectations of its initial supporters is the subject of this paper.

Throughout the Nixon years, supporters of détente outside the administration linked it to arms control. As Norman Cousins, head of the National Committee for a Sane Nuclear Policy (SANE), put it, the specter of nuclear war was "The nightmare that won't go away." He characterized "nuclear stockpiles as the world's number 1 problem."[3] Here was an unfortunate connection: Nixon and Kissinger considered arms control distinctly a secondary issue, part of a larger process of détente, but not the major goal. Kissinger himself believed that arms controllers took too seriously the danger of nuclear war. As he had charged in 1961, "the most vocal and passionate advocates of arms control have . . . [too often] given the impression that simply because the goal is important, it can be reached easily." He urged Americans to acknowledge that "without arms control stability will be more difficult to achieve. But it can probably be achieved even then."[4]

The Nixon Administration therefore conducted arms control negotiations with the Soviet Union with a view to larger political implications—both international and domestic. For some of the time, the fact that the two sides were engaged in serious dialogue was enough to show that détente worked. At other times however, the United States acted as if "our main requirement now was to be concrete," as Kissinger told Soviet Ambassador Anatoly Dobrynin.[5] As a result, détente engendered the greatest public support when it appeared to be a process with momentum. When actual arrangements emerged, however, critics pointed to specific flaws. Eventually, their skepticism swamped détente.

In 1969 and 1970 the president and national security adviser moved to control the process of negotiations with the Soviet Union in the face of congressional and public concern over deployment of the antiballistic missile system proposed at the end of the Johnson Administration. Lobbies of scientists predicted disaster if the United States deployed an ABM. The Soviets were bound to do the same. ABM systems could not knock out every incoming missile, so each side would have an incentive to build more missiles and flood its adversary's defenses. More destabilizing still was the prospect of the side behind in the development of ABM toying with the idea of a preemptive strike before the other's defensive system was operational. Such objections led Senators Frank Church (D-Ida.), Albert Gore (D-Tenn.), Edward M. Kennedy (D-Mass.), Edmund Muskie (D-Me.), Walter Mondale (D-Minn.), and John Sherman Cooper (R-Ky.) to oppose funding for further development of ABM.[6]

Nixon and Kissinger resented congressional interference even as they acknowledged the salience of some of the criticism. The president described ABM as a vital bargaining chip in arms negotiations. He announced that far from "complicat[ing] an agreement with the Soviet Union," a version of the ABM modified to defend U.S. missile bases would "give the Soviet Union even less reason to view our defense efforts as an obstacle to talks." The NSC chief dismissed concerns about the seemingly destabilizing effects of ABM, since "Soviet leaders and military theorists have never espoused the western academic notions that vulnerability was desirable or destabilizing." At the same time, he resisted letting Congress dictate U.S. arms policy. He lamented that "we could sell an ABM program to Congress apparently only by depriving it of military effectiveness against our principal adversary." Kissinger notified Congress that interference with ABMs or the development of Multiple Independently Targeted Reentry Vehicles (MIRVs) would wreck delicate conversations with the Soviets. He mourned that congressional meddlers pressed the administration to "abandon our ABM without reciprocity . . . and postpone our MIRV deployment as a unilateral gesture—in short to forego both our missile defense and the means to defeat that already deployed by the Soviet Union." Eventually, Nixon and Kissinger's arguments barely prevailed, and the Senate backed further work on the ABM by a one-vote margin in August 1969.[7]

Such close decisions in Congress forced Nixon and Kissinger to move forward with direct presidential initiatives in arms control. These appeared all the more necessary as Gerard Smith, head of the Arms Control and Disarmament Agency who was meeting with the Soviets in Vienna, differed with the White House regarding the most important issues facing the two powers. Unlike Nixon and Kissinger, who thought of arms control and détente as a means toward the goal of projecting U.S. interests in a changed environment of "superpower parity," Smith considered limiting strategic arms a valued end in itself. Specifically, he argued that the ABM should not stand in the way of an effective settlement of the more nettlesome question of the number of missile launchers. Smith told his counterpart Vladimir Semenov that both sides recognized that ABM was an ineffective device that frightened its owner as much as a potential adversary. He wrote Nixon that his opposite number, Semenov, shared this view and "strikes me as a man bent on serious business. . . . He spoke of nuclear war as a disaster for both sides—of the decreased security as the number of weapons increases—of the costly results of rapid obsolescence—of the dangers of grave miscalculation—of unauthorized use of weapons—and of hostilities resulting from third power provocations."[8]

While Smith, a representative of the Department of State, conducted the official and publicly acknowledged negotiations with Semenov over the future of strategic missiles, Kissinger, encouraged by Nixon, pressed forward with his own quiet talks with Soviet Ambassador Anatoly Dobrynin. These backchannel negotiations had several advantages from the White House's point of view. First, they kept Congress outside the process. Since Kissinger did not admit the conversations, Congress did not know what to ask. Had they done so, the Nixon Administration's adherence to executive privilege would have prevented the testimony of the president's personal advisers. Second, the backchannel permitted Kissinger to maneuver around Smith and the State Department. He informed Dobrynin that final decisions rested in the White House, which could overrule initiatives from other parts of the bureaucracy. The backchannel permitted the White House more flexibility in private than Nixon and Kissinger considered possible in the official sessions.

During two years of backchannel talks from 1969 to 1971, Kissinger outlined the American view of superpower parity. He noted the many developments that bound the two countries to one another more than to any other. Unlike their allies and lesser states in the Third World, the United States and the Soviet Union alone could wreck the planet with the nuclear weapons. They, and not their allies, could project armed forces far beyond their shores. (Here, however, the United States stood above the Soviets, with more aircraft carriers, more ships capable of transporting troops, and more soldiers stationed in overseas bases.)[9]

In May 1971 the backchannel brought positive results. Kissinger and Dobrynin divided the issues of ABMs (the primary Soviet concern) and offensive arms (up to that point the foremost American issue and the issue that Smith's team of negotiators found crucial). They announced that their countries would "concentrate this year on working out an agreement for the limitation of the deployment of antiballistic missile systems. They have also agreed that, together with concluding an agreement to limit ABMs, they will agree on certain measures with respect to the limitation of offensive strategic arms." In effect, the United States and Soviet Union had decided that it was easier to reach firm commitments banning ABMs, which did not yet exist, than it was to draft a treaty setting limits on nuclear weapons already deployed. As one observer noted later, "left unresolved in the 'backchannel' discussions were the specific limitations to be placed on offensive arms."[10] This flaw became serious later, as the specific limits never materialized in the Nixon or Ford administrations. In 1971, however, it appeared to Nixon and Kissinger as if a breakthrough had been achieved, one that advanced the momentum of détente.

The White House wanted to demonstrate to the rest of the bureaucracy its control over the course of U.S.-Soviet relations. Kissinger and Nixon believed that rivals within the government had parochial interests that overlooked larger, if less clearly definable, issues of the process of détente. "Don't tell them anything," Nixon explained to Defense Secretary Melvin Laird and Secretary of State William Rogers. "Russians [were] very sensitive" about American leaks. How different the White House's position was from that of Gerard Smith who claimed that the major issue facing the two parties was reaching an agreement on arms. "We should avoid wasting time on obviously inequitable propositions—especially when that time is being better used by the other side," he recalled.[11]

The White House hoped to focus on the political aim of creating better feelings between Moscow and Washington. Nixon informed Kissinger shortly before the

Moscow summit how important appearances were. "I believe that the expectations for the Moscow trip are being built up too much," the president wrote his national security adviser in an Eyes Only Memorandum. "What I am concerned about is not that we will fail to achieve the various goals about which there has been speculation but that when we do make the formal agreements there will be no real news value to them because of their having been discounted by an enormous amount of discussion prior to the summit." To heighten the drama, Nixon ordered "that no final agreements be entered into until we arrive in Moscow." For Kissinger, who projected rivalry between the two powers indefinitely into the future, it hardly mattered which side held formal superiority. As Nixon put it at his first press conference after becoming president, the United States wanted "sufficiency," not superiority, in strategic weapons. Neither side was likely to press any advantage to the point of actual warfare. Accordingly, it was more important that the two sides reach some agreement, demonstrating that the relationship could be properly managed, than it was to make certain that every military precaution was taken. Kissinger later patronized Smith's concerns for his delegation's technical expertise: "It was only human that they wanted to play a central role at the turning points of which they and their dedication had made possible. It was not their fault that the key decisions were political, involving domestic and foreign policy considerations for both sides. At the same time, we could not slow our efforts to resolve deadlocked issues simply to maintain the morale of our delegation."[12]

For his part, Smith resented being undercut by the White House in the latter part of the negotiations. He preferred greater caution on technical issues, with less attention to the political repercussions of the talks. Accordingly, he thought an agreement on strategic arms more important than an ABM treaty. The goals of an ABM agreement, he believed, could be better accomplished by a unilateral U.S. decision not to proceed with ABM. Smith believed that the president and national security adviser had pressed ABM in order to appear tough before hardline members of Congress and conservative spokesmen. Smith feared that politicians, carrying water on both shoulders, eventually would be unable to make the hard choices necessary for getting a SALT treaty. When Kissinger first let him know that he had been speaking to Dobrynin for over a year and showed him the draft of the May 1971 announcement, Smith sputtered that "the drafting was imprecise and the 'agreement to agree' would be criticised." For Smith, Kissinger's position could easily result in endless conversation without reaching an agreement.[13]

All the while, Smith thought the United States had to be thorough while negotiating limits on strategic forces already built. He took seriously objections raised by Pentagon officials who worried that the Soviet Union, relying on the greater destructiveness of their bombs to compensate for the American advantage in accuracy, might seek high limits on numbers of missiles. Under such circumstances, the Soviets could overwhelm U.S. forces.

Central to Smith's view was an alternative to the White House conception of détente. In Smith's opinion, arms control was an end in itself, not a part of a process of gradually improving U.S.-Soviet relations. To avoid a catastrophic nuclear war, it was important to count accurately the number of missiles and warheads on each side. The official delegates to the arms control talks believed that only highly qualified technical experts possessed the skills to make the count. The NSC, with a staff of fewer than forty professionals, lacked enough information. The endemic rivalry between Kissinger and the Defense Department only made the isolation of the NSC worse. Every proposal Smith presented to the Soviets seemed in danger of being undercut by counteroffers emanating from the White House and NSC. Smith's anxiety became acute during the May 1972 Moscow summit when Nixon and Kissinger took control of the final negotiations leading to SALT.

Kissinger thought that Smith was nitpicking and overlooked the appropriate reason for holding a summit and reaching an agreement on arms. The actual content of these agreements was less important than the signal that the two sides could agree on something. Under this view, arms control had symbolic importance demonstrating the concrete accomplishments of détente. When Nixon and Kissinger hammered out an Interim Agreement on the Limitation of Strategic Arms (SALT-I) at the May 1972 summit, the two American diplomats considered the signing more important than the content of the agreement. Smith, on the other hand, believed that the cavalier disregard for the work of his technical negotiators produced a worse agreement than the one his team was preparing. Specifically, Smith disputed the way in which the United States allowed the Soviets advantages in the size and numbers of land and sea-based missiles. "I questioned," he recalled, "whether we should accept an SLBM (submarine launched ballistic missile) freeze on terms that to many would look so unequal."[14]

These concerns proved prophetic after May 1972, but in the euphoria of the Moscow summit it appeared that the Arms Control and Disarmament Agency head was more interested in his own subordinates than in the overall policy of détente. Smith complained to the president that Kissinger would not show him copies of the translator's notes of the NSC head's April conversation with Brezhnev. He told Nixon he was "flabbergasted that Kissinger had once again gone off on his own and bypassed the delegation and others with SALT responsibilities." Nixon cut him off. Smith's objections were "bullshit," he informed the surprised Smith, and he should confine his inquiries to the White House to "matters of substance."[15]

When Smith pointed out that Brezhnev's position, eventually accepted by the administration, could "cause trouble in the future," the president told him once more that he was out of order. Kissinger, for his part, diverted attention from Smith's foreboding with some banter to a highly supportive press corps. He joked at the news conference explaining the limits in the SALT agreement, "Well, some of the great minds of the bureaucracy, which is not necessarily saying a great deal [laughter], have addressed this question."[16] Kissinger implied that Smith, upholding the desires and professional reputation of his subordinates, overlooked the importance of arms control as a vehicle for improved relations, not as an end in itself.

Arms control was to be part of a process of détente, and the continuation of the process dwarfed the contents of any actual agreement. If the president and general secretary of the Communist party could sign agreements, as occurred in each of the three summits, that alone had greater impact than any particular clause.

At the May 1972 summit, Nixon and Brezhnev signed three important documents: the ABM treaty, the Interim Agreement on the Limitation of Strategic Arms (SALT-I), and the Basic Principles of United States-Soviet Relations. The ABM pact committed each party to construct no more than two ABM sites, one protecting a missile base and one guarding the capital or National Command Authority (NCA). SALT I was a vaguer pact, restricting each side's offensive missiles approximately to the number deployed to date and regulating the size of replacement weapons. It was silent on the important issue of MIRVs and some kinds of offensive bombers. The interim agreement had a term of five years, with a provision that the two countries would use that period to work out a full-fledged treaty. The Basic Principles represented a Soviet effort to gain Western recognition as a legitimate and equal power. Nixon and Brezhnev agreed that "there is no alternative to . . . peaceful coexistence" (a standard Soviet formulation). Both acknowledged "the principle of equality and the renunciation of the use or the threat of force."[17]

Neither Nixon nor Kissinger made much of the Basic Principles either in Moscow or in their public explanations of the summit upon their return home.[18] Nonetheless, the innocent-sounding words of the Basic Principles later came back to haunt American exponents of détente. By the end of the summer of 1972, critics of détente, led by Senator Henry Jackson (D-Wash.) had seized on the Basic Principles as a stick to beat the administration for its supposed willingness to allow the Soviets "superiority" in strategic arms. Sixteen months later, during the October 1973 Mideast War, the Basic Principles once more became a contentious issue between supporters and critics of détente. Supporters of détente used them as guides to U.S.-Soviet relations during the crisis, while the critics considered the Soviets to have taken advantage of détente to threaten Israel, America's friend. In the long run, the critics' views prevailed in the domestic political debate, seriously wounding détente.

The reception in the summer of 1972 of the three documents signed at Moscow set the tone for later political evaluation of détente in the United States. By the time both houses of Congress adopted joint resolutions favoring SALT-I at the end of September, much of the original euphoria over the fruits of the Moscow summit had dissipated, and critics challenged the administration's hopeful assessment of détente as a process leading to a predictable international order.

Kissinger briefed Congress in June on the administration's understanding of the Moscow summit, stressing the political importance of détente and SALT beyond the specific contents of the accords. "The agreement on the limitations of strategic arms is not," he reported "merely a technical accomplishment, although it is that in part, but it must be seen as a political event of some magnitude." Kissinger warned of earlier failures by diplomats to seize the moment. "Catastrophe has resulted far less often from conscious decisions," he said, "than from the fear of breaking loose from established patterns through the inexorable march toward cataclysm because nobody knew what else to do. The paralysis of policy which destroyed Europe in 1914 would surely destroy the world if we let it happen again in the nuclear age."[19] Before Congress, Kissinger pursued the same arguments he had made in his disputes with Gerard Smith. He wanted to deflect attention away from what he and Nixon considered sterile questions of whether the United States or the Soviet Union were "ahead" in the number of nuclear weapons. Sufficiency was the new American goal. As Kissinger told Senator Jacob Javits (R-N.Y.), a prominent backer of détente and arms control, "beyond a certain sufficiency, differences in numbers . . . are not that conclusive."[20]

But Kissinger failed to persuade congressional skeptics that sufficiency in strategic weapons was good enough. Led by Senator Henry Jackson, detractors of détente focused on the ambiguities of the interim SALT accord. Jackson lectured Defense Secretary Melvin Laird that

the total number of ICBM missiles [listed in SALT] represents a unilateral position on our part and does not represent a bilateral understanding with the Russians. . . . In all of my experience, I must say, I have not heard of an agreement which involves such a serious substantive matter as the whole of our land-based strategic force not being set out in detail in the agreement. This kind of ambiguity can breed suspicion and lead to an unstable situation rather than to a more stable one.

Jackson continued his attack as he questioned Paul Nitze, the Defense Department's expert on arms control and a man generally recognized as very skeptical of Soviet intentions. When Nitze, backing the administration's conduct at the Moscow summit, denied that SALT allowed the Soviets to juggle the number of their heavy missiles, Jackson shot back: "All you are saying is that there is no ambiguity about the fact that the number is not specified. That is not the point. Without a specific number, there is uncertainty and ambiguity because the Soviets cannot be held to a specific number of ICBM launchers."[21]

During the remainder of the summer, Jackson sought to alter the future direction of the United States' SALT negotiations. He developed an amendment to the Joint Resolution supporting SALT in which he used the Basic Principles of "equality" in U.S.-Soviet relations. Instead of considering equality a stock Soviet phrase denoting Western acknowledgment of Moscow's legitimacy, Jackson substituted the affirmation that equality required that the missile forces of each side be equal in every particular. The Jackson amendment required that in the forthcoming negotiations for a SALT treaty U.S. diplomats maintain "the principle of United States-Soviet equality reflected in the antiballistic missile treaty.'' The reservation warned that pending a permanent restriction on offensive arms set by treaty, the United States would consider new Soviet deployments endangering American weapons to be contrary to U.S. interests. Jackson also called for continued developments of the next generation of American missiles.

About forty senators joined Jackson in sponsoring this amendment. For those concerned that Nixon and Kissinger had promised more than détente could deliver, the amendment seemed a good way of hedging a bet. What could be more acceptable and innocent than an appeal to equality between the United States and the Soviet Union? Sponsors of the amendment could have it both ways—supporting détente while demanding additional U.S. weapons.

Yet supporters of détente and further progress on SALT, led by Senators J. William Fulbright (D-Ark.) and John Sherman Cooper (R-Ky.), perceived that Jackson's amendment actually undermined Kissinger's Moscow arrangements and weakened détente. Kissinger and Nixon had reached an agreement with Brezhnev precisely because U.S. and Soviet forces were ''asymmetrical.'' The United States relied on a triad of land-based ICBMs, SLBMs, and manned bombers. The Soviets, on the other hand, had invested almost exclusively in ICBMs. Fulbright and Cooper wanted the United States to be able to exploit these asymmetries in future discussions, and so they altered Jackson's amendment, dropping references to specific weapons the United States would develop in response to new Soviet deployments.

Thus modified, Jackson's amendment passed along with the Joint Resolution of support for SALT in September 1972. The Washington senator's objections had turned the debate away from Kissinger's and Nixon's accomplishments at the Moscow summit into a debate over the future of arms control. The lawmakers leaned more toward Jackson's skepticism than toward administration optimism. While Congress did not threaten specific weapons in retaliation for Soviet moves, it went on record favoring equality of forces. The eventual resolution also indirectly chided Kissinger and Nixon for not going very far toward actually reducing arms. It asked for the beginning of Strategic Arms Reduction Talks (a Jackson locution later adopted and popularized by President Ronald Reagan in 1981). Finally, Congress insisted that any new treaties include ''concrete agreements,'' a recognition of Jackson's disappointment with the slipperiness of Kissinger's numbers.[22]

Congressional resistance to SALT I in the summer of 1972 delivered a blow to détente from which it never recovered. The Washington summit of June 1973, held in the midst of the Watergate revelations, bore few concrete results, with the exception of a Prevention of Nuclear War Agreement (PNW). This four-part arrangement resembled the Basic Principles in that the Soviets considered it ''profoundly important'' while U.S. officials regarded it only as ''a bland set of principles.''[23] In either case the PNW agreement implied that the two powers had a common interest in seeing that regional conflicts did not escalate into nuclear war. As a general principle, no one could dispute PNW's validity, but in specific crises, PNW, like the Basic Principles, created problems. As Garthoff observes, the two statements

contributed to the launching and development of détente, but before long they also contributed to its failure. For these agreed documents on a code of conduct did not really reflect an agreed understanding or consensus on the *substance* of policy restraints. This discrepancy was bound to emerge and create strong feelings that the understandings were being violated and that détente was being betrayed.[24]

A major test for détente came four months later during the October Mideast War. In diplomatic terms, détente worked during this crisis, but the way it worked further eroded political support for the process in the United States. Briefly, during the war both the United States and the Soviet Union cooperated in arranging a cease-fire between Israel and Egypt and nearly came to blows themselves as each side alerted its forces. Neither Kissinger nor Nixon at the time charged the Soviets with violating the terms of détente. Indeed, Nixon went so far as to observe on October 26, a few days after the alert, that "without détente, we might have had a major conflict in the Middle East. With détente, we avoided it."[25] Kissinger noted that "we are not yet prepared to say that they have gone beyond these limits [of détente]."[26]

Nevertheless, critics of détente, led by Senator Jackson, charged that the Soviets delivered a "brutal" note to the United States at the height of the crisis, thereby provoking a worldwide alert of American forces and violating the terms of détente.[27] It was Jackson's view that prevailed in the aftermath of the Mideast War. Opinion leaders who had been skeptical of détente since the Moscow summit now found confirmation that the Soviet Union would use détente to take advantage of the United States. The ambiguities of the participants' understanding of the obligations of détente encouraged detractors to believe that détente was not worth preserving.

Détente stalled completely in 1974. Most observers credit Watergate with derailing the Nixon's Administration's foreign policy in its last six months.[28] This was very true, but Watergate alone does not explain the meager results of the June 1974 summit in Moscow and the Crimea. Many of the pressures on détente in 1974 continued trends begun at least two years earlier. A preliminary trip by Kissinger to Moscow in March yielded far less than the "conceptual breakthrough" on a SALT treaty he had expected. The *Los Angeles Times* advised that a "U.S. Soviet summit this summer is of dubious wisdom."[29] The third summit did not produce a SALT agreement, although progress was promised later in the year. The powers signed a Threshold Test Ban (TTB), prohibiting underground nuclear explosions greater than 150 kilotons, but this agreement was never submitted to the Senate for ratification. The two agreed to open consulates in Kiev and New York to handle the greater economic, commercial, and industrial contact between them. Nixon pressed Brezhnev privately for greater Jewish emigration, but no deal was struck. (Six months later, the Jackson-Vanik Amendment to the Trade Expansion Act, requiring the Soviets to permit as many as one hundred thousand Jews a year to emigrate, provoked the sharp Soviet retaliation of abrogation of its trade agreements with the United States.)[30]

Whatever progress was made toward "modestly sustaining [the] momentum" of the process of détente at the June summit was swallowed by public interest in the impeachment hearings before the House Judiciary Committee in July.[31] As soon as Nixon returned from Russia, impeachment absorbed him. Kissinger, too, had more immediate questions, notably renewed public, press, and congressional interest in his role in wiretapping and the Cyprus crisis of July-August 1974.

When the Senate held hearings on détente in August, September, and October 1974, the Nixon Administration was over, and the discussion resembled a post-mortem on a policy. At these hearings George Meany, long a critic of détente, derided support for the policy. "This great idea—this 'conceptual breakthrough' to use one of Henry Kissinger's phrases is like gossamer. You cannot grab hold of it," he said. "[H]ow could we have gotten so excited about something that wasn't much of anything anyway?" Later, Meany observed that détente really was only "cold war under another name."[32] Meany's views were extreme, and Senator Fulbright tried during the hearings to argue the case for détente.

Yet the AFL-CIO leader had put his finger on the sorest spot in the policy of détente. From the very beginning, advocates of détente had been purposely ambiguous about what the new policy was designed to achieve. As long as Nixon, Kissinger, or other backers of the policy could focus attention on the process of the United States and the Soviet Union, despite their political differences, working out their disagreements, they gained political supporters. When Senator Jackson and other critics of détente turned their attention to the specific details of agreements, however, the domestic consensus over détente broke down.

NOTES

1. Raymond Garthoff, *Detente and Confrontation: American-Soviet Relations from Nixon to Reagan* (Washington, D.C.: Brookings Institution, 1985), pp. 27–28; U.S. House of Representatives, *Hearings before a Subcommittee of the Committee on Appropriations*, 94th Cong., 1st Sess., November 14, 1975, p. 14; U.S. Senate, Committee on Foreign Relations, *Detente*, 93rd Cong., 2nd Sess., August 15, 20, 21, September 10, 12, 18, 19, 24, and 25, and October 1 and 2, 1974, p. 373.

2. Garthoff, *Detente and Confrontation*, p. 29.

3. Quoted in Milton S. Katz, *Ban the Bomb: The History of SANE* (Westport, Conn.: Greenwood Press, 1986), p. 128.

4. Henry Kissinger, *The Necessity for Choice* (New York: Harper & Row, 1961), p. 296.

5. Henry Kissinger, *White House Years* (Boston: Little, Brown, 1979), p. 544.

6. The congressional debate over ABM is discussed in Alton Frye, *A Responsible*

Congress: The Politics of National Security (New York: McGraw-Hill, 1975), especially pp. 15–46.

7. Kissinger, *White House Years*, pp. 207, 208, 210, 212.

8. Gerard C. Smith, *Doubletalk* (New York: Doubleday, 1980), p. 84; Garthoff, *Detente and Confrontation*, pp. 53–60.

9. Kissinger, *White House Years*, pp. 147–150, 522–526.

10. Roger Labrie, "Overview," in Labrie, ed., *SALT Handbook* (Washington, D.C.: American Enterprise Institute, 1979), p. 13.

11. H. R. Haldeman, Notes, May 20, 1971, White House Special Files, Staff Members' Office Files, H. R. Haldeman, box 43, Notes May 2–June 30, 1971, part 2; Nixon Presidential Materials Project, National Archives; Smith, *Doubletalk*, pp. 62–63.

12. Eyes Only Memorandum, Nixon to Kissinger, March 11, 1972, White House Special Files, Staff Members' Office Files, Haldeman Files, box 45, HRH Notes, January–March 1972, part 2; Nixon Presidential Materials Project, National Archives; Kissinger, *White House Years*, p. 1217.

13. Smith, *Doubletalk*, p. 222.

14. Ibid., p. 459.

15. Ibid., p. 376.

16. Kissinger, *White House Years*, p. 1243.

17. "Basic Principles of Relations between the United States of America and the Union of Soviet Socialist Republics," *Department of State Bulletin*, June 26, 1972, p. 898.

18. Garthoff, *Detente and Confrontation*, pp. 290–291; Richard Nixon, *RN: The Memoirs of Richard Nixon* (New York: Grosset & Dunlap, 1978), p. 618; Kissinger, *White House Years*, pp. 1205, 1209, 1213.

19. "Congressional Briefing by Dr. Henry A. Kissinger," June 15, 1972, Frank Church Papers, box 166, folder 14, Boise State University Library.

20. U.S. Senate, Committee on Foreign Relations, *Strategic Arms Limitation Agreements*, 92nd Cong., 2nd Sess., June 19–22, 1972.

21. U.S. Senate, Committee on Armed Services, *Military Implications of the Treaty on the Limitations of Anti-ballistic Missiles and the Interim Agreement on the Limitation of Strategic Offensive Arms*, June 20–July 8, 1972, 92nd Cong., 2nd Sess; see also Henry M. Jackson, "Weapons Agreements: A Senator Questions U.S. Concessions," *Los Angeles Times*, June 25, 1974, part F, p. 7.

22. PL 92-448, as amended by Senator Jackson, approved by House on September 25, 1972, and Senate on September 30, 1972, U.S. Congress, Senate, *Congressional Record*, 92nd Cong., 2nd Sess., 1972, V. 118, no. 138, p. 514280.

23. Garthoff, *Detente and Confrontation*, p. 334; Kissinger, *White House Years*, p. 1152.

24. Garthoff, *Detente and Confrontation*, p. 338.

25. *Department of State Bulletin*, November 12, 1973, p. 583.

26. Ibid., p. 591.

27. "Kissinger Shuns Hard Line Despite Alert, Sees U.S. and Moscow on 'Parallel Peace Course,' " *Christian Science Monitor*, October 26, 1973, p. 1.

28. Kissinger, *White House Years*, p. 1254; Garthoff, *Detente and Confrontation*, pp. 409–411.

29. "Drawbacks of a Summer Summit," *Los Angeles Times*, March 29, 1974, Part II, p. 6; Garthoff, *Detente and Confrontation*, p. 420.

30. "Brezhnev Mystery," *Christian Science Monitor*, January 17, 1975, p. 1; "Kissinger and Congress," ibid., January 22, 1975.

31. Garthoff, *Detente and Confrontation*, p. 429.

32. U.S. Senate, Committee on Foreign Relations, *Detente*, 93rd Cong., 2nd Sess., August 15, 20, 21, September 10, 12, 18, 19, 24, and 25, and October 1 and 8, 1974, pp. 1–11, 373.

Discussant: The Honorable
Aleksandr M. Belonogov

Bearing in mind that we are on the eve of Soviet-American talks at the highest level, it appears relevant and significant that Hofstra University is currently holding a conference on the period of the Nixon Presidency—a period when after many years of Cold War and confrontation the first serious positive changes occurred in Soviet-American relations, particularly in the sphere of nuclear arms. The period of Nixon's presidency could be examined from different angles and from different political positions. It is common knowledge that here, in the United States, the attitudes to Nixon's political heritage are rather mixed. Of course, for our part we also see both pluses and minuses in Nixon's policy in the Soviet direction. At the same time, on the whole we rate highly that period in Soviet-American relations as the most fruitful and productive in the forty postwar years. I say exactly forty years so that no one would doubt that everything I say also applies to the current stage in Soviet-American relations. Here, as they say, everything is still ahead.

Speaking of the period of Nixon's presidency, I would like to single out as the most significant the following aspects. First, I would like to emphasize the importance of the changes in Washington's conceptual approach to mutual relations with the Soviet Union. For almost a quarter century after the end of World War II, the American establishment's political thinking was firmly in the grip of exaggerated notions about the power of the United States when, to use the words of Senator Fulbright, "the arrogance of power" prevented Washington from seeing the reality and taking into account the profound changes that were happening in the world. The realistic trends were latent and had a great difficulty in making themselves manifest in Washington. Suffice it to recall the slogans under which Nixon himself conducted his election campaign in 1968. But the fact that Nixon as a conservative politician upon taking office opted for improving relations with the USSR stresses, in our view, precisely the objective necessity of the course that he took at easing international tensions. Under Nixon, the line toward securing and consolidating strategic superiority, which had been in effect for several decades, gave ground to the strategic sufficiency concept. Although this sufficiency does not imply giving up the United States' strategic buildup and the improvement of its components, at the same time it would be erroneous to believe that the concept of sufficiency did not introduce anything new. Even though the strategic arms race went on, its platform was substantially reduced, which found its reflection in the relevant Soviet-American agreements.

Parallel to the strategic sufficiency concept, the American leadership then adopted the strategy of realistic deterrent which did not differ much from the flexible response strategy from the standpoint of the principles involving the use of military force, but there were also some significant nuances. The distinction lay first and foremost in a greater linkage of military strategy to foreign policy and diplomacy. In this sense the realistic deterrent was a peculiar reflection of the need for the United States to move away from confrontation toward negotiations.

The retreat from old concepts was not prompted, of course, by any personal peculiarities of President Nixon, although, unquestionably, his pragmatism and sense of reality did play a positive role here. The principal and decisive factor that resulted in a revision of both U.S. foreign policy doctrines and practices was the change in the balance of strategic forces between the Soviet Union and the United States and the establishment of a military parity between them.

In this connection, I would like to stress emphatically the significance of the document on basic principles of relations between the USSR and the United States, which was signed in 1972. Mr. Schulzinger asserts that "the Basic Principles represented a Soviet effort to gain Western recognition as a legitimate and equal power." The above quotation is correct in the sense that the initiative for drafting this document indeed originated with the USSR. But the aims of this document were not at all what they were asserted to be. At any rate they were not so simplistic and narrow. The Soviet Union did not need American recognition of the legitimacy of its existence and of its status as a great power whose military might had become equal to that of the United States. This was an objective fact, and no one disputed it.

It was important for us that Washington recognize something else (and this was recorded in the Basic Principles of relations): namely, that Washington recognize an obligation to do everything possible to avoid military confrontations and to prevent an outbreak of nuclear war; to exercise restraint in the conduct of its relationships and to conduct negotiations and settle differences through peaceful means in a spirit of reciprocity, mutual accommodation of positions and reciprocal restraint, and to understand that any attempts to gain unilateral advantages directly or indirectly at the expense of the other side were incompatible with these purposes.

It was also important that Washington recognize that the principle of equal security and nonuse or threat of force was an indispensable condition for maintaining and strengthening relations of peace between the United States and the Soviet Union. The provision in the Basic Principles of relations to the effect that differences in ideologies and social systems are not an obstacle to the development of normal bilateral relations between the USSR and the United States, based on the principles of sovereignty, equality, noninterference in internal affairs, and mutual benefit, is still relevant today. The document on the Basic Principles of relations—if subsequent American administrations had not turned away from it—could have played an outstanding role in strengthening relations of peace and cooperation between the two superpowers. To our deep regret, Soviet-American relations developed in zigzags, with attendant and at times very substantive retreats from the level achieved. At this time, Washington is gradually coming back to the recognition, in particular, of the code of relations between our two countries, which was laid down fifteen years ago. This, of course, is a positive change.

My second comment is that during the Nixon Presidency it proved to be possible for the first time to reach agreement on such an extremely complicated and delicate problem as nuclear arms. In this context, I would like to single out the ABM Treaty. I believe that if the Nixon Administration had done nothing else in the international sphere other than the conclusion of this treaty, it would still have the moral right to be recalled in a positive vein. This treaty contains a vast potential of beneficial effect on the strategic situation. Had there been no ABM Treaty, it would be difficult even to say at what level of the nuclear arms race the Soviet Union and the United States would find themselves now—or whether you and we would exist at all because there would, of course, be no SALT-I or SALT-II Treaties or the prospects that have opened now in terms of radical reductions in strategic arms. The importance of the ABM Treaty, as we all know too well, has not diminished over the years but rather has even increased. The ABM Treaty is perhaps the main monument to the Nixon Presidency in the sphere of international relations.

But I do not want to overlook the other substantial accomplishments of that time. What I have in mind is the 1971 Treaty on the Prohibition of the Emplacement of Nuclear Weapons and Other Weapons of Mass Destruction on the Sea-Bed and the Ocean Floor and in the Subsoil Thereof, the 1971 agreement on measures to reduce the risk of outbreak of nuclear war between the USSR and the United States, the agreement on measures to establish a direct communications link between the USSR and the United States, the 1972 agreement on the prevention of incidents on and over the high seas, the 1973 agreement on the prevention of nuclear war which binds the USSR and the United States to avoid actions capable of bringing about dangerous aggravation of their relations, the 1974 treaty on the limitation of underground nuclear weapons tests, and the 1974 agreement on nonuse of environmental modification techniques for military purposes. As you see, the list is impressive. And, of course, it should also include the quadrilateral agreement on West Berlin, which remains a factor important to Europe's military and political stability.

My third comment is that, in speaking of the period of the Nixon Presidency, we should not forget that in those years a legal foundation was laid for Soviet-American relations and cooperation in a variety of fields. The purpose of building such a foundation was embodied in the document on Basic Principles of relations. That period gave birth to agreements on cooperation between our two countries in the exploration and peaceful uses of outer space, environmental protection, health care, science and technology, transportation, exploration of the world's oceans, and peaceful uses of atomic energy. The list, as you see, is also a solid one. Moreover, these agreements did not remain on paper but initiated broad, mutually beneficial cooperation in various spheres. It is another matter that this entire structure was substantially dismantled under the subsequent administrations. Not much remains of this structure today, and this is too bad. For mutual understanding and trust are not born in a vacuum. If they are to grow and become stronger, what is needed is an appropriate and sufficiently broad field of co-operation.

Finally, a word about détente. It was born in Europe or, to be more precise, in Soviet-West European relations. The United States embarked on the path of détente later than did its European allies, and in contrast to Europe détente did not have enough time to take sufficiently deep root on American soil. The word "détente" was taken out of the lexicon of American political leaders for a whole number of years. To my mind, that happened not because détente originally generated an unwarranted euphoria and, as a consequence of that euphoria, swift and deep disappointment about détente itself. I do not, of course, rule out, that in the United States there were possibly some elements of euphoria and disappointment. But they were not the principal cause. In the United States, détente failed to stand up to the blows of influential forces that either from the very beginning launched an attack against it or regarded the period of improving relations with the USSR as the temporary and forced breathing space necessary for the United States to recover after its defeat in Vietnam. The forces that I referred to were formidable, and they operated actively both within the administration itself and in the Congress as well as outside official American institutions.

As to the euphoria which Mr. Schulzinger referred to, I do not agree either because in declaring its retreat from the policy of confrontation, the Nixon Administration was not at all ready to abandon in all areas the methods and tactics characteristic of that course, give up its designs to weaken the USSR, and drive a wedge between the socialist countries. What store should be set, for example, on the well-known Kissinger policy of so-called linkages, which actually impeded the momentum in the development of Soviet-American relations, specifically in the field of economic cooperation and trade. Mr. Schulzinger is correct in pointing out that the goal of arms limitation was not a top priority for the Nixon Administration.

Those of us who in those days worked in the foreign ministry of the USSR on American affairs remember very well the great efforts and the great patience and tolerance that it took to ensure progress at Soviet-American talks. But on the whole the bottom line was positive, and here we cannot fail to pay tribute to Nixon's farsightedness in matters of foreign policy strategy. In spite of all the existing constraints at the time, in spite of the conservatism and anticommunist bias of President Nixon himself, the agreements and treaties concluded between the USSR and the United States in 1970–74 signified substantial progress on the road of strengthening international security and mutual trust. The decisions that were taken jointly at the time have demonstrated not only the possibility of achieving tangible results through negotiation, but also the fact that in the nuclear age this is the only reasonable and realistic path.

We are currently in the midst of a new upsurge in Soviet-American relations. The upcoming meeting between Mikhail S. Gorbachev and Ronald Reagan, which will begin in Washington two weeks from now, will be marked by signing an agreement eliminating an entire class of nuclear weapons. The important thing, however, is not to stop at this borderline, but to create conditions for further progress so as to make real 50 percent reductions in strategic nuclear arms—provided, of course, that the antiballistic missile treaty is strictly adhered to. Ahead of us is a time of major and crucial decisions. It is important that the attitude toward them, here in the United States, be based on a sense of responsibility with due regard for the experience gained in Soviet-American relations, including the experience of the first half of the 1970s.

Discussant: Hedrick Smith

Thank you very much. It is a pleasure to be here at Hofstra. I am particularly grateful to my friend Leon Friedman for the invitation to take part.

The discussions thus far in this panel have been on so lofty a plane that I hesitate as a journalist to get down to what it was like to have a ringside seat to the summit of 1972, when I was in Moscow as a correspondent. I had hoped that the ambassador, who had been in the foreign ministry at that time, might have done what we saw recently done when the Kennedy Library got together a number of the participants of the October 1962 Missile Crisis, and we got a bit of historical replay, including some new facts from Fedyor Burlasky, one of Khrushchev's advisers, about the internal maneuvering within the Soviet Union. Concerned about the shooting down of a U–2 plane over Cuba, they rushed to the radio station to get a statement broadcast. They hoped there would not be an American invasion of Cuba. But that episode as well as the present perils of Pauline of the current summit, when Secretary Shultz is about to go to Geneva to meet with Mr. Shevardnadze to wrap up those last ninety-five bracketed items in the new arms agreement, remind me of the days just before the 1972 summit and suggest that some of the patterns that we had back then have not changed all that much now.

Just a few days before the summit was about to begin in late May 1972, a number of American bombing raids were staged around Hanoi, and then finally the harbor of Haiphong was mined. Sitting in Moscow were a number of American diplomats, and perhaps some of those I see in the front row here were in the White House at that time. There was a considerable question as to whether or not the whole process would collapse right then and there, and the Soviets would call off the summit and withdraw the invitation to Nixon. We scurried around, but in those days we didn't have the advantage of glasnost. There was next to nobody to talk to, and the foreign ministry did not have a spokesman who had daily press conferences. The information department of the foreign ministry dealt in anything but information, and we were greeted by silence. We did manage to talk to our contacts at *Pravda* and *Izvestia*, but they had nothing to say for twenty-four hours. They didn't know what to say, and so they kept quiet. Then finally on the second day after the mining of Haiphong Harbor, the Soviet press came out with a number of rather stern commentaries about the action, but simply did not deal with the question of whether or not there would be a summit.

So, I sat down in the evening, as many American correspondents did, and wrote my story indicating the Soviets had spoken rather harshly and denounced the U.S. action but had seemed to leave open the question of the summit. Then, I went off to dinner, and, as we often do in Moscow, I came back to work at midnight because we have what is called the time advantage in Moscow—which for a correspondent is a time disadvantage. It means that you can work until 2 A.M. and still make the deadlines in New York. So I was there checking the Tass wire updating and refreshing my story a bit. So it went on until 2:00 in the morning when I got a call from a friend of mine, a journalist who had been in Moscow for about twenty years. He had a number of high contacts in the Soviet Communist party and in the Soviet government and, I believe, in the Soviet KGB (the intelligence) as well. He told me that he wanted to give me some advice from his Soviet sources. He also said that they had told him that there was indeed a high-level argument within the Soviet Politburo. In those days, we didn't have Boris Yeltsin and other people coming out afterward to tell us everything that was going in central committee meetings, or at least part of it. He said that there was a group of hardliners in the Politburo led by a man named Piotr Shelest, the Ukrainian party boss and a senior member of the Soviet Politburo. Shelest was reportedly so deeply opposed to going ahead with the summit that they regarded the mining of Haiphong Harbor as an insult to the Soviet Union and to Soviet leadership, as well as a provocative act by Nixon. In fact, his Soviet source told him that the invitation would be withdrawn.

This was about two or three days before the summit, and I said. "Well, if that is the case, why hasn't there been some kind of a hint in public from the Soviet press that this would happen?" There had been these commentaries and so forth, and I said, "Yes, but there has been no linking of the events in Haiphong Harbor with the summit itself." My source said, "Don't be misled by that." I asked the same question of my Soviet contacts, who told me, "Remember the shooting down of the U-2 under Eisenhower and Khrushchev in 1960? Remember that Khrushchev was quiet and sandbagged Eisenhower for twenty-four to forty-eight hours? He let Eisenhower make a public statement, and then after Eisenhower had exposed himself, Khrushchev lowered the boom and revealed that Gary Powers and the Spirit of Détente of that period was sundered at that point." He also said that he was filing this story and that the Soviets would withdraw the invitation to his news organization in the West. He also said that his Soviet sources very much wanted to be sure that *The New York Times* was informed and had the advantage of filing the same story if it wished.

Well, this sounds like a very unusual story, and indeed it was. Only in places like Moscow do these kinds of journalists exist and make these kinds of calls. It was also remarkable to me, and to the point of a testimonial to the possibility that this story was true, that this man was sober at 2:00 in the morning. I had seen him on other occasions, and he would not have been able to be anywhere as coherent and as logical about the question. So, I hung up the phone and did what all foreign correspondents do in the middle of the night in Moscow when they get something that could be a news break: I stared at the wall and thought. Because there was nobody else to talk to, nobody else to consult with, no informed sources to go talk to, I finally decided to put it in the eighth paragraph of my story. I wrote that some Soviet sources had said that an argument had taken place at the top of the Politburo and that the Soviet Union would withdraw the invitation. It was a hell of a scoop, a hell of a temptation, but I resisted it and filed it down to my story.

The next day there was not very much more in the Soviet press. I went to the American Embassy, but there was not much more there either, although they were quite interested in the story I had to tell them. But I didn't tell them the source any more than I am telling you at this moment. I knew nothing more until about 2 A.M., and then there was a small item two paragraphs long that came across on the Tass wire. The next morning *Pravda* said that Piotr Shelest, the Communist party first secretary for the Ukraine, had just been relieved of his post and that he would be assigned some other job. We had just read about Gelssen, the first deputy chairman of the State Committee of Construction (or something like that), and obviously he would lose his Politburo seat.

I filed that story and indicated that I had been informed that there had been some kind of argument at the top level, although I was not able to confirm it in any reliable way. This story tells you that every once in a while the items a journalist is most proud of are the ones he doesn't file. But it also tells you that at times we get to the brink of agreement and to the brink of action, and can meet with the interference of a very substantial clash. This is particularly so in regions of the world where the leaders of the two countries can decide that the need to give a signal of reassurance to each other or to their respective countries and to the world overrides all other priorities, and I think that is what exactly happened in 1972.

I would agree with the professor that there is no question that an exaggerated sales job was done on détente in the early 1970s. The notion that it was going to produce a durable peace was simply too much for any kind of agreement or set of agreements to carry. It is also true, as both the professor and the Soviet ambassador said, that there were hardline skeptics in the United States, particularly in Congress, and certainly Scoop Jackson was prominent among them, who were opposed to this line. They were weary of this pacific condition and worked very hard to make sure it didn't go any further. But I do think that détente was more than a handful of smoke as George Meany suggested. I do think its substantial achievement was the ABM Treaty, which is still with us today. I think the ambassador is right that the concept of strategic parity of military sufficiency, rather than the superiority of the notion of equal security, is very interesting in that Gorbachev has not gone beyond that to talking about mutual security, which is a very non-Leninist, non-Soviet concept. That those concepts were adopted and talked about and were pervasive during that time is a very important legacy that is still with us today.

But there were basic flaws and misconceptions in the concept of détente at the time of the 1972 summit, which probably had more to do with the later failure of détente than with what the professor has singled out. The most important thing was that neither side was willing to give up anything substantial and important that was within reach. The ABM Treaty was achievable because any decent ABM system was so far down the road that neither side saw itself giving up anything very important. The ABM system that we had wasn't very good, and it was very limited, and what the Soviets had wasn't worth talking about for quite a while. The important point is that in 1973 and 1974, there were no followup agreements on the process of arms control or on regulating or managing the U.S.-Soviet relationship. In other words, there was harassment in Congress, and there was an overall sales job. Yet the critical fact was that the two leaderships had no agreement to make the kinds of sacrifices necessary to build a durable relationship.

Each side was operating with very important misconceptions. For its part the United States was guided by the misconception that technology would save us. I remember the briefing from Henry Kissinger well after midnight on the night they actually achieved the SALT Agreement in the Intourist Hotel in downtown Moscow. What Henry told those of us who were in that room was essentially that the bargain that was going to be struck on strategic offensive weaponry was Soviet-sized versus American-sophisticated. The accuracy of our missiles and, more important, the multiple warheads on our missiles were going to offset and protect against the massive megatonnage of what was then the Soviet SS-9 missiles. Now that was a misconception, and it was the conception that American ingenuity and innovation, and ultimately technology, were going to hold an edge permanently. Obviously, however, what had happened was that later the Soviets got the MIRVs and began to catch up. People forget what happened—that we jumped from roughly 2,500 nuclear warheads on our offensive weapons systems to about 7,500 during the 1970s, and the Soviets were late in coming along. But once the concept was accepted, MIRVing was part of the international strategic balance between us. Then the Soviets were going to get it slower, later, and less efficiently than we, but they were going to get it, and it became menacing. So we had a basic flaw in our notion and that was no security in the deal and there was no safety in the deal for us.

The second problem was that we believed that if we signed détente-type agreements, somehow, through that process, we were going to change Soviet society and the equation. There, basically, was the attraction of trade with the West. We thought we were going to get the Soviets to open up and let the Jewish emigrants, the refuseniks, come out in large numbers, and Jackson and Vanik jumped on that in the Congress. They succeeded in passing a law that required certain levels of immigration, or the Soviets would not get most-favored-nation treatment. They assumed that Nixon bank loans—that kind of thing—was attractive to the Soviets. That was too much of a burden for the relationship to bear at the time, and so talks broke down.

The Soviets talked about zigzags, but they had their misconceptions too. They believed somehow that their behavior would not affect us, and so disillusion and disenchantment set in for the whole process of arms control and détente. They carried out the buildup of their SS-17, 18, and 19 so far that we began to fear a threat not only to our land-based ICBMs, but also the Democratic administration of Jimmy Carter. Defense Secretary Harold Brown and others began to feel that the Soviets were no longer content with sufficiency and parity, but were striving for superiority. When you get to that point, the possibilities of agreement go out the window.

The Soviets also forgot that we watched their behavior around the world and that our retreat and their advance through Hanoi, Ethiopia, Angola, Yemen, and, eventually, Afghanistan was more than we could bear. The notion of restraint had broken down totally, and, of course, Afghanistan was the straw that broke the camel's back.

What are the lessons? The first lesson is that concepts are still important—sufficiency, parity, and mutual security are absolutely crucial, and they are still with us. The ABM Treaty is vital in telling both sides that there are limits to the arms race. Thus, there is some predictability to what the other side can do without, and it becomes much more unpredictable. Initially, we may be at an advantage because of our technology. We were ahead in the advance technology—SDI—but I believe that it is an illusion. Eventually, the Soviets will catch up, and we will have the same kind of problems we had before.

The second lesson is that regional issues can indeed undermine the effort to strike a deal and strike confidence between the two capitals—Afghanistan and all the things that ran before it. It was enough to blow up the Moscow-Washington détente.

The third and most fundamental lesson is that establishing a durable relationship requires substantial compromises, with each side putting something into the pot or on the table, and actually giving up what it would like to have in order to make the process work.

Discussant: Helmut Sonnenfeldt

Ladies and Gentlemen, like everybody else, I am happy to be at Hofstra. I used to make a big circle around this place because I never forgave it thirty-five years ago for seducing away our championship lacrosse coach at Johns Hopkins, Howdy Meyers. Anyway here I am, and I understand that there are so many new buildings here now compared to 1952 that I wouldn't recognize the place.

I have listened with interest to the remarks that were read by the Soviet permanent representative commenting on Mr. Schulzinger's paper. I note that Ambassador Belonogov remarked that it was common knowledge that the American attitudes toward President Nixon were rather mixed, but that in the Soviet Union, he is still held in high regard. I kept waiting, as the text unfolded, for comments on who the other fellow was who sat across from Richard Nixon through all those talks and wondered what the status of his reputation was in the Soviet Union. In fact, I was waiting for Rick Smith to tell us who that individual was, but he seems to have disappeared. I am, of course, referring to Mr. Brezhnev, who somehow didn't make it into the relationship between the United States and the Soviet Union in the version that we had from the Soviet ambassador today.

He did, however, observe that the notion of strategic sufficiency was propounded by President Nixon early in his presidency in 1969. As you are perhaps aware, sufficiency has now become the Soviet watchword in regard to their military posture. Indeed, I think the ambassador mentions it. If Mr. Gorbachev, who has started using this term, was running for president in the United States, he would long since have been accused of plagiarism for not mentioning his source. But in the Soviet Union, the standards of politics quite clearly are different from those in the Democratic party in this country.

There is a serious point that relates in my mind, at least, the comments that the Soviet ambassador made and what I think is a flaw in Professor Schulzinger's otherwise interesting rendition of the ups and downs of the U.S.-Soviet relationship. The Soviet ambassador refers in several places to the sense of realism that ruled President Nixon and his administration during that period—a sense of realism especially about the change in the balance of forces. Moreover, he argues that a great deal of the difficulty in American-Soviet relations before the Nixon Administration had to do with the American belief that it was the stronger of the two powers and the strongest power in the world. The ambassador refers to Senator Fulbright's well-known comment about the arrogance of power. Incidentally, Mr. Gorbachev owes the senator something too, for he has recently taken to referring to the arrogance of power without citation.

One of the serious problems we encountered in the 1970s, and it is reflected in the ambassador's comments, is a Soviet assessment that this so-called American sense of realism would lead us to tolerate assertive forms of behavior on their part, because we could no longer muster the power and the will to deal with them. This element is missing in Professor Schulzinger's paper. He remarks correctly that many people have attributed the failure of détente or at least the disenchantment with it, to Vietnam and in particular to Watergate. But neither of those tragic episodes would have made a great deal of difference if Soviet behavior during this period had not included precisely the kind of things Rick Smith was referring to—namely, an underestimation of American public reactions, despite the ordeal we were going through, despite the trials and tribulations we were experiencing over the disaster in Vietnam, with all its domestic implications, and the domestic political crisis associated with Watergate.

I am not certain what Soviet behavior would have been in 1973 and 1974–75 if we had not ended the war in Vietnam as we did, and if we had not had the Watergate crisis. I think, however, that it is at least conceivable that the Soviet assessement of American reactions to things, especially public American reactions, might have been more accurate in the event. I think they grossly miscalculated and indeed ultimately contributed to the backlash that came into being in this country. That backlash powerfully contributed to the election of Ronald Reagan in 1980 and to much of what we have seen after 1980, with respect to the American defense budget, the so-called Reagan doctrine, involving precisely those places where the Soviets came to be present during the period of uncertainty and political division in this country in the mid–1970s. I hope that in a revised or later version of his paper Professor Schulzinger will give greater weight to these aspects.

Since Rick Smith started reminiscing, let me recall two aspects of his story. First, we in Washington were keenly concious of the possibility that the 1972 summit would go down the drain after the decision had been made to mine Haiphong and its approaches, and to bomb the harbor and Hanoi, particularly while Soviet ships were in the harbor. I had written a draft statement for President Nixon in which he would have deeply deplored the Soviet decision to break off the summit. In fact, at one point I had even written a draft statement in which he himself would have broken off the summit as part of the decision to mine Haiphong and bomb Hanoi. President Nixon's instinct was much better than that of any us in this regard; he turned out to be correct in believing that the Soviets wanted this summit and that it was going to happen.

As to Rick's reference to the Soviet internal debate about whether to go forward with the summit and to the removal of Shelest as head of the Ukrainian party, we now know that this debate was a pretext. Shelest was removed for other reasons having to do with politics in the Ukraine. He had actually not been removed from the Politburo by the time we arrived in Moscow. I don't know whether there are in any of the exhibits out here pictures of that particular event. Every night we had staged for us in the Kremlin what we called signing ceremonies, because that summit in 1972 was associated with a host of agreements—from the ABM Treaty to SALT, to the statement of agreed principles, and some eleven bilateral agreements which, as if by magic, we managed to get completed in time for the summit meeting. The Politburo would be trooped out in precise rank order for each one of these and would be lined up behind Brezhnev and Nixon at the table where they were signing these documents. The line started at the far end with the next highest person to Brezhnev and went down to the center, to the lowest level. At this point, Shelest was the lowest. He was totally bald and consequently, the klieg lights that shone down on this particular scene night after night all bounced off his head. If you look at the pictures, he stands out in every one of them, smack at the center with a halo around his head, despite the fact that he was about to be dispensed with and consigned to whatever you were consigned to when you were dismissed in the Soviet Union, and not immediately given a new job.

One of the things that President Reagan and future American presidents may have to work with in dealing with Soviet leaders is that we may know a little more about the internal politics and the lines of force that operate within the Soviet Union. Perhaps the kind of discourse we used to be able to maintain with Brezhnev for hours and hours can extend to other leaders. (I myself spent over two hundred hours with Brezhnev in the various meetings I attended with President Nixon, President Ford, Henry Kissinger, and various other cabinet members whom I used to accompany from the White House.) I would hope that the new era will offer the chance to have that kind of dialogue, not only with Gorbachev, but also with many people in the Soviet leadership. While I do not generally accept the notion that the problems of American-Soviet relations are little more than misunderstandings and miscalculations, I do think that the conceptions and goals that went into the making of policy in the two capitals were so markedly different and occurred in such peculiar circumstances that they were bound sooner or later to lead to disenchantment.

Perhaps the risk can, at least at the margin, be reduced by a more complex and widespread kind of dialogue between those who have political responsibilities and political influence in our two countries. I don't know whether this will happen quickly because I don't know that glasnost has gone quite far enough. But if it does, it may contribute not so much to an amicable and tranquil relationship between the two countries, but at least to a relationship without illusions and a relationship in which judgments as to what is tolerable on the other side will come a little closer to the mark than they did in the 1970s.

While the Soviets were guilty of underestimating us, we were unable to recognize the limits of what could be achieved in a short time through our efforts. In the relationship with the Soviet Union, we lacked sufficient ability to present the Soviets with the sorts of risks of which they must always be conscious, when they attempt to act out their sense of entitlement to which the Soviet ambassador of the United Nations referred in his remarks—a sense of entitlement to being what they consider a great and equal power. Such notions of entitlement do not confer the right to recklessness, but rather the necessity of judgment and of calculating risk as well as benefits. In that respect Brezhnev and his associates were ill advised and failed, while we failed in presenting a credible image to him. I hope that does not recur in the future.

THE MIDDLE EAST AND THE
ENERGY POLICY

7

Peace or Oil: The Nixon Administration and Its Middle East Policy Choices

GIDEON DORON

Traditionally, the United States has had three main goals in the Middle East: the prevention of Soviet entry and increase of influence in the region; the preservation of the security and existence of Israel; and the protection and guarantee of a constant and uninterrupted supply of oil from the Gulf to the West. Other American goals in the area have been either temporary and thus replaced from time to time, or derivative of these three main goals. These three general objectives are not mutually exclusive. Indeed, as the American diplomatic, economic, and military experience in the area since World War II shows, they sometimes overlap and at other times stand in contradiction to each other. The order of priority, the saliency of each goal, and the intensity in which they are being pursued may differ from one administration to another, affected by changes in governmental ideologies, perceptions, and personal preferences. Regional events, such as wars, economic crises, and peaceful or violent changes in governments in Middle Eastern countries, also affect the order of priority of the various American administrations in their efforts to obtain their goals.

Stability in general and political stability in particular are often cited as the ultimate goals of the Americans in the Middle East because they reinforce favorable conditions for the achievement of the three permanent goals. They represent but one among many forms of means, or strategic considerations, that enable the accomplishment of the real American interests.[1] At times, events that introduce instability to established patterns of politics and collective life in the various regional countries were rather favorable to American interests and were therefore encouraged.[2]

The shifts in the attention given by the different administrations to the three general objectives often generated some measures of instability in the region and resulted in undesired consequences for the Americans. Thus, for example, the Eisenhower Administration paid little attention to the security of Israel. Consequently, Israel established an alliance with Great Britain and France and entered the fiasco of the 1956 Suez War. This incident forced the Americans to take sides against its three allies, so that its other objective, limiting the influence of the Soviets in the region as much as possible, would not be further damaged.[3] On the other hand, to use another example, in its first two years the Carter Administration had paid much attention to the Israeli situation by emphasizing the Palestinian problem as an international and not a local one.[4] Consequently, undesirable domestic and international pressures were imposed on the administration, affecting its ability to maximize its other two objectives.

The central thesis of this study is that, between the years 1969 and 1974, the Nixon Administration's Middle East policy had followed a "muddling through" policy strategy that supplied tentative solutions to two out of the three goals presented here. This policy overlooked the third goal of insuring a constant flow of oil to the West. This oversight and its consequences can be partly attributed to leadership style, to sets of beliefs and interests, and to errors in evaluating the significance of regional events to the achievement of desired ends.

The structure of this paper is as follows. First, I examine the meaning of the three goals that summarize the American interests in the region in the relevant period. Second, I present an analysis of the American oil policy in the region in the said period, concentrating on domestic as well as international factors. The analysis leads to a conclusion of policy "failure," that is, the oil embargo of 1973–74, which is perceived as a sort of tradeoff that the administration made between the oil objective and the other two. Finally, I will draw some tentative conclusions and present some reflections on the operation of the administration and U.S. policies in the Middle East in general.

AMERICAN OBJECTIVES IN THE MIDDLE EAST

The conduct of American policies in the Middle East during the Nixon Administration can be perceived as an attempt to obtain three main objectives: (1) to reduce the influence of the Soviets in the region; (2) to preserve the security of the state of Israel; and (3) to preserve a constant and uninterrupted flow of oil from the Gulf to the United States and to the West.

Because of a number of considerations, the Nixon Administration chose to concentrate mainly on the accomplishment of the first and second objectives. These considerations included personal orientations and competition among the members of the administration, including the president; the structure of the administration; regional and international crises; domestic political calculations; and real or perceived maneuvers of other players in the international arena. Only at the end of 1973, when the West was entering a real crisis in the form of an oil embargo, imposed by OAPEC (the Organization of Arab Petroleum Exporting

Countries) did the administration take serious steps to remedy the problem. This section explains why the first two objectives took priority and dominated the attention that should have been given to the third one as well.

Politically, the most important issue that the United States had to address when Nixon came to power was the solution to the Vietnam problem. For Nixon as well as for many in the administration and in the public, the war in Vietnam represented a point of confrontation between the two superpowers: the Americans and the Soviets. It was perceived as a zero-sum game in which the winner (i.e., the Russians, not the North Vietnamese) takes all. Hence, the administration was willing to increase the stakes until immediate domestic costs—which included, of course, public reactions and potential voter response in the presidential election—exceeded potential benefits that could have been derived from the war.

Similarly, the Middle East was also perceived as another area of confrontation between East and West. By 1969, when Nixon took office and appointed William Rogers as his secretary of state and Henry Kissinger as his principal adviser in the National Security Council, the United States and the West lost considerable influence in the region. During the 1950s and until about the middle of the 1960s, Western interests in the region were met by the presence of Great Britain and to some degree the French. But Great Britain's decision in 1968 to complete the process that began in the mid-1940s of transferring power and control to the various countries and to abandon, no later than 1971, its role as a mediating superpower which it had assumed at the end of World War I, left a political vacuum in the area. The Americans and the Soviets did not fail to gradually enter and consolidate their position in this vacuum. By 1968 the Soviets showed considerable presence in Egypt, Iraq, and Syria, countries that were traditionally under the influence of Great Britain and France. During the first year of the administration, the Russians were able to gain a foothold in the Gulf (i.e., in the People's Republic of South Yemen) and in Libya, and assumed some control over the Palestinians who were considered to be an extremely destabilizing regional force.

In its confrontation with the East over regional influence, the United States could choose to rely on an array of very small or militarily weak Arab countries such as Jordan, Lebanon, Saudi Arabia, and the tiny Gulf countries; it could depend completely on itself to block Soviet penetration into the area; or it could complement its military strategy with an alliance with the two militarily powerful non-Arab countries in the region: Iran and Israel. In reality, the actual strategy that was adopted consisted of a mixture of elements of these three possibilities. Implementation of this strategy had to be responsive and reactive to the nature of the problems that had to be addressed at any given point of time.

The tactical procedure was simple: when a problem, which Washington perceived as either endangering the "balance of regional power" or threatening to change the status quo, developed in any of the pro-Western countries, the local governments were expected to solve it. When they failed to do so, the Israelis or the Iranians were expected to lend a shoulder, deter the antagonist(s), or even intervene in the conflict for the preservation of their "local" interests. The Americans were kept on alert in such situations, ready to engage in the conflict if the first or the second "lines" failed to produce satisfactory results. This readiness was assumed to be a sufficient deterrence against the possibility that the Russians might score additional gains in the region.

The important point is that the administration chose to perceive much of the ongoing local conflicts in the Middle East as a confrontation between the Soviets and themselves. Therefore, they believed that the Russians were behind almost every local dispute, ready to exploit every opportunity to increase their influence in order to damage American interests, or merely to embarrass the administration and the president. The president could not afford, especially with the Vietnam affair in the background, to be perceived as less credible in the eyes of supporters at home and abroad.[5] The incidents that occurred in Jordan in September 1970 nicely illustrate some of the main characteristics of the American strategy in the Middle East.[6]

In 1970 the Palestinian Liberation Organization (PLO) led by Yasser Arafat, felt strong enough to attempt a challenge against the policies and the domination of King Hussein of Jordan. The king, who gradually lost his tolerance toward his insubordinate guests, decided on September 20 of that year to unleash his fifty-thousand-men-strong, British-trained, Bedouin Army against the rebels. Consequently, according to some accounts, about twenty thousand Palestinians were killed, and many more were wounded or fled the kingdom. The PLO headquarters and their "ministate" in Jordan were demolished. During the fights in that "Black September," Syrian tanks and armored vans moved into Jordan. The Jordanian Air Force attacked these advancing caravans and caused them to retreat home. Thus, the local pro-Western power was able to successfully confront opposition from within, and without the need of intervention and assistance from another greater force.

During that event, the Americans, that is, especially the president, believed that the Russians were behind the September incidents, waiting to score an additional gain in the region by instituting a pro-Soviet Palestinian state instead of a pro-Western Jordan. Since the Americans did not have viable channels of independent intelligence in the area, they had to rely heavily on data supplied by the Jordanians and the Israelis. The information received reinforced the administration's perception that the PLO and, later, the Syrian's actions were being orchestrated by the Soviets. Hence, Israel was asked and permitted to initiate moves that would enable actual engagement in the situation against the advancing Syrian troops. The United States, for its part, ordered the Sixth Fleet to move into the area, and also kept on alert its forces in Europe, Turkey, and even in mainland America. Middle East experts in and out of the administration had concluded that, at the time, the Soviets had very little to gain from instability in Jordan, let alone from the formation of a Palestinian state, and that the PLO had initiated the rebellion independently of the Russians and for that matter the other Arab countries themselves. But their assessment made very little impression on the president and his main policymakers. They chose to see even this low-magnitude conflict as another round in the East-West confrontation. Seymour Hersh had summarized this event as follows:

The legacy of Jordan was a new American policy in the Middle East—never formally stated. . . . The policy was tilted toward Israel. Kissinger and Nixon, exhilarated by their successful showdown with the Soviet Union, would continue—until forced otherwise, to view the basic problem in the Middle East as one of containing the Soviets and its client states, especially Egypt. Israel was seen as a bulwark of that policy, a regional American partner willing to intervene without questions on behalf of the Nixon-Kissinger view of the world.[7]

Because of the said objectives and the type of political and military resources (i.e., the pro-Western countries) available in the region, the United States had to design a policy that simultaneously maximized the probability of obtaining its objectives while minimizing the tensions and differences among its partners. That was not an easy task, and it naturally had to involve a considerable effort of mediation between adversarial partners. Compensations in the form of military and other types of assistance and commitments, as well as passive acceptance of demands and local interests that did not contribute to the general American objectives, were part of the price paid for maintaining a pro-Western coalition. Independent oil policy conducted by essential regional partners seemed to fall into this last category of payments.

Consequently, a two-heads approach to confront potential problems had been developed. In the east of the region, the area labeled as the Gulf, the United States relied on the concept of the Twin Pillars: Iran and Saudi Arabia. Iran, ruled by the shah, had been, of course, the militarily stronger of the two. Iran could serve as a block against Soviet attempts to advance directly toward the Gulf, or, indirectly, through the services of Iraq and local forces to interfere or even prevent the supply of oil to the West.[8]

The Saudis, the spiritual leaders of the Muslim world, were important in guaranteeing that the West receive its growing dosages of oil. They also helped to pacify and stabilize local adversaries. Their position as keepers of the faith and generous financiers of various Arab causes put them in an excellent position to serve as mediators in regional disputes that erupted from time to time. At times, of course, the Saudis had to take an active stand or get directly involved in a conflict that potentially could damage their interest. Such was their support of the Oman forces in the Yemen War during the 1960s.

On the western side of the region, the area often referred to as the ''Levant,'' Israel became a reliable force and ally that could protect and advance U.S. interests. American traditional commitment to the preservation of the Jewish state, and the special military and economic relationship that was initiated during the Johnson Administration, was intensified and became much more intimate during the Nixon Administration. Israel, the decisive victor in 1967, defeated

Table 7.1
U.S. Military and Economic Aid to Israel, 1967–74 (current million dollars)

| Fiscal Year | Military Aid | | | Economic Assistance | | | % Change In Total Aid |
	Loans	Grants	Total	Loans	Grants	Total	
1967	7.0	--	7.0	75.5	0.6	76.1	--
1968	25.0	--	25.0	51.3	0.5	51.8	- 9
1969	85.0	--	85.0	36.1	0.6	36.7	58
1970	30.0	--	30.0	40.7	0.4	41.1	- 42
1971	545.0	--	545.5	55.5	0.3	55.8	845
1972	300.0	--	300.0	53.8	50.4	104.2	- 34
1973	300.0	--	300.0	59.4	50.4	109.8	8
1974	980.0	1600.0	2580.0	--	51.4	51.4	645

Sources: For the years 1967–71, Paul Rivlin, "The Burden of Israel's Defense," *Survival* 20 (July/
August 1978); For the years 1972–74, Comptroller General of the United States, *US Assistance
to State of Israel* (Washington, D.C.: GAO, June 24, 1983).

and embarrassed the Soviets' clients—Egypt, Syria, and Iraq. During that war, Israel gained control over the Sinai Desert, which was captured from Egypt, the Golan Heights from Syria, and the West Bank from Jordan. Because of that war, Israel lost its special relationship with France, which was also a source of military supplies. The Nixon Administration was more than willing to compensate Israel for that loss. Table 7.1 provides summary data of U.S. military and economic aid to Israel during the last two years of the Johnson Administration and the entire period of the Nixon Administration.

In 1969 Gamal Abdul Nasser, the Egyptian president, decided to affect Israeli policies by imposing additional costs on their forces in the Sinai. Consequently, a practically two-year war of attrition erupted between the two antagonist countries. The new American administration considered that war as another incident in which the West could not permit itself to be defeated by the Communists. This position, and the traditional commitment and public sympathy to the Israeli cause, geared the administration to side with the Israelis against the pro-Soviet Egyptians. As shown in Table 7.1, immediately after assuming office, the administration beefed up the support to Israel. In special years, the special relationship materialized in manyfold increases in assistance. Thus, in 1970 when Secretary Rogers proposed his second peace plan and Israel cooperated with the United States against the Syrian invasion to Jordan, the administration increased its combined level of military and economic aid to Israel for the fiscal year 1971 by about 845 percent as compared to the previous year. Similarly, in 1974 after the Yom Kippur War, the administration increased its aid by about 645 percent, almost 70 percent of it being transferred in the form of grants.

The administration could afford to be generous with Israel for at least three important reasons. First, compared to the many billions of dollars of military aid the United States invested in Southeast Asia, South Korea, Japan, and Western Europe, where it also maintained troops committed to actual combat, investment in Israel was much lower and did not involve American soldiers.[9] Thus, the United States could obtain its objective through the good services of the Israelis. This means that when Israel won in a local dispute against a pro-Soviet country, the United States was also being credited for the success.

Second, during the Nixon Administration the Congress was largely pro-Israeli. On several occasions Congress increased assistance to Israel above the levels requested by the administration. Thus, for example, in 1974 Congress appropriated $133 million to relieve Israel of debts incurred as a result of the resupply operation during the October War.[10] The administration often exploited this congressional sympathy to Israel in order to bypass obstacles that could have been raised against appropriations to other countries. On this matter, David Abshire reports that in 1970 "the White House felt that prospects for the passage of the supplementary request were improved because aid for Cambodia, and . . . for Vietnam were combined with assistance to Israel."[11]

Third, Israel did not get a "free lunch" in the American assistance. With the exception of parts of the 1974 transfers, assistance was earmarked and Israel was obliged to spend most of the military aid in the United States. This requirement, of course, was compatible with interests of the American military industrial establishment. In addition, Israel was one of the few American borrowers that paid its debts with regular precision.[12]

The United States' increasing reliance on Israel, which was legitimized by the notion of a "balance of local forces," paid off in the case of Jordan, as described earlier in this paper. This position affected Sadat's decision to expel the Russians in 1972 and to move into the American zone of influence. It did not, however, prevent a new war from breaking out in the Middle East in October 1973. From the U.S. point of view and interests, the tension between Israel and Egypt had several interesting consequences: it signaled to everyone that American political and military backing was sincere and that the United States could deliver concessions to be made by the Israelis—a signal that was well read and understood by Sadat. It also showed the Arabs that American weapons, when used effectively, were superior to the Russian ones they used. Finally, it showed that the prevalent assumption that the Soviets were always interested in destabilizing the Middle East and that the Americans' benefit from stability was at best tentative, often not grounded in reality, and many times simply wrong.

It is this assumption, or the perception of the "real" American interests in the Middle East, that caused much tension between the State Department, headed until 1972 by William Rogers, and the NSC adviser Henry Kissinger. This tension ultimately resulted in Kissinger's replacement of Rogers. Putting aside personal ambitions, Rogers sought the role of stabilizer in the conflict. Rogers' first (1969) and second (1970) plans for peace in the Middle East were aimed at achieving some form of status quo: an equilibrium of "no war no peace" between the antagonists. This objective, which could have been met, implied the active involvement of the Soviets in the process of negotiation. Neither the president nor his chief adviser for international matters in the NSC favored the plans. Both the president and Kissinger feared that Russian involvement in a peace process would consolidate and legitimize their presence in the area. This Nixon-Kissinger orientation was compatible with the policy position that the Israelis held at that time. According to some evidence, the president took much pleasure in Israel's ability to defeat and destroy Russian military equipment utilized by the Arabs.[13] In 1974, however, when Egypt decided to side with the West and Kissinger was the sole director of U.S. foreign policy, stability and peace negotiations became a high priority. Kissinger followed in spirit (if not in method) the essential principles of the Rogers plans for peace settlement between the two adversaries, thus paving the route for an eventual contract of peace to be signed in 1979 by President Carter, President Sadat, and Prime Minister Menachem Begin of Israel.

The administration may have been successful along the anti-Soviet and Israeli dimensions. Clearly, the Americans gained an important partner in Egypt, which offset the loss of Libya who, until 1969, was a pro-Western country that had turned toward the East after its military revolution. In other pro-Soviet countries, the administration did not gain new ground. The gain of Egypt to the West, which ultimately resulted in a peace treaty with Israel, is, of course, an important achievement of the administration, although the main benefactor—Israel—had to pay a very high price for this accomplishment, that is, the costs of the October War.

It is not difficult, however, to argue that the U.S. foreign policymakers failed to obtain their third objective: a secure route for a constant flow of oil to the West. This failure was dramatically illustrated by the oil embargo that the Arab oil-producing countries imposed on the West from October 1973 until March 1974. The embargo, which denied the consuming countries' economies the level of energy they were accustomed to prior to 1973, and the series of price hikes on a magnitude of hundreds of percentages that followed, produced devastating effects on world economics for several years.

Western Europe, Japan, and Israel, too, suffered from OPEC (Organization of Petroleum Exporting Countries) and OAPEC (which is the dominant subset of OPEC) policies. Third World countries in Africa, South America, and Asia which lacked energy and the resources with which to pay for energy had to bear particularly negative consequences of OPEC policies. For many of them, the high levels of inflation and interest rates on international debts put a real damper on already shrinking economies.[14] Increased dependency on others (including the Soviets) has been an unavoidable consequence. During this process, the United States lost considerable credibility from proponents and opponents alike.

The next section analyzes the American oil policy in the Middle East. More specifically, the analysis addresses itself to the reasons for the absence of such policy during the time of the Nixon Administration. It concentrates on the con-

straints, limitations, and the political-economic and personal dynamics that prevented a design of a comprehensive American oil policy.

AMERICAN OIL POLICY IN THE MIDDLE EAST
OR LACK OF IT

No policy or "zero policy," as it is often labeled, is also a form of policy.
That is, when policymakers do nothing about a problem that exists or may develop
in the future and that deserves public response in the form of policy, their very
indecisiveness should be considered as a policy.[15]

Until 1970 the United States was energy self-sufficient. Energy sources like
oil and coal were in abundance on the North American continent, and therefore
reliance on foreign countries was not necessary. An expanding economy coupled
with wasteful practices of energy utilization (on the part of both citizens and
industry) and inadequate future-oriented government policies led, in 1970, to a
shortage of energy supplies from domestic resources. The United States' excessive appetite for oil is reflected in the fact that with 6 percent of the world's
population, it accounted for almost 33 percent of the world's energy consumption
in the early 1970s.[16] The shortage necessitated the importation of an additional
15 percent in oil to satisfy the growing demand for energy.

Once the Americans entered the category of importers, they continued to do
so with increased magnitude. This upward trend of consumption was not sensitive
to the increases in oil prices that the oil exporters occasionally made. A good
indication of the price increases of oil is the average income derived by the
Saudis from an average barrel of oil (i.e., an "export barrel" which includes
different types of oil). Thus, while in 1960 they received 15 cents per barrel
and in 1970, 81 cents, in 1973 they received $1.57, and in 1974—$7.29.[17] For
some types of oil the rate increase was much larger.[18] In 1973 the United States
consumed almost 17 million barrels per day. Although in 1970 domestic oil
accounted for 11.2 million barrels, the level dropped to 10.8 million in 1973.
The difference was made by the import of oil.[19]

In the early 1970s, the United States chose to become more dependent on
external energy sources. The additional increments of demand were inelastic and
insensitive to increases in the price of the product, an economic phenomenon
that deserves some explanation. There are several ways to explain the consumption behavior and the exporting practices of the Americans following 1970.
One possible explanation is that the economy expanded so much as to exhaust
its domestic energy base. Thus, in order not to slow growth, policymakers had
to rely on external sources. This argument could hold water only if the external
source were cheaper than the one that could be developed domestically, and its
supply constant and uninterrupted. That is to say, a decision to import a vital
economic source such as energy should be based on the product of two important
considerations: reliability of supply and opportunity costs of the product supply.

Reliability of Supply: In order to be able to engage in medium- and long-term economic planning, producers need to be sure that some essential elements of production will remain constant. Thus, for example, a manufacturer of cars will presumably not invest in a production line of automobiles, knowing that the material for his product will not be available in the next two or three years. In his planning he has to rely on materials that will be available during the entire prospective planning period. Similarly, since oil is such an essential component for many American industries and for personal utilization, business and personal decision makers must assume the availability of this energy resource so that they can continue their routine practices.

It is often difficult to tell theoretically and practically which products should be considered as "public" (and hence fall under the responsibility of the government for their provision) and which are "private" (and hence are under the entire responsibility of the "market"). Nevertheless, it is commonly understood in the United States (but not in most other countries) that the production and supply of oil is a private matter. Government attitudes with regard to the American market of oil have not differed essentially from their attitudes toward other industries. The government treats the oil industry as a regular oligopoly (i.e., an industry that consists of three to eight large firms and many or no very small ones). Thus, when necessary, the government imposed its antitrust regulation (the Sherman Act) on the industry in much the same way that it later regulated the tobacco trust.[20] In general, regulatory agencies made observations in order to detect price collusion and other types of unlawful agreements that are incompatible with public interests. For consumer protection, regulations were designed to ensure an upper bound for prices that companies could demand from their clients. This meant, among other things, that the government shared the belief that market mechanisms in the domestic oil industry were less than perfect and hence that government should assist the public in obtaining oil products at reasonable prices.

The regulation imposed had another effect as well. Although the big firms in the oil industry were quite profitable in the 1950s and the 1960s, they could be more so if the price of oil were decontrolled and also if they could import additional oil from external sources. While the first point is somewhat trivial, the second one is more interesting. Of course, the regulation that cupped the prices of oil did not permit the companies to charge more than a fixed price. If control would be lifted, then they could charge more and make more profit. Moreover, if the domestic firms could charge more, assuming a growing demand, they could exploit wells that were more expensive to use or they could invest more resources in the drilling of new wells. The pool of available domestic oil would therefore increase, and dependency on external sources would not be necessary. The industry's campaign during the Nixon Administration, and after, was therefore justifiable in terms of economic reasoning and long-term domestic interests. The administration's insistence on maintaining that regulation was perhaps justifiable as a short-term anti-inflation measure, but not in its long-term effects.[21]

The fourfold increase in the price of oil and the embargo itself shifted the administration's attempts to curb inflation by a strategy of price control. Since the administration rejected a cabinet committee recommendation in February 1970 to liberalize import quotas and expand domestic supply as a measure against a potential oil cutoff, the embargo forced Nixon to boost the price of domestic oil. Of course, as argued earlier, the industry naturally welcomed an increase in price. However, the immediate effect of higher prices was not higher levels of supplies, which was, of course, the interest of the administration and the public.

For the main part, however, deregulation was not the manifest choice of the administration and the industry during the early 1970s. Rather, it was an importation of additional quantities of oil in order to supplement growing demand and constant or even diminishing domestic supply. This choice stands in partial contradiction to the conventional understanding of the government-industry relationship: that one of the regulated industry's two main objectives is to affect the government in such a way that it will impose practical or, even better, legal barriers on the entry of competitive firms and products to the market. (The other objective is a direct transfer of subsidies from the government to the industry.)[22] It would be naive to argue that the oil industry did not have enough political leverage in Washington to prevent importation of cheap oil from the Middle East. In fact, the industry was interested in such imports for at least two important reasons. First, since the 1960s with the establishment of OPEC (in 1960) and the gradual nationalization of the production end of oil, the American oil companies became mostly responsible for marketing Arab oil to the West. They served as middlemen between producer and consumer. Hence, profits made from the distribution of oil, whether domestic or international, benefited them. Second, the oil produced by the Arabs was much cheaper than the oil produced in America. Only when imported oil became more expensive than domestic oil, did it generate the desired pressures to deregulate prices. Consequently, the oil companies did not oppose the importation of Arab oil, as is expected by the conventional economic theory, but rather supported and benefited from it.

The government assumed the role of protector of safe routes for the supply of oil from other countries. This role had to be incorporated into the national foreign and security policies, but it did not include a guarantee for price stability. Thus, while energy policy in general and oil policy in particular were left to an array of small and decentralized units in the administration, the State and the Defense departments were expected to insure that no hostile forces (re: Soviets and/or Soviet supporters) would be able to interfere and prevent the flow of oil to the West. The doctrine designed and implemented was supposed to provide maximum reliability for a continual supply of exported oil. It did not, however, include in its formulation safeguards against potential political threats that might come from the friendly producers themselves. This is because the prevalent assumption in Washington was that the Arabs must sell their oil "since they cannot drink it."[23] The Middle East oil policy also ignored some aspects of the interstate dynamic among the Arabs and other OPEC countries, insofar as they did not threaten basic American objectives in the region. This negligence, or rather misunderstanding, of patterns of the behavior and intents of their oil suppliers is further analyzed below.

Opportunity Costs of Oil: A price of a good or service in general, and of an imported one in particular, is not necessarily the figure reflected in the market-place at any given point of time. The price may preclude costs that are not related directly to the product but that should have been included. To be more specific, the Nixon Administration did not take into consideration the indirect costs of oil, the benefits foregone by deciding to rely on exported oil, that is, the opportunity costs of oil. These costs include, among other things, the costs of the loss of economic and political independence and reliance on others. Although it seems extremely difficult, if not impossible, to put dollar tags on the costs of dependency, the following would argue just that: that the Nixon Administration did not try to assesss the real cost of dependency on external sources of energy, and consequently the administration and the public paid a very expensive bill for such a miscalculation.

How can we determine the price of dependency? Let us assume that the price of oil in the international market is $2 a barrel and that the cost of production of one domestic barrel of oil is $5. It will make perfect economic sense to buy the cheaper product and not to produce the expensive one. But good economic sense does not always make good political or security sense. A superpower like the United States cannot afford to permit others to develop essential weapons systems for them, the supply of which may be denied at these countries' whims— unless the United States can be completely certain that such "whims" will not take place. One possible method to insure that acts of "denial" will not occur is to control the other countries. A democratic superpower may find difficulties of all sorts—legal, philosophical, or structural—in developing an effective system of control. Alternatively, an insurance against potential threats could be self-reliance, although it might be more expensive. In the early 1970s the United States put itself in a real or perceived vulnerable position. During the Embargo of 1973, not only national interests were damaged but also international reputation and credibility.

To return to the earlier example, when an economy can buy a barrel of imported oil for $2 but chooses instead to pay $5 for the domestic barrel, it means that someone has evaluated the cost of independence to be worth $3. Decision makers in the Nixon Administration were not engaged in such calculations, partly because they neglected to see the "writing on the wall" and partly because they had a limited perception of their role as implementors of American interests abroad. Ideological orientation (i.e., "the market will take care of the problem of oil supply," "OPEC as a cartel will have to disintegrate soon"), the structure of the government which did not include a central decision-making unit responsible for oil and energy policy, misunderstanding with regard to Arab attitudes to oil and the West, and the nature of the historical position of the oil industry in American politics—these are but some additional factors that contributed to an incomplete foreign policy with regard to oil.

Next we briefly examine the historical setting of three of the above variables: (1) the Arab attitude toward oil and the West; (2) the lack of a central decision-making locus in the administration; and (3) the prevalent ideology in the administration with regard to oil.

Arabs, Oil, and the West: When OAPEC imposed its oil embargo on the West, tying it in with the October War and seeking to put pressure on Israel so that it would have to make concessions to the Arabs, it was presumably surprised by the effectiveness of oil as a political weapon. Its oil became not merely an important economic source but also a potent political bargaining instrument. This enabled OAPEC to seek advantages in areas unrelated to the resource itself. For the Arabs, and especially the Saudis, the timing was right because the West had not prepared sufficient safeguards that could serve as counterthreats to Arab demands.[24] This was unlike the 1969 incident, when Muammar Qaddafi of Libya demanded similar political concessions, and no one, including the Arabs themselves, took him seriously because he was too small to affect the world market and his timing was not ripe for such acts.

OAPEC in 1973 and Qaddafi in 1969 were not the first to point out the potential of oil as a political weapon. Others before them recognized its power. Most notably, Gamal Abdul Nasser, the Egyptian president, recommended in his book, *The Philosophy of the Revolution* (1953), that the Muslims should consider utilizing oil as a weapon against their enemies.[25] In 1973 OAPEC could use oil as a weapon because it knew that at least in the short run circumstances were ripe to achieve economic as well as political gains. Therefore, price hikes and restrictions on supply were linked to the Arab-Israeli conflict. After the desired effects were achieved, supply was renewed, but the prices nonetheless did not return to their original pre-October levels. The West and the Americans did not have the proper or the credible response in the short run. Therefore, they could not afford to antagonize or retaliate militarily against the Arabs for fear of pushing them into the hands of the Soviets or even causing a destruction of the oil fields. Throughout these developments, we should also note that the Arab strategy was not entirely incompatible with the economic interests of some industrial elements in the United States. As it turned out, the oil industry was not damaged by the embargo; rather, it benefited from it.

Lack of a Central Decision Locus: By 1973 forty-four federal agencies were involved in making energy decisions. Clearly, this bureaucracy could not come up with a comprehensive energy plan that would incorporate international and security interests. As a result of the embargo shock, Nixon took several measures. Among them, on a national television address on November 7, 1973, he called for the adoption of Project Independence, which was billed as a path to energy self-sufficiency for the United States by 1980. In 1974 two new agencies were created, the Federal Energy Administration (FEA) and the Energy Research and Development Administration (ERDA). Only in 1977 did President Carter create the Department of Energy (DOE).[26] A structure like DOE enabled a wider comprehensive look into the issues under consideration. Moreover, it provided an additional independent channel of information concerning energy issues to the president at the cabinet level. This, of course decreased the traditional reliance on the industry as the dominant source of data for public policy-making.

But these developments came after the crisis was at hand. In 1973, several months before the embargo, the media and European friends pressured the administration to do something about the gradual price increases of oil set by OPEC. Some even pointed to a possible Arab oil embargo.[27] The administration's response was to form a committee that consisted of the president's three chief aids—Kissinger, George Shultz, and John Ehrlichman, as well as other cabinet members—who were supposed to study the issue and offer a solution. None of the members of that committee had previous experience in the oil area. Their response reflected a toothless policy which was established in the form of a document of principles and intentions. In short, the administration's response in 1973 was too little, too late, and largely irrelevant to the potential problem.[28]

Prevalent Ideology in the Administration: Many members of the Nixon Administration supported the thesis of market domination with regard to oil. That is, at least with respect to imported oil, it was assumed that price could serve as a regulator and as a reflector of the forces of supply and demand for the product. This position ignored two important elements. First, with the establishment of OPEC, the international market for oil stopped being ''free'' in any practical or theoretical sense. Decisions for the increase in prices were made on the supply side and did not reflect a market equilibrium. Second, the administration itself, by continuing the regulation on domestic oil, abandoned its market position and created the incentive to import first cheap and then expensive oil. Thus faced with an increased need for foreign oil, in the spring of 1973 Nixon removed all import quotas on oil. This policy had been prevalent since 1959 when Eisenhower, understanding the vulnerability of the foreign oil supply, set an import quota equivalent to 12 percent of domestic production. The removal of such quotas generated an increase in imports of almost 35 percent of total oil consumption.[29]

CONCLUSIONS AND SOME LESSONS

The period between 1969 when President Nixon took office and 1974 when he had to resign encompasses many interesting occurrences in the Middle East. Nixon, with the assistance of his secretaries of state, Rogers and Kissinger, chose to get involved in the region with a mixture of passive and active steps. The administration sometimes succeeded and sometimes failed. It may be reasonable to conclude that the administration was relatively successful in obtaining two of its three objectives. The gain of Egypt to the Western side perhaps outweighed the inability to prevent Soviet presence in the Gulf (i.e., in the People's Republic of South Yemen). The other objective—the preservation of Israel—was also accomplished but with the Israelis bearing the high costs of war. In the third area, that of oil, it seems that the Nixon Administration failed. The "relaxed approach" toward oil interests in the Gulf during the Nixon Administration may have also stemmed from the president's perception that his role was to run the country's foreign policy, without making the connection to the effects of this policy on domestic affairs.[30]

The Nixon Administration made a tradeoff. Rather than optimize its three objectives, it chose to maximize two and pay the domestic price for the third. The payment, though very unattractive, was considered reasonable because it was perceived only partly as a product of foreign policy. Hence, the designers of the defense and diplomatic strategy with regard to the region could publicly point to their successful accomplishments and shift the blame for failures in the third area of concern to others.

A country's foreign policy should, of course, take into consideration elements that are directly related to the short- and long-term welfare of its citizens. The United States as a superpower which operates in a bipolar international system has additional responsibilities which touch on the welfare of citizens of other countries as well. In its design, the administration's policies in the Middle East failed to incorporate the potential adverse effects of OPEC's activities on the welfare of these citizens. Hence, in order to secure the overall interests of their people and to prevent similar negative affects, superpowers who choose to get involved in regional matters need to establish either a reliable system of domestic safeguards (such as, for example, the SPR—the Strategic Petroleum Reserve developed in 1975) or to rely on a firm system of regional control that can prevent problems before they materialize. The specificities of such a control system, especially within the framework of a democratic superpower, deserve a separate analysis.

The story of the 1973 oil embargo can repeat itself in other areas where the United States is short of essential natural resources such as uranium, chromium, and titanium, resources important for space age production. Much thought and preparation should be given to these and other areas in light of the Nixon Administration's experience in the Middle East.

NOTES

I wish to thank Alfred L. Atherton, Hermann Frederick Eilts, Jo-Anne Hart, Dale R. Tahtinen, and Aaron Klieman for their useful comments on an earlier draft of this paper.

1. Harold Saunders had suggested five points of American interests in the Middle East: (1) the independence, stability, and political orientation of key states in the area; (2) the prevention of Soviet predominance in the area; (3) assurance of the security and prosperity of Israel; (4) maintenance of the steady flow of oil; and (5) control of arms

sales and "imbalances" in the area. AEI, *Conversations with Harold Saunders: U.S. Policy for the Middle East in the 1980's* (Washington, D.C.: American Enterprise Institute, 1982), pp. 6–9.

The position of this article is that only points 2, 3, and 4 are American objectives, while 1 and 5 are means to obtain them. The confusion between goals and means is also being reflected in the Department of Defense position on the region. USICA, "US Defense Official Presents Rapid Deployment Task Force Mission," *Official Text*, March 16 (Tel Aviv, 1982).

2. A case in point is the Central Intelligence Agency involvement in Iran in 1954, which led to the downfall of Prime Minister Muhammad Mosaddeq and the return of the shah to power. See Don Peretz, *The Middle East Today* (New York: Praeger, 1983), pp. 125–126, 508–509.

3. Kenneth Love, *Suez: The Twice-Fought War* (New York: McGraw-Hill, 1969); Amos Perlmutter, "The Fiasco of the Anglo-American Middle East Policy," in Michael Curtis, ed., *People and Politics in the Middle East*, (New Brunswick, N.J.: Transaction, 1971).

4. Jimmy Carter, "Statement on Palestinian Rights," in Walter Laqueur and Barry Rubin, eds., *The Israeli Arab Reader* (Canada: Pelican Books, 1978), p. 608.

5. Seymour Hersh, *The Price of Power: Kissinger in the Nixon White House* (New York: Summit, 1983), ch. 19.

6. William Quandt, *Decade of Decisions: American Policy toward the Arab-Israeli Conflict, 1967–1976* (Berkeley: University of California Press, 1977), ch. 4.

7. Hersh, *The Price of Power*, p. 249.

8. Thus, for example, Iranian troops participated on the side of the government of Oman in the dispute over the Dhofar Province in western Oman in the early 1970s. See James Bill and Carl Leiden, *Politics in the Middle East* (Boston: Little, Brown, 1984), p. 284. They also affected a withdrawal, in 1974, of Iraqi troops which occupied the Kuwaiti border post of Smitah on the mainland. See John Antony and John Hearty, "Eastern Arabian States: Kuwait, Bahrain, Qatar, United Arab Emirates, and Oman," in David Long and Bernard Reich, eds., *The Governments and Policies of the Middle East and North Africa* (Boulder, Colo.: Westview Press, 1986), p. 118.

9. Nimrod Novik, *The United States and Israel* (Boulder, Colo.: Westview Press, 1986), p. 98.

10. *Congressional Quaterly Almanac*, 1974, p. 591.

11. David Abshire, "Foreign Policy Makers: President vs. Congress," in David Abshire and Ralph Nurnberger, eds., *The Growing Power of Congress* (Beverly Hills, Calif.: Sage, 1981), p. 79.

12. Harold Smith, "Our Aid to Israel Is a Super Bargain," *Chicago Sun Times*, July 22, 1983, p. 26; Sever Pluzker, "America Is Giving Us as Much as She Wants to Get Back," *Yediot Achronot* (Last News), September 9, 1987.

13. Hersh, *The Price of Power*, ch. 18.

14. It was estimated that the developing countries had to pay an additional sum of $10 billion for oil between 1973 and 1974. This sum exceeded all the foreign aid that these countries received in 1973. See John Stoessinger, *The Might of Nations* (New York: Random House, 1975), p. 219.

15. Gideon Doron, *To Decide and to Implement* (Tel Aviv: Kivonim, 1986), p. 14; Yehezkel Dror, *Public Policy Making Reexamined* (New York: Chandler, 1968), p. 15.

16. William Smith, "The Energy Crisis in the Middle East," in Seymour Finger, ed.,

The New World Balance and Peace in the Middle East (Rutherford, N.J.: Associated University Press, 1975), p. 107.

17. Eli Arom, "International Aspects of Saudi Arabia Oil Policy" (M.A. Thesis, Tel Aviv University, 1982), pp. 25–26.

18. Clarke Cochran et al., *American Public Policy* (New York: St. Martin's Press, 1986), p. 54.

19. Ibid., p. 56; Novik, *The United States and Israel*, p. 117.

20. Gideon Doron, *The Smoking Paradox: Public Regulation in the Cigarette Industry* (Cambridge, Mass.: Abt Books, 1979), p. 9.

21. Hobert Rowen, "The Economic Legacy: A Non Policy to Fight Inflation," in The Staff of the *Washington Post*, eds., *The Fall of the President*, (New York: Dell, 1974), p. 129.

22. George Stigler, *The Citizen and the State* (Chicago: Chicago University Press, 1975), pp. 108–141.

23. Albert Wohlstetter, "Half War and Half Policies in the Persian Gulf," European American Institute (June 1980).

24. Abraham Gur, "Oil as a Political Weapon: Myth or Reality" (M.A. Thesis, Tel Aviv University, 1982).

25. Gamal Abdul Nasser, *Eygpt's Liberation: The Philosophy of the Revolution* (Washington, D.C.: Public Affairs Press, 1955). As a matter of fact, one of the main reasons for establishing OAPEC within OPEC in September 1968 by Saudi Arabia, Kuwait and Libya was to oppose Nasser's demand to link oil policies with the Arab-Israeli conflict.

26. Cochran et al., *American Public Policy*, pp. 58–61.

27. Most notable among them was James Akins, who was the director of the Office of Fuels and Energy, Department of State, and, in 1973, U.S. ambassador to Saudi Arabia. See James Akins, "The Oil Crisis: This Time the Wolf Is Here," *Foreign Affairs* 51 (April 1973).

28. William Smith, "The Energy Crisis in the Middle East," p. 111.

29. Cochran et al., *American Public Policy*, pp. 55–56.

30. Sharman Chubin, "American Security Interest in the Persian Gulf," in John Reichart and Steven Sturn, eds., *American Defense Policy*, (Baltimore, Md.: Johns Hopkins University Press, 1982), p. 276. Evidence for such an orientation is found in a statement by Nixon: "I've always thought this country could run itself domestically without a president, all you need is a competent Cabinet to run the country at home. You need a president for foreign policy." *The Making of the President—1968*, by Theodore White, cited by Murrey Marder, "The Diplomatic Legacy: Accomplishments to Be Assessed for Decades," in Staff of the *Washington Post*, eds., *The Fall of the President*, p. 132.

REFERENCES

Abshire, David. "Foreign Policy Makers: President vs. Congress." In *The Growing Power of Congress*, edited by David Abshire and Ralph Nurnberger. Beverly Hills, Calif.: Sage, 1981.

AEI. *Conversations with Harold Saunders: U.S. Policy for the Middle East in the 1980's.* Washington, D.C.: American Enterprise Institute, 1982.

Akins, James. "The Oil Crisis: This Time the Wolf Is Here." *Foreign Affairs* 51 (April 1973).

Antony, John, and John Hearty. "Eastern Arabian States: Kuwait, Bahrain, Qatar, United Arab Emirates, and Oman." In *The Governments and Policies of the Middle East and North Africa*, edited by David Long and Bernard Reich. Boulder, Colo.: Westview Press, 1986.

Arom, Eli. "International Aspects of Saudi Arabia Oil Policy." M.A. Thesis, Tel Aviv University, 1982.

Bill, James, and Carl Leiden. *Politics in the Middle East*. Boston: Little, Brown, 1984.

Carter, Jimmy. "Statement on Palestinian Rights." In *The Israeli Arab Reader*, edited by Walter Laqueur and Barry Rubin, pp. 608–609. Canada: Pelican Books, 1978.

Chubin, Sharman. "American Security Interest in the Persian Gulf." In *American Defense Policy*, edited by John Reichart and Steven Sturn, pp. 274–296. Baltimore, Md.: Johns Hopkins University Press, 1982.

Cochran, Clarke, et al. *American Public Policy*. New York: St. Martin's Press, 1986.

Comptroller General of the U.S. *U.S. Assistance to State of Israel*. Washington, D.C.: GAO (June 24, 1983).

Doron, Gideon. *To Decide and to Implement*. Tel Aviv: Kivonim, 1986.

———. *The Smoking Paradox: Public Regulation in the Cigarette Industry*. Cambridge, Mass.: Abt Books, 1979.

Dror, Yehezkel. *Public Policy Making Reexamined*. New York: Chandler, 1968.

Gur, Abraham. "Oil as a Political Weapon: Myth or Reality." M.A. Thesis, Tel Aviv University, 1982.

Hersh, Seymour. *The Price of Power: Kissinger in the Nixon White House*. New York: Summit, 1983.

Love, Kenneth. *Suez: The Twice-Fought War*. New York: McGraw-Hill, 1969.

Marder, Murrey. "The Diplomatic Legacy: Accomplishments to Be Assessed for Decades." In *The Fall of a President*, edited by the Staff of the *Washington Post*, pp. 132–148. New York: Dell, 1974.

Nasser, Abdul Gamal. *Egypt's Liberation: The Philosophy of the Revolution*. Washington, D.C.: Public Affairs Press, 1955.

Novik, Nimrod. *The United States and Israel*. Boulder, Colo.: Westview Press, 1986.

Peretz, Don. *The Middle East Today*. New York: Praeger, 1983.

Perlmutter, Amos. "The Fiasco of the Anglo-American Middle East Policy." In *People and Politics in the Middle East*, edited by Michael Curtis. New Brunswick, N.J.: Transaction, 1971.

Pluzker, Sever. "America Is Giving Us as Much as She Wants to Get Back." *Yediot Achronot* [Last News], September 9, 1987.

Quant, William. *Decade of Decisions: American Policy toward the Arab-Israeli Conflict, 1967–1977*. Berkeley: University of California Press, 1977.

Rivlin, Paul. "The Burden of Israel's Defense." *Survival* 20 (July/August 1978).

Rowen, Hobert. "The Economic Legacy: A Non Policy to Fight Inflation." *The Fall of a President*, edited by the Staff of the *Washington Post*. New York: Dell, 1974.

Smith, Harold. "Our Aid to Israel Is a Super Bargain." *Chicago Sun Times*, July 22, 1983.

Smith, William. "The Energy Crisis in the Middle East." In *The New World Balance and Peace in the Middle East: Reality or Mirage*, edited by Seymour Finger, pp. 105–118. Rutherford, N.J.: Associated University Press, 1975.

Stigler, George. *The Citizen and the State*. Chicago: Chicago University Press, 1975.

Stoessinger, John. *The Might of Nations*. New York: Random House, 1975.

USICA. "U.S. Defense Official Presents Rapid Deployment Task Force Mission." *Official Text.* March 16 (Tel Aviv, 1982).

Wohlstetter, Albert. "Half War and Half Policies in the Persian Gulf." European American Institute, June 1980.

Discussant: The Honorable
Alfred L. Atherton

Thank you very much. It is a pleasure to be here this morning. I am going to be speaking basically from the perspective of Washington. During the period that we are discussing today, I was based in Washington the whole time; therefore, I will be trying to convey a domestic perspective.

I have read the full paper that Professor Doron has summarized, and I think I would like to start by saying I agree with much of his analysis. In particular, he is quite correct in emphasizing that Henry Kissinger in the Nixon Administration did conceive the Middle East and the Arab-Israeli conflict, at least until the 1973 war, largely in east-west terms. In other words, in that perception U.S. policies and actions in the Middle East were seen above all as a move on the global chessboard of U.S.-Soviet confrontation. Regional dynamics, the imperatives that drove the policies of the parties to the Arab-Israeli conflict and especially the Arab parties to the conflict, were largely ignored or at least subordinated to considerations of U.S.-Soviet relations in this way of looking at the Middle East. In fairness, Henry Kissinger was neither the first nor the last U.S. policymaker to look at the Middle East largely in terms of U.S.-Soviet relations or of the east-west confrontation. However, a point I would like particularly to bring out is that a different view of the Middle East prevailed within the Nixon Administration during this period.

This view was associated with the Department of State under Secretary Rogers and his very active assistant secretary for the Middle East and South Asian affairs, Joseph Sisco. In this view, it is important to pay attention to the regional dynamics—to deal with the parties to the conflict not simply as Soviet pawns or as American pawns on the chessboard, but as principals in a conflict whose continuation was seen as threatening American strategic interests in the region, including the American interest in the uninterrupted supply of oil to the West. In those days, those of us who spoke about our Middle East policy and its objectives had a qualifier. We used to speak about the uninterrupted supply of oil from the Gulf to the West at reasonable prices. That qualifier, or at least the definition of reasonable prices, went very much by the board, of course, in 1973–74. The emphasis since then has been much more on the supply than on what it cost to get it.

I did an article in 1974 for *Foreign Affairs* in which I likened U.S. Middle East policy over the years to a pendulum swinging between these two views of the Middle East—the view that sees it in East-West terms and the view that sees it in terms of regional conflict and of regional dynamics. In the early Nixon years, at least through 1971, it sometimes seems that this pendulum was trying to swing in both directions at the same time, with the White House at one end of it and the State Department at the other. The plans associated with Secretary

Rogers were the Rogers Plan of the 1969 and the subsequent proposals that brought a cease-fire in 1970—and in a sense the last gasp of efforts to find a negotiable settlement in the Nixon period—an initiative that was given the name Interim Suez Canal Agreement. All of these plans sought to deal with the regional conflict in its own terms.

I would say, parenthetically, that I don't entirely agree with Professor Doron's characterization in the paper—that the main thrust of the Rogers or the Department of State approaches was to try to maintain the status quo equilibrium of a no war, no peace situation. This may in fact have been the result of the policy, but the policy itself did look beyond simply trying to stabilize the status quo. All the initiatives—Rogers's Plan One, Rogers's Plan Two, and the Interim Suez Canal Agreement proposal—were regarded as steps to get a negotiating process started between the parties, the ultimate objective was not simply to stabilize the status quo, but to try to move toward a comprehensive Arab-Israeli peace settlement. During this same period this comes out very clearly to anyone who has read Henry Kissinger's memoirs. Kissinger was not in agreement with the State Department's approach to the Middle East, and this often led to tensions between the two, sometimes producing very mixed signals as to what American policy was. Professor Doron has referred to the Syrian invasion of Jordan in 1970 and to the American belief that the Soviets were somehow behind this action. Many of us working on the problem never saw evidence that could bear that out. The point is valid, however, that whether or not the Soviets were behind it, if the Syrians had in fact succeeded with the PLO in toppling the Jordanian regime, Soviet policy in the Middle East would probably have been one of the principal beneficiaries.

Let us turn to the other component of Professor Doron's thesis, that the United States had no oil policy and failed to protect American interest in the uninterrupted supply of oil during the Nixon Administration. I don't disagree with Professor Doron, but I would cast this thought in somewhat different terms. Essentially that was part of the Nixon Administration's larger problem of failing to pay attention to, or perhaps failing to understand, the political forces at work in the Arab world and the Arab perceptions of the conflict. For a long time American policy was able to insulate, to some extent, its relation with the Gulf and with Saudi Arabia from its policy toward the Arab-Israeli conflict at the other extreme. This was particularly true when the principal Arab protagonist was Egypt under President Nasser because the Saudi's viewed Egypt under President Nasser as a threat to their own sovereignty and territorial integrity.

By 1973, however, when the 1973 conflict broke out, there was a very different regime in Egypt, a different ruler, and Egypt was then perceived as not an enemy in Saudi Arabia, but as a country that was trying to erase the commonly perceived Arab sense of humiliation stemming from its defeat in 1967. In these circumstances U.S. support for Israel was seen as a political offense to many of our Arab friends, and not just to those Arab countries that were basically seen as our adversaries in the Arab world. In the 1972–73 period we failed to take seriously what were fairly clear signals coming out of Saudi Arabia about their relations with the United States—signals one had to read as meaning among other things that a supply of oil would not be assured in another Arab-Israeli conflict. We had pretty well convinced ourselves at that time that the Arabs, as Professor Doron says, would not drink their oil. We did not take the possibility of an Arab oil embargo all that seriously until very late in the game.

The fundamental question was not whether the Nixon Administration failed to protect our interest in oil supplies in 1973 and 1974, but whether it could have done so while at the same time taking actions that would have run counter to our interests in the other two areas—our commitment to Israel's security and our attempt to keep the Soviets from extending their influence in the Middle East. I am leaving aside the question of whether more could have been done to build up oil reserves or to increase domestic production. Instead, I am simply asking a political question as to whether or not the embargo could have been avoided by different policies beginning with Sadat's assumption of office in the years before the 1973 war. This is one of those fascinating "what if's" of history, and I think I will leave it unanswered.

Discussant: The Honorable
Hermann Frederick Eilts

Thank you, Madam Chairman. I join with Ambassador Atherton in congratulating Professor Doron on what I consider to be an excellent paper. One thought struck me, however, when reading the paper. It is an inevitable reaction that anyone who was involved in U.S. policy formulation and implementation anywhere in the world has when reading evaluations of policy as conducted, say, fifteen or sixteen years earlier. With the wisdom of hindsight, it is always much easier to simplify, to categorize, to explain, and to reach conclusions on the wisdom or otherwise of past U.S. policies than it was at the time the developments are actually taking place. Even with an options approach, when foreign policy developments are actually taking place in the Middle East or elsewhere, they do not look quite the same as they do later on. The choices that we political scientists see today on what could and should have been done fifteen years ago were not at the time as patently clear as they seem to be today. I consider Henry Kissinger to have been one of the great conceptualizers of the Nixon Administration. He was absolutely superb in this regard. Yet, even his excellent conceptualizing did not quite frame the problems that the nation faced in the early 1970s in the same fashion that we can write about them now.

I want to address particularly two elements of Middle East policy during the Nixon Administration: One is the Persian or Arabian Gulf situation; the other is the Arab-Israeli problem.

As I recall, when President Nixon first came in, the Arab-Israeli problem was put pretty much on hold. There were too many other things that had to be addressed, and, following the Arab defeat of 1967, the Middle East situation did not seem that urgent. There were, of course, exceptions. William Scranton was sent to the Middle East after President Nixon's election, but before he took office, in order to assess the area situation. His report, suggesting a policy of "evenhandedness" in the Arab-Israeli problem, was disavowed by the president as domestically impractical.

The so-called Rogers initiative represented yet another exception. Its objective was to try to develop a process that would end the Egyptian-initiated "war of attrition" against Israeli positions in Sinai and the subsequent Israeli deep-penetration air raids into Egypt, by partial Israeli withdrawal from the Suez Canal and separating the front lines of the two forces in Sinai. It was Rogers' hope that, if this could be done, a political climate might gradually develop from which more substantive negotiations might flow. But one certainly did not get the impression at the time that, apart from Secretary Rogers and those in the Department of State who worked on the effort, the Nixon Administration placed a great deal of emphasis on the effort. This was partly due to the personal animosity that existed between Secretary Rogers and the National Security Coun-

cil adviser, Mr. Kissinger, which made it difficult for the secretary of state to
conduct effectively his Middle East efforts. Secretary Rogers has reminded people many times that the Rogers Plan, as it came to be called, was a misnomer.
It was in fact the Nixon Plan since it had been cleared by the president before
Rogers even attempted it. When the rug was pulled out from under Rogers'
efforts by the National Security Council adviser, it became politic to call it the
Rogers Plan.

As far as Middle East policy in the first period of the Nixon Administration
was concerned, the emphasis was elsewhere. As Dr. Doron points out in his
paper, the British had announced in 1968 that they would give up their military
positions in the Persian Gulf three years later, in 1971. That intended withdrawal
was understandably a source of major concern to the Nixon Administration when
it assumed office. A security vacuum, it was felt, would exist in the Gulf area.
The Gulf, after all, as the main source of Western petroleum and with huge
petroleum reserves, was clearly a major American interest. Free and unimpeded
access to Gulf petroleum reserves had always been a major U.S. objective in
the Middle East. Related to this, as a potential threat to continued Western access
to Gulf petroleum, was the perceived Soviet desire to establish a position in the
Gulf. Once the Soviets had done so, it was assumed, they would seek to use
that position in order to exclude or at least neutralize the U.S. role in the Gulf
area.

The establishment of the Marxist People's Democratic Republic of Yemen in
1968 accentuated that worry. In fact, however, the Soviets had become a factor
in the Gulf as early as 1958 when the Iraqi monarchy was overthrown and a
nationalist, military government was established in that country. An immediate
result was that Soviet influence in Iraq replaced what had formerly been British
and American influence. From the end of 1958 onward, Soviet naval vessels,
not in great numbers to be sure, regularly visited the Gulf, particularly the Iraqi
port of Umm Qasr. Moreover, in 1963, much to the distress of the United States,
the Kuwaiti government established diplomatic relations with the Soviet Union.
In a sense, therefore, by the time the Nixon Administration took office, the
Soviets had already established positions in the Gulf. There was concern that
the Soviets would seek to expand these positions.

Out of this situation, as Dr. Doron and Ambassador Atherton have indicated,
the belief developed in Washington that the primary threat in the Middle East
came from the Soviet Union. In the Gulf, in particular, an immediate effort was
needed to try to redress the situation. The solution hit upon by the Nixon Administration was the so-called Twin Pillars policy. This concept called for promoting
cooperation between Iran, as the largest and strongest power in the Gulf area,
and Saudi Arabia, the major friendly Arab state in the Gulf, in order jointly to
assume the security role in the Gulf. The Twin Pillars policy is a thing of the
past and has been much maligned in recent years as shortsighted. But as we
look back to the situation as it existed in the early 1970s, it is easy to forget
how difficult it was in that period to persuade Iran and Saudi Arabia, both littoral

states of the Gulf, but both harboring vintage suspicions of each other's objectives, to change their attitudes and cooperate with one another.

For one thing, the personalities of the shah of Iran and of King Faisal of Saudi Arabia were totally different. For another, there existed long-term ethnic antagonisms between Iranians and Arabs. It was an extraordinarily difficult task to persuade the two leaders to cooperate. At one point, when we thought we had the beginnings of an arrangement between Iran and Saudi Arabia, it died aborning because of a statement the Saudi monarch made when visiting Bahrain. That island polity, which had long been under British protection, was at the time still claimed by Iran. The shah viewed Faisal's statement that Bahrain was independent as a personal insult. The Iranian monarch therefore canceled a proposed trip to Saudi Arabia. With much U.S. effort, the two rulers were finally brought together, and the Twin Pillars policy could eventually be achieved. It worked for a period of time, although the Gulf Arabs were always worried about Iranian hegemonic objectives.

Implicit in the Twin Pillars policy was the idea that Iran and Saudi Arabia, especially if they were better armed with U.S. help, could somehow defend the Persian Gulf area against a possible Soviet threat. That was illusory, but it was a major element in U.S. policy. Military assistance to Iran, and to a lesser degree to Saudi Arabia, represented the first implementation of the so-called Nixon Doctrine. That concept involved arming indigenous governments in critical parts of the world in order to avoid deployment of American troops as had happened in Vietnam. The shah of Iran, whose appetite for military equipment had long been a source of concern to previous administrations, was now allowed to purchase more military equipment—and indeed the most sophisticated and therefore the most expensive military equipment in the U.S. military inventory. The result was a situation in which Iran soon found itself short of funds to pay for such military equipment. As the shah sought ways and means of increasing Iran's oil income, one of his major themes was that the U.S. government should persuade American oil companies operating in the Gulf area to purchase more Iranian oil, even if this meant reducing their petroleum offtake from other Gulf countries in which they held concessions, such as Saudi Arabia and Kuwait. The United States was not prepared to urge the companies to do so, nor was it willing to incur criticism from Saudi Arabia and Kuwait by increasing offtake of Iranian oil and reducing offtake from their concessions in Saudi Arabia and Kuwait.

The shah's alternative was to try to raise petroleum prices as a means of increasing Iran's income. The United States tacitly accepted that idea. It recognized that, if Iran was to pay for the increased flow of expensive U.S. military equipment, it needed greater oil income. The Nixon Administration did little, if anything, to urge the shah to keep petroleum prices down. Rather, it tacitly accepted his objective of increasing oil prices. The issue here was not our longstanding concern about the continued availability of Gulf oil, but the price of such oil. In years past, U.S. policy papers had also spoken about retaining a reasonable commercial price for oil. That concept now went out the window.

Could the United States have stopped an increase in the price of oil in those early years of the Nixon Administration? I am not sure that we could have done so, but I do believe we could have slowed the rapid escalation of oil prices. Since the shah had to pay his bills, however, and those bills were due mainly to the United States for military materiel, Washington was willing to accept oil price escalation.

In connection with this willingness to acquiesce in the shah's designs, I would argue that the Nixon Administration made a miscalculation. At that point in time, in my opinion at least, the United States still had considerable influence with the shah and should have urged him to improve his domestic policies. I think now—and thought then—that such urgings would have been feasible without endangering our desire to involve Iran more in Gulf security concerns. Even at the time, I remember being struck by what appeared to be our desire to propitiate the shah rather than urge him, in his own self-interest, to adopt domestic policies that might have prevented his eventual downfall.

Since my time is limited, let me turn briefly to the Arab-Israeli problem. I have already indicated there was a considerable degree of disinterest in that problem when the Nixon Administration first came into office. It was not until the unexpected October War of 1973 that Washington's attention was refocused. Active American reinvolvement in the Arab-Israeli problem resulted. In connection with the 1973 war, I would contend that the United States, that is, the Nixon Administration, had some real policy choices. By late October 1973, after the Israeli beachhead had been established on the western side of the Suez Canal, Washington could have allowed Israel to defeat the Egyptians. Israel had already defeated the Syrians, and the Egyptian Third Army in Sinai was surrounded. Had the Israeli armed forces continued, they could have defeated the Third Army and could probably have taken Cairo had this been their wish. But however far Israel might have gone, Egypt would have been decisively defeated. The alternative option, as far as the Nixon Administration was concerned, was to stop the Israelis after they had crossed the Suez Canal and after they had shown that they could defeat Egypt.

The decision on which alternative to choose was a difficult one. In my judgment, it is to the credit of President Nixon and Secretary of State Kissinger that they recognized the potential opportunity to catalyze an Egyptian-Israeli peace process. Sadat, unlike Nasser, represented a new brand of Egyptian leadership. Prior to the 1973 war, he had signaled to the Nixon Administration his hope that the United States would reinvolve itself in what had become a stagnant peace process. It was recognized in Washington that his limited military successes during the October War, in crossing the Suez Canal and overruning the vaunted Bar Lev line, might make it possible for Egypt to participate in a peace effort without the humiliation of total defeat.

For the Nixon Administration, there was also the risk that if the decision had been made to allow Israel to defeat Egypt, a U.S.-Soviet Union confrontation might have taken place. There was evidence that the Soviets, who had not endorsed Egypt's idea of launching a military operation against Israel, were nevertheless not prepared to see Egypt's total defeat. At the time, they still had too much at stake in that country.

Yet a third risk for the Nixon Administration was that, if Israel had been allowed to inflict a total military defeat on Egypt, Saudi Arabia and other Arab oil producers would continue the oil embargo that they had imposed during the war on the United States. Such an oil embargo had also not been expected by Washington policy planners, who had failed to read seriously the repeated warnings of the Saudi monarch that an embargo would indeed be part of a new Arab-Israeli war.

The choice that the Nixon Administration made, and I believe it was the right one, was to stop the war through a joint U.S.-Soviet arranged U.N. cease-fire and thereafter to utilize the situation that flowed from the conflict in order to get peace negotiations started. No one tried to pressure Israel to desist from military action, but the consequences of failing to do so were indeed pointed out to the Israeli leadership. Suasion, not pressure, was used. The Israeli leadership, too, saw the wisdom of trying to get Egyptian-Israeli negotiations started.

In this context, the idea was that a U.N.-sponsored Geneva conference would be convened with U.S. and Soviet co-chairmanship. An initial meeting of such a conference actually took place just before Christmas in December 1973. Much to the Soviets' annoyance, the conference was not reconvened in early January, as they had expected. Instead, the Nixon Administration, which despite the beginnings of détente with the Soviet Union continued to distrust Soviet intentions in the Middle East, determined to continue the Arab-Israeli peace effort on its own. Kissinger's famous shuttle of January 1974 resulted in the first Egyptian-Israeli disengagement agreement, better known as Sinai I. Subsequently, in May 1974, a similar disengagement agreement was reached between Israel and Syria. Regrettably, no such agreement could be negotiated between Israel and Jordan. These two disengagement agreements were modest in scope, but they paved the way for subsequent agreements and ultimately for Camp David and the Egyptian-Israeli peace treaty of 1979. President Nixon also made a much publicized Middle East tour in June 1974, in the wake of Sinai I and Golan I. Alas, it was his swan song. Shortly thereafter, Watergate overtook him, and he resigned the presidency.

I would make one final point for the record. At the time President Nixon left office in the late summer of 1974, we had only two Arab-Israeli agreements: Sinai I between Egypt and Israel and Golan I between Syria and Israel. Today, in the light of what has since happened, they seem like very minor agreements. At the time, they were modest but major agreements. Symbolically, they had enormous importance, even though neither Egypt nor Syria recognized them as political agreements. Both states insisted they were military agreements, akin to armistice arrangements. It was Nixon's successor, President Ford, who could capitalize on the successes of these two agreements and furthered the peace process through a second Sinai disengagement agreement in 1975. Similarly, what Nixon had built enabled Ford to continue the effort to bring Egypt into the U.S. and Western camp. It was a slow and difficult process. Frankly, in late 1973, 1974 and early 1975, the Egyptian leadership retained grave doubts that the United States could be relied on to continue the peace process. But the United States did so under both Presidents Ford and Carter. The effort begun by Nixon and continued by his two successors, one Republican and one Democrat, had the effect of materially altering the balance of superpower influence in the Middle East and of significantly reducing Soviet influence in that area. Both Nixon and Kissinger deserve great credit for that achievement.

Discussant: Jo-Anne Hart

The United States has three broad goals in the Middle East: to limit Soviet gains; to guarantee access to oil for the United States and its Western allies; and to promote the security of Israel. The relative attention and priority each administration affords these goals are of great use in explaining policy choices. One strength of Gideon Doron's paper is his attempt to analyze the rank order these goals held in the Nixon Administration.

Doron's analytical structure highlights the tradeoffs between U.S. goals in the region during the Nixon Administration, with particular concern for the role of oil. The oil price increases induced by the Embargo of 1973 had a dramatic impact on the world economy. The severe consequences, including supply shortages, that affected millions of people daily put the Middle East on the map for many Americans. Oil has irreversibly been a prominent feature of the American public's attention to the Middle East ever since. Every subsequent administration has been obliged to concern itself with energy policy and guaranteed access to oil.

Doron's central focus in this paper is to explain how the U.S. decision-making process vis-à-vis oil failed in such a way that the country faced an oil embargo and a price shock. He discusses criteria appropriate for determining oil policy— the reliability of supply and opportunity costs. The paper argues that the Nixon Administration "muddled through" when it came to oil policy. Doron puts oil in context by analyzing the factors that explain the lack of priority given to oil policy in its relative competition with the other primary drives in U.S. Middle East policy.

Particularly useful in this paper is the attempt to bring the Cold War into the discussion of Nixon's Middle East policy. Nixon and Kissinger had a strongly ideological world-view that supported a hardline on the traditional postwar containment strategy toward the Soviet Union. The Nixon Administration was not "muddling through," as Doron suggests, when it came to issues that were perceived as competition with the Soviets. Nixon and Kissinger firmly saw the Middle East as an arena of East-West confrontation, and American policy toward the region was based on this premise. This view was a guide to U.S. policy-making in the Middle East before Nixon. Indeed, Doron notes the events in Iran in 1953 when the United States assisted in the overthrow of the Iranian prime minister. In the Nixon period, this mode of operations tolerated some local instability for broader objectives pertaining to superpower rivalry. Doron could have cited the U.S.-Iranian (and Israeli) collusion to assist a rebellion in Iraqi Kurdistan in the early 1970s. The United States wanted the Kurdish revolt to destabilize Iraq, not achieve victory, and schemed to falsely implicate Soviet support to the Kurds as a way to damage Soviet relations with a local client.[1]

The Nixon Administration policy toward the Arab-Israeli conflict is a prominent example of the Middle East perceived through the prism of East-West rivalry. Nixon and Kissinger were disinterested in the Arab-Israeli peace process prior to 1973, until the Egyptians would definitively join the U.S. camp and dismiss the Soviets. The lack of White House support for Rogers's peace plan is partially explained by the zero-sum view of the Middle East held by the administration: it was most important that the United States be the primary actor responsible for bringing about a peace settlement, excluding the Soviet Union, and on terms acceptable to the United States.

The critical dimension of Nixon's policy in the Middle East, which should be developed further, is the *link* that developed between the consequences of oil policies and the East-West conflict. With the oil price increases beginning in 1973, several Middle Eastern countries acquired enormous financial surpluses. This development stimulated an attempt by the United States to recapture some of the outflow of oil money. Thus, a crucial link was formed between a Cold War containment strategy and U.S. regional economic interests. Namely, the United States would cultivate pro-West, oil-rich client states in the Middle East, especially in Iran and Saudi Arabia, via huge U.S. arms sales. In particular, highly sophisticated weapons were sold to Iran. These arms sales recycled Middle East oil revenues while they brought down the unit costs of weaponry for U.S. industry. Though motivated by security concerns, Nixon and Kissinger saw the important connection between oil revenues and arms sales. Professor Eilts's comments here indicated a tacit acceptance by the White House of the oil price increases. U.S. arms sales were a key aspect of the Nixon Administration's dealings with the Middle East, and they need to be underlined as such.

The connection between U.S. oil policy and American objectives for regional client states became institutionalized under Nixon. It is useful to go further than Doron and point out some far-ranging consequences of this turning point. It was under Nixon and Kissinger that arms sales to Iran were removed from the established governmental review process. The White House instructed the arms sales bureaucracy that future decisions on the purchase of conventional weapons should be made by the government of Iran. Thus, the bureaucracy was not to "second-guess" Iranian arms sales.[2] The shah could buy whatever he chose from the U.S. conventional arms industry, and in the 1970s Iranian arms purchases exceeded $20 billion. These enormous sales had a positive effect on the U.S. balance of payments with Iran; they also had economic consequences for domestic Iranian politics, which exacerbated instabilities there.

Furthermore, in a show of respect for the shah as the most loyal and anti-Soviet American regional ally, all U.S. contacts with Iranian opposition, direct and indirect, were ordered to cease. This decision reflects the link between oil policy, Cold War motivations, and client state politics. However, this choice alone had critical ramifications for U.S. policy-making toward a turbulent Iran throughout the 1970s, particularly hobbling the administration that had to face the Iranian Revolution.

These issues addressed here in the context of the Nixon Administration can also be used to pose wider questions for U.S. Middle East policy. Doron points out that the failure of U.S. oil policy was due in part to errors in evaluating the significance of regional factors and their effect on U.S. interests in the Middle East. It is important to consider the ways in which this problem transcends the Nixon Administration and, indeed, any given administration. Some analysts recognize shifts between a global-dominant perspective and regional view in decision making. At this panel there has been discussion of a pendulum swing. It is important to ask how much variance actually exists through administrations. Significant evaluative errors seem to plague president after president. There is an extent to which the inadequate analysis of regional problems is an institutional phenomenon, the State Department notwithstanding. Following Nixon, Carter confronted the difficulty of understanding the force and direction of the Iranian Revolution and, unsuccessfully, the impact of ongoing regional factors on oil prices and long-term U.S. interests in the region. In the Reagan Administration, a misreading of Iran and local politics led to more hostage-taking and the covert arms deal that badly discredited the administration. Policies are partly idiosyncratic to a given administration's mix of motivations, priorities, and personalities in leadership. However, there is a clear sense in which the problem has become structural—part of the institutional standard operating procedure. The impulse to view the region in terms of East-West rivalry works against the understanding of local Middle Eastern politics. Furthermore, this basis for U.S. policy-making is inherited by each White House and is entrenched in the foreign policy establishment. Each new administration seems to accept more legacy than it redrafts. From this standpoint, connective links in U.S.–Middle East policy decisions— choices that have regularly misjudged the significance of indigenous factors and emphasized the overlay of superpower rivalry—are handed down through administrations and become integral to the fabric of decision making.

Finally, a word should be said about the visibility of oil in U.S. Middle East policy-making, particularly concerning the Persian Gulf. Doron argues that the failure of U.S. oil policy stemmed partly from the lack of a sufficient guarantee to the flow of oil to the West. The economic and financial consequences of oil shocks, together with the costs paid by the American public, amount to a special attentiveness to oil in U.S. Middle East policy. To an extent this has raised the stakes for presidents subsequent to Nixon. Oil was thrust into celebrity status in U.S. military, economic, and political policy in the Middle East, and presidents are obliged to protect Americans against another price shock. At the same time, consciousness about oil prices can easily be used to garner domestic political support with the public and Congress for various U.S. policies in the region. In this way, the oil issue can be used to camouflage other motivations behind a given policy.

For example, it is highly credible now to relate U.S. military activities in the Gulf to Western oil interests. Thus, Carter declared that the region was in the vital U.S. interest and began the development of a force specifically earmarked for responsibility in the region to guarantee the flow of oil. The new U.S. Central

Command uses a Soviet invasion of Iran as their primary planning scenario. The current U.S. military activity in the Persian Gulf falls into this same category. The United States decided to engage in military operations there immediately following an arrangement by which the Kuwaitis leased three Soviet tankers. The U.S. escort of eleven "reflagged" Kuwaiti tankers, which tripled the U.S. military presence in the Gulf, is explicitly justified on the basis of guaranteeing the flow of oil, along with freedom of navigation, through the war zone. This has been the case despite the fact that the course of the Iran-Iraq War has not resulted in any significant interruption in oil supplies. In fact, the price of oil has declined, and the market has been glutted. In this case oil serves as a salient legitimator for a policy strongly motivated by other goals in U.S. policy. Prominent is the U.S. interest in limiting Soviet influence in the Gulf. Doron's paper can be used to highlight the early consequences of this linkage between U.S. oil interests and the East-West conflict. This legacy of the Nixon period continues today, with an increased threat of triggering U.S. military involvement in the region. In the past this deliberate mix of superpower politics and oil insecurity has come with high and somewhat hidden costs. It is revelant to ask now whether it is desirable for oil and East-West issues to be so closely tied.

NOTES

1. Richard Cottam, "American Policy toward Iran," *Iranian Studies* 13 (1980), 290.
2. Henry Kissinger, *White House Years* (New York: Little, Brown, 1979), p. 1264.

Discussant: Dale R. Tahtinen

Thank you. I guess it is both an advantage and a disadvantage to be the last commentator because, if it has been a really good panel as this one has been up to this juncture—I would say an excellent one—everything that I wanted to talk about has been covered plus some additional items. The advantage is that I am able now to deal with a few fun things.

One point that I would like to focus on was discussed by Ambassador Eilts and the previous commentator. That is, the whole issue of how extensively the shah of Iran's appetite was whetted for greater arms sales so that we could recover the petrodollars. A significant amount was written about this matter at the time of the congressional hearings, and, I might add, however, the bureaucracy considered the issue in the Nixon Administration. The reality is that Congress still had a lot of influence over the process, and there were certainly a significant number of congressional hearings. While I am the last person to defend the Nixon Administration's policies in the Middle East, I would have to say that you cannot blame the administration totally for what happened in those years. Congress was not exactly standing back, demanding that the administration push harder for a peace process in the Middle East in the Arab-Israeli conflict. Congress was not unanimously saying, "No we don't want the shah of Iran to buy all of this sophisticated military equipment." About the only thing Congress could get interested in was the F-14s with the Phoenix Missile System, and there was some concern there as to whether or not the system would eventually be violated in a security sense regardless of whether the shah stayed in power.

Overall, a number of people were arguing very strongly outside of the Nixon Administration, and on the inside as well there was some worry. I recall that in ISA [International Security Affairs] as well as elsewhere in the Pentagon, there was considerable discussion regarding how many sophisticated weapons should be provided to the shah. There was a recognition then that the shah of Iran faced an enormous crisis in the sense that he didn't have enough money to pay for all the "goodies." It seemed to be fairly accepted knowledge in the early 1970s that Mr. Kissinger had certainly encouraged the shah to buy just about anything that was in *Jane's Weapons Systems* or any of the other Jane volumes, as long as it didn't have nuclear applications. All of this was occurring at a time when enormous expenditures were required in different parts of Iranian society for internal stability purposes.

Obviously, both the Nixon Administration and the Congress went along with the shah's weapons requests. Congress did not prevent the sales of the F-14s with the Phoenix Missile Systems, or the other exported weapons. Ambassador Ardeshar Zahedi hosted lavish parties attended by key members of Congress, the executive branch, press, and other key opinion influencers of policy. The ambassador even had relatives of some congressional members on his payroll as consultants. Well, history records what has happened since the shah's fall, and the scrutiny of arms exports has created a lot of problems for the Saudis where there was a lot more justification for some purchases of advanced military equipment for a later point in time.

I don't want to stray too far away from the Nixon Administration, but let me just briefly hit on two other points. First, Dr. Doron indicates that the oil companies didn't oppose the import of Arab oil during this time period. I would take issue with that idea. Indeed, I could probably even go back and find some of the old documentation from that period. As early as 1966, 1967, and 1968, oil companies, including some of those who were even members of ARAMCO, were warning that there was an impending crisis. The United States was relying on increasing amounts of foreign oil, and the companies were warning about the possible disastrous consequences. They weren't saying the United States should not import Arab oil, but they were warning about the import of foreign oil in general. That admonition did not get much media coverage, and what it did receive tended to appear more in the technical journals, the business publications, and the like.

A lot of it was apparently interpreted as the oil companies' attempt to obtain additional tax breaks or some other additional assistance from the government. Whatever the case, warnings did emanate from the oil companies and some of the oil associations. I remember reading some of them when I first joined the Defense Intelligence Agency in 1967, when we were examining some economic possibilities. The companies are not total villains in this process. Obviously, they wanted to make profits, but it is difficult to argue effectively that they were willing to sacrifice the national interest. They may not have been totally altruistic, but the private sector did sound the warning bells. Of course, they also had a program for what they wanted done.

Just a final point: the term *oil blackmail* was popularized in the press during the October War, and this led to the question of why the Nixon Administration allowed the United States to be victimized by the increased import of oil. On this issue, you have to view it in a broader context, and perhaps we can learn a lesson from it today. That lesson is that right now there is tremendous opposition to an oil import fee and that some legal problems are also associated with it. There is great opposition to such a fee because of a concern that it would mark the beginning of a real rollback to greater protectionism. Key opponents contend that if a cap is placed on how much oil can be imported into the United States or if extra fees are added to it, then why isn't it possible to do the same thing with Japanese computers, South Korean cars, Japanese cars, and so on. It is a much broader issue of trade that becomes of great concern. Whatever one's position is on those areas, I think we ought to put the Nixon Administration's efforts into context. The administration was fighting inflation, it had some real problems during that time period, and obviously one could argue that it was a short-term fix. However, allowing greater amounts of cheaper foreign oil to come into the United States could only be helpful in terms of the pure economic problems and challenges.

In the long run, we could contend that two serious mistakes occurred. We became too reliant on foreign oil, and then we allowed ourselves to become victims to the shah's acquisition policies, which exerted even greater price pressure on petroleum. In addition, some experts have asserted that, if the Nixon Administration had earlier pushed a lot harder for some type of peace settlement in the Arab-Israeli process, the October War and oil price increases would never have occurred. I have articulated these thoughts mostly because I feel that other pertinent ones have been well covered, but I believe we should put the background in which the Nixon Administration was operating into better context.

We should also remember that during this period there was little flexibility in terms of positive perceptions on Capitol Hill or throughout most of the country. We had just exited from Vietnam, and that conflict had truly preoccupied the administration. I can certainly attest to that from my five years with the Defense Intelligence Agency through which the president was made aware of everything that was going on. In my last two years I happened to be in charge of putting together the Daily Intelligence Summary, and the vast majority of it was oriented toward Vietnam, even during the war of attrition between Israel and Egypt. As important as other events were, Vietnam seemed always to dominate. It's not a matter that the administration didn't do enough. Rather, the situation has to be considered within the context of other key pressures occurring at the same time. Perhaps that called for a better functioning system, but I don't see one existing today and can't even imagine one that could have performed more effectively then, given all the problems confronting the existing bureaucracy.

_____ Part II _____

The Foreign Policy Process

It has often been argued that a nation's military and security policies are dictated by foreign policy concerns over and above any domestic considerations. The Nixon Administration put that idea to a severe test. The change in defense strategy and the comparative decline in defense spending during the Nixon years were undoubtedly reactions to the heavy expenditures of the Vietnam War. The shift from the draft to an all-volunteer army also reflected the nation's desire to escape the pressures of the Vietnam era. The consequences of this shift are discussed in the papers and discussions that follow.

In addition, the Nixon years showed a more flexible, balance-of-power approach to world affairs, a shift from the rigid bipolar confrontation of the superpowers that marked the Vietnam years. It is certainly an anomaly that Richard Nixon is viewed as a rigid Cold Warrior when, in fact, his administration was marked by a far more adaptable program toward dealing with the Communist world, as shown in the following section.

Finally, the most significant institutional change in dealing with foreign policy concerns in the Nixon era was the passage of the War Powers Resolution, in which Congress reasserted its constitutional prerogatives to be involved as a partner in the initiation of hostilities abroad. The manner in which Congress came to the conclusion that its constitutional war powers had been abrogated and had to be reasserted is also discussed in the section that follows.

DEFENSE AND NATIONAL SECURITY

8

The Defense Policies of the Nixon Administration: A Decade of Neglect or Prudent Readjustment?

LAWRENCE J. KORB

In assessing the defense policy of the Nixon Administration, we must look not only at what it accomplished, but also at the constraints under which it operated. After all it is much easier to improve U.S. military capabilities absolutely and relatively if the defense budget is going up significantly in real terms than if it is declining. Similarly, it is relatively easy to have a high-quality military force if the Department of Defense (DoD) has an unfettered claim on the nation's youth through conscription than if one must compete in the marketplace for volunteers. No administration, however, can merely be content to react to the environment it inherits. Presidents and their chief national security subordinates can alter the domestic and international environment through their own actions and policies.

There are two schools of thought regarding the defense policies of the Nixon Administration. One school holds that Nixon, and his chief national security advisers, Henry Kissinger, the assistant for national security affairs, and Melvin Laird, the secretary of defense, ushered in a "decade of neglect."[1] Their policies are said to have led to a precipitous decline in U.S. military capabilities that tilted the military balance in favor of the Soviet Union, emboldened the Russians to invade Afghanistan and the Ayotollah to seize our hostages, and led to such military debacles as the Mayaguez Rescue and Desert One. Proponents of that point of view hold that it wasn't until the ascendancy of Ronald Reagan to the Oval Office in 1981, and the massive increases in defense spending that occurred in his first administration, that this trend was reversed.

On the surface, the facts seem to support the thesis that Nixon did indeed decide to reorder priorities away from defense and toward domestic programs.

Figure 8.1
U.S.*/Soviet Defense Spending, FY 1969–FY 1974 (in billions of dollars)

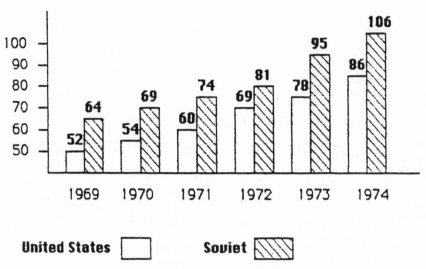

Sources: Arms Control and Disarmament Agency, *World Military Expenditures and Arms Trade,*
   1963–1973, and Melvin Laird, *Annual Defense Department Report, FY 1973*, February 17,
   1972, p. 33.
*excluding outlays for war in Southeast Asia

From 1950 through 1968, defense spending took about half of the federal budget
and just under 10 percent of our gross national product (GNP). In FY 1974
dollars, defense spending, exclusive of Korea and Vietnam, averaged about $78
billion per year throughout that period. By the time Nixon had turned over the
reins of power to President Gerald Ford, defense spending accounted for only
28 percent of the federal budget and only 5.8 percent of GNP. In the Nixon
Presidency, average military spending, exclusive of Vietnam, was about $57
billion, about $20 billion or 27 percent less than in the 1950–68 period.

Compounding the drop in U.S. expenditures for defense was the rapid increase
in the size of the Soviet military budget. Stung by the events of October 1962,
the Russians began to increase their defense spending substantially. By 1968
their defense expenditures surpassed those of the United States for the first time
since 1950. As indicated in Figure 8.1, during the Nixon Presidency they spent
approximately 20 percent more on defense than did the United States. Nor did
the Soviet defense effort slacken after the signing of SALT I; indeed, it accelerated. Between 1968 and 1979, cumulative Soviet investment in defense totaled
$270 billion more than ours.[2]

The massive Soviet expenditure did have a substantial impact on the strategic
and conventional balance. As indicated in Table 8.1, between 1968 and 1976

Soviet land- and sea-based missiles increased almost threefold, that is, from 750 to almost 2,400. During this same period, the number of U.S. missiles remained essentially static at about 1,700. A similar situation prevailed in the areas of ships, planes, and divisions. In 1968 the United States had 125 more surface combat ships than the Soviets; by 1976 we had 50 fewer. In 1968 the United States had over 2,000 more tactical aircraft; in 1976 we had 1,000 fewer than the Soviets. In 1968 we had ten more division equivalents, and in 1976, nine less. These comparisons also hold true if we go back to 1964.

The second school of thought rejects the decade of neglect thesis totally and argues that, given the environment in which they operated, the work of President Nixon and his subordinates in the area of defense policy was superb.[3] Proponents of this point of view point to several factors.

First, Nixon inherited a very unpopular war from the Johnson Administration. When Nixon took office, the United States still had almost 550,000 troops in Vietnam and was spending about $29 billion annually to prosecute that conflict. Nixon and Laird instituted the policy of Vietnamization, which allowed them to accelerate dramatically the process of withdrawal. As indicated in Table 8.2, by 1973 virtually all of the American troops were out of Vietnam and the war-related costs had dropped to $6 billion. This $23 billion "peace dividend" was transferred back into the baseline defense budget.

Second, it was the Vietnam War, not the actions of the Nixon Administration, which undermined support for defense. Indeed, were it not for the actions of Nixon and his advisers, the situation would have been far worse. During his time in office, Nixon did not even receive all the funds he requested for defense, in spite of the fact that in real terms he asked for less funding each year. As indicated in Table 8.3, the Congress reduced Nixon's request by an average of 6 percent per year, thus acting six times more negatively toward his requests than they did toward the requests of his four immediate predecessors.[4]

There was no doubt that Congress was responding to the public mood. During the Nixon Presidency, less than 10 percent of the American people supported an increase in defense spending, compared to nearly 70 percent at the outset of the Kennedy Administration.[5] As noted in Table 8.3, Congress itself transferred this "defense dividend" to the social areas of the budget, increasing those areas by about 5 percent over the level requested by President Nixon. Thus, it was the legislature more than the executive branch that was reordering priorities.

Third, Nixon had to contend not only with the lack of public support for increased defense spending, but also with the financial legacy of the War on Poverty and Great Society. Through these policies, Lyndon Johnson had created a host of social programs whose claim on the federal budget could be reduced only by changing the law. As indicated in Table 8.4, these relatively uncontrollable expenditures rose from $116 billion, or 63 percent of the federal budget in FY 1969, to $195 billion, or 72 percent of the budget by FY 1974. As a result, the truly controllable parts of the federal budget were reduced significantly. Moreover, by the early 1970s about 70 percent of the controllable expenditures

Table 8.1
U.S./USSR Force Levels for Selected Calendar Years

System	1964		1968		1972		1976		Change N		Change %	
	U.S.	USSR	U.S.	USSR	U.S.	USSR	U.S.	USSR	U.S.	USSR	U.S.	USSR
ICBMs	954	200	1,054	700	1,054	1,118	1,054	1,527	400	1,327	61	664
SLBMs	336	20	656	50	656	450	656	845	320	825	95	4,125
Bombers	630	190	650	250	569	140	387	140	-243	-50	-39	-26
Major Surface Combatant Ships	300	200	325	200	250	225	175	225	-125	25	-42	13
Tactical Aircraft	5,700	3,500	5,700	3,500	5,000	4,500	5,000	6,000	-700	2,500	-12	71
Division Equivalents[a]	19	7	20	10	16	25	16	25	-3	18	-16	255

Sources: Annual Reports to the Congress by the Secretary of Defense (for selected fiscal years).
[a]U.S. and Soviet divisions are not directly comparable. Soviet divisions are made equivalent to the United States in this comparison.

Table 8.2
War Costs and Troop Levels for the War in Vietnam (in billions of dollars)

Fiscal Year	Full Costs SEA War	Incremental Costs	Troop Levels
1968	26.5	20.0	549,500
1969	28.8	21.5	549,500
1970	23.1	17.4	434,000
1971	14.7	11.5	284,000
1972	9.1	7.1	69,000
1973	6.0	5.2	39,000

Source: Department of Defense (Comptroller), "The Economics of Defense Spending: A Look at the Realities," July 1972, p. 149.

Table 8.3
Congressional Changes in Budget Requests (percentages)

Fiscal Year	Total Budget	Defense Budget	Non-Defense
1970	-1.7	-7.7	+5.8
1971	+0.7	-3.4	+2.5
1972	-4.2	-4.4	+0.1
1973	+4.7	-7.2	+10.2
1974	+0.1	-6.3	+2.4
1975	+3.3	-7.0	+7.4
Average	+0.5	-6.0	+4.7

Source: Joint Committee on Reduction of Federal Expenditures, *1974 and 1975 Budget Scorekeeping Reports.*

in the federal budget were in the area of national defense. Therefore, defense had to be reduced to keep the federal budget under control.

Fourth, Nixon inherited a deteriorating force posture from the Johnson Administration. In order to attempt to dampen the impact of the cost of our involvement in Southeast Asia and to conceal the true costs of the war in Vietnam from the American public, Johnson's defense chiefs raped the baseline defense budget to prosecute the war. Thus, normal modernization of the conventional forces was either stretched out or postponed, and routine overhaul and maintenance projects were skipped in the 1964 to 1968 period.

An additional legacy of the war in Vietnam was an end to popular support for conscription. In the 1968 election, both candidates pledged to end the draft. Although the Selective Service System, which had existed since 1948, had many drawbacks, it did have the advantage of holding down the cost of military manpower, thus allowing DoD to spend additional funds on defense investment.

Table 8.4
Controllability of Budget Outlays (in billions of dollars)

	1969	1970	1971	1972	1973	1974
Relatively uncontrollable under present law:						
Open-ended & fixed cost:						
Payments for individuals	54.9	62.2	77.3	88.4	99.6	115.4
Net interest	12.7	14.4	14.8	15.5	17.4	21.5
General revenue sharing					6.6	6.1
Farm price supports	4.1	3.8	2.8	4.0	3.6	1.0
Other open-ended programs and fixed costs	2.8	3.8	5.2	6.4	6.3	6.8
TOTAL	74.5	84.3	100.1	114.3	133.4	150.8
Outlays from prior-year contracts and obligations:						
National defense	25.0	24.5	21.6	19.9	18.3	20.9
Civilian programs	16.9	17.0	18.6	19.4	21.3	22.9
Total, outlays from prior year contracts & obligations	41.9	41.5	40.2	39.2	39.6	43.8
Total, relatively uncontrollable outlays	116.4	125.7	140.4	153.5	173.0	194.5
Relatively controllable outlays:						
National defense	52.6	51.8	51.8	53.5	52.6	53.0
Civilian programs	17.6	21.5	21.9	27.7	23.8	24.2
Total, relatively controllable outlays	70.1	73.3	73.7	81.1	76.4	77.2
Undistributed employer share, employee retirement	−2.0	−2.4	−2.6	−2.8	−2.9	−3.3
Total budget outlays	184.5	196.6	211.4	231.9	246.5	268.4

Source: The Budget of the United States Government, Fiscal Year 1976 (Washington, D.C.: U.S. Government Printing Office, 1975), pp, 354–355.

The end of the draft would mean dramatic rises in costs in such areas as recruiting, pay, and living conditions within a declining defense budget. Moreover, in the Johnson Administration, the principle of pay comparability for military and civilian employees of the federal government was adopted. Essentially, this meant that the pay of half the civilians in the federal service and of all military people was now indexed to inflation and had to be absorbed in the DoD budget. Table 8.5 shows the dramatic rise in personnel costs both absolutely and as a· percentage of the defense budget. As that table indicates, these costs rose from about 42 percent in FY 1968 to over 55 percent in FY 1973.

Even if we accept the constraints under which Nixon had to operate, an

Table 8.5
Personnel Costs in the Defense Budget, FY 1968–FY 1974

	1968	1971	1971	1973	1974
Military Personnel	19.8	22.3	23.4	23.8	24.2
Civil Service	10.3	12.2	12.5	12.8	13.8
Military Retired	2.1	3.4	3.8	4.4	5.2
Total	32.6	38.4	40.3	41.6	43.0
% of Outlays	41.8	50.9	53.2	55.8	55.2

Source: The Budgets of the United States Government, for selected years.

Table 8.6
Department of Defense Manpower Levels (in thousands)

Actual	Active Military	Civilian	Total
1960	2,476	1,230	3,706
1965	2,655	1,155	3,810
1968	3,547	1,393	4,940
1969	3,460	1,391	4,851
1970	3,066	1,265	4,331
1971	2,714	1,190	3,904
1972	2,322	1,159	3,481
1973	2,252	1,100	3,352
1974	2,161	1,109	3,270

Source: Harold Brown, Annual Defense Department Report, FY 1979.

additional question must be asked. How well did Nixon and his aides deal with these constraints? Did they spend their funds wisely? Did they adopt policies and strategies consistent with the level of defense expenditures? On balance, the answer to these questions appears to be a resounding yes. This can be demonstrated by examining several actions taken by the Nixon Administration.

First, to provide funds for investment and to offset the rapidly increasing costs of manpower, Nixon and Laird reduced the number of active duty military and civilians in DoD some 35 percent below the levels they inherited and 15 percent below the levels that existed before the war in Vietnam. This is outlined in Table 8.6.

To compensate for this manpower reduction, Laird instituted the total force policy. This policy integrated the National Guard and Reserves into the total forces. No longer would these weekend warriors be a poorly equipped stepchild of the active establishment. Rather, they would now be integrated into U.S. war plans and would receive equipment based on their deployment date, not their

Table 8.7
Integration of Guard and Reserves into the Total Force

Service	Function	Percentage	
		Active	Reserve
Army	Combat forces	50	50
	Maneuver battalions	75	25
Air Force	Tactical airlift	44	56
	Tactical reconnaissance	60	40
	Strategic refueling	79	21
	Strategic airlift	57	43
Navy	Surface combat ships	75	25
	Patrol aviation	67	33
Average		63	37

Source: Office of the Assistant Secretary of Defense (Manpower and Reserve Affairs).

reserve status. As a result of this total force initiative, funding for the Guard and Reserves doubled in the Nixon years, and their share of the defense budget grew from 2.8 to 4.4 percent. As indicated in Table 8.7, this allowed the Guard and Reserves to take on a significant portion of the functions of the Total Force.

Second, the Nixon Administration made extremely wise investment decisions. For example, all the strategic programs currently being deployed had their origins in the Nixon Administration. These weapons, which Reagan has used to close the "window of vulnerability," include the MX missile, the B-1 bomber, the Trident Submarine and missiles, cruise missiles, and even the technology that could be deployed in the near term under the Strategic Defense Initiative (SDI).[6]

In the conventional area, Nixon and Laird made extremely wise decisions as well. It phased out some 175 obsolete weapon systems and reduced the overall size of the force structure by about one-third, compared to the pre-Vietnam level. This allowed it to reduce the percentage of the defense budget allocated to support costs from 29 percent in FY 1968 to 24 percent in FY 1974.[7]

In buying new equipment, the Nixon Administration pioneered the hi-lo mix policy, one that DoD uses to this day. For example, as noted in Table 8.8, instead of replacing tactical aircraft like the F-4 Phantom only with the high-performance but expensive F-14 Tomcats or F-15 Eagles, Laird also developed the somewhat less sophisticated but lower cost F/A-18 and F-16 aircraft. On average, the F-18 and F-16 cost about 33 percent less per unit than the F-14 and F-15. This has allowed DoD to purchase some 1,500 more planes over the past fifteen years.

Third, Nixon developed doctrines, policies, and strategies that were closely aligned and supportive of the defense budget. The Nixon Doctrine, with its

Table 8.8
Hi-Lo Systems in Tactical Aircraft

"Lo" Program	Number of Units	Program Cost[a]	Unit Cost[b]	Replaces	Number of Units	Program Cost[a]	Unit Cost[b]
F-16	1,388	13.8	10.8	F-15	749	13.2	17.6
F-18	1,366	17.4	17.6	F-14	500	12.1	23.8
A-10	733	4.5	6.3	F-15	749	13.2	17.6
Total	3,487	35.7	10.2[c]		1,249[d]	25.3[d]	19.5[c]

Source: Office of the Secretary of Defense (Comptroller), SAR Program Acquisition Cost Summary, February 14, 1977.

[a]in billions of dollars.
[b]in millions of dollars.
[c]average of all programs.
[d]F-15 counted only once.

emphasis on a Strategy of Realistic Deterrence and Vietnamization, allowed the United States to live up to its commitments abroad while enhancing U.S. defense strategy in spite of reduced defense spending. The basic theme of the Nixon doctrine was that the United States would participate in the defense of allies and friends only where it could make a real difference and where it was a vital U.S. interest. However, the United States would not conceive all the plans, design all the programs, execute all the decisions, and undertake the defense of all the free nations of the world. In other words, the United States would help its allies help themselves.[8]

The Nixon Doctrine allowed the Pentagon to modify its defense strategy from a two and a half war basis to a one and a half war commitment. The two and a half war strategy postulated fighting simultaneously a three-month, forward, conventional war in Europe, defending Southeast Asia against an all-out Chinese attack, and a minor contingency elsewhere. Under the one and a half war strategy, the United States pledged to maintain in peacetime adequate general-purpose forces for simultaneously meeting a major Communist attack in either Europe or Asia, assisting allies against non-Chinese threats in Asia, and contending with a contingency elsewhere.

This new strategy, which was referred to as Realistic Deterrence, allowed the United States to withdraw some troops from overseas. During the Nixon Administration, some fifty thousand troops were withdrawn from Europe and Korea. These allies compensated for these withdrawals by significantly increasing their own defense spending in the 1970s.

Fourth, through the skillful use of diplomacy, the Nixon Administration reduced America's defense burden. By normalizing relations with Mainland China, Nixon not only reduced the Chinese military threat to the United States and its allies, but he also pinned down some twenty-five Soviet divisions on the Chinese border. Similarly, by negotiating the ABM treaty and SALT I, Nixon not only reduced the necessity for spending on strategic defensive forces, but he also gave the United States time to catch up with the Soviets in the area of offensive weapons.[9] SALT I had much more impact on Soviet than on U.S. offensive systems.

The record of the Nixon Administration in the area of defense policy is not perfect. Despite Vietnamization, South Vietnam eventually fell to North Vietnam in 1975. The All Volunteer Force (AVF) nearly collapsed in the late 1970s. Despite the total force concept, the United States has still not attained the capability of fighting one and one half conventional wars. If anything, Soviet behavior after SALT I became more bellicose. Certain areas of the defense budget, like air and sealift, were virtually ignored. However, on balance the record of Nixon, Kissinger, and Laird in the defense area is a good one. This is especially true if one compares it to the Reagan Administration which spent without strategy in its first years in office and refused to accept the inevitability of fiscal constraints in its second.

NOTES

1. See, for example, Colin Gray and Jeffrey Barlow, "Inexcusable Restraint: The Decline of American Military Power in the 1970s," *International Security* (Fall 1985): 27–69.

2. Harold Brown, *Department of Defense Annual Report, FY 1982*, p. 16.

3. See, for example, Melvin Laird, "A Strong Start in a Difficult Decade: Defense Policy in the Nixon-Ford Years," *International Security* (Fall 1985): 5–26.

4. House Appropriations Committee, *Department of Defense Appropriations for 1964*, Part 2, p. 585, and Office of the Assistant Secretary of Defense (Comptroller).

5. William Kincade, "Period of Peril Revisited: A Public Opinion Perspective," Georgetown University and Access, September 1987.

6. Laird, "A Strong Start in a Difficult Decade," p. 14.

7. David Ott et al., *Public Claims on U.S. Output* (Washington, D.C.: American Enterprise Institute, 1973), p. 42.

8. Laird, "A Strong Start in a Difficult Decade," pp. 15–20, discusses the Nixon Doctrine and its strategic implications.

9. Henry Kissinger, *White House Years* (Boston: Little, Brown, 1979), p. 1245.

9

The Making of the All-Volunteer Armed Force

MARTIN ANDERSON

One of the most lasting legacies of Richard Nixon's presidency was the fundamental change he wrought in the defense manpower policy of the United States. Turning away from the heavy hand of conscription, on which we had relied strongly since the beginning of World War II to raise our armed forces, President Nixon embarked on a bold course—gambling that enough Americans would see that actively participating in the defense of this country was honorable enough, and important enough, that they would of their own free will enlist and serve their country. Nixon's new manpower policy has been strikingly successful, confounding the dire predictions of military weakness and social problems put forth by his critics. It has been successful even beyond the most optimistic hopes of many of his supporters.

The first responsibility of any president is the national security of the nation. Today we have a large, powerful armed force that—judged by the most important criterion, combat capability—can do what it is supposed to do: deter potential attackers and fight if necessary. The experience of the last fifteen years has shown us that men and women who have freely chosen a military career are, on balance, a more effective fighting force than one that is part volunteer, part forced service. And beyond that Nixon's new manpower policy achieved something precious and rare in the post-Vietnam years. Once again the military is an honorable profession.

When the United States abolished the military draft in the early 1970s it was the first time in its history that we had deliberately adopted a national policy of an all-volunteer, large peacetime armed force. Since then millions of young men have had the power to choose whether and how they would serve their country.

Ending the draft was a controversial policy. The move was strongly opposed by virtually the entire military establishment, by the Armed Services Committee in the Congress, by some of Nixon's most senior defense advisers, and by a large segment of the media. The ending of the draft was preceded by many years of debate in intellectual circles, in Congress, in election campaigns, and in the media. Conscription involves some of the most basic questions of individual rights and the relationship between the state and the individual. The issue has troubled our society from its very beginnings, flaring into controversy during times of war and subsiding during times of peace.

After the end of World War II, the idea of the draft was widely accepted. For most young men it became as much a part of growing up as graduating from school, finding their first job, and getting married. But a few voices in the intellectual world continued to hammer away at the idea, convinced that it was a fundamental violation of liberty and an ineffective way to man a modern armed force.

During the 1950s and the early 1960s, a number of articles appeared arguing the case for an all-volunteer force. They received little attention, although a few political figures did try to introduce the issue into presidential campaigns. Adlai Stevenson called for the abolition of the draft in 1956 and so did Barry Goldwater in 1964, but the arguments were not comprehensively developed and so their efforts faded away like spent aerial fireworks. But within the intellectual world, the idea of an all-volunteer force was spreading and gaining converts—all across the ideological spectrum from John Kenneth Galbraith to Milton Friedman.

In December 1966, I had dinner with a colleague from the Graduate School of Business at Columbia University. His other guests included a young lawyer who had recently joined Richard Nixon's law firm on Wall Street. As the evening progressed, so did the intensity of the political discussion we were having. Finally, in exasperation he looked at me and said, "With views like that you should be working for Nixon." I didn't think anything more about it, but a few days later I got a telephone call from Leonard Garment, one of Nixon's senior law partners, who invited me to join him and a few other fellows for dinner later that week. I went and gradually became part of a small, informal group—Leonard Garment, Patrick Buchanan, John Sears, and Raymond Price—that was deeply involved in the policy development of Richard Nixon's yet-to-be announced 1968 campaign for the presidency.

In March 1967 at one of our weekly meetings in a tiny room at the law offices of Nixon, Mudge, Rose and Guthrie, someone raised the issue of the military draft. For as long as anyone remembered, Nixon had consistently supported the draft, and since 1952 when he became Eisenhower's running mate, he had loyally supported Eisenhower's idea of establishing a universal military service that would try to ensure that all young males, not just a select few, served some time in the military.

What should Nixon's position be in the upcoming presidential campaign? Stay with universal military service? Propose modifications to the current draft system that was under increasing attack for being unfair? Or perhaps propose a radical new plan of universal national service for everyone?

I was familiar with the debate on the military draft and had just read an article by Milton Friedman that summed up the arguments in favor of ending the draft completely and changing to an all-volunteer system. Friedman was especially concerned about the draft's effect on personal liberty, making the point that

so long as compulsion is retained, inequity, waste, and interference with freedom are inevitable. A lottery would only make the arbitrary element in the present system overt. Universal national service would only compound the evil—regimenting all young men, and perhaps women, to camouflage the regimentation of some.[1]

As I looked around the table, it was clear that no one thought that having Nixon call for universal military training was going to be much of a political plus in 1968. But it was also clear that, unless there was a solid, substantial alternative, he would be forced to stay with his old views.

"I have an idea," I said, thinking about the powerful arguments in Friedman's article. "What if I could show you how we could end the draft and increase our military strength at the same time? Let me put together a paper on this." They were obviously a little skeptical but agreed that I should go ahead. In the next few days I combed my files for material on the draft that I had saved over the years and had spent hours on doing research in the Columbia University library. The result, finished a few weeks later, was a seventeen-page policy memorandum for Nixon that spelled out the essential arguments, pro and con, for ending the draft and setting up an all-volunteer force.

Nixon read it, indicated that he found it "very interesting," and said he wanted to think further about it. Almost no one else in the budding campaign seemed very interested, and the few who were thought it was a bad idea. But Nixon found the idea intriguing and sent the proposal to many of his old friends in the military and in the political world for their comments. For the next six months the comments rolled in, about half highly supportive of ending the draft and the other half, mostly from military officers, just as strongly opposed. Nixon never mentioned the issue, and nothing further happened until one day late in the fall.

On November 17, 1967, Nixon was returning to New York City from Washington on the Eastern Airline shuttle. Besides myself he was accompanied by a young reporter, Robert Semple, from *The New York Times*. At the time, Nixon's chances were perceived to be so dim that covering his campaign did not warrant the attention of one of the *Times'* senior reporters. Semple was new at the paper and had just recently been assigned to cover Nixon. After the plane took off, I switched seats with Semple so he could conduct the interview with Nixon that had been arranged earlier. The interview ranged over a variety of domestic and foreign issues. As it was winding down, Semple suddenly changed the subject. "What would you do about the military draft?" he asked, knowing that Nixon had openly and consistently supported both the draft and universal military service when he was the vice president of the United States.

Nixon smiled and replied evenly, "I think we should eliminate the draft and move to an all-volunteer force." As Nixon continued to elaborate in great detail about his new idea, Semple sat stunned, hurriedly scribbling notes. Nixon had just totally reversed his longstanding position on what could be a critical issue in the next year's campaign, and he was confidently explaining just why he now favored such a move.

It had taken six months, but Nixon apparently had been persuaded by the logic of the argument that it was possible to end the draft, enhance our freedoms, and do so without impairing our national security. From that day on, his policy was to end the draft. As his campaign gathered speed and his primary victories piled up, he elaborated on the idea more and more. His full policy on military manpower was finally laid out in an address to the nation on the CBS national radio network on October 17, 1968, which he concluded by saying, "Just as soon as our reduced manpower requirements in Vietnam will permit us to do so, we should drop the draft and put our Selective Service structure on stand-by."

When Nixon narrowly defeated Hubert Humphrey, who staunchly defended the Vietnam draft throughout the 1968 presidential campaign, the idea of the all-volunteer force had traveled from the intellectual world into the high-powered rhetoric of a presidential campaign and was now a major policy commitment of the newly elected president. Nixon knew that turning that campaign commitment into legislation was going to be extremely difficult. Key members of Congress, virtually the entire hierarchy of military leaders, and many of his own appointees—including his new secretary of defense, Melvin Laird, and his national security adviser, Henry Kissinger—had long supported the draft. The public's support for the idea was growing, but it was still nowhere strong enough to propel the Washington power structure to a change of heart on this issue. Faced with sure defeat if he proposed legislative change, Nixon quickly agreed to establish a presidential commission that would carefully review the whole idea and report directly to him within a year. The President's Commission on All-Volunteer Armed Force was established on March 27, 1969, by executive order.

Just after the election in 1968, I was appointed special assistant to the president, and one of my duties soon became coordinating the establishment of the Commission, compiling a list of candidates from which Nixon could select members, and acting as White House liaison to the Commission. It is possible to predetermine the results of any commission by carefully selecting the members who represent a particular viewpoint. But a stacked commission is usually obvious, and its conclusions and recommendations will be heavily discounted. Nixon was faced with the formidable task of changing the minds of respected military and political leaders and a deeply entrenched bureaucracy, so the credibility of the Commission's report was critical.

To assure credibility, it was decided to appoint Commission members who held independent views and had a reputation for integrity and honesty. The final number of members was fifteen—five of whom, including Milton Friedman and Alan Greenspan, were strongly committed to the idea of an all-volunteer force, five had not thought much about the idea one way or the other, and five members were opposed.

Nixon wanted Thomas Gates, who was secretary of defense when Nixon was vice president, to be the chairman and invited him to the Oval Office to discuss it. After he had explained to Gates what he wanted him to do, Gates reluctantly said,

"But Mr. President, I'm opposed to the whole idea of a volunteer force. You don't want me as the chairman."

"Yes, I do Tom," the president replied, "that's exactly why I want you as the chairman. You have experience and integrity. If you change your mind and think we should end the draft, then I'll know it's a good idea."

Gates was dubious but agreed. Very few have ever been able to say no to any president in the magic aura of the Oval Office.

Over a million dollars was appropriated for the work of the Commission, and with a professional staff of forty-four experts led by the executive director, Dr. William Meckling of the University of Rochester, they went to work. Less than one year later, on February 20, 1970, the Commission submitted its report to the president. Although the members were originally of very different persuasions, the intensive year of effort had wiped out their differences and each of them signed the letter of transmittal, which said in part,

We unanimously believe that the nation's interests will be better served by an all-volunteer force, supported by an effective standby draft, than by a mixed force of volunteers and conscripts; that steps should be taken promptly to move in this direction. . . . We have satisfied ourselves that a volunteer force will not jeopardize national security, and we believe it will have a beneficial effect on the military as well as the rest of our society. . . . The findings and recommendations . . . are unanimously agreed to.[2]

The report was widely distributed to the media and key policymakers in Washington. The Macmillan Company published a hardcover edition, which found its way into every major library in the country, and tens of thousands of copies of a small paperback edition went on sale in bookstores across the country. The report generated a great deal of discussion, articles, and radio and television commentary. As the debate went on, more and more people became convinced that the idea was a good one, and the public's support, as measured by national public opinion polls, rose steadily.

The path of any new idea is rarely straight and true. In this instance, the idea moved rapidly from the intellectual world into the campaign world and then into

Washington, where it would have died for lack of political support had not Nixon wisely deferred any attempt at action while the Commission worked. In effect, by creating the Commission, he sent the idea back into the intellectual world for a rigorous and comprehensive review. When it reemerged, the case was far stronger and more complete, and it had the necessary intellectual momentum to carry itself through the political gauntlet in the Congress.

Legislation incorporating the specific recommendations of the report of the President's Commission on All-Volunteer Armed Force was prepared for submission to Congress. After a long and hard struggle in the Congress, draft induction authority officially ended on July 1, 1973. Almost six years from the time Nixon announced publicly his support of the idea, the draft was dead and the all-volunteer force was the new defense manpower policy of the United States.

In terms of policy change, the establishment of an all-volunteer armed force was, in terms of importance and magnitude and lasting effect, one of the top accomplishments of the Nixon Presidency. In foreign policy, the ending of the military draft perhaps is surpassed on the scale of achievement only by the ending of the Vietnam War and the opening to China. There is nothing to compare with it on the domestic policy side. Before Watergate effectively prevented the Nixon Presidency from achieving most of its blueprint, little had been accomplished of lasting significance in any major area of economic and domestic policy.

Economic policy was shaky, interest rates and inflation were creeping up, unemployment was growing, there had been a disastrous experiment with wage and price controls, and we had abandoned the gold standard. A valiant effort had been made at welfare reform, but the plan Nixon had been persuaded to support by Daniel Patrick Moynihan and others was fatally flawed in concept and was soundly thrashed by the Congress.

The all-volunteer armed force that Richard Nixon established in the 1970s will go down in history as one of the few major accomplishments he managed to achieve before the Watergate scandal engulfed him.

In one of the major ironies of this century, it is also true that President Nixon has now changed his mind on the wisdom of ending the draft, and he has reverted to the earlier position he held when he was vice president under President Eisenhower. In an interview given on July 2, 1986, to C. L. Sulzberger he parted company with one of his most successful policies declaring,

I believe that from the standpoint of the country at this time, clearly apart from what the economics would be, it would be better to have the draft than the volunteer army. . . . At first, like others, I was inclined to support the argument that conscription was involuntary servitude. I backed the concept that military service should be voluntary. And I remember the day after we finished the Paris peace agreements on Vietnam, we got rid of the draft. But in retrospect I would say that today I believe that a draft across the board with no exceptions, except of course for health, would be good for the country, and I think it would be a very positive foreign policy move as well.[3]

Well, so far President Reagan has strongly supported the concept of an all-volunteer armed force in peacetime. Who we select as president in 1988 may well determine whether, in the future, we shall raise our armed force by persuasion or by force.

NOTES

1. Milton Friedman, "Why Not a Volunteer Army," *New Individualist Review* 4, no. 4 (Spring 1967): 3–9.

2. *The Report of the President's Commission on All-Volunteer Armed Force* (New York: Macmillan Co., 1970), Frontmatter.

3. C. L. Sulzberger, *The World and Richard Nixon* (Englewood Cliffs, N.J.: Prentice-Hall, 1987), p. 48.

Discussant: Martin Binkin

When I was asked to be a discussant on this particular panel, I thought it would be a good opportunity to set the record straight on the crucial role that Martin Anderson had played in the decision to abandon conscription. However, he did a good job not only of describing his own role in that process, but also in unveiling some new insights into the personal dynamics surrounding the decision.

I am pleased to be part of this event. Issues related to defense manpower are usually not accorded such prominent billing, but I'm certain that history will record that the Nixon Administration's decision to abolish conscription was one of the most important manpower decisions of our time. I might add that I find it ironic that of the relatively few legacies for which history will treat President Nixon kindly—opening relations with China, ending the Vietnam War, and adopting the all-volunteer force (AVF)—he has been so quick to renounce the volunteer force.

I can better understand President Nixon's reservations about the wisdom of abandoning conscription in the context of the sorry state of the volunteer forces when he first expressed them in *A Real War* in 1980:

I considered the end of the draft in 1973 to be one of the major achievements of my administration. Now seven years later, I have reluctantly concluded that we should reintroduce the draft. The need for the United States to project a strong military posture is now urgent, and the volunteer army has failed to provide enough personnel of the caliber we need for our highly sophisticated armaments. Its burden should be shared equally by all strata of society, with random selection and as few deferments as possible. Even so, it will cause hardships, and whatever its form, the draft is inherently unfair; it can only be justified by necessity. But as we look at the 1980s, necessity stares us in the face: we simply cannot risk being without it. To put off that hard decision could prove penny wise and pound foolish; our reluctance to resume the peacetime draft may make us weak enough to invite war, and then we will find ourselves imposing a wartime draft instead. (P. 201)

But his continued adherence to that position in 1986 (as expressed in C. L. Sulzberger's *The World and Richard Nixon*), even in the face of the dramatic recruitment successes in the early 1980s, indicates how fragile his commitment to the volunteer concept must have been and strongly suggests that his decision was a political expedient.

In any event, the consequences of that decision have been far-reaching. First, there has been a dramatic change in the composition of our military establishment: the volunteer forces consist of a larger proportion of minorities and women than did the conscript army. In contrast with 1971, for example, when 83 percent of all new recruits were white males, by the end of the decade 40 percent of the volunteers were nonwhites or women; today, roughly one of every three recruits is a minority or a female.

Second, by eliminating the "free good" element, the costs of military manpower became more visible under the volunteer system, thereby encouraging a more efficient use of manpower resources.

Third, and from my standpoint, the most worrisome consequence of the end of conscription has been the necessity to constrain the size of the armed forces to meet their limited ability to attract volunteers, and, in so doing, to increase dramatically the dependence on reserve forces. The decision to end the draft was accompanied by the decision to cut the U.S. Army to thirteen divisions and eight hundred thousand active troops instead of the larger force (one million troops and sixteen divisions) envisaged by military planners. The reduction was rationalized in large part by relaxing the assumption about the number of contingencies that the United States should be prepared to confront simultaneously. The two and a half war scenario was replaced by the one and a half war strategy largely on the basis of better relations with China and the Sino-Soviet rift. Moreover, under what was called the total force policy, U.S. reserve forces were assigned a much larger and much earlier role in contingency planning.

This heavy dependence on Reserves was actually a leap into the unknown, since historically reserve mobilizations have been fraught with difficulties and laden with a good deal of political baggage. The track record did not breed optimism about the prospects for the total force approach.

Both Presidents Ford and Carter went along with planning for one major and one minor contingency. President Carter tried, unsuccessfully, to withdraw the single remaining U.S. division from South Korea and to reduce the American involvement there. Even before that ill-starred attempt, successive oil shocks had made the Persian Gulf an area of increasing concern, and James Schlesinger, Jr., while secretary of defense, not only foresaw the need for a more ambitious planning concept, but also set out to restore the size of the active-duty Army to sixteen divisions, but without increasing active Army strength. In the late 1970s Harold Brown continued these endeavors, and by 1980 President Carter had declared the freedom of the Persian Gulf states a matter of vital interest to the United States. The stage was thus set for a return to the planning concept of the mid-1960s. The Reagan Administration distanced itself publicly from this kind of approach to force planning and talked in general terms about preparing for a worldwide war. It seems safe to assume, however, that the Joint Chiefs of Staff and the Army not only continued to do their force planning in relation to specific contingencies, but also recognized that the Persian Gulf and the Caribbean (or, more precisely, Cuba and Nicaragua) had effectively been added to Europe and Korea as theaters in which they might be called on to operate in the event of a major emergency.

Thus, rhetoric and reality appear to be drifting ever more widely apart. Rhetoric underlines the renewed importance of conventional forces, but the Army remains at the bottom of the budgetary totem pole. Rhetoric emphasizes worldwide U.S. interests, worldwide threats, and the possibility of what amounts to World War III. Yet the Army is not capable of conducting the kinds of campaigns implicit in the rhetoric. The Army, with some reposturing, can probably fight a war on the scale of Korea or Vietnam; it is not now in a position to provide the thirty-five to thirty-six divisions needed to deal with contingencies in Europe, the Persian Gulf, Korea, and the Caribbean while also standing guard in Iceland, Alaska, and the Panama Canal. In other words, the nation now has a three-to-four contingency rhetoric and a one-contingency reality. This is not to say that the gap between rhetoric and reality would not exist had conscription not been abandoned.

But it is safe to say that the cap imposed on Army strength by the volunteer concept has played a large role in shaping the contemporary U.S. Army. For those of us who believe that we now possess too thin a hedge against a worst-case threat (as low as its probability might be), the social benefits of the all-volunteer Army may have come at the expense of an overstretched Army.

Discussant: Adam Yarmolinsky

Some of you will remember that great takeoff on English history called *Ten Sixty-Six and All That*, which included among other things King John, who was a bad man but a good thing. Now at least in my book, Richard Nixon clearly was a bad man but in some ways a good thing. Some of the ways have been pointed out by previous speakers.

On military manpower I am inclined to agree with Martin Anderson that Nixon made the right judgment by ending the draft, if only because so limited a lottery as we had to operate after the end of the Vietnam War produced more discomfort and disagreement than it helped. I've always thought that there were a couple of arguments in favor of the draft too little voiced, one of them being that it is always a good idea in any organization to have at least a number of people there who'd rather be someplace else. It helps keep the organization on its toes. The other argument is the utility of the draftee's mother. Somehow volunteers don't have mothers in the same urgent sense that draftees do; and the draftee's mother can be a wonderful influence again in keeping the army and the military generally up to scratch.

Despite those arguments, I think the case for the volunteer forces has proved itself, even if we manage to maintain—perhaps even at some point to increase— the prosperity of the country and lower the unemployment rate further. I think we can make do, but I also believe that Nixon missed a great opportunity, to institute a real national voluntary service system. This system has been described by a number of commentators and has been proposed in legislation, some of which I believe is now still before the Congress. That legislation would create a major organizational effort using private voluntary organizations and the states and local government to mobilize not only military but also civilian volunteers; it would give to military as well as civilian volunteering the character of real voluntary service rather than what Charles Moskos has characterized as mercenary service. I'm not sure that voluntary service in the military now partakes of this character for those who do not make a profession of military service. That opportunity was never as great as it was when the draft ended, and it was the kind of opportunity that the Nixon Presidency was not large minded enough or imaginative enough to undertake.

By the same token, I am in vigorous agreement with Larry Korb that the Nixon years were no decade of neglect. In fact, they contrast sharply with the profligate policies of the Reagan Administration, which I regard as extremely dangerous to our national security. The legacy of the Weinberger era is a military loaded down with incomplete, unnecessary, wasteful, duplicative military systems, now constrained by the necessary and inevitable budget cuts that are not, I'm afraid, going to eliminate some of those unnecessary systems because they are too far down the road. Rather, they will cut the bone and muscle of military readiness and preparedness. We are in real danger of having what a number of commentators have described as a hollow military force. That didn't happen under Richard Nixon and Mel Laird: the combination of pursuing the B-70 and the Stealth Bomber, the C-5 Transport Airplane, and the C-7, and a six-hundred ship navy. It seems to me an absolutely absurd idea that we can build a navy that would be capable of attacking the Soviet land mass. All these expenditures were made without any overriding choice exercised among strategic alternatives.

I am not sure I can agree with Larry Korb that the famous shift from the two and a half war doctrine to the one and a half war doctrine was more than cosmetic, but at least it was a shift in the right direction. We could do with a bit of Nixonian prudence in purchasing and matching forces to strategies. But again I am afraid I also see in the administration and management of national security in the Nixon Administration some very important lost opportunities. We might have avoided MIRVing our strategic missiles. The MIRV, as most of you are probably aware, is a missile that acts like a Roman candle; it goes up, and then a number of warheads split off from the lifting body and go off targeted for different objectives. This was a technological development in which we were ahead of the Russians, which we generally are. Inevitably, they would catch up with us, and as they did, both we and the Soviets found ourselves in a less secure situation. The reason is that, if you have MIRVed your missiles, each missile is a more tempting target because it has so many warheads. The danger of escalation in a nuclear war by accident or miscalculation is thereby significantly increased. At the time SALT I was negotiated, we had an opportunity to agree that we would not develop the MIRVs and the Soviets would not follow suit. We could very easily have verified their compliance because one of the easiest things to verify is the testing of missiles. You can't deploy a new missile with additional warheads without testing it, because you don't know whether or not it will work. Henry Kissinger who I'm afraid has a way of changing his mind to suit his prospects, at one time observed that it was unfortunate we had not taken that step to agree with the Soviets not to deploy MIRVs. Now I believe he thinks differently.

Then, too, we might have stopped the cruise missile in its tracks. The cruise missile presents all kinds of problems of verification. It was clear that once we had developed the cruise missile the Soviets would develop one too. We missed that opportunity, and we missed the opportunity for a comprehensive test ban. I think too few people are aware of the fact that the famous atmospheric test ban treaty that was negotiated and signed back in the 1960s made no difference at all in the military posture on either side because the kind of testing that was performed in the atmosphere can be performed underground just as effectively. The atmospheric test ban treaty protected milk and grain products from pollution by radiation, but it hasn't reduced the danger of nuclear war. We could have had a comprehensive test ban treaty. I believe that it is less difficult for a Republican president to put an arms control agreement through Congress than for a Democratic president, but Nixon didn't do that.

We might have gotten out of Vietnam several years earlier, and many thousands of lost lives might have been saved. But there were more than missed opportunities in the Nixon national security policy that I think we have to remind ourselves of. There were the seeds in the national security policy itself of Watergate and of the Iran/Contra affair that were nurtured in the White House basement offices of the National Security Council staff. John Midgley, the distinguished former chief American correspondent of the *Economist*, has wisely observed that Henry Kissinger was the father of Watergate since he began the practices of wiretapping his own staffers. The plumbers were Ollie North's political and intellectual ancestors, and I am afraid Henry Kissinger anticipated the role of Bill Casey perhaps with a bit more panache. It is tempting to contrast Richard Nixon's prudence with Ronald Reagan's incredible insouciance about his constitutional obligations but we must never lose sight of Richard Nixon's betrayal of his own constitutional obligations. Even King John's signature of the Magna Carta failed to alter history's verdict that King John was not, in the last analysis, a good man.

FOREIGN POLICY DEVELOPMENT

10

The Nixon Doctrine as History and Portent

EARL C. RAVENAL

This paper examines large-scale change in foreign policy. It is a retrospective evaluation of the largest element in the foreign policy of President Richard M. Nixon and his assistant for national security affairs and later secretary of state, Henry M. Kissinger: the shift to a balance-of-power policy. This move represented the end of one era of American foreign policy-making and provided the impetus for the succeeding one—an era in which we still operate, a decade and a half later. In the broadest terms (the level of this inquiry), Nixon and Kissinger moved American foreign policy from rigid bipolar confrontation to the more fluid diplomacy of a multipolar balance of power. And they changed the correlative object of our foreign policy (again in the broadest terms) from a bipolar international system, clustered around opposing alliances, to a multipolar system. (The definitions of both the foreign policy and the objective international system are subject to appropriate qualifications, as we will see below.) In the process, they actually helped to move the international system from its prior state to the new objective state they envisioned.

Although I will have to explicate and defend these assertions, and give some account of my definitional criteria for foreign policies and international systems, my primary purpose is not to describe what Nixon and Kissinger did, or to narrate a sequence of events. Rather, I will try to explain *why* they attempted—and largely, though inchoately, fragilely, and temporarily, succeeded—in doing these things. In this inquiry, then, we have a chance to study the causative and motivational structure and process of large-scale foreign policy change and, more generally, the phenomenon and dynamics of foreign policy choice.

So much ink and blood and acid have been spilled in the fifteen years that have passed since the collective crest of the foreign policy-making of Nixon and Kissinger that we are in need of some revisionism—perhaps even counter-revisionism or post-revisionism—of the style and content of their policy. We need to characterize its achievements as well as evaluate its limitations and failures. I might say at the outset that I regard the main lines of their foreign policy—particularly the changes that they either initiated or facilitated in the orientation of the United States to the international system—as (1) real, not fictional, (2) substantial, not superficial, and (3) major, not trivial or marginal, but (4) transient and (5) ultimately unsatisfactory, or at least insufficient. The last two items of reservation do not, however, cancel the significance of the first three. I both commend and criticize the policy-making of the Nixon-Kissinger Administration, as a modification but also a continuation of the almost half-century-long attitude of containment of the Soviet Union and worldwide communism. This attitude of containment still dominates American foreign policy and national strategy.

The Nixon-Kissinger Administration's shift to a balance-of-power policy can be identified and defined as Phase II of the Nixon Doctrine. Phase I was the Nixon Doctrine more narrowly construed (the 1969 Guam Doctrine). Both of these phases were widely misunderstood in their time. Phase I, the Nixon Doctrine proper, was viewed as a retrenchment of American objectives in the world, whereas it was really a substitution of means—force substitution. Phase II, which was mistaken as shallowly tactical or even symbolic or merely rhetorical, involved nothing less than an attempt to alter the structure of the international system, from bipolar confrontation to multipolar balance of power.

Both the Nixon Doctrine and the balance of power were attempts to implement containment more efficiently and in a way that would not exactly command the support of the American people but, more accurately, would be minimally tolerable and largely unnoticed by it. That may be a requisite, and is certainly one of the aims, of a balance-of-power policy. It may also be one of the reasons why that policy style and orientation cannot endure within the American constitutional system. The latter judgment is supported by the events of the Nixon-Kissinger period, especially by the widespread reaction to Watergate, a scandal which I construe as an attempt by the executive branch of government to do what seemed to be "necessary" from a foreign policy standpoint in spite of the blunt and somewhat obstructive tendencies of the legislative branch, the press, and the public. In this respect, Watergate *is* a precursor of the extracurricular diplomacy of the second term of the Reagan Administration. The twin nemeses of this manipulative, secretive diplomacy of oblique but still militant and global confrontation with communism are, then, obstacles in the international system (such as military parity with the Soviet Union and resistance in the Third World) and constitutional tension at home. Much of the importance, as well as the interest, of the Nixon-Kissinger foreign policy attaches to this effort of grand architecture. It is rare for an American administration and rare for a nation in the world or in history. What it means for a nation to take the state of the international system as an object of its foreign policy-making deserves more theoretical comment. Such an effort constitutes large-scale foreign policy choice.

On another theoretical plane, the question of motive arises: Why did Nixon and Kissinger attempt to move the United States, and the international system, to a balance of power? For the Nixon-Kissinger Administration was distinguished, or marked, by two aspects: the notable shift in foreign policy and an impression of pathology in its political conduct. The syndrome includes Watergate, the extreme secrecy and deception in government, the covert employment of the National Security Council, the extensive use of quasiprivate diplomacy, the "lone ranger" approach, the autocratic administration, the attempt to circumvent domestic constraints, and indeed the subversion of the American constitutional system. In view of the general bent of our time toward psychohistorical explanations (Nixon and Kissinger have been subjected to rather frequent, not always careful, exercises in psychodynamics), we are drawn to a more fundamental theoretical critique of psychological determinants of policy behavior and policy outcomes. This is the issue of personality and politics, the interaction of psychodynamic and situational factors, the question of logic or "psycho-logic."

I maintain that it is the *logic* of policy, rather than the psycho-logic, that induced Nixon and Kissinger to shift, within the overall framework of containment, to a kind of multipolar balance-of-power policy. This shift was designed to extend the thrust of the more limited Phase I of the Nixon Doctrine and to mitigate the disabilities of implementing containment through bipolar confrontation with the Soviet Union and its regional proxies. By the same token, however perceptive Nixon's and Kissinger's evaluation of the situation they inherited and however intelligent their adaptation, the balance of power is itself a transient solution to a moving and unfavorable set of parameters, both international and domestic. The balance of power has disabilities, and it will likely give way to a further adjustment in the attempt by the United States to deal with an even more fragmented world in the future.

In evaluating the impact of personality variables on foreign policy choices and outcomes, it is well to recognize three enabling factors, which allow us even to entertain the question of the influence of psychodynamics on policy-making and policy outcomes. The administration of Nixon and Kissinger was a period of the supremacy of executive power (followed, of course, by its startling failure and curtailment). Therefore, it was an occasion in which the causative effect of personality factors of the key individual policy-makers could have been transmitted more directly into policy initiatives (or at least not considerably impaired or diluted). This period also happened to be one when the United States was (as it still is, to a large, but somewhat diminished, extent) an essential actor in the international system. And it was a time when the "shape" of the international system itself was in flux; that is, it was a "turning point," an occasion on which the United States could be influential in fixing the direction and configuration of the next period.

Not all historical junctures, and not all nations, provide these opportunities for the transmission of personality factors directly from individual psychological formation (to whatever extent we can discern that such nonrational factors, rather than rational choice, were operative) all the way to profound transformation of the structure of the international system. That is because, when we address the phenomenon of systemic change and fundamental foreign policy reorientation, we are dealing not just with variables, even with "policy variables," but with parameters. Most often, and to most nations, the international system presents a framework *within* which each nation must choose. That is to say that the international system is parametric. To *some* extent its characteristics are alterable by a few individual nations, more or less according to their power. The United States has had, and will continue to have, preeminent ability to set and modify those parameters through its own choices and acts. But to do so requires a further expense or effort. This effort is, at most times, arguably less efficient than a policy of operating within the parameters. That is, the system can be altered, and the parameters widened, but only with "meta"-methods, and at corresponding "meta"-cost. Such alteration amounts to fighting the system or, more grandly, reversing entropy, and such endeavors are always heroic.

Yet there are rare junctures, nations, and leaderships insightful and bold enough to recognize and seize opportunity, where an individual nation can feasibly hold the shape of the international system as an object of its own foreign policy. Such an occasion was the era of Nixon and Kissinger, from 1969 to 1974. Besides sufficient power—that is, essentiality within the international system—there was a favorable cost-benefit ratio attached to changing the system, as opposed to simply living with bipolarity and its burdens. In addition, the system was evolving in the favored direction anyway (that is, toward a multipolar balance of power, and a dissolution of alliances and blocs); and there were potential "collaborators"—other emergent powers, having a parallel interest in such systemic change (such as China). But these are the exceptions that demonstrate the point: It is usually better to work with the "grain" of the evolving international system; and it is always good to recognize the situation one is in.

When a nation, such as the United States, is beset by such problems as the Vietnam War and the overarching responsibilities of bipolar confrontation with the Soviet Union, it may seem more efficient to alter the parameters of the system than simply to accommodate to the system. And when, in addition, an individual nation has the capacity to change the structure of the system, such a policy may become both attractive and feasible. That describes the opportunity that, at least putatively, presented itself to the Nixon-Kissinger Administration, an opportunity that Nixon and Kissinger had the insight to recognize and the intellectual grasp and administrative authority (as least momentarily) to seize. This also describes the importance of this case and its more general relevance to the enterprise of foreign policy-making.

But the rarity and the transience of such personal and situational factors will also account for the failure, by successive American administrations—seduced, perhaps, by the glittering example of Nixon and Kissinger—to accomplish similar diplomatic feats, and, more generally, the evanescence and ultimate futility of balance-of-power politics in the context of the American constitutional system and political process.

Several other questions should emerge along the way. One is the matter of foreign policy "style"—or, more generally, political or administrative style. Style is not to be taken as a superficial and entirely psychological, or even symbolic, matter, something that can be invented by an individual or group, and mixed and matched in infinite and arbitrary gradations and variations. Quite the contrary, style is almost substantive; it must emerge in response to situation and to the range and structure of available choice. At any juncture there is not an infinite variety of subtle gradations, but rather a limited and stark choice of modes of conduct. The American people has traditionally imposed on its leaders a task that embodies a contradiction, like the biblical one that Pharaoh handed to the Israelites: to make bricks without straw. It wants a "successful" foreign policy, but it wants legality and constitutionality. Indeed, it has constructed this constraint in the tangible form of checks and balances and the separation of powers. What emerges is a "constitutional tension." An American administration—as long as it operates in the active, internationalist mode, and when it is faced with foreign policy challenges,—is typically drawn to extralegal, counterconstitutional executive behavior, and is tempted to use secretive, deceptive, and "private" diplomacy. This conduct has characterized administrations conceded by historical consensus to have been "good"—such as Franklin Roosevelt's on the eve of the United States' formal entry into World War II—as well as those imputed to be "bad"—that is, Richard Nixon's, and now Ronald Reagan's in the throes of the Iran/Contra affair.

What is at stake here is not mere criminality, but the larger antithesis of the American constitutional system and the ideal of government *under* law, on the one hand, and the "effectiveness" of foreign policy (that is, the relatively unfettered ability of the executive) *above* the law, to carry out a mandated foreign policy, on the other. Henry Kissinger himself, particularly since January 1977, has frequently, even obsessively alluded to this theme. It is more than the trivial matter of some figures in an administration getting caught in some technically illegal abuse of power, an infraction of some congressional restriction. It is a question that underlies any valid contemporary assessment of America's ability to continue to perform the four-decade-old mission of the containment of Soviet power in the world. Therefore, some abiding questions arise, from the record of the Nixon-Kissinger foreign policy-making and its less fortunate sequels, with regard to the entire American enterprise of containment.

For four decades, containment of Soviet expansion and international communism has been the main game in town. A succession of foreign policies and national strategies has been devised to implement containment. Containment can be seen as motivated by either strategic concerns or political values (or, of course, both, in some measure). Nixon and Kissinger saw containment as a strategic game. I think they were correct in their assessment of the strategic primacy of foreign policy activity. But what is conceived as strategic can fairly be judged strategically—that is, by macro-strategic criteria, a cold judgment of feasibility in the unfolding future, tasks against means, purposes against support.

At the advent of their administration, Nixon and Kissinger realized the peculiar burdens placed on the United States by the bipolar structure of the international system. They sought to change U.S. foreign policy and national strategy in order to ease those burdens and tilt the odds of containment toward success: initially, through the first-phase Nixon Doctrine of force substitution; then, as the limitations and disabilities of the Nixon Doctrine in its more restricted meaning were experienced, through the move to a broader balance-of-power policy.

I believe that the international system will evolve beyond the manageable configuration of a multiple but limited number of "controllable" and relatively "responsible" nations, to a more diffuse configuration of, say, a dozen-and-a-half autonomous national centers of political-military initiative, including some "regional hegemones" that dominate or at least aspire to dominate their regions. Concomitantly, I believe that the American system will become even less receptive to and supportive of international exercises by the United States, particularly against increasingly unfavorable odds of success or of enduring success at tolerable levels of cost and sacrifice.

Therefore, the prognosis for containment is dim. In this regard, the Nixon-Kissinger regime is a portent as well as a historical prodigy. It was exemplary because it fielded a conscious attempt, on a large scale, to carry out a foreign policy adjustment, to reconcile continued containment with the manifest constraints, foreign and domestic, on that exercise. It exhibited perhaps the most intelligent (though unconstitutional, technically illegal, and even, in some aspects, criminal) attempt to deal with the constraints that it clearly discerned. Therefore, the question of what the Nixon-Kissinger Administration was trying to accomplish, and why, is of enduring importance. After the ensuing mixed performance of the Carter Administration and the attempted "Reagan restoration" of American power and influence, we are faced again with strains on fiscal solvency and evidence of the intractability of international political-military problems.

We must remember that foreign policy adjustment is an extraordinarily difficult move. It is not simply "decreed" by the White House, least of all on the basis of some formal verbal study. It is (1) forced by circumstances, (2) grudging, (3) done on balance, that is, according to the costs and risks versus the advantages, and (4) accomplished within a country's situation and (5) in response to domestic pressures. These pressures are usually indirect and are often responses to "second-order" effects—that is, not even to the immediate costs and risks, but rather to fiscal and economic effects such as taxes and inflation. In this operational sense, there is *already* a considerable "objective" constituency for going beyond containment to a stance of nonintervention and strategic disengagement (what some prematurely saw as the early portent of the Nixon Doctrine). This move probably must be made, and will be made, over time, in order to accommodate to America's situation in the world. This is what, in the abstract Nixon and Kissinger attempted to do.

The large aggregate choices now are either endless conflict management, appropriate to the role of an active superpower, with the accompanying costs, or a transcendence of containment. This is not to say that the alternative of strategic disengagement and nonintervention amounts precisely to absolute national passivity. Rather, it is to say that a nation *can* act, though it must always act *within its situation*; and it can act *upon* its situation, though it must act in ways *appropriate* to its situation. Whatever the substantive divergences between this alternative prescription and the policy of the Nixon-Kissinger Administration, and whatever the unfolding differences of situation and circumstance, that is the enduring formal lesson of the diplomacy of Richard Nixon and Henry Kissinger.

A METHODOLOGICAL NOTE

In attempting to construct an explanatory scheme for macro-political choice and for determining our orientation to the international system, we come upon an old debate: the question of the relative influence of situational and psychological determinants on political behavior and in turn on political outcomes— the question of "logic or psycho-logic?" The literature is by now so voluminous that it would be tedious to cite it here.[1]

Can anything new be said about this topic? The debate about situation and personality reminds one of the children's game where the paper covers the rock, and the rock smashes the scissors, but the scissors cuts the paper. Everyone now understands that situation and personality operate on each other in determining political actions and outcomes. Everyone on "both sides" of the question now understands that politics in some fashion is a result or reflection or summation of human conduct, that political decisions are made by human beings and their institutions. No one contests the presence of psychological motives or determinants of one kind or another, whether normal or pathological—values, predilections, hangups, perceptions, and misperceptions. And no one challenges the fact that patterns of political action and political structures, including foreign policies and, by extension, the shape of the international system, must be accounted for in a multicausal scheme.

Particularly if we want to understand large-scale foreign policy moves, situational and psychological factors must be sorted out more precisely. The nature of their complementarity has to be made clearer, and they have to be integrated into a more comprehensive framework. We need not just more ramified and multivariate explanatory schemes, more lists of factors, more "panels" in taxonomies of causes, but also better models of the policy process and more articulate representations of the structure of choice on which the decisional system operates, whether that decisional system is conceived as a competent individual, an elite group, an organization, or a nation. After the ravages of nonrational explanations of national behavior—not only irrational models such as the psychological ones, but subrational or suboptimizing models such as the organizational (incremental or satisficing) and the bureaucratic—there is a need for more complex, comprehensive, and sophisticated, but still rational, explanations.

Moreover, we need models that explain foreign policy change and adaptation. Most of the research in personality and politics, especially in the area of typologies, has been devoted to discovering regularities, or patterns of political structures and action that derive from and can be explained by the personality configurations of leaders (or groups, in the case of "national character" studies).

The kind of model we need is one that will account not for accidental or casual change, but for "necessary" change; and not for marginal, incremental change, but for the large-scale reorientation of a nation to the international system. The corresponding questions are: Why does a leadership group desire a certain kind of international system? What functions will such a transformed international system perform to solve the problems of that leadership? In contrast, psychological studies ask: What is it about that elite group that gravitates toward that kind of system rather than its alternatives? We can see that the way the question is put predisposes the kind of answer: whether situational or psychological; whether a foreign policy object is seen as a telos or magnet and a reason for action, or a compulsion and a source of the motivation to action.

The framework of explanation that must evolve should meet two requirements. The first is that it should correspond more closely and morphologically to the actual activity of policy-making that is recognized by those who have participated in decision making in government or other complex collectives. The explanatory scheme should correspond in its descriptions of both the structure and the process of policy choice. The structure of choice refers to the array of available distinct alternatives and what they entail (their consequences, their costs in all dimensions of "cost"). The policy process incorporates a complex objective function, or set of goals that is to be optimized or maximized, and a list of constraints of all kinds. As a system encounters obstacles to its thrust toward a complex of goals, it will experience "feedback." Thus, it will be faced with a further set of alternatives that deal with widening the critical constraints, in order to improve the prospects for the overall satisfaction of its objectives. This framework of structure and process is one in which we can include and reconcile rational strategic factors and nonrational psychological factors.

A second requirement is that the explanatory framework should be useful in the enterprise of "policy science." It should give decision makers, at least in principle, a better idea of what must be changed and what can be changed, in order to bring about a more constructive foreign policy. It should indicate the "wiring diagram," and where the "levers" and "buttons" are: the active, working elements and the inert elements; the constraints or parameters, including the critical ones and the intractable ones; and the variables, including "policy variables."

As we develop this interest in more structured, comprehensive, and policy-relevant models, we have to focus on the question, not of the relative strength of psychological factors, but where they "cut in"—the various places in a more comprehensive framework where psychological determinants operate. This kind of inquiry will actually sharpen the significance of psychological factors, while delimiting their function.

That is one of the theoretical, or methodological, tasks that this paper projects. The other, more practical task is to explore a concrete case—the move of Nixon and Kissinger to a balance-of-power policy—that might throw light on the operation of situational and psychological factors. The fact that this shift was engineered and sponsored by two individuals who have become extraordinary objects of psychological—particularly psychodynamic or ego-defense-oriented—explanation, including their attitudes toward power, gives particular point to this discussion.

What does it mean for a nation to make a large-scale foreign policy choice or change, to "choose" an international system? Two complementary propositions suggest themselves. First, an international system is not transformed into another without the intervening variables of each nation's policy-making network or decision-making core. Second, systemic change is accomplished in and through the actions of individual, autonomous centers of national decision. It is in both of these ways that the international system determines the conduct of each nation's foreign policy, and reciprocally each nation seeks to determine the international system by influencing the acts of other states. Individual national choices (the foreign policies of nations) are the efficient causes of systemic change and the immediate objects of the foreign policies of other nations. Thus, there is a two-way relationship between foreign policy and the international system, which can be expressed this way: The international system is both object and determinant of the foreign policy of a nation.

The concept of choice is appropriate here for another reason: It is not inevitable or completely determined that a state take a certain unique course. No matter how strait or compelling its situation, and no matter how psychologically compelled its leaders or ruling groups, if more than one alternative can be brought about or refused, then a situation of choice exists. Of course, however, choice exists (1) within a constrained objective "menu" of external availability and (2) within a constrained internal system of influences and inhibitions on the policy process itself.

But nations do not "choose" international systems (or, for that matter, diplomatic or internal administrative styles) in a single act of unrestricted, direct decision. Rather, nations—certain essential, sufficiently powerful, and influential members of an international system—bring about transformations in the system by responding in certain ways to constraints. Just as a nation's orientation toward a certain type of international system, as object, is not free and unbounded (either externally or domestically), neither should this basic foreign policy "choice" be considered as direct and decisive. Rather, a nation proceeds "from here to there" in a kind of staged dialectic. A typical sequence would be the recognition of a gap between existing objectives and constrained resources and support; a substitution of particular means and resources designed to alleviate or avoid the constraints (the Nixon Doctrine); obstruction and denial (external and constitutional) of the newly required latitude and specific resources; a new attempt to adjust the external environment (balance-of-power diplomacy) and the internal ambience (evasive or repressive administrative style, even the extremity of "Watergate"), possibly bringing about a real, though temporary, transformation of the international system; further reaction, foreign and domestic, to the new diplomacy and the constitutional alteration; and frustration of the new international and domestic balances.

A BALANCE-OF-POWER APPROACH

The Nixon-Kissinger regime combined a secretive style of foreign policy-making with an expansive display of philosophical rationale. We are left with some interesting questions. For example, how can we characterize the Nixon-Kissinger foreign policy? Was it—and in what respects was it—a balance-of-power policy, as a foreign policy stance, and as an orientation to an objective international system? Why did that administration move to the series of dramatic and profoundly influential foreign policy measures? In other words, why did it attempt to change the international system through the foreign policy of our own nation?

The Nixon-Kissinger Administration's behavior and objectives for the international system were widely characterized, in a kind of shorthand, as a balance of power. This characterization proceeded, on the one hand, from the popular discovery of Henry Kissinger's works of scholarship and political commentary.[2] On the other hand, it proceeded from a few much-quoted scriptural utterances of Richard Nixon. In particular, there was the "five power" speech in Kansas City on July 6, 1971.[3] In this speech Nixon was frank, if premature, about the advent of five great concentrations of economic power, hinting at their evolution to political and even military significance. There was also the "even balance" interview in *Time* magazine, January 3, 1972, in which Nixon said: "I think it will be a safer world and a better world if we have a strong, healthy United States, Europe, Soviet Union, China, Japan, each balancing the other, not playing one against the other, an even balance."[4]

Despite these indications and the insistent use of such code-words as "structure" and "stability," admissions of a "balance-of-power policy" were studiously rare.[5] In any case, an administration's foreign policy is not described, let alone explained, by glossing scripture, but by discerning the thrust of its actions, at most in the light of those convincing statements of purpose that are associated with critical actions. The real point is that the United States moved toward a balance-of-power policy, not because of the Nixon-Kissinger Administration's assertions or suggestions or despite its denials or qualifications, but because its *operational propensities* shifted to this kind of system—as a recognized setting, an item of objective choice, and a set of rules that influence the process of foreign policy-making. From these indications, to what extent is it fair to call this a balance-of-power *policy*, with the object of creating and maintaining a balance-of-power *system*? What are the features of a balance-of-power system?[6] What are the features of the Nixon-Kissinger Administration's diplomacy? And how well do they match?

It might be useful to focus briefly on a way of conceptually defining the balance of power. First, we can generate, succinctly, four referents of the balance of power by analyzing and arraying two "dimensions" of the concept. The balance of power can be either (1) prescriptive or (2) descriptive, and can apply to either the international system or the foreign policy of nations. With these two dimensions, the concept can have four basic referents: an ideal equilibrium or an actual distribution of power; norms or "rules" of foreign policy or the actual motives and conduct of nations. Another way of approaching a conceptual definition of the balance of power, as an international system, is to lay out the criteria of international systems in general and to qualify the balance of power according to those criteria.

International systems can be identified, defined, and differentiated in terms of three kinds of operational elements: the configuration or distribution of power; the mechanisms or institutions for regulating or controlling power; and the behavioral "rules" that are internalized by each essential member of the system and reflected or exemplified in its foreign policy.

In these terms, a multipolar balance-of-power system represents an equilibrium among important independent nations, which act competitively in pursuit of national goals, but impartially—in an implicit sense—in support of the structural stability of the system as a whole. This system implies a high degree of coalition activity, either formal alliance or tacit alignment, but in either case flexible and shifting. (As Henry Kissinger has observed, however, alliance flexibility is inhibited or depreciated, in the contemporary context, by nuclear weapons, residual ideological attachments, and the existence of a thirty-year-old historical axis of primary confrontation.) The powers might ally to promote national ambitions, but also to counter the ambitions of other powers or coalitions that threaten to destabilize the overall system.

The balance of power is the limiting case of an international "system," in that restraints on the exercise of power are barely institutionalized, and then only by the distribution of power itself, and by the propensity of the essential actors to exercise their power against others who threaten the equilibrium of the system. This is both the beauty and the ultimate vacuity of the balance-of-power system. In one sense, "the hidden hand" is a perfect mechanism, because its equilibrating effect for the system is built into the incentives for the conduct of each individual member of the system. In a further sense, however, the diplomatic style appropriate to a balance-of-power system militates against concrete institutionalization.

Some theorists posit the existence of at least five essential powers as a condition for the existence and operation of a balance-of-power system.[7] Many observers of the Nixon-Kissinger diplomacy, from several items of evidence, inferred the specific propensity of that administration to create a pentagonal or five-power world.[8] In the galaxy of the Nixon-Kissinger (and the Ford-Kissinger) diplomacy, and in the accompanying state of the international system,[9] there were traces of several types of systems: There was still the central strategic axis of a *bipolar confrontation*, where the only nations, even among the nuclear powers, capable of destroying each other and the world, were the United States and the Soviet Union. And to the extent that nuclear protection constitutes the fulcrum of alliance systems, there was still roughly a bipolar configuration (with China, of course, on the periphery in such a description). Moreover, the framework of alliance institutions still existed. Elements of ideological, as well as strategic, "zero-sumness," were still apparent in the differential attitude of the major powers—certainly the United States—toward coups, revolutions, and invasions conducted by Communist, as distinguished from non-Communist, factions.

There were also evidences, accentuated by the present real or apparent détente, of *condominium*: the virtual concession of separate spheres in core areas; the evolution of rules of engagement (however imperfectly observed) in peripheral areas; the summit agreements, negotiated without the close collaboration of allies; the June 1973 agreement between Brezhnev and Nixon to inhibit nuclear crises. Indeed, President Nixon envisioned "an international system resting on the stability of relations between the superpowers."[10]

But the central tendencies were those of a *balance-of-power* system—more the dynamic Bismarckian than the supposedly "static" Metternichian.[11] The specific features of détente themselves helped to bring this about, in two rein-forcing ways. First, détente exacerbated intra-alliance frictions and promoted a scramble for diplomatic access, trade, and political accommodation. Second, it encouraged direct contact between the major adversaries, independently of the operation of alliance structures. (It also reduced the perceptions of common threat that create cohesion in alliances.)

The Nixon-Kissinger vision of the future, or objective, international system included the desire to bring about or codify a controlled pluralism in the inter-national system: (1) to establish "rules of engagement" among the principal actors, particularly adversaries; (2) to include a limited number of essential participants—the number arising not from some abstract geometry, but from the recognition of the power of certain entities and the treatment of others *as if* they were politically unified (Europe) and strategically weighty (Japan);[12] and (3) to exclude limited regional actors (such as India, despite its increasingly hegemonic role in its region), giving even shorter shrift to the rest of the Third, or developing, World.[13]

The Nixon-Kissinger policy also perpetuated a commitment to the formal integrity of our alliances. But the functions of alliances changed. As Nixon put it: "Our alliances are no longer addressed primarily to the containment of the Soviet Union and China behind an American shield. They are, instead, addressed to the creation with those powers of a stable world peace."[14] Increasingly, alliances were seen simply as relatively fixed points in a more multilateral frame-work—points where our common understanding, with our allies, of the rules of the system was further advanced, and where the behavior of our allies was more reliably benign. To this extent, our alliances were still seen as items of strength rather than as net liabilities.

Nevertheless, there was the perception that the friendly centers of power, Europe and Japan, were becoming increasingly independent, in the precise sense that is relevant to the structure of a multipolar balance of power. Their future orientation in crises would be less automatically determinable either from their ideological or historical antecedents.

Two tendencies could be discerned in all this, which equated roughly to a balance-of-power perspective and a balance-of-power world. The first was the stress on "*structure*" and its achievement and preservation through cultivating a certain behavior of the principal actual and potential participants, and giving them a stake in the system. In a balance-of-power system, only the large, capable nations "count" because only they can have enough of a stake in the system and enough resources to maintain the system, by exercising self-restraint and by restraining the exaggerated conduct of other nations.

The second tendency was the propensity to deal flexibly and directly with the major adversaries. This constituted a policy of *maneuver*, an attempt to create a more subtle and dynamic balance, rather than dealing through formal alliances, with the burden of attaining consensus, the risk of leaks or subversion by allies, the sufferance of vetoes by inferior and otherwise ineffectual powers, and the incurring of debts in return for support. It also constituted dealing in partial alignments, such as America's tacit—though, I suspect, not entirely adequate—reinsurance of China's northern border against the USSR.

In a literal sense, the classic mechanism of shifting alliances does not commend itself to modern powers in a nuclear age. Thus, we kept the institutional shell and the psychological facade of our alliances. But a certain distance was put between the United States and its principal allies. Exemplifying this distance were the first "Nixon shock" to Japan, caused by the unilateral, secretive, and sudden American approach to China; the tension between the demand for burden redistribution and the insistence on continued American control;[15] and the qual-ifications of U.S. support, making it less automatic in crises. This was the fruit of the Nixon Doctrine, which promised only air and naval and logistical support, not ground combat forces, over a wide range of contingencies, and a nuclear shield. Even the reliability of the nuclear shield was put somewhat in doubt by talk (no longer officially discouraged) of the devolution of nuclear capability to allies.

The two tendencies, structure (great power politics) and maneuver (flexible diplomacy), can be summed up in a single proposition: The Nixon-Kissinger Administration deliberately moved to rationalize relations with its two major adversaries, with the foreseen—perhaps even desired—consequence of unset-tling relations with allies, and inspiring them to make further moves that would increase their independence and their distance from the United States. This at once attenuated their need for our support and their claim on our support.

These features of the Nixon-Kissinger diplomacy, though not the "classic" formula, nevertheless describe a balance-of-power policy in objects and style. And it was a policy by deliberation, not by default or accident.

THE CULT OF PERSONALITY

To explain the Nixon-Kissinger Administration's move to a balance-of-power policy, we can consider two avenues of approach. One (which we will treat later) is a complex situational dialectic. The other is psychological determination, or the influence of personality. This approach emphasizes personal, subjective motives and drives, rather than situational, objective constraints. Often positing some pathology, it discounts rationality and the calculus of costs and benefits. It centers on a kind of causal determinism, and sometimes causal simplicity, rather than on the structured choice that matches the logic of each decision, or the explanatory richness that matches the complexity of the decisional process. In some of its cruder and less conscious applications, psychological analysis encourages the notion of unbounded volition or blind compulsion, rather than deliberation and calculation within perceived and actual limits. At times, it has degenerated into popular psychologizing about individual statesmen and their personal motives, particularly the compulsions that operate on them, usually arising from their antecedents and life-precedents.

I do not think it is worthwhile here to cite at great length the various psychological treatments of Nixon and Kissinger. It might be enough to suggest, in several quotations, the nature of the observations. Their range includes the journalistic, scholarly, and clinical; ad hoc studies and those based on general theories of personality dynamics and development.

A prime example of a psychological explanation of Nixon's behavior, particularly his crisis behavior, is Bruce Mazlish's work, *In Search of Nixon: A Psychohistorical Inquiry*.[16] Mazlish considers Nixon's behavior completely comprehensible, having its own inner rationality, "consistent and stable." Nixon has a tendency to overreact, overreach; a penchant to portray himself as "the injured party" (as in the "Checkers" speech and many sequels). The syndrome also incorporates "day-dreaming . . . dependency wishes . . . and isolation." Mazlish attempts to establish three significant mechanisms, grounded in character: acting and role-playing, ambivalence, and, most important, the use of "mammoth denial as a defense against unacceptable impulses and feelings." Mazlish's analysis (published in 1972) seemed to fit the crisis behavior of Nixon's first term, and it foreshadowed Nixon's reactions to Watergate and the revelation of the secret bombing of Cambodia. It suggested Nixon's probable responses to accusations and threats, both personal and national. But it is less useful in explaining his more diffuse orientations to patterns of world order, or the long-range manipulation of the power resources of the state to cultivate China and negotiate with the Soviet Union.

Psychological probes of the personality of Henry Kissinger have sprung from diverse motives and origins and have appeared on several levels of seriousness and complexity. He has been "Superkraut," "Metternich," "the lone ranger," and an "acrobat," as well as his own celebrated persona, the "cowboy leading the caravan [sic]"—the [sic] being the analytic contribution of George Ball.[17] In fact, more attempts have been made to account for Kissinger's style than for the objects of his policies.[18]

The gist of the psychological analysis of Kissinger is contained in the article by Dana Ward, "Kissinger: A Psychohistory."[19] According to Ward, Kissinger is an example of the "depressive or dysmutual personality." His penchant for secrecy, for isolated personal decisions, for repressing the bureaucracy, for bullying subordinates and deceiving Congress, for manipulating other nations, and for asserting American power in "test" situations—all arise from childhood and youthful experience and formative influences. Again, the Cambodian invasion, the mining of Haiphong, the coercive peace negotiations, and the Christmas bombing of Hanoi (and, presumably, the later case of the October 25 nuclear alert in the Middle East) would proceed from certain "basic tensions in Kissinger's psyche," particularly "a tension between the avoidance of, and compulsive confrontation with, risks." This tension in turn stems from an "undervalued sense of self which gives rise to depression, timidness, and lack of confidence."

Ward does confront the payoff question: "the process by which personal motives are transformed into political action" (as distinct from the antecedent question: "why a certain principle is believed or valued"). Thus, he notes that Kissinger's "inability to empathize with others, his compulsion to face risk in order to prove his worth, and his tendency to act alone have in fact become significant components of American public policy." This comes closer to the essence of Kissinger's conduct and stewardship of American foreign policy, since Ward draws extensively not only from clues of Kissinger's formative years, but also from his early work, A World Restored. This self-conscious and admiring study of the conservative diplomacy of Metternich and Castlereagh elaborates "the principle of balance and the role diplomacy plays in the control of this balance." It is important to see how Kissinger himself has read the lessons of history and has applied them to large decisions and directions, in which he was in a position to be instrumental.

Much of Ward's article reflects the state of play of the debate on Vietnam at the time of its writing (before and during the winter of 1974–75). Ward is insightful about Kissinger's mode of peacemaking in the face of North Vietnamese resistance. He notes Kissinger's need to use "tacit bargaining" and to leave the major issues "formally unresolved," in an exercise of conscious "ambiguity." And he draws attention to the demonstrative character of many of Kissinger's foreign policy moves—they were designed "not simply to do something, but also to *prove* something." These observations are closer to the concept and practice of the balance of power. The trouble is that Ward considers it obvious that these tactics were strategically gratuitous. By implication, they are all the more intimately derived from kinky psychological motives: "Had an administration been in office that did not view Vietnam as a test and which did not feel the need to demonstrate strength and face risks, there is a great probability that the war would not have lasted an additional four years." But it is well to reflect that all prior administrations viewed Vietnam as a test; it was never considered an intrinsic strategic interest. They could have come to this conclusion—whether right or wrong—on purely cognitive grounds, having to do with the "dominoes" or some other essentially intellectual image of strategic necessity (or, for that matter, from a number of other psychological biases and formations).[20]

So we see that psychological explanations of Nixon and Kissinger might not provide a sufficient explanation for the policies of the Nixon-Kissinger Administration. For a more comprehensive answer, we must look to the objective structure of choice and the objective features of the policy process.[21]

Ultimately, foreign policy-makers are limited by inescapable situational alternatives and are influenced by the bias that is built into the policy process. In any case, the policy process is collective, systemic, and complex, rather than individual, private, and simple, and is not "affective" in any ordinary sense.[22]

The question of the operation of psychological factors is now transformed into another series of questions: How do personality factors operate in the structure and process of choice? In other words, "where" do these factors "cut into" the structure or the process? Is it more correct to say that there is choice, rather than compulsion? And how can we construct a comprehensive framework that reconciles and integrates situational and psychological interpretations?

The answer to these questions would start with the elaboration of an overall approach to the structure and process of policy. I take *structure* to include the following considerations: the alternatives that are objectively available; the consequences of each alternative course; the possibility of contradiction within any of the alternatives that might be chosen; the inability to "choose" several courses at once, or to mix elements of several, if they are contradictory or if elements would lead to divergent courses of action in situations where they are tested by events.

The policy *process* is conceptually distinct from the structure of choice. A model of the policy process presents a complex objective function of the total system, which the system tends to optimize or maximize, and a series of constraints of various kinds. Such a model integrates environmental and actor elements. It can indicate whether a certain state of affairs that is "desired" by a system as part of its "objective function" is attainable within the multiple constraints (limits or costs) that must be observed by the system.

We can put structure and process together and try to discern the way psychological determinants enter this combined representation of the policy function. In an ultimate sense, what determines the output (the decision or action) of the system is the inability of individuals, elites, or the total decision-making system to choose a certain course, because they could not "live with" certain contingent outcomes or they could not stand certain entailed costs or side-effects. Thus, it is not so useful to explain directly, in terms of psychological causation, why certain decision makers wanted certain things, for their own sake. It is more useful to ascertain, more indirectly, why they could not live with certain contingent outcomes, and why they postulated certain constraints or took certain existent constraints seriously.

One virtue of the process model I propose is that it can preserve the overall framework of rational decision making, while admitting the operation of nonrational factors—whether institutional or personal, social or psychological. It does so by expressing them as constraints. This kind of model is able to combine nonrational constraints in a single calculus, alongside rational or semirational constraints, without confusing their disparate natures. In sum, what we see from this account of policy formation is that actors have attitudes and reactions, not simply toward alternative goals, but toward all aspects of the complex structure of the choices that are before them. Thus, invoking psychological factors does not allow us to avoid the analysis of the structure and process of policy choice.

RATIONALITY

We can now return to the assertion I made earlier in more cursory and dogmatic terms: that Nixon and Kissinger behaved rationally in their general strategic conduct, particularly in those moves that resulted in the shift to a balance-of-power policy. In short, they were responding to some very real objective constraints, while attempting to salvage as much of the "value" of our global status as they could within those constraints. (It should go without saying that one can affirm this judgment and still have fundamental substantive objection to the policies themselves.) In this view, even the complex of domestic moves encompassed in Watergate was a rational response among only a few available alternatives—no less rational, even though it was illegal and unconstitutional.

The gravitation to a balance-of-power policy can also be seen as a rational move, among alternatives, to obviate contradictions that remained even after the adoption of the Nixon Doctrine in its earlier, more limited, phase. It was a move to adjust the international system to permit continued control, but at lower cost. Of course, the recourse to this alternative might have been given impetus by psychological factors, but to stop with that statement is to miss several points. First, the whole sequence of moves, from the Nixon Doctrine to the balance of power, was more an adjustment than a pure initiative, even though its object was to retain control of the international system. Second, in those circumstances, any leader or elite group would have had to respond within the constraints, or widen the constraints, or give up national goals. To say that is *not* to say, crudely, that any leader in those circumstances would have made the same choice among the alternatives.

As for the constraints, they could not entirely be moved by Nixon and Kissinger's will. There is every reason to believe that Kissinger was correct when he drew that lesson from the inability of the total American decisional system to make a sufficient response to the challenge of Vietnam (and a series of other situations, culminating later in Angola). This judgment might well have been—as many liberal critics of Kissinger declaimed in the spring of 1975, when Vietnam was finally crumbling—a self-fulfilling prophecy. But the conclusions were nonetheless true.

As the constraints operating on the American posture became clearer to Nixon and Kissinger (they both had begun to pick up the clues even before they assumed office in 1969), their administration conceived the practical "necessity" to move, first to the ephemeral pose of the Nixon Doctrine and then to a multipolar balance-of-power policy that depended on accommodating Beijing and seeking détente with Moscow. On a large scale, this was a rational move to stabilize the United States' global status at a lower level of cost—a level on which goals and constraints could be reconciled, or a level on which the minimum tolerable policy would just attain its requisite domestic support.

As for the goals, they were widely shared by the nonpathological critics of Nixon and Kissinger. In fact, they constituted the consensus position, and then (as now, still) only a few "extreme" and "irresponsible" critics would accept derogation from these objectives of U.S. foreign policy. (In this sense, Vietnam did not shatter the "Establishment." The Establishment retained its rules of exclusion.)

The notion of rationality in policy-making has been subverted, in recent times, by several nonrational types of explanation: bureaucratic politics; psychological theories; certain cognitive assertions, such as the primacy and pervasiveness of perceptions and economic and institutional determinism, which allows only the illusion, or at most the tactical exercise, of choice, within a rigid, encompassing framework of necessity.

Fred Greenstein, for example, takes for granted "the fact that political behavior is not rational, in the sense of employing the appropriate means to the actor's perceived ends."[23] (He goes on to say that irrationality can stem not only from ego-defensive, inner mechanisms, but also from "cognitive" factors, such as "imperfect information," "cultural stereotypes," and "insufficient time to make the appropriate calculations.") These attacks on rationality pose the problem, for those who would reinstate it, of asserting rationality in a way that does not stretch the concept to the point of covering everything, and thus indicating nothing in particular.

I am asserting rationality in the specific sense that both the structure and the process of policy are essentially rational. The *structure* is rational in that the array of alternatives, their entailed consequences and costs, and even the cognitive bias in terms of which those alternatives and consequences and costs are considered and construed, constitute a process of weighing. The policy *process* includes the rational elements of the goal-orientation of the system to an objective function that is to be optimized; a set of constraints that are observed or taken into consideration, sometimes taken into explicit, detailed calculation; and a feedback mechanism, by which the system corrects its actions and orientations in response to information about the results of previous strategies and actions.

These rational aspects of the structure and process of choice are qualified and constrained, but not defeated, by the presence of nonrational elements such as cognitive (perceptual) distortions and psychological and organizational factors. We need a theoretical framework that has the ability to contain both rational and nonrational elements. One way of incorporating nonrational factors (the compulsions of psychology, the imperfections of perceptions, the distortions of bureaucratic motives, the force of economic and institutional determinants) is to consider them as sets of constraints within a larger, essentially rational model.

Actually, a model that is based on constraints[24] in a way finesses—just as it reestablishes—the notion of rationality. Once constraints, however they or their values, are derived—are "cranked into" the system of equations and inequalities, the system then behaves rationally. That is, it seeks to optimize or maximize its complex goal function within the entire series of constraints. If it cannot attain the necessary level of total value without violating constraints—or if the constraints tighten up (what could be called parametric change), as they did during the period of the Vietnam War—then, through a process of feedback, the system itself, or the elites operating the system, will make some kind of adjustment.

THE DIALECTIC OF POLICY SHIFTS

The dialectic that led the Nixon-Kissinger Administration to the balance of power runs like this, in bare outline: Surveying the domestic and international wreckage of Vietnam, it had to decide whether to prepare to fight such wars better (Option A), or to plan not to fight them at all (Option C), or to change the international system so that they become less likely, perhaps, but more feasible (Option B). Intuitively rejecting Option C, the course of disengagement, the administration first embraced Option A. This option was, in fact, the Nixon Doctrine in its initial phase of force substitution (the total force concept, relying on military assistance, allied ground forces, technological fixes, the threat of nuclear war, and more equitable burden-sharing). But the American political system and the recalcitrance, apathy, or incompetence of allies frustrated the application of this phase of the Nixon Doctrine, and again posed the contradiction of restricted means versus undiminished commitments and the heavy demands of contingencies. So the administration moved to the middle solution, Option B, the creation of a more favorable international environment, through overarching great-power diplomacy and a multipolar stalemate—in short, a balance of power.

This balance-of-power stance, in turn, contains its own contradictions. There is domestic blockage: the lack of social will and public comprehension, and the consequent lack of requisite support, if a balance-of-power policy is ever seriously tested by a difficult intervention.[25] And there are the tests of continuing external instability—nations and groups not behaving according to the "rules" of the balance-of-power system. This phenomenon has many dimensions: revolutions, willful nationalists, and opportunistic great powers with different senses of proper international objectives.

The Nixon Doctrine itself was a response primarily to certain domestic problems, which can be defined as economic stringency and lack of a concerted "national interest." The first represents the decreasing availability of resources (in constant dollars and as a portion of total national income) for defense, and especially for general-purpose forces. The second is an inner fact of American society; this is a tenuous national community, fractured (actually or latently) along multiple lines of fissure.[26] Historical impressions of consensus, such as the several-decade-long apparent support of the Cold War—and even the recent apparent return to congressional and public support for ample defense budgets— are not proofs to the contrary. There is no firm evidence of a consensus until it is tested—until the bill is presented, denominated in lives lost and dislocated.[27]

To all this, the Nixon Doctrine was a limited solution. Without openly acknowledging the societal premise, it groped for the maximum limit of pressure that such a society could stand. It was a constrained compromise—a shrewd and marginally economical way of continuing a foreign policy of involvement, control, and projection of power. It was not disengagement but a program of force substitution, the calculated replacement of U.S. troops with foreign forces, bolstered by our military and economic assistance, air and naval support, and nuclear deterrence. In a cool tradeoff, it relied on the indirect conduct of conflict, through proxy armies and remote weapons systems. It projected a lower direct American presence, a consolidated base structure, smaller overall forces, and perhaps more sustainable defense budgets. It offered the prospect of reduced conscription and fewer casualties. It favored covert presidential wars, such as Laos, that had less impact on, and required less support from, the American people.

But Congress implicitly rejected the essence of the Nixon Doctrine, even while accepting its rhetoric of "low profile." Signals were the Senate vote on October 29, 1971, defeating the foreign aid authorization bill, and the Senate and House votes in the summer of 1973 to cut off the bombing of Cambodia. The first example may not have been, as the press prematurely construed,[28] the death-blow to all foreign military and economic aid. Later, authorizations were partially restored;[29] in any case, until 1973, three-quarters of U.S. military aid (primarily the portion that had gone to South Vietnam, Laos, and until FY 1973, Thailand) had not even been included in the foreign authorization but had been integrated into the U.S. defense budget.[30] But the vote was a repudiation of the logic of the Nixon Doctrine. The essence of the Nixon Doctrine was the tradeoff between U.S. military assistance and U.S. troops: that they run in opposite directions—

the more we buy of one, the less we need of the other. Congress was insisting, rather, that military assistance and direct U.S. intervention run in the same direction: that one be a precursor of the other and make it more, rather than less, likely.

The Senate vote of October 1971 rejected the ploy of military assistance and proxy forces; the Case-Church Amendment, which took effect in August 1973, rejected the complementary role of U.S. air power. Altogether, by rejecting the premises of force substitution inherent in the Nixon Doctrine, Congress exposed the nerve of the Nixon Administration's policy. For if ambitious international objectives were to be retained, but the instruments of remote and economical warfare were denied, then the United States would have to confront contingencies with revived conventional force, or residual reliance on nuclear threat, or the grace (and perhaps the wisdom) to disengage.

But the Nixon-Kissinger Administration was unwilling or unable to consider any of these a solution. To resolve the contradiction of objectives and instruments, then, it required a restructured international system—one in which conflict would be contained and risk would not be magnified. To bring about this condition, the administration cultivated the emerging multipolar balance of power and made a series of overhead deals with major adversaries, accepting the full spectrum of effects on allies.

Several analysts have suggested that the Nixon Doctrine and the balance of power were antithetical solutions.[31] Actually, the Nixon Doctrine was a phase of a dialectic that led to an attempt to restructure the international environment, to apportion power among several reliable, capable, independent nations. Such a dispensation would diffuse the responsibilities and burdens of mutual deterrence to the point where the United States could limit defense preparations and yet contain its adversaries and maintain the stability of the international system.

In short, the balance of power was a dynamic corollary—or a dialectical fulfillment—of the Nixon Doctrine. It was the single condition of the international system which (if it worked) could dissolve the contradiction between objects and means. This was the underlying rationale for the "emerging structure of peace." The balance of power was Phase Two of the Nixon Doctrine.[32]

The objectives and the approach of a balance-of-power policy, in turn, contain structural and procedural flaws. Those flaws can be briefly described:

1. A lack of the requisite domestic support for such a policy, based on the substantially "isolationist" American tradition (which, in turn, has real geographical and deep historical sources), and the constraints that it places on the conduct of limited wars. A balance-of-power policy, because of its sensitivity to barely perceptible and perhaps ambiguous "threats," and its reliance on minute, discriminating, and closely guarded decisions, is particularly likely to offend against the domestic processes of a constitutional democracy.

2. The possible inoperability of a balance-of-power policy in a democratic system of

unstable and revolving elites. It has been charged that only a Kissinger could operate an intricate global policy of maneuver, and coordinate, discipline, or outwit the bureaucracy to the extent necessary to bring the political-military power and influence of the United States consistently and reliably to bear on international situations.

3. The prospect of intractable international disorder, of a kind, moreover, that is not amenable to the regulatory devices of the balance of power.

4. The necessity for demonstrative small wars to prevent larger ones. A balance-of-power policy is peculiarly sensitive to the necessity of responding to symbolic challenges, even if they are strategically peripheral.

5. Finally, the liability of overdependence on information. This flaw might not be unique to one type of policy, but it is of the essence of a balance-of-power policy to identify threatening intentions and destabilizing actions early and accurately, and to make timely, discriminating, and appropriate responses. All of these requisites imply a special reliance on information—which is likely, however, to be confused, or undependable, or lacking.

We have begun to see, then, the realization of another round of constraints that apply to the balance-of-power policy, arising from the flaws I have cited. They also arise from congressional assertions of control in the spirit of those that Congress made during the Vietnam War, including the War Powers Act; reactions to the high budgetary costs of keeping up our end of a balance-of-power policy; and lack of sympathy for, or interest in, certain countries, whether on humanitarian, moral, or other grounds, that are designated as "proxies" in the new scheme to stabilize regions. These constraints will inhibit, or at least render unreliable, the balance-of-power policy. So the dialectic—of policies, constraints, partial responses, new contradictions, revised policies—will proceed to other forms of foreign policy orientation and other forms of international system as partial consequences, and partial causes, of these changes in our foreign policy.

In the last analysis, the underlying condition for relieving the constitutional tension—for reconciling the United States Constitution with the conduct of foreign policy, and for avoiding the continual temptation of the executive branch to strain the political system and abuse its institutions—is a noninterventionist foreign policy. For that, we must look to the transcendence of containment and the arrival at a policy of strategic disengagement. There would have to be a change in the gross decision-rules of our own system and a shift in the ambient world in which American foreign policy has to operate.

EPILOGUE: PORTENTS FOR THE FUTURE

There may be a particular point in this analytic retrospection of the Nixon-Kissinger regime. It comes at a time when we have to contemplate another change in government. The question of situation or personality, logic or psychologic, with regard to large-scale foreign policy choice translates into the question of whether automatic change will derive from the predilections and personality structures of different incumbents, or pervasive similarity of basic policy orientation, despite the rhetorical expressions and even the real intentions of the protagonists of a new administration.

Just as the explanation of the behavior of the Nixon-Kissinger Administration turns not on its psychological or moral qualities, a prognosis for the foreign policy of any successive administration depends less on the personality and predilections of its protagonists than on the evolution of the total pattern of challenges and constraints, including the peculiar characteristics of our own political system. Thus, successors to the Nixon-Kissinger Administration, holding much the same objectives for the international system and beset by many of the same constraints, have been likely, despite themselves, to maintain the recognizable structural features of their predecessors' foreign policy, however qualified they might have been by "stylistic" differences. Indeed, although it initially dismantled some of the stylistic "excesses" of its predecessors, even the Carter Administration—and certainly the Reagan Administration—under pressure, recovered and utilized many of the same devices of diplomacy and even internal governance.

Therefore, voters and analysts should discern what "correct" policy means, in objective terms, regardless of who is making it—whether a secretive, reclusive president and a subtle and difficult secretary of state, or an attractive and open president and any of a host of direct and honorable aspirants to the top foreign policy positions. Critics should not try to pass off the foreign policy directions of the past several administrations as products of aberrant or defective personal impulses—with the implication, or the expectation, that "right-mindedness" or "whole-mindedness" will automatically rectify our national policy and restore the American position in the world.

NOTES

1. It would also be unnecessary, thanks in part to the painstaking and structured list of relevant publications presented by Michael Lerner, "A Bibliographical Note," in Fred I. Greenstein, *Personality and Politics: Problems of Evidence, Inference, and Conceptualization* (New York: W.W. Norton, 1975).

2. Notably *A World Restored: The Politics of Conservatism in a Revolutionary Age* (New York: Universal Library, 1964), a work that exalts the structure of Metternich—supposedly a static system, based on shared conceptions of political and social legitimacy; and "Bismarck: The White Revolutionary," *Daedalus* (Summer 1968), a work that leans toward a more dynamic and aggressive concept of power balancing, stressing daring diplomacy backed by decisive force, and resting on no necessary common ground of legitimacy or shared political values, but on pragmatically shifting coalitions and exploited opportunities.

3. *Department of State Bulletin*, July 26, 1971, pp. 94–95.

4. "An Interview with the President," *Time*, January 3, 1972, p. 15.

5. In various contexts, Kissinger affirmed, qualified, or denied the existence of a

balance-of-power world and the waging of a balance-of-power policy. It may be worth extensive quotation: February 1, 1973), CBS News interview (*Department of State Bulletin*, April 2, 1973), commenting on Nixon's "five power" speech:

... when I arrived in China, Chou En-lai asked me ... 'What about this five-power world that your President mentioned?' ... I said, 'What about it?' So he had to get a copy of the speech, and showed it to me. The balance of power in the 19th-century sense about which I wrote is obviously not applicable to the contemporary situation. In the 19th century, you had a large number of states of approximately equal strength that were trying to prevent marginal changes in the international situation because they believed that any marginal change could be transformed into an overwhelming advantage sooner or later. In the nuclear age the biggest changes in the situation can be achieved without any territorial acquisition at all. No amount of conquest could have given the Soviet Union as much additional power as the development of the nuclear, and, later, the hydrogen bomb. So we are talking about a completely different world than the one that existed in the 19th century. You can't have these shifting alliances; you can't have these endless little wars. But there is something in the balance of power in two respects. One, no nation can make its survival dependent on the good will of another state if it has a choice about it, especially of a state that announces a hostile ideology. So you must have a certain equilibrium of strength in order to retain some freedom over your fate. ... Now, what this administration has attempted to do is not so much to play a complicated 19th century game of balance of power, but to try to eliminate those hostilities that were vestiges of a particular perception at the end of the war and to deal with the root fact of the contemporary situation—that we and the Soviet Union, and we and the Chinese, are ideological adversaries, but we are bound together by one basic fact: that none of us can survive a nuclear war and therefore it is in our mutual interest to try to reduce those hostilities that are bureaucratic vestiges or that simply are not rooted in overwhelming national concerns.

May 3, 1973, "U.S. Foreign Policy for the 1970's: Shaping a Durable Peace" (Washington, D.C.: U.S. Government Printing Office, May 3, 1973; the fourth State of the World message, hereinafter cited as Nixon IV), pp. 194, 232–233:

In the classical balance of power system, most national leaders were concerned with accumulating geopolitical and military power that could be translated into immediate advantage. In the nuclear era, both the United States and the Soviet Union have found that an increment of military power does not necessarily represent an increment of usable political strength, because of the excessive destructiveness of nuclear weapons in relation to the objective.... We seek a stable structure, not a classical balance of power. Undeniably, national security must rest upon a certain equilibrium between potential adversaries. The United States cannot entrust its destiny entirely, or even largely, to the goodwill of others. Neither can we expect other countries so to mortgage their future. Solid security involves external restraints on potential opponents as well as self-restraint. Thus a certain balance of power is inherent in any international system and has its place in the one we envision. But it is not the overriding concept of our foreign policy. First of all, our approach reflects the realities of the nuclear age.... Secondly, our approach includes the element of consensus. All nations, adversaries and friends alike, must have a stake in preserving the international system.... Negotiation with adversaries does not alter our more fundamental ties with friends.... Our alliances remain the cornerstones of our foreign policy.... Although their forms must be adapted to new conditions, these ties are enduring.

September 24, 1973, address to the United Nations General Assembly (*Department of State Bulletin*, October 15, 1973):

We have no desire for domination. We will oppose—as we have consistently opposed throughout this century—any nation that chooses this path. We have not been asked to participate in condominium; we would reject such an appeal if it were made. We will never abandon our allies or our friends. The strengthening of our traditional ties is the essential foundation for the development of new relationships with old adversaries. We will work for peace through the United Nations as well as through bilateral relationships.

October 8, 1973, address before the Third Pacem in Terris Conference (*Department of State Bulletin*, October 29, 1973):

Today's striving for equilibrium should not be compared to the balance of power of previous periods. The very notion of "operating" a classical balance of power disintegrates when the change required to upset the balance is so large that it cannot be achieved by limited means. More specifically, there is no parallel with the 19th century. Then the principal countries shared essentially similar concepts of legitimacy and accepted the basic structure of the existing international order. Small adjustments in strength were significant. The "balance" operated in a relatively confined geographic area. None of these factors obtain today. Nor when we talk of equilibrium do we mean a simplistic mechanical model devoid of purpose. The constantly shifting alliances that maintained equilibrium in previous centuries are neither appropriate nor possible in our time. In an age of ideological schism the distinction between friends and adversaries is an objective reality. We share ideals as well as interests with our friends, and we know that the strength of our friendships is crucial to the lowering of tensions with our opponents. When we refer to five or six or seven major centers of power, the point being made is not that others are excluded but that a few short years ago everyone agreed that there were only two. The diminishing tensions and the emergence of new centers of power have meant greater freedom of action and greater importance for all other nations. In this setting, our immediate aim has been to build a stable network of relationships that offers hope of sparing mankind the scourges of war.

December 27, 1973, news conference (*Department of State Bulletin*, January 21, 1974):

... the great task before this administration, as it will be before its successors, has been to construct an international system based on a sense of justice so that its participants would have a stake in maintaining it, with a sufficient balance of power so that no nation or group of nations would be dependent entirely on the good will of its neighbors, and based on a sense of participation so that all nations could share in the positive aspirations.

June 7, 1974, statement before the Senate Committee on Foreign Relations (*Department of State Bulletin*, July 8, 1974): "If we are to move toward a world where power blocks and balances are no longer relevant, where justice, not stability, can be our overriding preoccupation ... "

6. It is not novel to observe that the term *balance of power* is used in many senses. In fact, scholars have spent an inordinate amount of time stuffing and mounting and labeling the varieties. For a much-noted exercise in these directions, see Ernst B. Haas, "The Balance of Power: Prescription, Concept or Propaganda," *World Politics*, July 1953, pp. 442–477; and "The Balance of Power as a Guide to Policy-Making," *Journal of Politics*, August 1953, pp. 370–397. See also Martin Wight, "The Balance of Power," in Herbert Butterfield and Martin Wight, eds., *Diplomatic Investigations: Essays in the Theory of International Politics*, (Cambridge, Mass.: Harvard University Press, 1968), pp. 132–178. A more operational attempt to distill meanings of the balance of power, in propositions or hypotheses that could be tested, is Dina A. Zinnes, "An Analytical Study of the Balance of Power Theories," *Journal of Peace Research* 3 (1967): 270–288.

7. These theorists include Morton A. Kaplan, *System and Process in International Politics* (New York: John Wiley, 1957), p. 22.

8. See, for example, James Chace, "The Five-Power World of Richard Nixon," *The New York Times Magazine*, February 20, 1972.

9. To a certain observable and appropriate extent, these characteristics still persist in the present international system.

10. Richard Nixon, "U.S. Foreign Policy for the 1970's: The Emerging Structure of Peace" (Washington, D.C.: U.S. Government Printing Office, February 9, 1972, p. 25, the third State of the World message, hereinafter cited as Nixon III).

11. On this point, see Chace, "The Five-Power World of Richard Nixon."

12. Note Kissinger's comment in a news conference on March 21, 1974 (*Department of State Bulletin*, April 8, 1974, p. 355): "Anybody reading the President's annual reports knows that it has been the fixed principle of American foreign policy to encourage other centers of decision."

13. A stance hardly remedied by Kissinger's belated posturing at Lusaka, April 25, 1976.

14. Nixon III, p. 6.

15. See Kissinger's remarks, "The Year of Europe," directed at our NATO allies, at the annual meeting of the Associated Press editors, New York, April 23, 1973, and published in the *Department of State Bulletin*, May 14, 1973, pp. 593–598.

16. New York: Basic Books, 1972. Other treatments are Arthur Woodstone, *Nixon's Head* (New York: St. Martin's Press, 1972); Eli S. Chesen, *President Nixon's Psychiatric Profile* (New York: Peter Wyden, 1973); sections of James David Barber, *The Presidential Character: Predicting Performance in the White House* (Englewood Cliffs, N. J.: Prentice-Hall, 1972); and Stanley Allen Renshon, "Psychological Analysis and Presidential Personality: The Case of Richard Nixon," *History of Childhood Quarterly: Journal of Psychohistory* 2, no. 3 (Winter 1975).

17. *Diplomacy for a Crowded World* (Boston: Atlantic-Little, Brown, 1976)—too crowded, evidently, for both Ball and Kissinger.

18. One of the most comprehensive of the psychodynamic accounts of Kissinger's behavior is Bruce Mazlish, *Kissinger: The European Mind in American Policy* (New York: Basic Books, 1976).

19. *History of Childhood Quarterly: The Journal of Psychohistory* 2, no. 3 (Winter 1975): 287–348.

20. For an earlier psychologically oriented study of Kissinger, and one that addressed more specifically the interaction of personality and strategic problems, see David Landau, *Kissinger: The Uses of Power* (Boston: Houghton Mifflin, 1972).

21. Certainly the Soviets, with their Marxist concentration on objective conditions, do not seem to have been influenced, in predicting the authoritative behavior of their adversaries, by their judgment of Nixon's (or Kissinger's) personality antecedents. An account by Joseph Kraft, in the aftermath of the Moscow summit meeting of May 1972, illustrates this ("Letter from Moscow," *The New Yorker*, June 24, 1972):

When . . . I visited Georgy Arbatov, the head of the U.S.A. Institute in Moscow, who often speaks for the Soviet leadership, Arbatov said, "As a Marxist, I was never much interested in psychoanalyzing your President. I didn't think the talk about the New Nixon or the Old Nixon was very interesting. What mattered was his response to circumstances—particularly to two changed circumstances in your country. One was the growing complexity of international affairs, which showed, especially Vietnam, that it was not possible for a single power, however strong, to have everything its way. The other was the change of priorities—the lesson that rulers cannot neglect domestic business."

22. If anything, *foreign* policy is even more subject to the kind of complex, structured analysis I suggest. In the area of foreign policy, (1) there are a greater multiplicity and

complexity of variables and parameters; (2) the determination of issues depends more on other parties; (3) there is more uncertainty, particularly about the behavior of other parties, and this necessitates more general "meta-strategies" to deal with problems; and (4) the activity proceeds on two levels of administration, domestic and foreign, and elites must confront other countries as if their own nation were a unitary rational actor, whether or not that is strictly the case. (Although distinctions between foreign and domestic policy are increasingly blurred, these points, I believe, remain clear.)

23. Greenstein, *Personality*, p. 146—although this particular statement is made in an oblique context.

24. A "constraint," in the most general sense, can be seen as any condition that pertains or must be satisfied. A typology of constraints would be useful. There might be three elements in such a scheme: (1) the kind of constraint, or its origin—for example, economic, political, physical, legal, moral, and so on; (2) whether the constraint is a limit or a tradeoff, and whether, in turn, the tradeoff is measured in cost, effectiveness, or utility; and (3) how "fixed" or "movable" the constraint is, over time, and by various amounts of effort or expense.

25. In this matter, see Stanley Hoffmann, "Will the Balance Balance at Home?" *Foreign Policy* (Summer 1972). My point is slightly different: (1) A balance-of-power policy initially requires only acquiescence, and might well attain this shallow level of support, at first; but (2) in the test, social fractures will inhibit intervention, probably just at the critical point. "Enough" support for covert operations and modest interventions might well exist, given certain presidential adjustments and instrumental fixes. But intervention will not be steady or effective in the more important and demanding cases.

26. My point is not that this is not a nation, or that it will fall apart, but rather that the possibility of fission will limit external adventure.

27. Lyndon Johnson's reading of American history is instructive: "There never was a President with a major war who didn't have a rebellion. Washington had one-third of the country against him. Lincoln was sure he wouldn't be reelected. Roosevelt was shooting zoot-suiters on the West Coast" (quoted in Hugh Sidey, "The Presidency," *Life*, November 5, 1971, p. 4). Also indicative is a citation in Seymour M. Lipset, "Polls and Protests," *Foreign Affairs* (April 1971): 555:

... it may also be important to note that antiwar activity during wars has also been a recurrent American trait. Sol Tax of the University of Chicago sought to estimate the extent of such opposition to different wars, and concluded that Americans had opposed a number of other wars more extensively than they had Vietnam, at least up to the time the United States agreed publicly to negotiate the end of the war in March 1968. The War of 1812 witnessed a large-scale secession movement by antiwar New Englanders. Battalions of American deserters actually fought with the Mexican Army during the Mexican War. There were massive antidraft riots during the Civil War. The antiwar Socialists obtained over 20 percent of the vote in municipal elections shortly after we entered World War I, while hundreds of thousands were involved in violations of the draft laws in that conflict. Opinion polls registered early extensive adult and student opposition to the Korean War.

The contention that *all* potentially demanding foreign policies contain, implicitly, the conditions for creating dissensus, when tested, is further illustrated in John Mueller, "Calculating the Costs," *The New Republic*, February 10, 1973:

"(F) or comparable periods the two wars (Korea and Vietnam) inspired almost exactly the same amount of support and opposition from the American public.... Support for the wars ... dwindled according to the same pattern for both wars: when US casualties grew by a factor of 10—from 1000 to 10,000 or from 10,000 to 100,000, for example—support declined by some 15 percentage points. In absolute terms, the popularity of Vietnam did finally fall below that of Korea, but only after the losses of the later war had considerably exceeded those of the earlier one.

28. And largely deplored, because the Senate vote affected economic as well as military aid. *The Washington Post*, October 31, 1971, commented: "The Senate's vote to kill foreign aid was capricious and blind. . . . The isolationist 'signal' to the world is disastrous."

29. On March 2, 1972, Congress finally cleared a combined military and economic appropriation for FY 1972, at a level of $2.6 billion, almost a billion dollars less than the administration's original request. For military assistance alone (including government credit sales but excluding "service-funded" assistance integrated into the U.S. defense budget), administration requests and eventual congressional authorizations were: for FY 1972, asked $1.242 billion, given $.935 billion; for FY 1973, asked $1.347 billion, given $.989 billion (under continuing resolution authority).

30. In FY 1970 $2.272 billion out of $2.731 billion, or 83 percent; in FY 1971 $2.427 billion out of $3.914 billion, or 62 percent; in FY 1972 $2.596 billion out of $3.531 billion, or 74 percent; in FY 1973 $2.875 billion out of $3.864 billion, or 74 percent; in FY 1974 (proposed) $2.899 billion out of $4.229 billion, or 69 percent; in FY 1974 (actual) $1.803 billion out of $5.098 billion, or 35 percent; in FY 1975 $.239 billion out of $2.570 billion, or 9 percent; in FY 1976 (proposed) $.560 billion out of $3.261 billion, or 17 percent. (Figures are derived from the secretary of defense annual reports to various congressional committees; figures for the same year vary somewhat among the reports.) But for FY 1975, Congress started putting limits on the amount of military assistance that could be located in the U.S. defense budget.

31. Robert E. Osgood (in Osgood, Robert W. Tucker, et al., *Retreat from Empire? The First Nixon Administration*, Baltimore, Md.: Johns Hopkins University Press, 1973, pp. 8–10) reasoned that the Nixon Doctrine (reducing expense and burden while maintaining commitments and influence) depended on maintaining essentially a bipolar management of confrontation and negotiation, and that therefore the Nixon Doctrine conflicted with and precluded a full-scale multipolar balance of power.

32. Secretary Kissinger himself characterized the policy of the Nixon Administration in two phases—although he asserted that the second phase, a restructured international system, had been Nixon's goal from the beginning:

. . . with the war in Viet-Nam ended, the major focus of our foreign policy attention could turn to the design of the structure of peace that has been the President's principal goal since he came into office. In its first phase, this meant that the United States had to reduce many of its overextended commitments and that the United States had to disengage gradually from any foreign involvement and, above all, that the United States should evoke a sense of responsibility for its own sake in many areas of the world. This was the so-called Nixon doctrine which characterized the first two or three years of the President's first term. It was the prelude to the initiatives toward China and the detente with the Soviet Union that were to lay the basis for a fundamental realignment of the postwar period which had been based on a rigid division between opposing hostile blocs. (News conference, December 27, 1973; *Department of State Bulletin*, January 21, 1974, pp. 45–46).

11

Richard Nixon as Summit Diplomat

ELMER PLISCHKE

As president, Richard Nixon continued and augmented the practices of summit diplomacy that were introduced and refined by his predecessors. These practices included communicating directly with other world leaders, appointing special presidential envoys as his surrogates to deal with the chiefs of state and heads of government of other countries, receiving and conferring with such leaders when they come to the United States on summit visits, undertaking presidential trips and visits abroad, and engaging in summit meetings and conferences in the United States and foreign countries.

The president's personal involvement in diplomacy blends the powers and activities of his office with the conduct of foreign relations. It is clear that the latter—called diplomacy—consists of the making and implementation of foreign policy. When the president engages actively in this capacity in dealing with other world leaders, elevating the conduct of foreign affairs to the highest level, he functions as summiteer and often as his own ambassador.[1] In short, summit diplomacy constitutes presidential, personal involvement in diplomatic communication, conferral, and negotiation at the chief of state/government level, both in the United States and abroad. Of all the powers and responsibilities of the president, according to Clinton Rossiter, "In recent years, the role of the Chief Diplomat has become the most important and exacting of all those we call upon the President to play."[2]

NIXON'S PREPARATION FOR SUMMITRY

Volumes can be written on Nixon's preparation for his functioning as summiteer. After serving in the Navy during World War II and in Congress for six years,[3] he had the benefit of two active terms as vice president, often substituting for President Eisenhower in important meetings and ceremonies and representing him as his personal emissary abroad. As early as the Republican nominating convention in 1952, Eisenhower told Nixon: "I don't want a Vice President who will be a figurehead. I want a man who will be a member of the team."[4] And he carried out this aspiration. Aside from the social affairs at which Nixon substituted for the president, he performed a number of summit ceremonial duties, welcomed or met and consulted with various foreign leaders during their summit visits to the United States,[5] led the delegation that welcomed Eisenhower on his return from the Geneva Summit Conference in 1955[6] and, accompanying the president, joined Queen Elizabeth II in dedicating the Saint Lawrence power project in 1959.[7]

More important were his experiences as a member of both the cabinet and the National Security Council and his subsummit tours abroad. He not only participated regularly in cabinet and National Security Council meetings, but also if the president had to leave before adjournment, he asked the vice president to substitute as chairman.[8] During Eisenhower's illnesses (1955–57), he deputized Nixon to summon and lead these sessions.[9] In addition, in 1960 the White House announced that if the four-power (United States, France, the Soviet Union, and the United Kingdom) Paris Summit Conference continued beyond its scheduled time, he would have the vice president take his place because the president was committed to visit Portugal on his return trip, or if "domestic requirements" in Washington prevented his remaining at the conference. This unprecedented proposal evidenced the president's confidence in his vice president.[10]

Most notable for preparing him for his later role as diplomat in chief were Vice President Nixon's foreign ventures. He performed such ceremonial services as representing the United States at the inaugural of President Juscelino Kubitschek in Brazil (1956), flying to London to dedicate the American Chapel in Saint Paul's Cathedral (1958), and participating in the independence celebration of Ghana in 1959.[11] At the time of the Hungarian uprising and the Soviet repression in late 1956, he was designated by the president to lead an American delegation on "Operation Mercy," going to Austria to investigate and report on the situation and facilitating the immigration to the United States of more than twenty-one thousand Hungarian refugees that had found temporary sanctuary in Austria.[12]

Especially noteworthy was his eleven-day visit to the Soviet Union in the summer of 1959, to open the American National Exhibition in Sokolniki Park, in return for Deputy Premier Frol Kozlov's visit to the United States to open the Soviet Exhibition of Science and Culture in New York City earlier that year. This was the first such high-level visit by an American leader to the Soviet capital, and it paved the way for a planned exchange of visits by the American president and the Soviet premier. During Nixon's two-week stay, he conferred with top Soviet officials, toured Russia and Siberia, engaged Nikita Khrushchev in the highly publicized "Kitchen Debate," and delivered his unprecedented television address to the Soviet people.[13]

Nixon made several grand tours as vice president. At the request of the president, in October 1953 he set out on the first of his five subsummit good will ventures. Traveling more than 45,500 miles, he spent sixty-nine days visiting fourteen Asian, Pacific, and Mideast countries to confer with their leaders, explain American policy, reassure Allies, and assess attitudes toward Asian affairs. Later, he confided in his memoirs that this venture "established my foreign policy experience and expertise in what was to become the most critical and controversial part of the world."[14] During the next four and one-half years, also at the behest of the president, Nixon undertook similar trips to Mexico, Central America, and the Caribbean (1955), to Southeast Asia (1956), to Northern Africa (1957), and to South America (1958).[15] All told, as the personal representative of the president, he visited approximately fifty countries and therefore was more widely traveled than any vice president in U.S. history.[16]

In addition, during the eight-year interim from 1961 to 1969, as a private citizen Nixon continued his interest in international affairs and his foreign travels. Accompanied by his family, he took a six-week vacation trip to Europe and the Middle East in 1964, and he returned to Asia three times, during which he focused substantially on the Vietnam problem.[17] But in 1967 he also returned to Europe (including the Soviet Union and Romania) and traveled to Latin America, the Mideast, and Africa.[18] During these trips he was received by and conferred with many ranking officials, including opposition political leaders, and also a good many younger officers who later rose to positions of prominence.

To summarize, President Eisenhower deliberately made the vice presidency an important office and included Nixon in his inner team. At a news conference as early as 1955, he declared: "Never has there been a Vice President so well versed in the activities of government" who "has gone to numerous nations where he was widely and favorably accepted," and he called him "the most valuable member of my team."[19] In all, as the president's chief summit surrogate, and subsequently as a private citizen, Nixon visited at least 60 of the 126 then independent nations, as well as the Vatican and four additional territories and dependencies. Aside from the advantages of his first-hand learning experience, this extensive acquaintanceship with foreign nations gave him the opportunity to confer with dozens of world leaders and many of those who would later become reigning monarchs, presidents, and prime ministers.

The relationships Nixon established through these contacts, he later reported, "were tremendously important to the development of my thinking about foreign affairs." In short, he "met the leaders, met the people, and saw first hand the problems, opportunities, and dangers confronting the United States."[20] More particularly, as a consequence of his experiences in the Far East, in his article on Asia in *Foreign Affairs* (1967) he concluded that the United States needed to launch an era of negotiation and rapprochement. Specifically, he observed that the People's Republic of China should be persuaded that dialogue was essential and that China ought to return to the world community.[21]

NIXON AS SUMMIT COMMUNICATOR

Like other recent presidents, Nixon maintained considerable personal communication with other world leaders. Aside from a variety of feelers and unwritten "signals"[22] intended to preface communication by more concrete means and ceremonial messages such as New Year greetings,[23] these fall into three main categories. The first encompasses occasional or intermittent summit messages concerning a variety of subjects. These are illustrated by the exchanges between Washington and Moscow respecting negotiation of the SALT I Treaty, U.S. military operations in Vietnam, Soviet-Chinese border clashes, the Indo-Pakistani War, and other functional and regional problems.[24]

The second type consists of summit communications in times of crises involving the United States. For example, to produce a negotiated termination of the Vietnam War, the president frequently communicated with President Nguyen Van Thieu of South Vietnam, several European leaders, and even Ho Chi Minh and Pham Van Dong of North Vietnam,[25] although the chief burden of negotiation devolved upon other processes, especially the use of presidential special emissaries and negotiations at the conference table in Paris.[26] Nixon's exchanges with Soviet leaders—initially with Aleksei Kosygin and later with Leonid Brezhnev—dealt with the Kremlin's endeavor to surreptitiously establish a naval base at Cienfuegos Bay in Cuba in 1970.[27] He also interchanged messages with Arab, Israeli, Soviet, and European allied leaders at the time of the Yom Kippur War in October 1973.[28]

The third category of summit communication was employed during the tortuous negotiations preparing the way for President Nixon's trips to Beijing and Moscow. The maneuvers—sometimes simulating an exciting "suspense story"—to achieve agreement for his trip to China in 1972 involved a combination of subtle signals,[29] confidential third-party intermediaries (especially Agha Yahya Khan, president of Pakistan),[30] and other neutral channels,[31] Henry Kissinger's dramatic "Polo" trips to Beijing,[32] and direct summit exchanges between the president and Premier Chou En-lai.[33]

The road to Moscow was less convoluted but equally delicate, and the prelude to his 1972 trip paralleled that leading to the summit meeting in Beijing. But these negotiations were facilitated by the availability of regularized diplomatic channels in Washington and Moscow and by the momentum of earlier meetings of U.S. and Soviet leaders since the Roosevelt Administration. Agreement for the first presidential visit to Moscow was consummated by the exchange of letters of the president with Kosygin and Brezhnev in August 1971. On the last day of the 1972 meeting, President Nixon endorsed the continuance of transmitting messages via their "private channel," and at the end of the Moscow meeting in 1974 he stressed the need for not only continued but also increased Soviet-American summit communication.[34]

In addition to his written messages,[35] President Nixon occasionally resorted to other means to communicate with foreign governments. For several decades it had been common practice for the president to telephone the prime ministers of Canada and Great Britain, the leaders of friendly European countries, and others to discuss matters of mutual concern.[36] During the 1973 Mideast War President Nixon telephoned both Golda Meir and Anwar Sadat to congratulate them when they agreed to end the war.[37]

He also employed the Washington-Moscow hot line to cope with serious crises. In December 1971, at the time of the Indo-Pakistani War, in which the Soviet Union backed India and China supported Pakistan, he conferred with Brezhnev by this means to localize the conflict and obtain a cease-fire. Two years later, during the Yom Kippur War, the Soviet leader initiated hot line exchanges concerning the ruptured cease-fire that had been agreed to by the United States, the Soviet Union, Israel, and the Arab states.[38]

Thus, President Nixon was an avid summit communicator with the leaders of friendly powers, adversaries, and others. He may not have been an eager pen-pal, but he utilized this summit technique freely and effectively. Many of his exchanges were confidential, and his objectives—as in the case of opening channels of communication with Hanoi during the Vietnam War, paving the way for his trips to Beijing and Moscow, and mediating in foreign crises, especially in the Mideast and Indo-Pakistani wars—might have been aborted had his initiatives been subjected to American public pressures or debate in advance.

NIXON'S SPECIAL SUMMIT SURROGATES

Since the days of George Washington, presidents have appointed hundreds of special diplomatic envoys.[39] This time-tried practice, unique to the United States and referred to as Rover Boy Diplomacy, enables the president to commission a particular person to a specific foreign mission, serving as his personal surrogate at the highest level.

These presidential emissaries may be officeholders—such as the vice president, the secretary of state, other cabinet members, or professional diplomats on special assignments, or they may be appointed from outside the government. Their assignments vary, are usually limited in duration, and range from good will and information gathering to troubleshooting, conflict mediation, and even the negotiation and signing of diplomatic settlements and international treaties. Often the president uses such special agents to satisfy his desire for expedition and confidentiality, to accord the mission an aura of importance, urgency, and stature, or to respond to pressures from other world leaders who wish to escalate the level of negotiations.[40]

As noted, when he was vice president, Nixon served as one of President Eisenhower's principal special representatives—for ceremonial and information-gathering purposes and to undertake a series of foreign good will tours. After becoming president, Nixon appointed many special envoys to a variety of missions. Naturally, Vice President Spiro Agnew and Secretary of State William P. Rogers were utilized in this capacity. The vice president was asked to embark on a number of ceremonial, fact-finding, good will, and other trips—mostly to Asia and the Pacific, but also to Europe, the Mideast, and Africa.[41]

Aside from accompanying the president on certain summit ventures abroad (such as Nixon's trips to Beijing and Moscow), Secretary Rogers conferred with world leaders (including foreign ministers) who came to the United States, signed several treaties and agreements (embracing the hot line accord in 1971 and several agreements consummated at the United States-Soviet summits in 1972 and 1973), and attended the ministerial meetings of ANZUS, CENTO, NATO, SEATO, and the Organization of American States. He also was deputed to visit Mexico in 1970 to attend the inaugural of President Echeverría Alvarez (1970) and undertake trips to South Vietnam (1969), Africa (1970), the Mideast (1971), Europe (1972), and Latin America (1973), as well as a world tour in 1972.

In addition, New York Governor Nelson Rockefeller (former assistant secretary of state) was sent by the president on a major fact-finding tour of Latin America in 1969. It proved to be a two-month, violence-plagued, twenty-country odyssey intended to improve inter-American relations. Since the Arab-Israeli War of 1967, special shuttling emissaries were also employed by the White House in a mediatory role in the Middle East. In 1970 President Nixon named Assistant Secretary of State Joseph J. Sisco as his personal representative to discuss U.S. policy and plans with President Gamal Nasser, Premier Golda Meir, and other officials in the area.[42]

Other special agents included David M. Kennedy (ambassador at large and former secretary of the treasury), who was selected to help resolve an economic conflict with Japan and to negotiate a three-year trade agreement in October 1971. A year later Ellsworth Bunker (then ambassador to Saigon) accompanied Henry Kissinger in an attempt to get President Nguyen Van Thieu to agree to a draft agreement which Kissinger had worked out with the North Vietnamese to end the war in Southeast Asia.[43] Alexander Haig, who served on Kissinger's White House staff and later as an aide to the president, went to Beijing in January 1972 to handle technical and logistical preparations for the president's visit, was sent on several trips to Southeast Asia, and assisted Kissinger in the Paris negotiations with the North Vietnamese.[44]

When Nixon became president, negotiations to end the war in Southeast Asia were under way in Paris. Initially, he selected Henry Cabot Lodge (former ambassador to the United Nations, South Vietnam, and Germany) as his emissary to represent the United States. In July 1970 Lodge was succeeded by Ambassador David K. E. Bruce (former representative of the United States in France, Germany, and Great Britain), and a year later by William Porter (former deputy ambassador to South Vietnam and ambassador to Korea).

But President Nixon had more confidence in top-level "private talks." In a public address from the Oval Office in January 1972, he revealed that Kissinger (then assistant to the president for national security affairs) had been his special envoy for confidential discussions with Hanoi representatives since August 1969.[45] In any case, it was Kissinger who conveyed a comprehensive American peace plan to the North Vietnamese in Paris in May 1971, handled the critical discussions with Le Duc Tho in the fall of the following year, and finally consummated and signed the Paris peace accord in January 1973. Kissinger and Tho were awarded the Nobel Peace Prize for 1973, but the North Vietnamese leader declined it.[46]

It was Kissinger on whom President Nixon relied most heavily as his chief ambassadorial surrogate. As a ranking member of the White House staff, he served as personal adviser to the president on such foreign policy matters as the SALT negotiations, as courier to pave the way for the president's trips to Beijing and Moscow, and as adviser in important Soviet, Japanese, European, and NATO affairs.[47] He also became an eager, peripatetic White House envoy who traveled some 560,000 miles to more than fifty countries, although he concentrated particularly on Beijing, Moscow, Paris, and the capitals of Israel and its neighbors.

As the president's superemissary—called Nixon's "diplomatic superstar"—Kissinger focused on developing effective channels of communication with top foreign leaders, dealing personally at the highest levels, developing broad policy strategy, managing events and negotiations in favor of the United States insofar as possible, maneuvering relations to the point of negotiability, and producing livable (though not necessarily preferred) accommodation and compromise. Historically, he proved to be a four-star presidential special representative and President Nixon's right-hand agent in the conduct of foreign affairs.[48]

SUMMIT VISITS TO THE UNITED STATES

Since King Kalakaua of Hawaii came to the United States for the first summit visit during the Grant Administration in 1874, American presidents have received more than a thousand foreign leaders. President Nixon hosted some 140 during his five and one-half years in the White House, the largest number to that time.[49] He averaged approximately twenty-five per year, which is the norm for recent administrations. Chiefs of state and heads of government came from sixty-seven countries—from nearly thirty American allies, all of the major Western industrial powers, several Communist states (the Soviet Union, Romania, and Yugoslavia), a number of newly independent nations, and such distant lands as Botswana, Fiji, Laos, Mauritania, Mauritius, and Singapore. (For a list of countries, see Table 11.1.)

More than eighty of these visits occurred during the first two years of his presidency—explained in part by the eleven ceremonial visits to attend former President Eisenhower's funeral in 1969 and the twenty-nine visitors who, in New York to attend the twenty-fifth anniversary of the United Nations the following year, were invited to a gala commemorative dinner at the White House.

Table 11.1

List of Countries and Visitors to the United States and President's Visits Abroad

Country	Foreign Visitors	President's Visits	Country	Foreign Visitors	President's Visits
Algeria	1		Liberia	1	
Austria		2	Malaysia	2	
Australia	3		Malta	1	
Belgium	2	2	Mauritania	1	
Benin (Dahomey)	3		Mauritius	1	
Botswana	1		Mexico	2	2
Brazil	1		Morocco	3	
Cambodia	2		Netherlands	3	
Cameroon	1		New Zealand	3	
Canada	2	1	Nicaragua	2	
Ceylon (Sri Lanka)	1		Norway	2	
Chad	1		Pakistan	2	1
China, Dem. Rep. of		1	Panama	1	
China, Republic of	1		Peru	1	
Colombia	1		Portugal	1	2
Costa Rica	1		Philippines	1	1
Cyprus	1		Poland		1
Denmark	2		Romania	2	1
Egypt		1	Saudi Arabia	1	1
Ethiopia	3		Senegal	2	
Fiji	1		Sierra Leone	1	
Finland	2		Singapore	3	
France	2	3	Somalia	1	
Gabon	1		Spain		1
Germany, Fed. Rep.	7	1	Sweden	2	
Ghana	3		Syria		1
Iceland		1	Thailand		1
India	1	1	Tunisia	1	
Indonesia	1	1	Turkey	3	
Iran	3		U.S.S.R.	1	2
Ireland	3	1	United Kingdom	6	4
Israel	7	1	Upper Volta	2	
Italy	3	2	Vatican City		2
Ivory Coast	1		Venezuela	1	
Jamaica	2		Vietnam	2	1
Japan	6		Yugoslavia	2	1
Jordan	6	1	Zaire (Congo)	2	
Korea, Rep. of	3				
Laos	4		Total	142	42

Geographic Areas	Countries	Visits to U.S.	President's Visits
Africa	16	26	0
Asia and Oceana	18	36	7
Europe	22	42	26
Mideast	10	24	7
Western Hemisphere	10	14	2
Total	76	142	42

Source: Extracted from Elmer Plischke, *Presidential Diplomacy: A Chronology of Summit Visits, Trips, and Meetings* (Dobbs Ferry, N.Y.: Oceana, 1986), chs. 2 and 4.

Table 11.2
Summit Visits to the United States (January 20, 1969–August 9, 1974)

A. Visits Per Year				B. Number of Days Per Visit		
Year	No.	%		Days	No.	%
1969	33	23.24		1	76	53.52
1970	49	34.50		2	37	26.06
1971	26	18.31		3	14	9.86
1972	7	4.93		4	3	2.11
1973	25	17.61		5	1	0.70
1974	2	1.41		6	2	1.41
				7	4	2.82
				8	2	1.41
				9	2	1.41
				12	1	0.70
Total	142	100.00			142	100.00

C. Rank of Visitor				D. Type of Visit		
Title	No.	%		Type	No.	%
Monarch: Emperor,				State Visit	2	1.41
King, Queen, Shah	17	11.97		Official Visit	41	28.87
President	39	27.47		Informal/Unofficial		
Prime Minister,				Visit	48	33.80
Premier, Chancellor	81	57.04		Ceremonial Visit	43	30.28
President-elect	1	0.70		Private Visit	6	4.23
Others	4	2.82		Summit Meeting	2	1.41
Total	142	100.00			142	100.00

Source: Based on Elmer Plischke, *Presidential Diplomacy: A Chronology of Summit Visits, Trips, and Meetings* (Dobbs Ferry, N.Y.: Oceana, 1986), Tables 3 and C, pp. 105–115, 147.

But the frequency of visits declined substantially during 1972, when the president concentrated on his trips to Beijing and Moscow, and in 1974, when he was busy with two major foreign trips, SALT negotiations, and the Watergate affair. (See Table 11.2, Part A.)

A majority of these summit visitors (57 percent) were heads of government (prime ministers, premiers, and chancellors) who normally are accorded less ceremony and protocol than chiefs of state, although a substantial number (39 percent) involved the latter (reigning monarchs and presidents). In keeping with precedent established by Presidents Kennedy and Johnson, most visits (80 percent) during the Nixon era were of short duration—for parts of one or two days—but a few ran for as long as seven to twelve days. (See Table 11.2, Parts B and C.)

President Nixon hosted an unusually large number of ceremonial visits, for reasons already noted, and by comparison with his immediate predecessors (Eisenhower, Kennedy, and Johnson), there were very few formal state visits. On the other hand, the preponderant majority (63 percent) were either official or unofficial/informal visits designed to provide opportunity for serious discussion of public policy issues at the highest level.[50] (See Table 11.2, Part D.)

As indicated in the breakdown by geographic areas in Table 11.1, more than half of the summit visitors came from European and Asian/Pacific countries, whereas the fewest were from the Mideast and, surprisingly, from Western Hemisphere nations. Aside from the traditional periodic exchanges of visits by the president and the prime minister of Canada and the president of Mexico, the most frequent summit visitors during the Nixon Administration were from the Federal Republic of Germany (7), Israel (7), and Great Britain, Japan, and Jordan (6 each).[51]

The individual leaders who came most frequently were King Hussein of Jordan (6 visits), Emperor Haile Selassie of Ethiopia (3), Shah Reza Pahlavi of Iran (3), and Prime Ministers Golda Meir of Israel (6), Willy Brandt of West Germany (5), Edward Heath of Great Britain (4), and Souvanna Phouma of Laos (4). Other reigning monarchs included Emperor Hirohito (Japan) and Kings Baudouin (Belgium), Faisal (Saudi Arabia), and Olav V (Norway). President Nixon also received such other leaders as Leonid Brezhnev (Soviet Union), Charles de Gaulle (France), Indira Gandhi (India), Archbishop Makarios (Cyprus), Chung Hee Park (Korea), Suharto (Indonesia), Nguyen Van Thieu (South Vietnam), and Josip Broz Tito (Yugoslavia).

Summit visitors are usually received in the national capital, but there are exceptions. Thus, President Nixon met with Vietnam's President Thieu at Midway Island in June 1969, and, when he came to the United States on an official visit for six days in April 1973, they met at the president's retreat at San Clemente, California. The president also met with others at alternative sites—with President Chung Hee Park of Korea at San Francisco (August 1969), Emperor Hirohito at Elmendorf Air Force Base in Alaska (September 1971),[52] Chancellor Willy Brandt at Key Biscayne, Florida (December 1971), Prime Minister Kakuei Tanaka of Japan in Hawaii (August 1972), and General Secretary Brezhnev at Camp David in nearby Maryland (June 1973).

Naturally, foreign leaders come to the United States for a variety of reasons— to get to know one another—to meet face to face, to promote good will, understanding, and favorable relations, to achieve acceptance by the United States and the world in the case of newly emergent nations, to confer on economic needs, political problems, national security issues, and the strengthening of alliances, and to cope with crises or, sometimes, for more concrete and particularized reasons, including private medical attention.[53]

To cite a few illustrations, President Nixon hosted more than twenty-five visits with the leaders of eleven Pacific and Asian allies during the Vietnam War. Early in 1970 he sought to mend fences with several major European powers— especially Britain, France, and West Germany. When Prime Minister Harold Wilson came in January, Wilson informed the president of British plans to remove its forces from the Persian Gulf and discussed how the United States might fill the power vacuum there. President Georges Pompidou of France arrived the following month for an extended visit that took him throughout the United States, and he publicly pressured the president to end the Vietnam War quickly (while he also was quietly helping to arrange secret talks by Kissinger with the North Vietnamese). Chancellor Brandt, who came for eight days in April, proved to be the most difficult, owing to disagreement over his *Ostpolitik*, the possibility of reducing U.S. forces in Europe, and uncertainty respecting the future of NATO. And when the president met with Japanese Prime Minister Tanaka in Hawaii in 1972, they agreed to maintain indefinitely the United States-Japanese Mutual Security Treaty and debated ways to improve festering trade relations.[54]

Sometimes the president's summit guests come to express appreciation for American assistance, but more frequently to solicit it. In 1973, following the cease-fire in Vietnam, President Thieu wished to personally thank the United States for its help and to commend the American people for their sacrifice in seeking to stem Communist aggression in Southeast Asia. It is well known, however, that many summit visitors seek United States assistance in the form of improved trade relations, financial grants, loans, and technical assistance. The roster of foreign leaders who discuss this subject with the president and other officials in Washington tends to parallel the list of those who visit Washington.[55]

The most highly publicized summit visit during the Nixon Administration was that of Brezhnev, who came for an East-West summit meeting as part of the exchange of visits between the two leaders, which is discussed later. Such summit visits hosted by the United States continued until April 1974, just a few weeks before President Nixon left for his two trips to the Mideast and Moscow, and only four months before he resigned from the presidency. The president believed that these visits contributed to the shaping of his foreign policy, augmented American credibility and good will, and constituted an integral, highly visible, and sometimes valuable component of his personal conduct of American foreign affairs.[56]

NIXON'S FOREIGN VENTURES

Since Theodore Roosevelt, the first president to leave the United States and enter foreign jurisdiction (to inspect construction of the Panama Canal and to deliver an address in the city of Panama in 1906), every president (except Herbert Hoover)[57] has gone abroad in some capacity. But it was Franklin Roosevelt who incorporated foreign trips, primarily for purposes of conferencing, into the presidential summit repertoire. In the past eighty years, presidents have undertaken some 110 trips and made more than 250 summit visits to foreign lands.

Their purposes have been mixed, varying from occasional vacationing (as in the case of Franklin Roosevelt, 1934 to 1940) and purely ceremonial responsibilities to conferring and negotiating with foreign leaders. The obvious goals of presidential summit visits include getting to know and taking the measure of other leaders personally, promoting good will, improving the climate of inter-

Table 11.3
President Nixon's Summit Trips and Visits Abroad (January 20, 1969–August 9, 1974)

Trips

A. Trips Per Year

Year	No.	%
1969	3	20.00
1970	3	20.00
1971	2	13.33
1972	3	20.00
1973	1	6.67
1974	3	20.00
Total	15	100.00

B. Types of Trips

	No.	%
To single country	9	60.00
To 2 or more countries	2	13.33
Grand tours	4	26.67
	15	100.00

Visits

C. Type of Visit

Category	No.	%
Conference	0	0.00
Meeting	5	11.91
State visit and meeting	2	4.76
Ordinary state visit	10	23.81
Official visit	5	11.91
Informal visit	14	33.33
Ceremonial visit	4	9.52
Audience with Pope	2	4.76
Total	42	100.00

D. No. of Days Per Visit[a]

Days	No.	%	Total No. of Days
1	7	16.67	6[b]
2	24	57.14	48
3	7	16.67	21
4	1	2.38	4
7	1	2.38	7
8	1	2.38	8
9	1	2.38	9
	42	100.00	103

Source: Based on Elmer Plischke, *Presidential Diplomacy: A Chronology of Summit Visits, Trips, and Meetings* (Dobbs Ferry, N.Y.: Oceana, 1986), Tables 1 and A, pp. 21–24, 37.

[a]The duration of visits represents full or partial days.

[b]Discrepancy due to papal audience occurring during a three-day visit to Rome and, therefore, is not counted as an additional day.

national diplomacy, expounding U.S. interests and policies, aligning national positions, invigorating alliances, and, occasionally, signing agreements.[58]

President Nixon was an unusually active summiteer abroad. He undertook fifteen summit trips to foreign lands which involved forty-two summit visits. To date, this represents the largest number of foreign trips (except for the seventeen summit trips taken by President Eisenhower, but exceeding even those of President Roosevelt) and the highest number of foreign visits. These consist of ten formal state visits (the largest number for any president), four ceremonial trips, nineteen official and informal/unofficial visits, seven summit meetings, and two audiences with the Pope.[59] (See Table 11.3, Part C.)

On these summit trips, the president visited thirty different countries. Beginning with his "voyage of reconciliation" to Europe early in 1969, he concentrated his foreign ventures on European states (some nine Western and four Communist countries, plus the Vatican). But he also visited seven Asian and Pacific nations (including Vietnam and China), six in the Mideast, and only Canada and Mexico in the Western Hemisphere.[60] (See Table 11.1.) Complementing the summit visits of foreign leaders to the United States, the president therefore met and dealt with the chiefs of state and heads of government of some seventy-six nations, which amounts to approximately 60 percent of the independent countries (with which the United States dealt diplomatically) at the time. These trips and visits, in conjunction with his vice presidential trips and those taken during his eight intervening years as a private citizen, mean that his foreign travels and personal association with the world's leaders of his day were more extensive than those of any other president in our history.[61]

Nine of President Nixon's trips were for limited purposes, taking him to a single country—such as (aside from his purely ceremonial visits)[62] his conferral with the presidents of Mexico (Puerto Valarta in August 1970) and France (Azores in December 1971 and Reykjavik, Iceland, in May 1973) and with the prime ministers of Britain (Bermuda in December 1971) and Canada (Ottawa in April 1972). In several of these cases, he appears to have preferred meeting in "neutral" sites. In addition, when he went to Beijing, he avoided pickaback stops in other countries, whereas when he flew to Moscow in 1972 and 1974 he combined these with visits to other countries.[63]

Four of Nixon's foreign ventures became grand tours, each of which aggregated visits to some six to eight countries. These took him to Europe (shortly after his inauguration in 1969 and in the fall of 1970), to Asia and the Pacific (including Vietnam in the summer of 1969),[64] and to the Mideast (in June 1974, shortly before his second trip to Moscow).[65] In addition to his two trips to Europe (an area ignored by President Johnson during his foreign travels),[66] these grand tours included a nine-day globegirdling odyssey to Asia (beginning with the splashdown of Apollo IX on July 23, 1969) coursing among five Asian allies and India, and returning from the Far East via Romania and the United Kingdom,[67] and his ten-day tour of the Mideast, primarily to improve relations between Israel and the Arab powers.[68] (For types of trips, see Table 11.3, Part B.) But his most historic trips took him to China and the Soviet Union.

On three-fourths of his foreign visits, the president spent merely a day or two, but, understandably, he extended his stay to a week or longer when he went to Beijing and Moscow.[69] All told, in his foreign summitry he aggregated more time—totaling 103 days—than any other president, except for Woodrow Wilson.[70] (See Table 11.3, Part D.)

Such presidential trips and visits have become common practice since World War II. They vary considerably in their objectives and achievements, occupy a substantial amount of White House time and energy, and need to be assessed in terms of whether this technique of summitry is better suited than other diplomatic practices to achieve the nation's objectives, which can best be determined on a case-by-case basis.[71] Nevertheless, Hugh Sidey, who has frequently commented on the presidency and summitry, has written: "The cynics can deplore the modern summit ritual, with its posturing and pomp, but nobody has thought of a better idea."[72]

NIXON'S SUMMIT CONFERENCING

During his five and one-half years in the White House, President Nixon participated in fewer summit meetings than any of his predecessors since Franklin Roosevelt, except for President Truman. However, he surpassed them all in the number and significance of his meetings with the leaders of Communist China and the Soviet Union—a daring and risky venture in post–World War II diplomacy. He preferred bilateral conferencing and attended no major multipartite conclaves (like Woodrow Wilson at Paris to draft the World War I peace treaties), but he averaged two summit meetings per year.[73]

Of Nixon's nine summit meetings, only two were held in the United States, and the sole multilateral gathering involved his attendance at a North Atlantic Treaty Organization session in Brussels (February 1969). On two occasions he joined others in simultaneous bilateral sessions (with President Georges Pompidou of France and Prime Minister Marcello Caetano of Portugal in December 1971 and with Pompidou and Iceland's Prime Minister Olafur Johannesson in May 1973). None of the meetings he attended were purely ceremonial. The primary role he played at these summit meetings was devoted to discussion and conferral, except for his conclaves with Chinese and Soviet leaders, in which he also engaged in negotiation and the consummation of agreements. All told, he spent forty-one days in summit conferencing, usually limiting himself to only one or two days per meeting, but his East-West conclaves in Beijing, Moscow, and Washington lasted from seven to nine days. (See Table 11.4 for statistical data.)[74]

The president's first summit meeting, with President Thieu at Midway Island on June 8, 1969, was scheduled to persuade the Vietnamese government to support President Nixon's plans for Vietnamization of the fighting in Southeast Asia and for beginning the withdrawal of American combat troops from the area.[75] In December 1971 the president decided on a series of bilateral meetings with the leaders of our principal European allies to deal with a global financial crisis and pressing NATO issues. He met with President Pompidou of France on Terceira Island in the Azores and with British Prime Minister Heath at Bermuda—both neutral sites.[76] Subsequently, in May 1973, he met again with Pompidou in Reykjavik to discuss the president's "new Atlantic Charter" proposal for economic cooperation of the NATO powers and continuing allied problems.[77]

The remaining four summits President Nixon participated in constituted his most noteworthy summit ventures. His trips to Beijing and Moscow in 1972 are technically classified as joint state visits/summit meetings, whereas the exchange

Table 11.4

President Nixon's Participation in Summit Meetings (January 20, 1969–August 9, 1974)

A. Meetings Per Year		B. Location		C. No. of Days
Year	No.	U.S.	Abroad	
1969	2	1	1	3
1970	0	0	0	0
1971	2	0	2	4
1972	2	0	2	17
1973	2	1	1	10
1974	1	0	1	7
Total	9	2	7	41
%		22.22	77.78	

D. Participants			E. Primary Presidential Role	
Year	Bilateral	Multilateral	Discussion	Negotiation
1969	1	1	2	0
1970	0	0	0	0
1971	1	1	2	0
1972	2	0	0	2
1973	1	1	2	0
1974	1	0	0	1
Total	6	3	6	3
%	66.67	33.33	66.67	33.33

Source: Based on Elmer Plischke, *Presidential Diplomacy: A Chronology of Summit Visits, Trips, and Meetings* (Dobbs Ferry, N.Y.: Oceana, 1986), Tables 5 and E, pp. 242, 253.

of visits by Brezhnev and Nixon in 1973 and 1974 lacked the stature of such formal visits. In any case, ceremonies were of secondary importance to serious, in-depth discussion of policy matters and negotiation of mutual understandings.

The road to these conclaves was as intricate, time consuming, and precarious as it was in earlier administrations. President Nixon used both personal communications and special emissaries—especially Kissinger—in addition to traditional diplomacy to facilitate the way to the summit. East-West summit conferencing was begun by President Roosevelt during World War II, and every subsequent president has engaged in such gatherings, establishing a conferencing momentum. Prior to his election in 1968, Nixon asserted in August that, if nominated for the presidency, he might go to Moscow immediately, but it took nearly four years to prepare the way.[78] Eventually, he accelerated the process, meeting with Brezhnev in three annual sessions, 1972–74, and before his resignation he planned another (to which Gerald Ford fell heir).[79]

The ascent to the summit with China's leaders was even more tenuous. Diplomatic relations between the countries had been severed following the Communist takeover in 1949, complicating the process of communication. The principal purposes of establishing official contact were to instill mutual confidence and eventually normalize relations, including the reestablishment of resident diplomatic representation. Although initially limited and unfruitful exchanges were maintained at the diplomatic level for more than fifteen years in neutral sites (Geneva, 1955–57, and Warsaw, after 1957), President Nixon initiated the march toward normalcy by a series of signals and probes in January 1970. But it took more than two years, including Kissinger's two "Polo" trips, to consummate arrangements for the president's journey to Beijing.[80]

While in China, February 21–28, 1972, Nixon was the first American president to be treated by the Communist government to various elements of the formal state visit—including the customary banquets and toasts, attendance at a performance of the Beijing Opera, a gymnastics and table tennis exhibition, and side excursions to the Ming tombs, the Forbidden City, the fabled Great Wall, Hanchow, and Shanghai. But the main objective of the trip—serious Sino-America conferencing—involved the president in preliminary talks with Mao Zedong for an hour and more than fifteen hours of informal policy discussions with Premier Zhou Enlai. These were paralleled by Kissinger's negotiations at the end of each day on the final version of the summit communique and Secretary Rogers' meetings with Chinese Foreign Minister Chi Peng-fei. Subjects discussed ranged widely, embracing U.S. and Chinese national concerns in Asia, the American military presence in Japan, Soviet expansion and hegemonism, the war in Indochina, Indian-Pakistani relations, and the Mideast. The status of Taiwan (Nationalist China) proved to be the most contentious and difficult issue on the agenda.[81]

The principal concrete result was the signing of the 1,800-word Shanghai Communique, a landmark in presidential diplomacy. It specified Chinese and American positions and differences, and it identified those bilateral issues on which the leaders could agree, such as that neither country sought hegemony—an expression the Chinese insisted on—in the Asia/Pacific area and both opposed imperial domination by the Soviet Union. In the communique they recognized the sovereignty and integrity of other countries in the Far East (reminiscent of the American Open Door policy at the turn of the century), supported peaceful coexistence, and undertook to facilitate future contacts and exchanges. Finally, they agreed to continue the diplomatic process "for concrete consultations to further the normalization of relations."[82]

Kissinger called the China initiative a bold "historic opening to China" and "a genuine historic achievement." In *The New York Times* James Reston commended the president for ending "one of the great problems of United States foreign policy—the isolation and hostility of China." On his return to the United States the president declared that it had been his principal goal to reestablish communications with the People's Republic and that he achieved this goal. In his final banquet toast in China he exulted: "This was the week that changed the world."[83]

President Nixon's objectives for meeting with Soviet leader Brezhnev three times were more ambitious and complex. In addition to ameliorating Soviet-American differences (détente), stablizing geopolitical relations on the basis of mutual advantage, and acknowledging shared responsibility for maintaining world peace, these objectives included discussing methods of cooperation and area problems and crises, and especially concluding nuclear arms limitation treaties and a series of "technical agreements." Each of the three meetings was comprehensive in scope and depth, conferencing organization was more sophisticated than at Beijing, discussions were wide ranging, negotiations and bargaining were vigorous, often protracted, and sometimes heated, and in view of the difficulty of reconciling apposing national interests and achieving accommodation, the results were impressive.

The president personally engaged in many hours of discussions—averaging some thirty to forty hours at each of the three meetings—but, reflecting his style, he generally left detailed negotiations to Kissinger, Secretary Rogers, and other members of his delegation. Late in these visits the president was given the opportunity to deliver a radio-TV address to the Russian people and when Brezhnev came to the United States he spoke to the American public. As customary, at the conclusion of each meeting, the leaders signed a communique describing the encounter and its results.[84]

The significance of these Soviet-American summits is attributable especially to the progress made in negotiations on nuclear arms limitation. To summarize, eight treaties and agreements concerned with nuclear affairs were signed. These dealt with the Limitation of Anti-Ballistic Missile Systems (ABM Treaty) and the Limitation of Strategic Offensive Arms (SALT Treaty), in 1972; Basic Principles of Negotiation on Strategic Arms Limitation and on the Prevention of Nuclear War, in 1973; and a Protocol to the ABM Treaty, a Threshold Test Ban Treaty to limit underground nuclear weapons tests, and agreements prescribing procedures governing replacement, dismantling, or destruction for both strategic offensive arms and the ABM systems, in 1974. President Nixon and General Secretary Brezhnev personally signed the first six, whereas Kissinger and Soviet Foreign Minister Andrei Gromyko signed the last two.

In addition, evidencing progress in other areas, the U.S. and Soviet governments also signed some twenty "technical" treaties and agreements at these three summit meetings. They covered a broad spectrum of subjects, ranging from a series of separate agreements to cooperate with respect to agriculture, cultural exchange, energy, environmental research, exploration and use of outer space, heart research, peaceful use of atomic energy, science and technology, the study of world oceans, and transportation, to a general Convention on Taxation (similar to the treaties on double taxation already signed by the United States with thirty-five other countries), and an important Agreement on Basic Principles of Mutual Relations, signed in 1972 to govern subsequent negotiations, somewhat comparable in purpose and essence to the Shanghai Communique.[85] These Nixon-Brezhnev summit meetings became a practical and promising paradigm for constructive conferral and agreement in future years.

By means of the East-West summit meetings, President Nixon and the leaders of China and the Soviet Union not only got to know and understand one another better, but they also created an ongoing, top-level process for discussing and assuaging differences. At a cabinet review of Nixon's trip to China, Kissinger confided that the dialogue between the president and the Chinese leaders in Beijing could not, in his judgment, have occurred at any lower level. The president concluded that its most crucial aspect turned out to be the mutual exchange of views on the respective American and Chinese sense of national purpose and commitments which, he said, could only be addressed effectively at the summit.[86]

Although unprepared to sign a permanent offensive nuclear arms limitation treaty (SALT II) at Moscow in mid–1974—which the president called "a holding pattern summit"—Nixon and Brezhnev had developed mutual credibility and rapport. This was evidenced in part by their discussion of broader, more philosophical matters and issues of national leadership in addition to the agendas at hand. They had also come to taste and value the utility of private, informal discourse, the advantage, if not the necessity, of diplomatic incrementalism, and the momentum of their personal deliberations.

THE VERDICT

President Nixon was an active, often enthusiastic summiteer. He not only employed the traditional summit practices established by his predecessors, but he also introduced a number of important variations and refinements. He was the first president to engage in a bilateral summit with Communist Chinese leaders, the first to visit Beijing and Moscow, and the first to venture to East European countries (Poland, Romania, and Yugoslavia) and to Egypt and Israel on regular summit visits.[87] He initiated annual Soviet-American summit meetings "to limit the miscalculation that can lead to war."[88] He also engaged in regularized summit negotiations with the principal Western industrialized powers to deal with mutual economic problems,[89] and he elevated summitry beyond the amorphous "Spirits" of Geneva (1955), Camp David (1959), Manila (1966), and Glassboro (1967).[90] At the same time he downplayed purely ceremonial and prestige visits to the United States.

Equally impressive evidence of his enthusiasm for presidential diplomacy is the extent of his reliance on certain summit practices. As noted, in addition to the most foreign trips and visits before he became president, these embrace the largest number of special ceremonial visits to be hosted in the United States,[91] the most presidential visits abroad with the highest annual average, as well as the largest number of presidential state visits, papal audiences, and countries visited while president (including the largest number of Communist states), the most meetings with leaders of Communist governments since World War II, and the signing of the largest number of treaties and agreements at the summit.

Contemporary popular assessment of a president is based, in part, on public opinion polls, which provide a rule-of-thumb depiction of his popular image. Since the second Roosevelt Administration, periodic Gallup polls have asked respondents whether they approve or disapprove of the way the president is handling his job; these polls measure a blend of his performance and emotional support for him. Cumulative reports in these samplings indicate a high of 67 percent approval for President Nixon, a low of 24 percent, and an overall average of 49 percent.[92]

Presidents often receive their highest rating immediately after inaugural and sometimes following reelection. President Nixon duplicated his highest popular approval at the time of the Vietnam peace arrangement and his second inaugural, in January 1973, when his rating shot up 16 points in less than a month. Public support was confirmed at the time by endorsement of the peace arrangement by more than a majority of two to one and by overwhelming popular satisfaction with the Vietnam settlement by 80 percent of those polled.[93]

Relating President Nixon's popular image in these polls specifically to his summit experience, we see that his rating increased 7 points immediately following his China trip and 9 points when he returned from the Moscow meeting in 1972. However, his approval score remained unchanged at the time of his meeting with Brezhnev in Washington, and it declined 2 points following his second trip to Moscow. Therefore, the notion that the public uniformly reflects reflexive support for the president's summit ventures cannot be sustained.[94] On the other hand, the record also indicates that, except for such major developments as the Vietnam War, the Watergate affair, and similar matters, a president's prospects of improving his popular image by ascending the summit generally tend to be favorable.

By way of comparison, it is interesting to note that at the time of President Nixon's popularity slide during the Watergate era, when his rating sank to 26 percent in June 1974, his foreign affairs ranking was nevertheless more than twice as high (54 percent), perhaps because of his successful consummation of the Arab-Israeli cease-fire and his impending second visit to Moscow. Moreover, in 1976—two years after his resignation from the presidency—a special Gallup poll asked "what three U.S. Presidents do you regard as the greatest," in which the respondents ranked Nixon among the top ten.

As far as assessment by "experts" is concerned, in the surveys of historians and social scientists, which rank presidents by categories, Nixon's appraisal is uncertain. But ranking presidents as noteworthy diplomats in chief is quite another proposition. They tend to be remembered in diplomatic history for particular reasons—their major policy initiatives and management, the quality of their foreign relations strategies, their concrete contributions to specific aspects of summit diplomacy (thereby augmenting the opportunities of their successors), their credibility to and stature and success of their personal surrogates, and their practical summit accomplishments.

The principal legacies for which President Nixon as summiteer is remembered include rapprochement with China and the Soviet Union and the amelioration of the Cold War, the attempt to fabricate a structure of peace and international stabilization based on pragmatic treatment of the negotiable, the Nixon Doctrine, such sanguine end-products as the Shanghai Communique and the SALT, ABM, and other nuclear treaties, the unprecedented and unmatched package of U.S.-Soviet technical agreements, and, for more sophisticated analysts, the sagacious and productive use of the linkage principle in his summit negotiations.[95] On the basis of these criteria, achievements, and legacies—leaving opinion polls, predisposition, polemics, and partisanship aside—President Nixon bears the distinction of joining George Washington, Theodore Roosevelt, Woodrow Wilson, Franklin Roosevelt, Harry Truman, and Dwight Eisenhower in America's Summit Hall of Fame of most notable diplomats in chief.[96]

It is freely acknowledged that President Nixon was knowledgeable in the field of foreign affairs,[97] that he was determined to control major policy considerations and developments in the White House,[98] and that he intended to institute significant changes in both foreign policy and its implementation. This, one of his biographers has written, "set the United States . . . on a wholly new course in its foreign relations" and "marked a most momentous shift in America's posture toward allies and adversaries alike."[99]

Equally significant, the president understood and mastered the foreign relations equation—supported by many theorists and analysts—that to succeed in foreign affairs it is essential to keep policies in balance with objectives, commitments commensurate with capability, and action in equilibrium with opportunities, possibilities, and potential consequences. According to Raymond Price, President Nixon's foreign policy "depended absolutely on American strength—not only military and economic strength but also strength of will and strength of purpose."[100] Kissinger recounts that the president and he "wanted to found American foreign policy on a sober perception of permanent national interest."[101] These factors, relating interests and capability with objectives and feasibility, produced a unique amalgam of ideals, realism, and pragmatism in Nixon's foreign relations. While the language of his policy espousal confirmed basic American ideals, in practice his actions reflected equally the constraints of the possible. In short, in his conduct of foreign affairs, Nixon was fundamentally a pragmatist with a staunch regard for basic goals and principles.[102]

"Essentially, what Nixon sought as President," concludes Price, "was to seize the opportunity presented by a particular confluence of forces in the world that might not be repeated, and to use this opportunity to create a new structure that could maintain peace among the major powers for the balance of the twentieth century and beyond." This personal and policy aspiration of contributing to peace and being remembered by posterity as peacemaker motivates all presidents. Nixon was no exception. In his memoirs Kissinger writes: "Richard Nixon wanted nothing so much as to go down in history as peacemaker."[103] In the early 1970s Nixon wrote that his greatest goal was "the development of a new structure of international relationships leading to a more peaceful world." By this he meant "not only the absence of war, but a peace based on new, creative and conciliatory global relationships containing rational arrangements for the containment of tensions . . . and measures for the negotiation of confrontations."[104]

In pursuance of this and other national objectives, Nixon wore the mantles of policymaker in chief and the country's chief ambassador with enthusiasm, imagination, and credibility. And, like other recent presidents, he espoused the stewardship (rather than the caretaker or purely administrative) theory of the presidency, which regards the president, unless forbidden by the Constitution, as empowered to do what is necessary for the people to whom he alone is responsible.

It has been written that, as a "relentless traveler," Nixon "played out his strategies publicly as a consummate actor with a flair for the dramatic on practically every world stage," that he was "a passionate believer in personal diplomacy," and that "his personality thrived on extraordinary foreign exposure,"[105] that he "never left summit meetings to chance,"[106] and that his "approach to personal diplomacy was extremely meticulous."[107] With hindsight, in 1982 Nixon emphasized the particular need for and value of summitry between the leaders of the major powers. "In the nuclear age," he wrote, "leaders who do not meet, who do not talk out their differences, who do not understand each other, run the risk of inadvertently pushing each other over the brink—not because they want war, but because they miscalculate what actions will provoke war."[108]

Driven by his desire to initiate an era of negotiation to ameliorate the Cold War and construct an interlocking "structure of peace," in less than two and one-half years President Nixon engaged in four historic East-West summit meetings. Although his goal of rapprochement with both Communist China and the Soviet Union was only partially achieved, his summit legacy of creating a strategy of refining basic areas of mutual concern and negotiability, and resolving issues incrementally is impressive—and remains without parallel in the post–World War II era. There is no way of knowing what might have happened had he enjoyed the freedom and vigor of his first term for another two and one-half years. And yet, in the judgment of Kissinger, who was closest to him in the formulation of foreign policy and his summit ventures, Nixon "met the test of his encounter with destiny" and "the judgment of history . . . would remember his major achievements."[109]

As an epilogue, it needs to be added that during his post-presidential years Richard Nixon has continued his avid interest in U.S. foreign policy and relations, evidenced by his favorable reception abroad by many foreign leaders during his continuing travels, especially to China and the Mideast but also to Eastern Europe,[110] by his lectures and addresses on foreign affairs, and by his reflective publications. In addition to his memoirs, he has published an impressive series of volumes presenting his commentary and judgments on the presidency, American foreign policy and strategy, and the foreign dignitaries with whom he dealt at the summit, and an exponential and edifying discourse on "superpower summitry."[111] In this fashion, he has contributed more to the understanding and appraisement of summitry than any other president.

Also illustrating his introspective and assessory contribution is the ten rules he would carve into the walls of the Oval Office of the White House to guide future presidents. On the positive side, for example, he counsels: always be prepared to negotiate but never negotiate without being prepared, always remember that covenants should be openly agreed to but privately negotiated, and always leave an adversary a face-saving line of retreat. Negatively, he warns that the president should never give up unilaterally what may be used as a bargaining chip but make the adversary give up something in return, never seek publicity that would destroy the ability to achieve results, and never let an adversary underestimate what you would do in response to a challenge but never tell him in advance what you would not do. To these he sagely adds an eleventh commandment as a caveat, namely: while posing these postulates as absolutes, "never foreclose the unique exception," but "always leave room for maneuver," and remember that the president always must "be prepared for what he thought he would never do."[112]

Commenting on summitry, Nixon also warns that, in contemplating an ascent to the summit, the president must weigh carefully and systematically his goals and capabilities, his policies and expectations, and possible benefits, risks, and disadvantages. When dealing with adversarial powers, he acknowledges that in his experience the chief benefits of summit meetings with Soviet leaders were that they enabled him to take their measure and thereby reduce the possibility of miscalculation in the event of a future confrontation. They also gave him the opportunity to use his presidential powers of persuasion.

With hindsight, in 1985 former President Nixon wrote that for five years he had strongly urged the holding of annual summit meetings with adversaries. Even though major substantive agreements might not be ready for consummation, in his view these meetings could be useful for several reasons: to "reduce the risk of war from miscalculation," to inhibit "one side from engaging in actions that would be clearly against the interests of the other during the period before the meeting" (providing an incentive to avoid conduct that would poison the atmosphere and impede momentum), to "get a bureaucracy moving" (which is stimulated by the deadline of the impending summit), and hopefully to mitigate oscillation in American policy development from administration to administration.[113] But, he also cautions, "a President should go to a summit only if the stakes are worth the risks," and "no American President should go to a summit with an adversary unless he knows what is on the other side of the mountain."[114]

NOTES

1. It must be realized that, technically, the president serving as his own ambassador differs substantially from the allegation that a president functions as his own secretary

of state. For commentary, see Elmer Plischke, *Diplomat in Chief: The President at the Summit* (New York: Praeger, 1986), pp. 451–455; hereinafter cited as *Diplomat in Chief*. Also see Elmer Plischke, *Conduct of American Diplomacy*, 3rd ed. (Princeton, N.J.: Van Nostrand, 1967), pp. 178–80.

2. Clinton Rossiter, *The American Presidency*, 2nd ed. (New York: Harcourt, Brace, World, 1960), p. 28.

3. As a member of the House of Representatives, Nixon went to Europe in 1947 with the Herter Committee to review the practical applicability of the Marshall Plan.

4. Quoted in Ralph de Toledano, *Nixon* (New York: Holt, 1956), p. 151.

5. Such as Prime Minister Winston Churchill (and Foreign Minister Anthony Eden) in 1955, as well as the leaders of France, Japan, and other countries.

6. To avoid any semblance of another "Munich," the press reported that Vice President Nixon, despite a summer shower, insisted that no umbrellas—the symbol of Neville Chamberlain's appeasement of Adolf Hitler at Munich in 1938—be displayed at the president's arrival ceremony. See *Washington Post*, July 25, 1955, and Keith Eubank, *The Summit Conferences, 1919–1950* (Norman: University of Oklahoma Press, 1966), p. 158.

7. The day preceding this joint ceremony President Eisenhower joined the queen in dedicating the Saint Lawrence Seaway.

8. James Keogh, *This Is Nixon* (New York: Putnam, 1956), p. 16.

9. When President Eisenhower was stricken with his heart attack in 1955, he regularized this arrangement by letter to the vice president. The president was in Denver for forty-eight days during which Nixon handled various executive functions, including the signing of ceremonial documents ("in behalf of the president"). The same arrangement was employed when the president was incapacitated by his ileitis surgery the following year and when he suffered a stroke in 1957.

For Nixon's account, see *The Memoirs of Richard Nixon* (New York: Grosset & Dunlap, 1978), pp. 164–166, hereinafter cited as *Memoirs*; also see his *Six Crises* (New York: Pyramid Books, 1968), pp. 139–194, with the text of the president's letter specifying procedures for a possible vice presidential takeover of presidential functions on p. 191. On this matter, also see Fawn M. Brodie, *Richard Nixon: The Shaping of His Character* (New York: W. W. Norton, 1981), pp. 348–350, 355–359; and Earl Mazo and Stephen Hess, *Nixon: A Political Portrait* (New York: Harper & Row, 1968), ch. 12.

10. For the White House announcement respecting this summit conference procedure, see *Public Papers of the Presidents of the United States: Dwight D. Eisenhower, 1960–1961*, (Washington, D.C.: U.S. Government Printing Office, 1961), pp. 361–362, 363–364; hereinafter cited as *Papers of Presidents*. This was a unique precedent if it was intended that the sessions were to continue at the summit, with the vice president serving as subsummiteer. In response, Premier Nikita Khrushchev, sensitive to the matter of equality of treatment, let it be known that he objected to this proposal because, as he put it, this would "leave the cabbage to the care of the goat." In any case, as a consequence of the U–2 incident, this contingency never materialized because the 1960 Paris Conference was aborted and the president made his visit to Portugal as scheduled.

11. *Memoirs*, pp. 186, 200–201. While in London, for example, he conferred with British officials, delivered his "Guildhall Address," lunched with Queen Elizabeth, hosted a Thanksgiving Day dinner for the queen, and visited aging Winston Churchill. Ghana became the first black African nation to become independent after World War II. See Richard Nixon, *Leaders* (New York: Warner Books, 1982), pp. 259–260.

12. This was a seven-day trip during which Nixon visited the Hungarian boundary; he returned via Munich and Iceland, arriving in Washington the day before Christmas. See *Memoirs*, pp. 181–184; Richard Nixon, *The Real War* (New York: Warner Books, 1980), p. 22; Brodie, *Richard Nixon*, pp. 378, 381; de Toledano, *Nixon*, pp. 151–152.

13. On his return trip he also visited Poland. See *Papers of Presidents: Dwight D. Eisenhower, 1959*, pp. 330–332; *Memoirs*, pp. 206–214; Nixon, *Six Crises*, pp. 253–314, which relates discussions in detail; Nixon, *The Real War*, p. 48 for his visit to Poland; Brodie, *Richard Nixon*, pp. 379–388; Mazo and Hess, *Nixon*, ch. 14, especially p. 191.

14. *Memoirs*, pp. 119–137, with the quotation on page 134. On this trip the vice president traveled by Constellation, helicopter, limousine, jeep, tractor, oxcart, and imperial coach. For additional commentary, see Keogh, *This Is Nixon*, p. 64. Also see de Toledano, *Nixon*, pp. 160–164, which describes Nixon's preparation, his experiences, and his report to the National Security Council and the public on the trip, and his recommendation for creating a military crescent coursing from the Mideast to the Pacific.

15. For commentary on Nixon's harrowing trip to South America, which includes his mistreatment by volatile, sometimes vicious mobs in Peru and Caracas, Venezuela, in 1958, see *Memoirs*, pp. 185–193. Also see Nixon, *Six Crises*, pp. 195–252; *Leaders*, pp. 190, 211; and *The Real War*, p. 47; also Mazo and Hess, *Nixon*, ch. 13; Brodie, *Richard Nixon*, pp. 362–376; and Keogh, *This Is Nixon*, p. 66.

16. These included all Asian and Western Pacific countries (except the People's Republic of China, Afghanistan, and Singapore), all but two Latin American states, Iran and five other Mideast nations, the Soviet Union and several other European countries, and half a dozen sub-Saharan African nations, plus Hong Kong, Majorca, Puerto Rico, and the Vatican.

17. *Memoirs*, pp. 248–250, 256–258, 271.

18. *Memoirs*, pp. 280–283, and Nixon, *Leaders*, pp. 280–283.

19. Quoted in Keogh, *This Is Nixon*, pp. 14, 17, and de Toledano, *Nixon*, p. 157.

20. *Memoirs*, pp. 137, 280.

21. In this article Nixon suggested that Asia would pose the greatest threat to world peace in the final third of the twentieth century, which would be of grave concern to the United States, a major Pacific power. See Richard Nixon, "Asia After Viet Nam," *Foreign Affairs* 46 (October 1967): 111–125. For commentary, see *Memoirs*, p. 285; and Henry Kissinger, *White House Years* (Boston: Little, Brown, 1979), pp. 164, 331, 334, hereinafter cited as *White House Years*.

22. Such as Nixon's interview published in *Time* magazine on October 5, 1970, in which he indicated that he was anxious to visit China before he died. He emphasized the desirability of Sino-American rapprochement to several foreign leaders who came to the United States to celebrate the twenty-fifth anniversary of the United Nations in October 1970. See *Memoirs*, p. 546; *White House Years*, p. 699.

23. Aside from ceremonial greetings, these usually are congratulatory, condolence, appreciation, and other courtesy messages. Examples include congratulations to Israel on its twenty-first anniversary (1969), and to the Organization of African Unity on its tenth anniversary (1974); condolence on the death of Charles de Gaulle (1969), the death of three Soviet cosmonauts (1971), and the murder of Israeli athletes at the Munich World Olympics (1972); appreciation to France on accepting its gift commemorating the American Bicentennial (1974); and the message to the Soviet president informing him of the

United States' acceptance of the SALT I Treaty (1972). For texts of such documents, see *Papers of Presidents: Richard Nixon, 1969–74.*

24. U.S.-Soviet communications were commenced by President Franklin Roosevelt during World War II and were revived by President Eisenhower and continued by subsequent presidents. For background on important U.S.-Soviet exchanges, see Plischke, *Diplomat in Chief,* pp. 31–52 and Elmer Plischke, ''Eisenhower's 'Correspondence Diplomacy' with the Kremlin—Case Study in Summit Diplomatics,'' *Journal of Politics* 30 (February 1968):137–159.

25. *Memoirs,* especially pp. 393–397 for Ho Chi Minh, and pp. 402, 695, 702–705 for Pham Van Dong.

26. To launch the diplomatic process, the United States also sought to establish communications with Hanoi through half a dozen ''third countries'' and via a number of ''special connections'' or ''channels,'' such as Jean Sainteny, a French businessman who had lived in Vietnam and had high-level contacts in Hanoi. See *Memoirs,* pp. 349, 393–394; *White House Years,* pp. 258, 277–279, 462; with summary in *Diplomat in Chief,* pp. 86–87.

27. In some respects this was similar to the Cuban Missile Crisis of 1962 in that American intelligence obtained information on which diplomatic action could be taken. It differed, however, in that quiet diplomacy, mostly at the subsummit level, resulted in Soviet agreement to abandon the project. See *Memoirs,* pp. 485–489; *White House Years,* pp. 635–652.

28. These included Golda Meir, Anwar Sadat, and Soviet leaders Aleksei Kosygin and Leonid Brezhnev. For commentary on the Mideast crisis, see *Memoirs,* pp. 478–485, 920–943; *White House Years,* pp. 582–593, 598–600, 609–631.

29. Such signals included his 1967 *Foreign Affairs* article (see note 21), a number of low-level probes in 1969, Nixon's observations in his first report to Congress, entitled *U.S. Foreign Policy for the 1970's: A New Strategy for Peace* published in February 1970, and Sino-American diplomatic discussions in Warsaw. See *Memoirs,* p. 545; *White House Years,* pp. 163–193; *Diplomat in Chief,* pp. 342–344.

30. Premier Zhou Enlai called this initiative ''The first time that a proposal has come from a Head [of State] through a Head, to a Head.'' The Nixon-Zhou exchanges were funneled through the Pakistani president. For quotation, see *Memoirs,* p. 547.

31. On the development of these special summit channels, including the use of secret ''backchannels,'' see *Memoirs,* pp. 544–557; *White House Years,* pp. 699–701, 714, 718, 722–725, 728, 738; *Diplomat in Chief,* pp. 342, 344. For discussion of the Kissinger-Anatoly Dobrynin (Soviet ambassador to the United States) special channel, see *White House Years,* pp. 138–147. For discussion of ''backchannels,'' which bypass normal Department of State technical global communications facilities and must be distinguished from special summit intergovernmental channels of communication, see *White House Years,* pp. 722–723; see also *Diplomat in Chief,* pp. 343–344.

32. There were two preparatory ''Polo'' trips, July 1–13 and October 16–26, 1972. See *Memoirs,* pp. 552–557; *White House Years,* pp. 733–763, 774–784; *Diplomat in Chief,* pp. 344–347. Also see note 80.

33. *Memoirs,* pp. 544–557; *White House Years,* pp. 701, 714–715, 724–728; *Diplomat in Chief,* pp. 342–347.

34. *Memoirs,* pp. 617, 1038.

35. For comprehensive analysis of presidential summit communications, see *Diplomat in Chief,* ch. 2, and for assessment of the use of this summit technique, see pp. 58–62.

36. This is reminiscent of President Roosevelt's telephonic exchanges with Prime Minister Churchill and with McKenzie King of Canada during World War II. For general commentary on telephonic summitry, see *Diplomat in Chief*, pp. 52–54.

37. *Memoirs*, p. 982.

38. The establishment of the Washington-Moscow hot line (called "Molink") was agreed to in June 1963. Originally, communication was by Teletype messages across ten thousand miles of undersea and land cables, supplemented by an emergency backup radio circuit. During the Nixon Administration, by supplementary agreement in 1971, more reliable facilities were established, including transmission via space satellites. See *Memoirs*, pp. 527–530, 931, 933, 936–942; *White House Years*, pp. 909, 911, and Henry Kissinger, *Years of Upheaval* (Boston: Little, Brown, 1982) pp. 568–591, hereinafter cited as *Years of Upheaval*; and *Diplomat in Chief*, pp. 54–56.

39. Special emissaries bear various generic titles—such as presidential special representatives or envoys—and in our early history they were called "secret agents." Their accreditation may be denominated as "ambassador," "commissioner," or "plenipotentiary." For commentary, see *Diplomat in Chief*, p. 65.

40. For historical and analytical commentary, see *Diplomat in Chief*, ch. 3, and for assessment of presidential usage, see pp. 112–118.

41. These embraced two Asian trips in 1969 and 1970, a ten-nation thirty-two-day sweep of Asia, Africa, and Europe in 1971, and a trip to the Pacific to participate in the ceremony commemorating the return of Okinawa by the United States to Japan in 1972.

42. *Memoirs*, pp. 477, 482, 1047; *Diplomat in Chief*, pp. 84–85; Tad Szulc, *The Illusion of Peace: Foreign Policy in the Nixon Years* (New York: Viking Press, 1978), pp. 175, 314, 440–441, 796; Rowland Evans, Jr., and Robert D. Novak, *Nixon in the White House: The Frustration of Power* (New York: Random House, 1971), pp. 87–91.

43. *Memoirs*, pp. 750–751; *White House Years*, p. 339; Szulc, *The Illusion of Peace*, pp. 459, 628–630.

44. *White House Years*, pp. 435–436, 1039–1040, 1049–1051, 1309–1314, 1338–1341, 1411–1415, 1459–1460, 1469–1470. Alexander M. Haig, *Caveat: Realism, Reagan, and Foreign Policy* (New York: Macmillan, 1984), deals with Haig's tenure as secretary of state during the Reagan Administration, but see pp. 201–202 for his 1972 China trip.

45. *Memoirs*, p. 585.

46. *Memoirs*, pp. 687–707, 717–758; *White House Years*, passim, especially pp. 1315–1318, 1331–1338, 1341–1356, 1415–1444, 1462–1466, 1472–1473.

47. See comment in *Memoirs*, p. 477. Also see notes 30–32.

48. For commentary on, and comparison of, Kissinger with other four-star presidential special emissaries, see *Diplomat in Chief*, pp. 96–108.

49. For detailed statistical data, chronologically arranged in columnized form, for this section on summit visits to the United States, see Elmer Plischke, *Presidential Diplomacy: A Chronology of Summit Visits, Trips, and Meetings* (Dobbs Ferry, N.Y.: Oceana, 1986), pp. 105–115, with comparative summary statistics on p. 147; hereinafter cited as *Presidential Diplomacy*. For historical analysis and assessment of summit visits to the United States, see *Diplomat in Chief*, ch. 4.

50. These practices illustrate Nixon's style of generally preferring short working visits to ceremonious and protracted visits. He tended to discourage ceremonial or prestige visits—except for such special occasions as President Eisenhower's funeral, the celebration of the twenty-fifth anniversary of the United Nations, and President Truman's

funeral. Also see note 91. The United States normally limits state visits, the most for-malized, to a maximum of four per year, although they sometimes exceed this number. During the Nixon Administration, however, according to the Department of State, there were only two—President Lleras Camargo of Colombia in 1969 and, surprisingly (because these are restricted to foreign chiefs of state), Prime Minister Eisaku Sato of Japan in 1972.

Furthermore, President Johnson used the designation "informal" rather than "unof-ficial" visits, which has generally been continued except for a time during the Nixon Administration when they were again designated "unofficial." These types of summit visits, initiated by the foreign guest, are similar if not identical, and they normally involve a minimum of ceremony.

For historical and analytical commentary on the distinctions among and development of the various categories of summit visits, see *Diplomat in Chief*, pp. 134–136.

51. From the time of Nixon's inaugural through the 1980s, the countries that ac-counted for the highest number of summit visits to the United States include: Australia, Canada, Egypt, West Germany, Israel, Italy, Japan, Jordan, New Zealand, and the United Kingdom—each with eight or more such visits.

52. On rare occasions an invitation for a summit visit is declined or aborted, as in the case of Emperor Hirohito of Japan. Early in the 1970s, President Nixon extended several invitations to him, and apparently he wished to come to Washington and had the approval of the Japanese cabinet. The White House considered the visit an important prelude to a presidential trip to Tokyo. But because of the extremist opposition in Japan, the Imperial Household Agency rejected the proposal. Consequently, the president and the emperor only met briefly in "neutral" Alaska in September 1971 as Hirohito was en route to Europe—his first foreign venture—and his formal state visit to the United States was delayed until 1975. See *Diplomat in Chief*, p. 164; Szulc, *The Illusion of Peace*, p. 458.

53. For general discussion of purposes of summit visits to the United States, see *Diplomat in Chief*, especially pp. 156–161.

54. *White House Years*, pp. 416–425; Szulc, *The Illusion of Peace*, pp. 217–219, 616–618.

55. *Diplomat in Chief*, p. 158; and see John Osborne, *The Fifth Year of the Nixon Watch* (New York: Liveright, 1974), ch. 10, for President Thieu's second summit visit (1973).

56. For general assessment of this summit technique, see *Diplomat in Chief*, pp. 161–170.

57. However, as president-elect Hoover toured ten Latin American countries in No-vember-December 1928.

58. For commentary on the general planning and purposes of such presidential trips and visits abroad, see *Diplomat in Chief*, pp. 189–198.

59. Such presidential audiences with the Pope were begun by President Wilson as early as January 1919 and have been continued by every president since Eisenhower, but Nixon had two such audiences. He also had an audience as a private citizen in 1967; see Mazo and Hess, *Nixon*, pp. 302–303.

60. Nixon went to Britain four times, to France three times, and either once or twice to each of the rest. For a complete list, see Table 11.1.

61. In addition, since resigning the presidency, Nixon returned to China in 1976, 1979, 1982, and 1985, and flew to Egypt for President Sadat's funeral (as President

Reagan's special emissary, together with former Presidents Ford and Carter), followed by a private tour of Saudi Arabia, Jordan, Tunisia, and Morocco (in October 1981). He also met with Chinese leaders when they came to Washington in 1979 and 1984. He visited ailing Shah Reza Pahlavi of Iran in Mexico in 1979 and attended his funeral in Egypt in July 1980.

For a comprehensive treatment of Nixon's post-presidential career, to 1984, see Robert Sam Anson, *Exile: The Unquiet Oblivion of Richard M. Nixon* (New York: Simon & Schuster, 1984); for his foreign trips, see especially pp. 127–133, 214–215, 267–268 for China trips; 223–224, 245–246, 259–260, 263, 267 for European trips; 250–259 for Sadat's funeral; and 210–211, 224–225 for the Iranian Shah.

62. Nixon's only purely ceremonial presidential trips include the dedication of the Amistad Dam (Mexico, 1969) and attendance at memorial services for French Presidents de Gaulle (1970) and Pompidou (1974).

63. Thus, in 1972 he also went to Austria, Iran, and Poland. In 1974 he combined his Moscow visit with attendance at a NATO Council meeting in Brussels and separate conferral there with the leaders of four of our principal European allies.

64. While in Saigon, he also met with U.S. military personnel (as President Johnson had in 1966 and 1967); see *White House Years*, pp. 276–277.

65. For a detailed listing of Nixon's foreign trips and visits, see *Presidential Diplomacy*, pp. 21–24, and for comparative statistics, see p. 37. For a comprehensive historical account of presidential trips, see *Diplomat in Chief*, ch. 5.

66. See Nixon, *Memoirs*, pp. 370–374, for his 1969 eight-day "working trip" including his conferral with de Gaulle in France to seek his assistance in ending the Vietnam War, Prime Minister Harold Wilson in Britain, and the leaders of West Germany and Italy, and his papal audience. For details, see *White House Years*, pp. 73–111, 936–938. Also see John Osborne, *The Second Year of the Nixon Watch* (New York: Liveright, 1971), ch. 29.

67. *Memoirs*, pp. 394–396; *White House Years*, pp. 155–158, for the Romanian visit.

68. *Memoirs*, pp. 1008–1018; Nixon, *Leaders*, pp. 295–298; *Years of Upheaval*, pp. 1124–1143; John Osborne, *The Last Nixon Watch* (Washington, D.C.: New Republic Book Co., 1975), ch. 21.

69. Nixon's trips to Beijing and Moscow in 1972 were combined state visits and U.S.-Chinese and U.S.-Soviet summit meetings, a technique introduced by President Johnson in 1966 when he went to the Far East to participate in the Manila Conference.

70. President Nixon averaged nearly nineteen days per year, whereas President Eisenhower averaged thirteen days, President Kennedy fourteen days, and President Johnson less than ten days. Participating in the World War I Peace Conference at Paris, President Wilson set a record for American presidents when he went to Europe for 168 days which, plus travel time, means that he was out of the country for more than six months.

71. For general assessment of presidential trips and visits, see *Diplomat in Chief*, pp. 266–277.

72. Hugh Sidey, *Time* Magazine, June 14, 1982, p. 21.

73. To distinguish conferences and meetings, Department of State designations, when available, are employed. The criteria that help to distinguish among them are the number of participants (bilateral conclaves are meetings rather than conferences), the formality of advance preparation, the complexity of functioning, the nature of the end-products, and sometimes their sites and duration. For commentary, see *Diplomat in Chief*, pp. 218–219, 222–224.

74. For detailed and comparative data, see *Presidential Diplomacy*, pp. 242, 253.

75. *Memoirs*, pp. 392–393 and *White House Years*, pp. 272–274. Kissinger reports that the setting in Midway was surrealistic in the sense that for seven hours the atoll, no more than two square miles in size, was inundated by a presidential entourage of over five hundred officials, security officers, communicators, journalists, and supernumeraries—a spectacle monitored by a cadre of beady-eyed gooney birds.

76. *Memoirs*, p. 529. The president had conferred bilaterally with British Prime Minister Heath over a seven-day period in Washington, and for two days with West German Chancellor Brandt shortly after the Bermuda meeting. See *White House Years*, pp. 958–967.

77. In the meantime, President Nixon also conferred bilaterally with British Prime Minister Heath twice and with West German Chancellor Brandt, who came on summit visits to Washington. For commentary on the Iceland meeting, see *Years of Upheaval*, pp. 170–180.

78. For Nixon's statement, see *Washington Post*, August 7, 1968.

79. This was billed as an interim "mini-summit," convened at Vladivostok on November 23–24, 1974; for commentary, see Gerald R. Ford, *A Time to Heal: The Autobiography of Gerald R. Ford* (New York: Harper & Row, 1979), pp. 213–219; also *Diplomat in Chief*, pp. 385–392.

80. *Memoirs*, pp. 544–557; *White House Years*, pp. 684–732; Lloyd C. Gardner, ed., *The Great Nixon Turnaround* (New York: New Viewpoints, 1973), pp. 101–118; *Diplomat in Chief*, pp. 342–347. For "Polo" trips, see note 32.

81. *Memoirs*, pp. 557–580; *White House Years*, pp. 1053–1096; *Diplomat in Chief*, pp. 348–354; Gardner, *The Great Nixon Turnaround*, pp. 119–122; Frank van der Linden, *Nixon's Quest for Peace* (Washington, D.C.: Robert Luce, Inc., 1972), pp. 139–166.

82. For the text of the Shanghai Communique, see *Papers of Presidents: Richard Nixon, 1972*, pp. 376–379 (and Chapter 3 of the present volume); and for ceremonial documents, see pp. 368–384. For commentary, see *Memoirs*, pp. 576–577; *White House Years*, pp. 1079–1086, 1091–1096; *Diplomat in Chief*, pp. 350–352.

83. *Memoirs*, p. 580, and also see Nixon's later assessment in *The Real War*, pp. 136–141; *White House Years*, pp. 1086, 1095; James Reston, *New York Times*, March 1, 1972.

84. For commentary on the prelude to and conduct of these meetings, see *Memoirs*, pp. 524–525 and 609–621 (for 1972), 875–887 (for 1973), and 1023–1039 (for 1974), and Nixon, *The Real War*, pp. 48–49, 208, 290–291; *White House Years*, pp. 1124–1164 (for Kissinger's secret 1972 mission to Moscow) and pp. 1202–1257, and *Years of Upheaval*, pp. 286–301 (for Washington 1973 meeting) and pp. 1151–1178 (for 1974 meeting in Moscow); *Diplomat in Chief*, pp. 354–385; van der Linden, *Nixon's Quest for Peace*, pp. 187–238; Gardner, *The Great Nixon Turnaround*, pp. 222–235. For texts of the toasts, addresses to the public, and communiques, see *Papers of Presidents: Richard Nixon, 1972*, pp. 619–643; *1973*, pp. 594–619; *1974*, pp. 553–582.

85. For lists of U.S. and Soviet signatories of these nuclear and other treaties and agreements, with commentary, see *Diplomat in Chief*, pp. 360–361, 371, 380–381. Also see *Memoirs*, pp. 617–618, 886, 1035–1036; *White House Years*, pp. 1241–1246, 1252–1253, and *Years of Upheaval*, pp. 1165–1173.

86. William Safire, *Before the Fall: An Inside View of the Pre-Watergate White House* (Garden City, N.Y.: Doubleday, 1975), p. 414.

87. Although Franklin Roosevelt went to Egypt in 1943 and 1945 to confer with

Prime Minister Churchill, Generalissimo Chiang Kai-shek, and other leaders, these were not, strictly speaking, summit visits to Egypt to deal with its leaders.

88. Quoted in Nixon, *Leaders*, p. 210.

89. These summit sessions with the leaders of France, West Germany, Italy, Japan, and the United Kingdom numbered twenty-eight in less than six years (not counting an additional five ceremonial visits) and may have contributed significantly to the commencement of annual Western multipartite economic summits in November 1975.

90. Referring disparagingly of such "Spirits" in 1972, President Nixon observed: "What they all added up to was cosmetics . . . all froth and very little substance." See *Newsweek*, May 29, 1972. During the presidential campaign of 1960, Vice President Nixon declared that before going to the summit, a president should be sure that he had some reasonable assurance "that something is going to come out of it other than some phoney spirit of Geneva or Camp David." *Washington Post*, October 22, 1960. And in 1980 he warned that the creation "of a willowy euphoria is one of the dangers of summitry." See Nixon, *The Real War*, p. 266.

91. These, as noted, were all related to such special events as President Eisenhower's funeral ceremony in 1969, the United Nations' twenty-fifth anniversary White House reception in 1970, and President Truman's funeral in 1973. Also see note 50. In keeping with his general policy, none of the other summit visits to the United States during his administration were purely ceremonial. Even the formal state visits of the president of Colombia (1969) and the prime minister of Japan (1972) were restricted to only two days.

92. Both Presidents Truman and Carter sank to lower ratings than did President Nixon, and his overall average exceeded that of Presidents Truman, Ford, Carter, and Reagan (during his early years in the White House). Moreover, in terms of disparities between highs and lows, President Nixon's record of 43 points also was exceeded by those of Presidents Johnson (45 points), Carter (54 points), and Truman (64 points).

93. These and the following paragraphs are based on Elmer Plischke, "The President's Image as Diplomat in Chief," *Review of Politics* 47 (October 1985): 544–565, and "Rating Presidents and Diplomats in Chief," *Presidential Studies Quarterly* 15 (Fall 1985): 725–742; also see *Diplomat in Chief*, pp. 480–485. For a comprehensive profile of poll statistics on the involvement of the United States in international affairs in the early 1970s, see William Watts and Lloyd A. Free, eds., *State of the Nation* (New York: Universe Books, 1973), ch. 10.

94. It must be realized that often these rating changes cannot be attributed solely to such solitary developments. As a matter of fact, during the past forty-five years the patterns relating poll ratings to presidential involvement in major summit events have been unpredictable. For a table, with commentary, of such rating changes in twenty-one cases (1941–81), see Plischke, "The President's Image as Diplomat in Chief," pp. 556–559.

95. On President Nixon's views on the linkage principle, see *The Real War*, pp. 267–269; also see *White House Years*, pp. 127, 129–130, 132–137, 143–144, 161, 966; *Years of Upheaval*, pp. 247–251, 986; Henry Kissinger, *For the Record: Selected Statements, 1977–1980* (Boston: Little, Brown, 1981), pp. 87–91; *Diplomat in Chief*, pp. 340, 354, 361, 383, 424–425.

96. For commentary on this American Summit Hall of Fame, see *Diplomat in Chief*, pp. 483–485; and Plischke, "Rating Presidents and Diplomats in Chief," pp. 737–739.

97. Dan Rather and Gary Paul Gates pay Nixon the compliment of saying that he "was deeply knowledgeable in foreign affairs, in terms of both historic perspective and

contemporary realities"; see *The Palace Guard* (New York: Harper & Row, 1974), pp. 270–271. Ron Ziegler, the White House Press secretary, has observed that Nixon "had an unbelievable grasp of issues and a great awareness of subtleties in foreign affairs"; quoted in Szulc, *The Illusion of Peace*, p. 32.

98. Kissinger reports that the president took over "not simply the planning but also the execution of major initiatives"; see *White House Years*, p. 840.

99. Szulc, *The Illusion of Peace*, p. 7. Raymond Price devotes a whole chapter of his biography *With Nixon* (New York: Viking, 1977, ch. 8) to "The Nixon Revolution," in which, he contends, the president waged battles not only over "the proper role of the United States in the world," but also over issues of power and primacy. Also see note 109. For Nixon's modus operandi in National Security Council sessions, see *White House Years*, p. 48.

100. Price, *With Nixon*, p. 374. Emmet John Hughes, in *The Living Presidency*, maintains that presidents like Theodore and Franklin Roosevelt were effective leaders because they understood and enjoyed the use of power and the management of foreign affairs; cited in Osborne, *The Fifth Year of the Nixon Watch*, p. 181.

101. *White House Years*, p. 914. Nixon and Kissinger agreed that foreign policy "had to be related" not to the idiosyncrasies of decision makers, but "to some basic principles of national interest that transcended any particular Administration," p. 12. Also see Richard Nixon, "Our Resolve Is Running Strong," *Life* 49 (August 29, 1960): 86–88, 91, 93, 94, which is one of twelve essays by different authors on the American national purpose published by *Life* in 1960.

102. Ideals need to be distinguished from idealists, and they differ from ideology and idealogues. For an assessment of a major aspect of ideals and idealism, see Price, *With Nixon*, ch. 7, entitled "Not with Woolly-Headed Idealism." On this matter, Nixon said: "I'm a pragmatist with some deep principles that never change." See interview quoted in Mazo and Hess, *Nixon*, p. 316.

103. Quotations in Price, *With Nixon*, p. 108 (also see note 109); and *Years of Upheaval*, p. 414. "The final verdict of history is not rendered quickly," Nixon has said. "It takes not just years but decades or generations to be handed down. Few leaders live to hear the verdict." Quoting de Gaulle's favorite line from Sophocles, he added: "One must wait until the evening to see how splendid the day has been." See Nixon, *Leaders*, pp. 344–345.

104. Quoted in van der Linden, *Nixon's Quest for Peace*, p. 237. This volume emphasizes the peace objectives and programs of President Nixon. In his first inaugural address, Nixon said: "Peace does not come through wishing for it. There is no substitute for days and even years of patient and prolonged diplomacy." See *Papers of Presidents: Richard Nixon, 1969*, p. 3. Also see his four annual reports to Congress on *U.S. Foreign Policy for the 1970s*, which have subtitles referring to aspects of peace, and *Real Peace*, cited in note 111. Illustrating his post-presidential views on peace, see his address entitled "The Pillars of Peace," Los Angeles World Affairs Council, March 6, 1986 (processed).

105. Szulc, *The Illusion of Peace*, p. 4. Evans and Novak report that President Nixon's early moves in summitry "established a dramatic style and an extraordinarily fast pace in global affairs"; see *Nixon in the White House*, p. 101; their Chapter 4 is entitled "A Very Personal Diplomacy."

106. *White House Years*, p. 769.

107. Szulc, *The Illusion of Peace*, p. 32.

108. Nixon, *Leaders*, p. 210.

109. *Years of Upheaval*, pp. 1208, 1209. These achievements Kissinger defines as "a revolution in American policy so that it would overcome the disastrous oscillations between overcommitment and isolation" and the dream of "a new international order that would reduce lingering enmities, strengthen friendships, and give new hope to emerging nations," to which he adds that Nixon "brought us by a tremendous act of will to an extraordinary moment when dreams and possibilities conjoined." See *White House Years*, pp. 1475–1476 which is repeated in *Years of Upheaval*, p. 1184. In 1979 Gary Wills wrote: "Moynihan tries to cast Nixon as Disraeli; Kissinger would like him to be Metternich; Nixon himself yearns for Woodrowfication. But the historical parallel that must be most convincing to Nixon himself is . . . Churchill: the man and the moment came together." See Gary Wills, *Nixon Agonistes: The Crisis of the Self-Made Man* (New York: Mentor, 1979), p. 535.

110. For a summary of Nixon's post-presidential "summit" tours and visits, see note 61.

111. These include Nixon's *The Real War* (1980); *Leaders* (1982); *Real Peace: A Strategy for the West* (New York: private edition, 1983), and (Boston: Little, Brown, 1984); and *No More Vietnams* (New York: Arbor House, 1985); also see his "Superpower Summitry," *Foreign Affairs* 64 (Fall 1985):1–11.

112. *The Real War*, p. 250. Szulc notes that President Nixon "frequently did what he professed he would never do" and that he "used his unpredictability as a diplomatic weapon"; see *The Illusion of Peace*, p. 7.

113. Nixon, "Superpower Summitry," pp. 9–11.

114. Nixon, *The Real War*, p. 266.

12

Continuities and Contradictions in the Nixon Foreign Policy

KENNETH W. THOMPSON

The rediscovery of Richard M. Nixon has been primarily focused on the Nixon foreign policy, and it is foreign policy in which he enjoyed his most notable successes. His conduct of foreign policy gives clues to the nature of his presidency and the differences between national and foreign affairs. The Introduction to the Miller Center volume on the Nixon Presidency begins:

The presidency of Richard M. Nixon stands apart from other postwar presidencies. Two images persist in the minds of most Americans. One is of a leader whose foreign policy may possibly have offered the best hope for peace with the Soviet Union. The other is of a President, disgraced and rejected by the people, boarding a helicopter to leave the White House forever.[1]

How are we to reconcile these two conflicting viewpoints? Of the many and varied explanations of the Nixon Presidency, which one is most helpful in squaring the circle with these two seemingly irreconcilable views? Are the failures of President Nixon, if they are failures, those of policy and practice or the result of the perceptions Americans have of him?

One explanation that deserves scrutiny is the proposition that a president's strengths in one area may prove his downfall in another. We may ask if President Reagan's failure to explain his role in the Iran/Contra affair would have stood out in as glaring a fashion in his November 1986 press conference if he had not up to then been seen as "The Great Communicator?" Does the idea of Greek tragedy and its sources bear on the problem? With Richard Nixon was his commitment to secrecy both a possible explanation of his success in foreign policy and the cause of his downfall once Watergate struck? Did his capacity for homework lead him to seek too much control over the flow of events culminating in the break-in?

With Nixon, secrecy was a product of both personality and experience. Secrecy and personal isolation may have been one of the traits that led Bryce Harlow to say: "Eisenhower would never have picked him as his favorite bridge companion."[2] Related to his secretiveness was his apparent fear and dislike of most people and of extended social intercourse. In John Ehrlichman's phrase:

He's not the sort of fellow that you'd find fascinating as a next door neighbor. He wouldn't come over and play Scrabble or talk to you about a new record that he just bought. . . . His major weakness was in interpersonal relations. . . . He tended to avoid controversy by presenting an aspect of himself which he probably subconsciously calculated would be acceptable to the person he was dealing with.[3]

Ehrlichman and others have discussed Nixon's distaste for relations with some of his associates: "We've [the White House staff] got the reputation . . . of building a wall around the President. The fact is that he was down under his desk saying 'I don't want to see those fellows,' and we were trying to pull him out."[4] He especially resisted those meetings with associates from whom he felt he had nothing to learn. His staunchest defenders attribute his keeping his distance from most people to that fact.

The majority of his intimates who participated in the Miller Center's oral history apparently feel that something deeper, some traumatic event or experience shaped his attitudes and character. The late Bryce Harlow asked himself: "What about so many people disliking him most of his life? There must be a reason?"[5] Harlow reports numerous conversations in which people were saying "I just don't like him" but were unable to explain why. Responses like these drove Harlow and his friends to distraction until finally he hit on a possible explanation:

People didn't like him for the simple reason that he didn't like people. . . . In the case of Richard Nixon, I suspect that my gifted friend somewhere in his youth, maybe when he was very young or in his teens, got badly hurt by someone he cared for very deeply or trusted totally—a parent, a relative, a dear friend, a lover, a confidante. Somewhere I figure someone hurt him badly, and from that experience and from then on he could not trust people and by implication they couldn't trust him.[6]

Harlow who would have railed against the excesses of psycho-history concluded that he had never talked with Nixon about this thesis but added that he would welcome the opportunity, an opportunity now foreclosed by death.

Tendencies feed on one another and are mutually reinforcing, and this was true of Richard Nixon's relations with the press. "The press was hooked on an anti-Nixon drug and could never break the addiction. It was a terrible drag throughout Nixon's political career."[7] In the 1960 campaign, he discontinued press conferences. He lived with the antagonism he engendered but could not trace it to its source. Bryce Harlow sought an answer and came closest during the 1968 campaign at a lunch with John Osborne of the *New Republic*, whom Harlow considered the best political reporter in Washington. Harlow asked: ''Just why do you hate my guy so much?'' Osborne admitted to a sense of loathing for Nixon but confessed he had no real basis for the dislike. Finally, after long reflection, Osborne responded: ''I'll tell you one reason a reporter has trouble liking Nixon. Bryce, we've never really met him. None of us have. Do you know what we call him in the press corps—the cardboard man.'' Harlow asked why ''the cardboard man?'' Osborne responded:

He conceals himself somewhere behind a cardboard image of himself. He never comes out. I've talked to him in all kinds of ways. But I've never seen nor met the real Nixon. I keep trying. Now, Bryce, you can't trust a man, you can't like a man . . . who hides himself from you. You suspect him.[8]

Secrecy and distrust spread to other areas and poisoned the atmosphere. The ordinary citizen with little more than newspaper coverage sensed this was happening, but a more reliable, less impressionable source again is Bryce Harlow. In his words:

The grouping that shaped up in the 1970s—Nixon, Haldeman, Ehrlichman, Colson, Magruder and so forth—took on an eerie quality, like the man with wax wings who flew so close to the sun that he and his son fell to the earth; these people did that. They started vying for favor on Nixon's dark side. Colson started talking about trampling his grandmother's grave for Nixon and showing he was as mean as they come. The same with Haldeman and Ehrlichman. Everybody went *macho*. It was the ''in thing'' to swagger and threaten.[9]

Harlow told of a small White House meeting on campaign strategy in the spring of 1972. The group was an inside group that met semimonthly, and the president asked Harlow to attend. At one meeting, the summary firing of two men in the Agriculture Department was discussed. When Harlow asked what the men had done, he was told ''nothing.'' They were a couple of innocent victims whose firings would be publicized for political purposes. Harlow, who was by then out of the government, threatened to report their design and its motivation to the president. To his surprise, the ''insiders'' dropped the plan. Later at a breakfast with Henry Kissinger at the Metropolitan Club, Harlow commented: ''Henry, we are lucky it was Watergate, because if it hadn't been that, it would have been something much worse, the way things were going.''[10]

The source of the problem antedated the Nixon White House and went back to 1932. Watergate was bound to happen to a president sometime in the 1960s or 1970s. To quote Bryce Harlow again:

The sins of the fathers visiting upon their sons is what did in the Nixon generation. It had been endlessly building up. . . . There had to be a reckoning. The White House had proven too powerful, too irresponsible, too independent, too self-satisfied and arrogant. It felt too big, it acted too big. It was dangerous. It had to be restrained and reformed.[11]

The defects of the White House extended beyond secrecy, but it was secrecy that reinforced an atmosphere of individual arrogance and of a group standing above and outside the law.

President Nixon's distrust of the bureaucracy was well known, and he spoke of it as being "ninety-nine percent against us." Thus, from the outset, his administration was destined to seek channels other than the traditional bureaucratic ones such as the Department of State. One obvious channel was the National Security Council adviser and the NSC, but other forms of backchannel diplomacy presented themselves as well. The point is that all this and more were entirely in keeping with Nixon's character and world-view. As one of his political associates said, he was an introvert trying to be an extrovert. He was at his best in private meetings. In diplomacy as in politics, success may depend on one side or another imposing its will. Politics and diplomacy involve psychological relationships, not physical relationships as in the use of force. For the effective leader, they involve manipulating people and situations to his own ends. Of Nixon, Elliot Richardson could say: "His manipulative characteristics are things that historians will have to recreate.... I was a victim of his manipulative tendencies in the week leading up to the so-called 'Saturday Night Massacre' to a degree that I didn't even realize until months after it was all over."[12] Moreover, "It's hard . . . to be successfully manipulative in a situation where you are dealing with a whole lot of people who talk with each other and take notes."[13] Nixon turned to the arenas of power because he loved to wield power or, in Richardson's judgment: "Nixon and a handful of others over the last thirty years really have had an overriding desire to exercise power, but that is not a common characteristic in Washington" which is described as generally "a city of cocker spaniels."[14]

Diplomacy and private negotiations require secrecy, flexibility, and a certain subtlety of mind. A sometime critic of President Nixon observes: "The distinction fundamentally between Nixon, Carter and Reagan . . . is that Nixon was capable of a much greater degree of subtlety. . . . [The] Reagan administration came into office in somewhat the way an individual trained to fly a fixed-wing airplane might try to take over the controls of a helicopter."[15] Reagan was capable of dealing with the likes of Clark Kerr or Helen Gaghagan Douglas in state or national politics. As Lou Cannon has noted, Reagan had a sixth sense of what appealed to a majority at any given time and could deflect criticism of himself to others. He was adept at turning accusations against his accusers. Nixon had that sense in international politics, and it paid dividends in his diplomacy.

That subtlety manifested itself especially in foreign policy. American values and the overlapping grievances and dislikes of the great mass of the people for communism made Nixon's unequivocal anticommunism good politics domestically. The homogeneity of American society made a monistic approach to good and evil a possibility on the national scene. When Nixon turned to international politics, single-factor analysis and discourse went by the board. In place of communism as the sole all-consuming enemy, Nixon in foreign policy came to think in terms of dualities and sometimes antinomies (opposites that do not cancel each other out): détente and deterrence, conflict and cooperation and peace as a process of living with conflict and arms buildups and political tensions. Nixon is saying that international relations is not the pursuit of a single goal. "International relations are not like lunch at the club or a round of golf with friends. They are more like entering a snake pit where good intentions and good manners, adhered to slavishly in the face of your enemy's malevolence, are bound to be distinct hindrances."[16] Indeed, Nixon reserves some of his harshest criticisms for fellow presidents and world leaders who fail to recognize the dualities. Carter pursued détente without recognizing that it must be paired with deterrence. Advocates of disarmament fail to understand that wars result from unresolved political differences and territorial ambitions, not possession of arms. Complete nuclear disarmament, despite Reykjavik, is an impossible dream. And on summitry, while recognizing that face-to-face meetings may sometimes be useful, Nixon states:

No leader should meet with an adversary unless he is fully aware of his own strengths and weaknesses and those of his opponent; unless he has something he wants to bargain for and something to bargain with; and unless he is prepared to be worked over by professionals.[17]

The shift in temper and perspective from Nixon's view of domestic politics to his sense of international politics is capsulated in his advice to leaders in foreign policy.

The criticism is made that President Nixon in national affairs had difficulty distinguishing between politics and governance. Given his experience in the Congress and the Senate and as vice president, President Nixon was perhaps the best and most experienced executive in the history of the republic. Yet few presidents have had more problems than Nixon had in establishing the balance between politics and governance. At one extreme, some presidents or heads of state assume politics has little or nothing to do with governing. From different points on the political spectrum, Herbert Hoover and Woodrow Wilson may have suffered sometimes from this illusion. Richard Nixon is said to have fallen prey to the opposite misconception. In his eyes, the law of politics was the law of the jungle and Marquis of Queensbury's rules did not apply. Evidence mounts that he carried over this viewpoint from politics into governance. Because politics was for him a continuing struggle raw in tooth and claw, he was disposed to engage in overkill, as in instructions to John Ehrlichman to cut off all federal money to MIT or to firebomb the Brookings Institution. Ehrlichman notes that: "He was given to these kinds of excesses and you just simply had to know the difference."[18] Haldeman comments that "some people give me some credit . . .

and I think it was a valid function I performed—in not doing some of the things that the President wanted done."[19]

Others were less skilled in discriminating between orders that should or should not be carried out, and the example most often cited is Charles W. Colson. In Ehrlichman's words: "One place the Nixon administration got into difficulty was that there were people around who didn't know the difference. . . . They saluted and went out and did what they were told. . . . I wouldn't be at all surprised to learn that Colson saluted, did an about-face and went out to collect fire bombs [to bomb Brookings]."[20] These views may lend credence to a *New York Times* dispatch of May 29, 1987, occasioned by the release of some 267,500 pages of documents made public that day by the National Archives. In a memorandum dated January 14, 1971, from Air Force One, President Nixon wrote: "It would seem that the time is approaching when Larry O'Brien is held accountable for his retainer with Hughes [O'Brien had once done some public relations work for Howard R. Hughes]. Perhaps Colson should make a check on this."[21] The *New York Times* report concludes: "Many believe that Mr. Nixon's desire for information about Mr. O'Brien was behind the break-in and burglary of the Democratic party headquarters in the Watergate office and apartment complex on June 17, 1972. Charles W. Colson . . . later pleaded guilty to a charge of obstructing justice and served a prison sentence."[22]

Whatever the merit of such interpretations and reports, they suggest that Richard Nixon was capable of highly ambiguous moral and political actions. There follows the question whether acts of this kind are not more necessary and commonplace in the half anarchic society that is international politics. For centuries, rulers employed court poisoners whose function was to dispose of their rivals. Cavour declared: "If we had done for ourselves what we did for the State what scoundrels we would be." It is fair to ask whether President Nixon was not better equipped to cope with such an environment than presidents who preceded and followed him.

In this connection, *Time* columnist Hugh Sidey has put forward two related suggestions. The first involves a comparison of Lyndon B. Johnson and Nixon. The second constitutes a reflection on evil and international politics. Sidey reports that President Johnson spoke of his wish of meeting Chinese leaders and observed that "you never get a deal until you get two at a table." Sidey asked him why he didn't initiate such contact. Johnson replied that his diplomats told him "the time was not right." Sidey took note of the answer and later wrote: "You know what Nixon would say if somebody told him about the diplomats' opinions; you couldn't print it. He'd just tell them to stick it in their left ear. That is what he did with China."[23]

On the subject of evil and international politics, Sidey wrote:

I said, "Mr. President, it is kind of an enigma for us that in the minds of many people in the world you are the incarnate of evil. You've been thrown out of office and you've done all these bad things, and yet people are saying you have a better grasp of the world now and you are more honored for your foreign policy than anybody. On the other hand, Jimmy Carter who was a man who was supposed to be the incarnate of good, who walked among the people in his sandals and brought love, is rejected now. He is condemned and reviled. How do you explain that?'' I paused and watched him. Nixon looks like an evil person. He has a hunch. On that occasion his nose and eyebrows were going up and down, and he looked evil. He took a long time to answer and it was rather incoherent but what he said was: ''You've got to be a little evil to understand those people out there. You have to have known the dark side of life to understand those people. I only know half a dozen corporate chief executives that I would trust in a room with a healthy Brezhnev. Yet, I know twenty or thirty labor leaders I'd let in there.'' It was a view of the world. It all kind of figured. He didn't trust anybody.[24]

Ray Price sums up the phenomenon: ''Americans hire presidents to look after the nation's interests in a brutal, dangerous, lawless world. . . . The worst thing a president can do is to be so paralyzed by propriety that he shrinks from bending the rules when the nation's security requires it.''[25]

Thus, certain of Richard Nixon's least praiseworthy human qualities as far as national culture and politics are concerned may have been his most important assets in foreign policy. They were perhaps reinforced by a few of his ablest foreign policy lieutenants who had no qualms about taking liberties with virtue and truth. For those who doubt the utter ruthlessness of the NSC adviser and secretary of state, Henry Kissinger, Joseph Sisco's comments are instructive: ''The President gave Bill Rogers the responsibility for taking the lead in all of the Middle Eastern policy, and all the way along the book [Kissinger's memoirs] cites chapter and verse as to how Kissinger and the NSC sought to undermine the policy. He was very frank about it.'' Sisco concludes: ''One would have to cite not only the dozens of incidents that are known but the eight dozen incidents that aren't known'' in relations between Kissinger's NSC and the State Department and the deliberate discrediting of Secretary Rogers. To give the devil his due, Sisco credits Kissinger with being the world's foremost policy talent but with a dark side about which Sisco writes at length. It was the same dark side historians had found in Bismarck and Metternich. It gave Nixon and Kissinger both important foreign policy strengths and shadows, which as with Plato's cave were often all the public saw in their actions.

Lenin had spoken of idealists in the West as ''useful idiots'' who were misled about communism and filled with illusions that Soviet leaders could exploit. Nixon held that only hard-headed policymakers were capable of responding to the Soviet threat. He quoted Charles Bohlen's comment about the Soviets: ''They are pure materialists. You can no more describe them as being sincere than you could describe that table as being sincere.''[26] In Nixon's words: ''We must develop a policy of hard-headed détente that will convince Kremlin leaders that they stand to lose far more than they could possibly gain by threatening our interests.''[27] The West and especially the United States was handicapped in the struggle by the fact that ''their policy is one of sheer, ruthless opportunism; the

West, meanwhile, struggles to find ways to combat covert Soviet aggression that are in accordance with accepted rules of traditional warfare."[28]

Even the needs of humanity were approached in this spirit. Peace in Nixon's view can never be based on mutual friendship. Its sole foundation must be "mutual respect for each other's strength."[29] Good personal relations do not ensure good state relations, although Nixon favors annual summit meetings of the leaders of the United States and the Soviet Union. His reason, however, is to ensure that they take one another's measure before a crisis in order that they can respond in a more reasonable way. Anyone who would deal with the Soviet Union must understand power because the Kremlin leaders have never won a free election, but they are "masters at getting and keeping power."

What Nixon finds unacceptable are the two prevailing views for dealing with the Soviets, which he identifies with "superhawks" and "superdoves." The superhawks call for military superiority and look forward to the collapse of the Soviet system. They forget that confrontation and isolation can strengthen a dictatorship and that a democracy cannot sustain such a policy without the hope that international tensions can be reduced. "It is irresponsible for the world's two greatest military powers not to have maximum communication and not to try to negotiate their disputes."[30] We live in "a highly combustible atmosphere of semi-belligerency, with both sides building up armaments without restraint while firing salvos of hot rhetoric."[31] Without negotiations, our interests could rub together in powder keg areas such as the Middle East and set off a spark that could ignite a nuclear war.

The superdoves explain Soviet actions as stemming exclusively from fear. They excuse Soviet aggression and falsely believe that if we cut our defense budget the Soviets will do the same. The superdoves with whom Nixon identifies President Carter before Afghanistan do not recognize the Soviets for what they are. We do not have to convince the Soviets that we want peace, but they must know they cannot win a war.

Opposed to the prescriptions of superhawks and superdoves, Nixon urges a policy of hard-headed détente which combines détente with deterrence. "It is not an entente, which is an agreement between powers with common interests, nor is it a synonym for appeasement."[32] It does not mean the superpowers agree but that we profoundly disagree. "It provides a means of peacefully resolving those disagreements that can be resolved, and of living with those that cannot."[33] From 1969 to 1974, hard-headed détente worked. Some issues like arms control and the settlement of World War II debts were negotiated on the basis of mutual interests. Others such as most-favored-nations status and American grain purchases were appealing to the Soviets and gave the United States diplomatic and political leverage. Not a single nation was lost to the Soviet bloc during this period. The Soviets backed down from establishing a submarine base in Cuba, from overthrowing King Hussein, from supporting India's efforts to gobble up West Pakistan in 1971, and from sending Soviet forces into the Middle East during the Arab-Israeli War of 1973.

The character of hard-headed détente is best illustrated, Nixon argues, by the bombing and mining of Haiphong on the eve of the 1972 summit meeting to stop the North Vietnamese offensive. Nixon writes that "Those who did not understand hard-headed détente thought it would torpedo the summit. They were wrong. It strengthened our hand and helped pave the way for a broad range of agreements."[34]

Why then did hard-headed détente fail? Why did the people turn against Nixon and Kissinger? Nixon blames the Congress and the Carter Administration. Congress reduced military assistance to Vietnam, passed the War Powers Act, and denied the president the power to enforce the Paris peace accords. The Carter Administration canceled and delayed major arms programs. But Nixon's explanation has to be measured against the standards he himself put forth. He had warned that leaders sometimes go to international conferences in pursuit of good press at home. The handling of the opening to China had many of these characteristics when Nixon claimed it was the twentieth century's greatest diplomatic triumph. Détente was oversold to the American people and invited a reaction. Friendly critics (Hans Morgenthau) warned that, while nations might achieve détente on a specific problem, global détente was an illusion. Nixon knew that "history is a pathetic junkyard of broken treaties,"[35] yet he defended some of his agreements as though they guaranteed perpetual peace.

Beyond the specifics of the ongoing conflict, neither Nixon nor Kissinger succeeded in generating public confidence in their approach and policies. Whatever the successes or failures, the American people were uneasy with Nixon's approach and perhaps always will be when leaders achieve an approximation of political realism. But neither Kissinger nor Nixon did much to reassure the public that the shadowy and ambiguous course they were following had a moral purpose. Increasingly, both were denounced as wholly immoral. Their secrecy and cynicism about which Bryce Harlow spoke turned back on them. It may be that all was inevitable and that explaining a realistic foreign policy to a mass public is impossible, but the dual judgment of the public that the Nixon policy was a combination of crafty atmospherics and cynical and Machiavellian statecraft devoid of *virtue* led to the repudiation of his policies. The tragedy is the deeper because no president before or since has possessed the same geostrategic sense and overall grasp of foreign policy that Nixon achieved.

NOTES

1. Kenneth W. Thompson, "Introduction," in Kenneth W. Thompson, ed., *The Nixon Presidency: Twenty-two Intimate Perspectives of Richard M. Nixon* (Lanham, M.D.: University Press of America, 1987), p. xi.

2. Bryce Harlow, "The Man and the Political Leader," in Thompson, ed., *The Nixon Presidency*, p. 6.

3. John Ehrlichman, "The White House and Policy-making," in Thompson, ed., *The Nixon Presidency*, p. 139.

4. Ibid., p. 132.

5. Harlow, "The Man and the Political Leader," in Thompson, ed., *The Nixon Presidency*, p. 9.

6. Ibid., pp. 9–10.

7. Ibid., p. 11.

8. Ibid., p. 13.

9. Ibid., p. 15.

10. Ibid., p. 16.

11. Ibid., p. 26.

12. Elliot L. Richardson, "The Paradox," in Thompson, ed., *The Nixon Presidency*, p. 59.

13. Ibid.

14. Ibid., p. 60.

15. Ibid., pp. 66–67.

16. Richard Nixon, *Real Peace* (Boston: Little, Brown, 1984), p. 13.

17. Ibid., p. 13.

18. John Ehrlichman, "The White House and Policy-making," in Thompson, ed., *The Nixon Presidency*, p. 129.

19. H. R. Haldeman, "The Nixon White House and Presidency," in Thompson, ed., *The Nixon Presidency*, p. 95.

20. Ehrlichman, "The White House and Policy-making," in Thompson, ed., *The Nixon Presidency*, p. 129.

21. *New York Times*, May 29, 1987, p. A19.

22. Ibid.

23. Hugh Sidey, "The Man and Foreign Policy," in Thompson, ed., *The Nixon Presidency*, p. 311.

24. Ibid., pp. 311–312.

25. Raymond K. Price, Jr., "Nixon's Reassessment Comes Early," in Thompson, ed., The *Nixon Presidency*, p. 388.

26. Nixon, *Real Peace*, p. 17.

27. Ibid., p. 53.

28. Ibid., p. 76.

29. Ibid., p. 16.

30. Ibid., p. 24.

31. Ibid.

32. Ibid., p. 26.

33. Ibid.

34. Ibid., p. 28.

35. Ibid., p. 15.

Discussant: Lloyd S. Etheredge

These papers are stimulating, and they arrived a full month in advance, so I have had the opportunity to go over them as well as to listen to them. I think we all would like to engage, now, in a judgment of Richard Nixon and his practices: My comments will be brief, and I will hope to leave time for questions and the sharing of ideas.

DR. PLISCHKE'S PAPER

Mr. Nixon really does merit recognition for his professional preparation to make foreign policy—to make his own judgments about other national leaders, foreign countries, and trends. Dr. Plischke's paper documents Mr. Nixon's extensive preparation, during his years as a private citizen, to equip himself for foreign policy decision making. The numerous trips he made on his own initiative—with personal funds and from various other sources—gave him an unusual background that contrasts very sharply with the current occupant of the White House and, to their disadvantage, a good many of the people now running for the presidency.

As we talk about secrecy and a closed decision process—and Mr. Nixon often *was* closed and secretive about what he was doing—we should acknowledge that he had a basis for confidence in his own judgments. In the White House, as Dr. Plischke records, he kept channels of communication open, through personal diplomacy and through envoys. The process was secretive and closed, but as a result of this mechanism, Mr. Nixon was not isolated in his own world.

We must leave to future historians the task of finding out what was actually said in these high-level meetings with other foreign leaders and how important these meetings were. But the meetings may have been consequential: the record does suggest that Mr. Nixon could speak with frankness and directness in these meetings, that they were different than ordinary diplomatic communications, and that he genuinely tried to build a basis for understanding a logic of American foreign policy among the various leaders he was dealing with. I will return to this issue in a moment, but we should note that dramatic changes *have* taken place in Soviet and Chinese perceptions of the United States, and especially of the politics and concerns of the American right. Mr. Nixon's policies and his explanations of them, via the summitry Dr. Plischke documents, likely played an important part in these changes.

DR. RAVENAL'S THESIS

Dr. Ravenal's paper asks: "What difference did it make, to the *outcomes* of American foreign policy decision making, that Mr. Nixon was president

and Dr. Kissinger was his secretary of state and national security adviser?''
As a method to answer this question rigorously, I suggest we extrapolate a
trend, or baseline, of American foreign policy and ask ''What would the
logic of events have led *any* American president to do?'' We can ground the
analysis by inserting another imaginary president, who under other circumstances might have been in office, and we can run through these years and
their events using this thought experiment.

To be specific, it seems to me that Hubert Humphrey, as president, would
have made many of the same types of decisions leading (for example) to an
opening to China, although he might not have been so dramatically successful
or persuasive in bringing along American conservatives. Under Humphrey, I
think we certainly would have seen a much earlier end to the Vietnam War that
did not require American withdrawal and defeat to be stretched out into a slow-
motion defeat, purchased at the cost of tens of thousands of lives. Under Humphrey, this would have been done with less brutal demonstration, on the receiving
end, of the destructiveness of American military power that an angry, hardball-
playing American president and secretary of state brought to bear. Mr. Humphrey
would also surely have spoken more articulately and genuinely of Third World
and humanitarian concerns. Because he cared more deeply, he would probably
have been a bit more effective in inducing the Congress to pass appropriations
to further these causes.

Dr. Ravenal's paper raises direct questions about the importance of personality
in decision making, and he suggests a separation between psychodynamic explanations and rational decision-making explanations. Technically, I think it's
wiser not to separate rationality from other aspects of psychodynamics. It is a
great tribute to our political system, to its technical character of decision making,
to our substantial agreement about America's interests and how the world works,
that we *do* use the concept of rational choice. But, to a psychologist, an individual's capacity for rationality is part of personality: it takes a hell of a lot of
work, personal maturity, professional commitment, and (perhaps) apprentice-
ships and other experience to end up with what we call a rational decision maker.
To the extent that rational decision processes and professional judgments were
made during the Nixon Administration, these were a product of a great many
characteristics of individual personality and background, and of our institutions,
which supported these characteristics.

Mr. Nixon, being who he was, probably did make a unique contribution
that Mr. Humphrey would not have made. I suspect, as I mentioned earlier,
that the most dramatic consequence from the Nixon years was a changed
image, among Soviet and Chinese leaders, of the character of American
leaders, of our political system, and (especially) of our hardline conservatives. In candor, it must be said that we will not know, until many years in
the future, whether this hypothesis is correct. However, I suspect Mr. Nixon
clearly demonstrated that ideological confrontation would be sold out and
even hardline American conservatives, such as himself, would operate by a

realpolitik sensibility. And the evidence seems to suggest that, during the Nixon-Kissinger years, the Soviet leaders were persuaded that at least a part of détente was genuine and that their earlier fears of a possible American preemptive nuclear attack were unrealistic.

To analyze the story of this Soviet learning, I think scholars will have to look at the nature of institutional memory and learning in the Soviet Union, especially to the learning of Soviet diplomats who served in Washington during the Nixon-Kissinger years and who were engaged in continual conversation with Mr. Nixon and Mr. Kissinger. I suspect that both men invested substantial time and energy in these discussions and sowed seeds that have begun to bear fruit.

I think Mr. Nixon was consequential in another area: it seems to me that the boldness and drama of his opening to China—and his delivery of the American right ("playing the China card") as part of the public acclaim—has inspired other world leaders to similar acts of statesmanship. President Sadat's boldness is an example. World leaders do, I think, pay attention to one another, and one hopes that the extraordinary boldness Mr. Nixon displayed will enter the canons of statesmanship and, like Sadat (or Gorbachev), inspire other politicians with the thought that such peacemaking boldness can be acceptable even to hardline conservatives.

There is one additional aspect of personality and decision making I want to mention. I suspect one of the greatest foreign policy legacies of Mr. Nixon's administration was achieved almost by inadvertence because he was interested only in what he thought to be power relations rather than economics. By all reports, neither Mr. Nixon nor Dr. Kissinger was interested in economics—and they readily signed off when their technical advisers said it was time to drop the gold standard and shift to the market mechanism of freely floating exchange rates.

What happened, as it turns out, is that a major portion of our national sovereignty was given away by a stroke of the pen, and it probably will never be regained. We've ended up with a *world* money supply, a complete change of the older rules of nationally based macroeconomic policy, and other massive changes that are still spinning their way out in the international system. It is going to take quite a while to understand the consequences of what Harry Johnson, Herbert Stein, and other economists put through. But it is probably a result of Mr. Nixon's personality that one of his most consequential acts of political statesmanship did not seem that way at the time.

Thus, in assessing Dr. Ravenal's thesis, I would argue that personality characteristics—in addition to a capacity for pragmatic and rational judgment in the national interest—did make a selective difference in policies. And I would suggest that Mr. Nixon, with his background as a tough-minded Cold War warrior and conservative, did achieve results for these policies which Mr. Humphrey would not have accomplished as readily.

DR. THOMPSON'S THESIS

Dr. Thompson's paper asks whether the sources of success in Mr. Nixon's foreign policy were the sources of his ultimate failure—impeachment—in the domestic arena. He suggests *secrecy*, in both arenas, as a common denominator.

Secrecy was certainly present in both arenas. But the relevant traits spelled out in Dr. Thompson's paper are more numerous than the secretiveness he emphasizes. For example:

- An extraordinary ambition, coupled with a sense of higher justification that made it possible for Mr. Nixon to engage in lying, deception, and manipulation. (I prefer to talk about this behavior candidly rather than use Dr. Thompson's diplomatic phrasing that Mr. Nixon was "capable of highly ambiguous moral and political actions.") We are all aware of the professional rationales that explain why, "rationally," morality should not determine foreign policy. But in Mr. Nixon's case of *realpolitik* sensibility, I believe ordinary morality was not a constraint, and this was an expression of his personality.

- Mr. Nixon was tough-minded, and indeed single-minded, about power. He often viewed other political players in a similar way—as ambitious and manipulative to the point of being Machiavellian—and was highly mistrustful of their intentions.

- Mr. Nixon's extraordinary self-confidence, ambition, and single-mindedness about power also reflected a detached personality with few other public emotions. He spoke with, and perhaps felt, little warmth for others.

Such elements, implicit in Dr. Thompson's paper, suggest we should talk about a wider syndrome. I will not go into a full discussion of all the interlocking elements that psychologists have nominated and still argue about. But it is the full syndrome, I think, that must be analyzed to assess whether Dr. Thompson's analysis of identical sources of success and failure—a compound of irony and Greek tragedy in the interpretation of Nixon—works well.

Whatever one may think of these traits—and obviously many people would not find some of them personally attractive—they included elements that served Mr. Nixon well in foreign affairs. It would have been easy as well as politically acceptable for him to continue the simple, unthinking, ideological formulas of his earlier career. His genuine accomplishments—his statesmanship and commitment to construct a more vital and enduring world order—come, in part, from his extraordinary ambition and other elements of his personality. Mr. Nixon's personality *did* help him to abandon ideological hostility to communism as a basis of foreign policy. His logic was power, not ideology: he *used* ideology, but he cared more about power.

How much of this personality system was necessary or critical to his success? Extraordinary self-confidence, pragmatism, and his ambition for political mastery served Mr. Nixon well in foreign policy. But were other (e.g., the more mean-spirited, duplicitous, and callous) elements necessary? To answer the question,

I think we must decide whether Mr. Nixon's stark image of Soviet leaders was accurate, and, thus, whether Mr. Nixon's instincts related to it were necessary.

Mr. Nixon reminds us of the critical issue in a quotation included in Dr. Thompson's paper. Thompson is quoting an interview of Mr. Nixon by Hugh Sidey. Sidey paraphrases Nixon: "You've got to be a little evil to understand those people out there. You have to have known the dark side of life to understand those people. I only know half a dozen corporate chief executives that I would trust in a room with a healthy Brezhnev. Yet, I know twenty or thirty labor leaders I'd let in there."

This view is quintessential Nixon. It is Mr. Nixon's self-made myth that he was one of the *only* Americans tough enough to deal with the Russians. The quotation also refers to the experience of the dark side of life, and Mr. Nixon certainly knew, both as a politician and from the receiving end of the instincts his operating style aroused in the American political system, more about hatred and personal vilification than most politicians. It identifies *the* perception that is key to understanding Mr. Nixon's foreign policy: that is, that the Russian leaders are themselves so ambitious and tough-minded that one must, of necessity, deal with them the way Mr. Nixon dealt with them.

Primarily, I want to underscore this issue as a question. Political scientists today are rightly concerned about possible misperception in international relations. They often focus on simple and general psychological biases that may be at work. But if there is one lesson, one message, from these papers, I believe it is that Russian and Chinese leaders need to address the perception of themselves expressed by Mr. Nixon. Only they and the historians in those countries can tell us whether the logic of Mr. Nixon's policies—including the tens of thousands of lives he expended in Southeast Asia to demonstrate his toughness to Russian leaders and others—was a necessity.

If Mr. Nixon's perception was a major *mis*perception (and I suspect it was overdramatized), this is important to know.

To give a brief summary: I suggest Mr. Nixon's chief foreign policy failure was to continue the Vietnam War unproductively and unnecessarily. Thus, differing from Dr. Thompson, I would suggest that Mr. Nixon's failures, foreign *and* domestic, came from a similar source—and I would call it a broader personality syndrome similar to what James David Barber has pointed out in his analysis of "active-negative" politicians like Mr. Nixon. The consequence of the interlocking elements of the syndrome was to make Mr. Nixon more combative, committed to dominance, and very rigid when his power was openly challenged in a public power drama, foreign or domestic. The domestic handling of Watergate reflects the same pattern of a vivid challenge in a public drama, a heightened combativeness and instinctive commitment to domination associated with rigidity.

Discussant: Roger Morris

I wanted to address myself first to Professor Thompson's quite superb paper and the provocative point that he raised from Bryce Harlow about the early wound in President Nixon's life. If one really wants to excavate that aspect of American foreign policy, you'll probably have to look to love letters written to young Richard Nixon at some time during the autumn of his junior year at Duke Law School. The figure in question was named Ola Florence Welch, and he was indeed deeply wounded. She wasn't the first to hurt him. His father plays a role in that, and I think that emphasizes the importance of biography as background in these matters.

It is also true that Professor Thompson's remark about the anti-Nixon press in foreign policy relates very much to the man's background and his origins in American politics. In fact, for the better part of Richard Nixon's political career, he was very much the darling of the America media. He had indeed been a cardboard figure both in his early campaigns and on Capitol Hill. But he was eminently successful and was treated lavishly by the local press in the Los Angeles basin, especially by the *Los Angeles Times*. He was also treated very well indeed by the *New York Herald Tribune*, the *New York Times*, by other major papers, and even on occasion by the *Washington Post* in his earlier incarnation. So when the worm turned, it was Mr. Nixon who tended to be astonished at the caprice of the American media, and not the politican himself who changed so much.

Those two comments having been made, let me go on to address Professor Ravenal's point, which I think is very well taken—that this indeed was the Nixon-Kissinger regime, noting that one of those gentleman was not elected to office. I think that points to the basic paradox in their foreign policy: that it was fundamentally antidemocratic. The coup d'etat which they staged at the Hotel Pierre during the transition period was designed to achieve, and did indeed accomplish, the rule of these two men in foreign policy, substituting for the wider bargaining and the sometimes raucous and ineffectual brokering of foreign policy which had been the nature under previous administrations, certainly under the Johnson regime. I do want to say, however—because all of my colleagues seem quite intent on criticism of the Nixon record—that there were reasons for that. And I think these reasons are very germane to the dilemmas we still face in American foreign relations. Nixon and Kissinger came into office facing a more profound misrule, a much more profound stagnation than any of us then imagined. The Johnson Administration was effectively crippled on every front. Its foreign service had ceased to function as an intellectual resource for government. Its decision making was lurching at best. Its relations with the Congress were awful, and its communication with the public had all but ceased.

The Nixon revolution in foreign policy also took advantage of the unique weaknesses of the regime Mr. Nixon himself assembled. He brought into the Department of State, as you may recall William P. Rogers whose chief quali- fication was his friendship with Nixon through the Eisenhower Administration, a man who had no previous experience in foreign affairs and who was now called to govern an inherently unruly and unprofessional bureaucracy. Nixon assembled around him other people in the cabinet who were similarly handi- capped: Melvin Laird in Defense whose chief virtue was as a Wisconsin dells politician, and not as an administrator; Richard Helms at CIA, a professional who continued the bureaucratic self-interest of that agency; and on and on, so that the Nixon-Kissinger coup d'etat proceeded in a vacuum. I think it is important to remember, too, that their accomplishments can be traced in large measure to their ruthlessness and to their ability to conquer in many instances the paramount weaknesses of their opponents. I shudder to think what we would be discussing here in terms of the record of the Nixon Administration had foreign policy been left in the hands of the rest of the cabinet.

They did not, of course, subdue every problem of American foreign relations, but they did manage to humiliate the secretary of state and the Department of State. They left very much intact a problem I haven't heard discussed in these papers and that is still very relevant. That is the whole covert world of American foreign affairs. The CIA thrived in the Nixon years. Its operations were far- flung, reaching every region of the world and very seldom tampered with. Sometimes the operations were extended and expanded as in Chile and elsewhere. Sometimes they were done subtly and with long-term consequences, as in the establishment of something called the Office of Public Saftey. It was one of those wonderful little misnomers in American foreign relations, which, as you may recall, was programmed to advise foreign police departments on the suppres- sion of dissent in Latin America and elsewhere. It ended up being disbanded by bipartisan action in the Congress when the agency was implicated in widespread torture and abuse of political prisoners.

I think the worst thing one can say about the Nixon foreign policy, the Nixon- Kissinger foreign policy (aside from its ruthlessness and its antidemocratic es- sence) is that it was very largely irrelevant. Despite its broad coming to terms with the Russian and Chinese revolutions, it did not manage in any way to anticipate the challenges that would come after, the challenges that chase us now into the 1980s and 1990s. The reason is simply that it was old-fashioned *realpolitik*, an old-fashioned diplomacy that was directed at rearranging borders and arrangements among states. It was inherently unable to deal with those forces that were roiling within national boundaries, the great economic changes in Western Europe and Japan, the forces of economic and social justice emerging in Africa and Latin America. It was also unable to overcome its own fundamental political defects here at home. By that I mean the intrinsic ideological and intellectual limits of its architects. It was inherently racist in a number of ways. It did not understand economics or sociology. It was almost everywhere intolerant of political dissent and of changes in the status quo. Its record in human rights and humanitarian aid affairs was utterly abominable, whether one takes the case of Bangladesh, Burundi, Chile, or Greece. The list goes on and on and on, including literally millions of people who perished in part because of the indifference of this government during those years of grand diplomatic accomplishments.

At the same time, however, so much changed within the American government. By that I mean the developments that we addressed here regarding détente in the Soviet Union and the opening of China. So I want to leave my colleagues with a subject that I hope they will address in future scholarship: that is the question that the Nixon foreign policy, which may have been his greatest single accomplishment as a leader, may also have been his undoing. There is a very dark side indeed to that foreign policy which has nothing at all to do with the president or Henry Kissinger. It has to do with opposition within the American government to what the president was doing, an opposition that now turns out to be right and honorable. I am talking here about the Pentagon spy ring in 1971 and 1972 and the role of military officers on the Kissinger staff whose story is only beginning to dribble out in terms of how much the Nixon regime itself may have been subverted from within, how much these forces may have played a role indeed even in the final unfolding of Watergate.

In the end, of course, neither Nixon nor Kissinger—for all their gifts or all their ruthlessness—was able to institutionalize their own role in foreign policy. They left behind very largely the same anarchy they found. They left behind a foreign ministry that has abdicated responsibility and can no longer play an effective role even when challenged by a semiliterate lieutenant colonel in the Marine Corps. They left behind the whole capricious play of press and of a Congress that interacts in the process when convenient or when headlines are to be gained. They left behind, too, a public indifference that is challenged only when a scandal makes the evening news. The basic conditions in American life and the basic imbalance in American political and governmental institutions that make possible both the achievements and the abuses of the Nixon-Kissinger foreign policy are still very much with us.

THE WAR POWERS RESOLUTION

_____ 13 _____

Nixon Versus the Congress: The War Powers Resolution, 1973

PHILIP J. BRIGGS

"The congressional bombing cutoff, coupled with the limitation placed on the President by the War Powers Resolution in November 1973, set off a string of events that led to the Communist takeover in Cambodia and, on April 30, 1975, the North Vietnamese conquest of South Vietnam."[1] So stated Richard M. Nixon, thirty-seventh president of the United States, in what is arguably one of the strongest indictments ever leveled by a president against the Congress in the formulation of foreign policy.

The following case study will examine the context, issues, and political positions taken by leading members of the congressional and executive branches of government in the development and enactment of the War Powers Resolution, which placed restrictions on the president's ability to "make war." A final section will summarize and evaluate why passage of this act occurred despite the president's veto.

THE CONSTITUTIONAL SETTING

Beginning with the Constitutional Convention of 1787 in Philadelphia where the war power was briefly discussed on August 17, a determination was made empowering the Congress to "declare" war, with the president retaining the power to "make" war as recorded:

"To make war"
Mr. Pinkney opposed the vesting this power in the Legislature. Its proceedings were too slow. It wd. meet but once a year. The Hs. of Reps. would be too numerous for such

deliberations. The Senate would be the best despositary, being more acquainted with foreign affairs, and most capable of proper resolutions. If the States are equally represented in Senate, so as to give no advantage to large States, the power will notwithstanding be safe, as the small have their all at stake in such cases as well as the large States. It would be singular for one-authority to make war, and another peace.

Mr. Butler. The Objections agst the Legislature lie in a great degree agst the Senate. He was for vesting the power in the President, who will have all the requisite qualities, and will not make war but when the Nation will support it.

Mr. M(adison) and Mr. Gerry moved to insert "*declare*," striking out "make" war; leaving to the Executive the power to repel sudden attacks.[2]

Therefore, the completed Constitution provided in Article I, Section 8, that the Congress "shall have the power . . . to declare War, grant Letters of Marque and Reprisal, and make rules concerning Captures on Land and Water." Letters of marque and reprisal authorized private individuals to prey on the property and shipping of enemy nations without being considered pirates. This practice was banned by the Pact of Paris in 1865.

In Article II, Section 2, of the Constitution, it is stated that, "The President shall be Commander in Chief of the Army and Navy of the United States." The Congress shares with the president authority over the armed forces by supplying the necessary appropriations and regulations for its governance. Nevertheless, the president's authority to "conduct" war was not in question at the Constitutional Convention, as evidenced by Connecticut's change of vote on the substitution of "declare" war for "make" war as a congressional power. The Connecticut delegate had first cast one of the two votes against the substitution, but, "on the remark by Mr. King that 'make' war might be understood to 'conduct' it which was an Executive function, Mr. Elseworth gave up his objection (and the vote of Cont was changed to—ay.)"[3]

The treaty power and the power to appoint ambassadors are given as shared powers to the president and the Senate. It is the sharing of these foreign policy powers, including the war power, that the eminent constitutional authority Edward S. Corwin described as "an invitation to struggle for the privilege of directing American foreign policy."[4] And struggle they have since the first administration of George Washington to the present day. Nevertheless, an historical pattern clearly emerged with reference to the war power: Declarations of war by the Congress would be infrequent—there having been only five such declarations since the inception of the Republic to the present day. Involvement of the armed forces in hostilities abroad as directed by the president and without a declaration of war would be frequent—with 199 such cases being documented for the time period 1798 to 1972, one year prior to passage of the War Powers Resolution.[5]

In addition, successive presidents have interpreted the power of the commander in chief as one of their most important in formulating foreign policy, and the Supreme Court has upheld their position as sole judge and responsible actor in several landmark cases. In *Martin v. Mott* (1827) the Court held that the president, when acting under the authority of a 1795 congressional act, is the only judge as to when an exigency has occurred that necessitates action by the militia.[6] On the eve of the Civil War in *Durand v. Hollins* (1860), Supreme Court Justice Samuel Nelson held that naval Captain Hollins had acted correctly in 1854 when his ship bombarded a Central American port in the execution of his orders from the commander in chief, President Franklin Pierce, although no congressional sanction for the bombardment had been obtained. In the *Prize* cases (1863), during the Civil War, the Court upheld President Abraham Lincoln's action in seizing blockade runners in violation of a presidential proclamation, but once again without any special legislative approval by declaring: "He [the president] does not initiate the war, but is bound to accept the challenge without waiting for any special legislative authority."[7]

In the Senate debate over the War Powers Resolution during July 1973, both its opponents and proponents included in their arguments the positions of certain Founders during the ratification period following the Constitutional Convention of 1787. Republican Senator Barry Goldwater of Arizona, a former presidential candidate for his party, was the chamber's leading opponent of the resolution. Goldwater referred to Federalist No. 38 in which James Madison, the principal architect of the Constitution itself, revealed that the Framers had intentionally removed the direction of war from Congress, where it had been placed under the Articles of Confederation, because, in his words, it is "Particularly dangerous to give the keys of the Treasury and the command of the army into the same hands."[8]

Senator Jacob Javits, Republican of New York and architect of the War Powers Resolution, countered Goldwater's reference with the following excerpt from a letter of Thomas Jefferson to James Madison in 1789: "We have already given in example one effectual check to the Dog of war by transferring the power of letting him loose from the Executive to the Legislative body, from those who are to spend to those who are to pay."[9]

THE POLITICAL CONTEXT

The immediate political context in which to view the passage of the War Powers Resolution is the legislative-executive conflict over the power to conduct the Vietnam War. Yet, earlier events in the long history of conflict and cooperation between the two branches are also highly relevant and include certainly President Franklin D. Roosevelt's relations with the Congress during the World War II period. Roosevelt, recognizing the necessity of maintaining supply convoys to England during the summer and autumn of 1941, issued his famous "shoot-at-sight" order to the Navy for their protection in the North Atlantic. The president's order was issued without congressional consent, but according to Arthur M. Schlesinger, Jr., in *The Imperial Presidency*, "His choice was to go to Congress and risk the fall of Britain to Hitler or to proceed on his own."[10]

President Roosevelt was also a committed internationalist who wished to avoid the bruising and fruitless conflict that ensnared Woodrow Wilson in his epic struggle with the Senate over consent for the League of Nations following World War I. It was FDR's tactic to commit the United States to an international peacekeeping organization before victory was achieved. Initially, the president proceeded toward his goal without congressional involvement, but Republican Senator Arthur H. Vandenberg of Michigan "won for the Republicans the right to be consulted, and thus made bipartisanship possible."[11] The result was full congressional support for internationalism via passage of the Fulbright and Connally resolutions in 1943. Importantly, the methodology for this historic turn away from isolationism was bipartisanship.

An era of bipartisanship had begun in the formulation of U.S. foreign policy which, during a "brief but generative" period from the middle to the late 1940s, would produce the hallmarks of American post–World War II foreign policy. This period would end with the so-called loss of China issue beginning in 1949, followed by the Korean War and the onset of McCarthyism. While the bipartisan era had passed, its practice by President John F. Kennedy in 1963 played a critical role in obtaining Senate approval for the limited nuclear test ban treaty, thus demonstrating its utility for various kinds of foreign policies on the eve of the Vietnam debacle.[12]

During early 1964, Walt W. Rostow, a presidential adviser to Lyndon B. Johnson, suggested the usefulness of a bipartisan congressional resolution that would give the president "discretionary authority to conduct war in Asia." This resolution would be similar to the Formosa Resolution obtained by President Dwight D. Eisenhower in 1955, in the eventuality that the People's Republic of China might attack Formosa, the Pescadores, and related positions. William P. Bundy, assistant secretary of state for Asian and Pacific affairs, supported the congressional resolution plan and drafted one for a floor debate in June. By mid-June the president decided to postpone the congressional request until after the November presidential election because he did not wish to appear eager to expand America's military role in Vietnam before the election.[13]

While the presidential campaign between President Johnson and Republican Senator Goldwater was underway in the summer of 1964, two American destroyers reported attacks on them by North Vietnamese PT boats in the Gulf of Tonkin. Although subsequent congressional hearings would cast some doubt on the authenticity of the attacks, the president seized the moment to gain congressional support for future military actions via the previously prepared congressional resolution.

The Tonkin Gulf Resolution that resulted was steered through the Congress, at the president's request, by Democratic Senator J. William Fulbright, chairman of the Foreign Relations Committee. Later, Fulbright would become a severe critic of the resolution and the Vietnam War, but under his guidance it received almost complete support by the Congress with a Senate vote of 82 to 2 and a House vote of 416 to 0. The sweeping language of the joint resolution itself read in part that "the United States is, therefore, prepared, as the President determines, to take all necessary steps, including the use of armed force, to assist any member or protocol state of the Southeast Asia Collective Defense Treaty requesting assistance in defense of its freedom."[14]

The year 1965 saw a fateful turning of the American role in the Vietnam War from that of advisers to major participants in numerous combat operations, accompanied by a large-scale buildup of U.S. forces on the ground, at sea, and in the air. The Americanization of the war occurred despite the fact that, during the previous year's election, Johnson had appeared less willing to commit American forces to the Southeast Asia imbroglio than his opponent Goldwater. By the summer of 1965, the president's top advisers considered a formal declaration of war, but Johnson "was afraid that it would provoke retaliation by Communist China and also provoke opposition in Congress."[15]

The remaining years of the Johnson Administration witnessed a developing spiral of hostility between the president and the Congress, as well as ever increasing student demonstrations against the war. Escalation of the war also continued, with more and more U.S. troops embarking for Vietnam and, in 1965, the ordering of a substantial air war against North Vietnam code-named Operation Rolling Thunder. Casualties continued to mount, with four thousand Americans losing their lives in 1966, and the draft becoming ever more unpopular at home.

By 1967 Senate Foreign Relations Committee Chairman Fulbright was claiming that the Congress had abandoned its constitutional role in foreign policy to presidents who acted in foreign affairs without consulting Congress.[16] On the executive branch side during the same time period, *The Pentagon Papers* described the administration as divided into three camps: a "dove" group led by Secretary of Defense Robert S. McNamara who wished to limit and reduce the war; a military group led by the commander in Vietnam, General William C. Westmoreland and the Joint Chiefs of Staff, who wished to widen the war; and a third group led by the president and civilian officials at the White House and State Department who took a middle of the road position.[17]

All the military and political efforts of the Johnson Administration in Vietnam received a severe jolt when seventy thousand Viet Cong troops broke a late January 1968 truce proclaimed to celebrate Tet, the lunar new year holiday, and attacked thirty provincial capitals and five major cities, including Saigon. Militarily, the Tet Offensive was a failure for the Viet Cong and North Vietnamese who suffered forty thousand killed. Yet, its psychological impact on the American public and the administration was devastating. In the New Hampshire Democratic primary during February 1968, Senator Eugene J. McCarthy of Minnesota came close to defeating Lyndon Johnson. McCarthy's unprecedented voter strength against an incumbent president soon brought a more formidable Democratic opponent into the nomination contest—Senator Robert F. Kennedy of New York. It was all over for Johnson, and on March 31, 1968, he announced a cessation of the bombing campaign against most of North Vietnam, the sending of veteran diplomat Averell Harriman to Paris to negotiate a peace with the North Vietnamese, and his own plan to withdraw from politics.

NIXON AND THE WAR

> The main subject was Vietnam. The travail of the long war was etched on the faces around me. These were all able and intelligent men. They had wanted desperately to end the war before leaving office, but they had not succeeded.[18]

So observed President-elect Richard Nixon on his visit to the Cabinet Room of the White House and a meeting with Johnson's top advisers. Nixon had just accomplished one of the greatest "comebacks" in American electoral history, given his defeats at the polls in 1960 for president and in 1962 for governor of California. His 1968 presidential election had nevertheless been a narrow popular vote victory that had left the Democrats in full control of the Congress. In fact, he was the first president in 120 years to assume the office with both chambers of the Congress controlled by the opposition party. He had made a significant promise to the American people upon receiving the Republican nomination: "And I pledge to you tonight that the first priority foreign policy objective of our next Administration will be to bring an honorable end to the war in Vietnam."[19] The war was now his to direct and end as commander in chief, but the mood in Congress was increasingly restive, assertive, and critical of the war.

The withdrawal of American troops from Vietnam, already begun during the waning months of the Johnson Administration, continued during the Nixon Administration and was clearly tied to the administration's policy of Vietnamization. According to this policy, the United States would gradually reduce its troop strength in Vietnam while training and increasing the troop strength of the Saigon forces. Concurrent with this process would be strong diplomatic efforts to bring a negotiated peace, plus direct military pressure against North Vietnam. Under these conditions, the American withdrawal could occur in an "honorable" fashion as pledged by Nixon at the Republican nominating convention.

For Richard Nixon and his chief foreign policy adviser Henry A. Kissinger, who served as national security adviser during the president's first administration, the strategic significance of Vietnam as a bulwark against Chinese Communist expansion had been significantly altered by the growing Sino-Soviet rift and developing rapprochement with the People's Republic of China. President Nixon also redefined U.S. foreign policy in Asia by the enunciation of the Guam Doctrine (later called the Nixon Doctrine) on July 23, 1969. Nixon declared that in the future the United States would aid only those countries with economic and military assistance that were ready with their own military forces to defend themselves. The doctrine's emphasis on a lower profile for U.S. military forces dovetailed well with the Nixon-Kissinger policy of Vietnamization of the Southeast Asian war.

Bringing an "honorable end to the war in Vietnam," as promised by the new president, would nevertheless be very costly. As Nixon took office in January 1969, "there were 550,000 American troops in Vietnam, 30,000 men were being drafted every month, and combat casualties were as high as 300 a week."[20] The administration's policy of gradual withdrawal of U.S. ground troops from the high-water mark established by President Johnson was not matched by a deescalation of the air war. U.S. bombing campaigns escalated, particularly in technically neutral Cambodia which the North Vietnamese had long used to send troops into South Vietnam. These "secret" bombings were soon discovered and reported in the *New York Times* during March 1969. The president then established a "Plumbers" unit to stop such leaks to the press. Eventually, this decision led to a series of criminal acts by the Plumbers, especially an attempted break-in at the headquarters of the Democratic party in Washington's Watergate Hotel in 1972.[21]

But the "Side-Show"[22] in Cambodia was not over. Following a successful coup against the Cambodian leadership in early 1970, South Vietnamese and U.S. forces crossed into Cambodian territory in an effort to disrupt North Vietnamese supply lines. The administration's decision to enter Cambodia with ground forces was taken without any consultation with the Congress, even though a national frontier had been crossed (however ill defined) by U.S. armed forces. The U.S.-South Vietnamese incursion touched off a new wave of student demonstrations and tragic incidents on American campuses and led to an ever deepening conflict between president and Congress. At the same time, American ground forces were continuing their slow withdrawal from Vietnam.

CONGRESSIONAL ASSERTIVENESS

The War Powers Resolution, which eventually became public law in 1973, was passed by the Congress during a period of reform and assertiveness that roughly coincided with Richard Nixon's years in office as president of the United States. The major fueling mechanism for congressional assertiveness and reform during this period was clearly the Vietnam War. Yet, earlier incidences, such as the previously noted "shoot-at-sight" orders by FDR in 1941, and the use of joint resolutions such as the Formosa Resolution in 1955 and the Tonkin Gulf Resolution in 1964 on which to justify future war actions, also played an important role.

During Nixon's first year in the White House, the Senate fired an opening salvo against the presidential commitment of troops to battle without an explicit authorization from the Congress. The Senate offered a resolution claiming that a "national commitment" could only come about through a concurrent action by the president and the Congress. The Senate resolution failed in the House, but the long march culminating in the War Powers Resolution had begun.[23]

The Cambodian incursion had acted as a lightning rod for the antiwar members of Congress. In 1970 it attempted to ban the use of funds for operations in Cambodia via passage of the Cooper-Church Amendment, and the Senate repealed the 1964 Gulf of Tonkin Resolution on which the Johnson Administration had Americanized the war. Yet, the Nixon Administration, in a May 30, 1970, letter to Senator Fulbright, claimed that it "does not depend on the Tonkin Gulf Resolution, as legal or constitutional authority for its present conduct of foreign relations, or its contingency plans." Instead, the president acted on "his constitutional authority as Commander-in-Chief." From the standpoint of international law, according to the letter, "the action in Cambodia was an exercise by the United States and the Government of Viet-Nam of their right of individual and collective self-defense under Article 51 of the UN Charter."[24]

Congressional assertiveness in the foreign policy area was also expressed by passage of the Case Act in 1972, which required that executive agreements between the president and foreign governments be reported to the Congress for its information. This form of agreement, which is similar to a treaty but does not require Senate consent, had long been controversial. President Franklin D. Roosevelt had made several such agreements during World War II—most notably at Yalta—and a series of such agreements had been made between Washington and Saigon during the 1950s and 1960s, "promising American support for the government of South Vietnam."[25]

In the presidential election of 1972, Richard Nixon's opponent came from the U.S. Senate. Liberal Senator George McGovern of South Dakota was a strong antiwar critic, and his dovish positions aided him enormously in gaining the Democratic nomination. But in the general election his strong stance against the war, which included a quick withdrawal of American troops and the refusal of future military aid to South Vietnam, became a liability. "Thus the issue that may have been McGovern's trump card in winning the nomination could only do him harm if it remained salient in the general election."[26]

The result was a Nixon triumph at the polls as American units continued to withdraw from Vietnam. Yet the president was in a melancholy mood on his own victorious election night. In an effort to explain why, he added: "To some extent the marring effects of Watergate may have played a part, to some extent our failure to win Congress, and to a greater extent the fact that we had not yet been able to end the war in Vietnam."[27]

Independent congressional efforts to reduce the role of U.S. military forces in the war continued in the Democratic-controlled Congress, despite the president's strong endorsement at the polls in November. In May 1973, the Senate passed a supplemental appropriations bill for the Defense Department, with an attached amendment by Senator Thomas Eagleton, a Missouri Democrat, prohibiting the use of any funds for combat activities in Cambodia or Laos. By June the House had agreed to a similar-language bill that President Nixon vetoed. However, the Eagleton Amendment was soon attached to other appropriations bills that Nixon could not veto without interfering with normal government operations. By the end of June the president, increasingly besieged by the un-folding Watergate scandal, accepted the Eagleton Amendment.

THE WAR POWERS RESOLUTION

As various war power proposals were working their long way through the legislative process, the American phase of the Vietnam War was finally ending. On January 11, 1973, a cease-fire agreement was reached with North Vietnam, and on January 16, 1973, Richard Nixon made a commitment to South Viet-namese President Thieu that "we will react strongly in the event that the agree-ment is violated." He also added his "firm intention to continue full economic and military aid."[28] However, the Congress would later cut appropriations for South Vietnam, and after Nixon's resignation in August 1974, the Saigon regime was defeated during the spring of 1975.

On March 7, 1973, a House Foreign Affairs subcommittee opened hearings, with both Senate and House sponsors of different war powers proposals appearing as witnesses. These hearings in the 93rd Congress would represent the final phase of the legislative effort, begun in 1969 with the Senate introduction of the National Commitment Resolution, to reassert the congressional war power.

The clear relationship of the Vietnam War to the perceived necessity for a war powers resolution to curb the chief executive's ability to commit American forces into hostile actions was evident in the statements of witnesses such as Democratic Representative Spark M. Matsunaga of Hawaii. According to Mat-sunaga, "we need definite, unmistakable procedures to prevent future undeclared wars. 'No more Vietnams' should be our objective in setting up such proce-dures."[29]

On July 18 the House passed H.J. Res 542, sponsored by Wisconsin Democrat Clement J. Zablocki, leader of the war powers movement in the House. The Zablocki bill set a 120-day limit on the commitment or enlargement of American fighting forces abroad unless the Congress specifically so authorized. In addition, it would allow the Congress to terminate military commitments at any time by passage of a concurrent resolution not requiring presidential signature and thus avoiding the veto. President Nixon's opposition to both of these provisions was spelled out in a June 26 telegram sent to House Minority Leader Gerald R. Ford, a Michigan Republican and future president. Ford read aloud from the Nixon telegram on July 18 during the debate over the Zablocki bill. The president declared that he was "unalterably opposed to and must veto any bill containing the dangerous and unconstitutional restrictions."[30]

In the same telegram, however, Nixon also noted that he would "fully support the desire of members to assure Congress its proper role in national decisions of war and peace," and that he "would welcome appropriate legislation providing for an effective contribution by the Congress."[31] But as to what that "proper role" should be the president did not elaborate, and Minority Leader Ford could offer almost no specifics, except that he thought the president was in "sympathy"[32] with a substitute bill offered by Indiana Republican David W. Dennis, which would require approval or disapproval by the Congress within ninety days of a presidential report of U.S. involvement. The Dennis proposal was subsequently defeated on a recorded teller vote of 166–250.

The president had failed to coordinate his resistance to the Zablocki bill with representatives who were opposed, and the House Republican Policy Committee failed to agree on a Republican amendment alternative and issued no policy statement. Therefore, House opponents of the bill, whose efforts remained scattered, went down to final defeat on July 18—despite the fact that those opposed claimed that the use of a concurrent resolution to end a U.S. troop commitment was both unconstitutional and not binding on the president.[33]

In the Senate a similar pattern of Republican members either supporting their chamber's war power measure or not coordinating their opposition was repeated despite strong opposition from the president. The Senate bill (S440) was sponsored by Senators Eagleton, Javits, and John C. Stennis, a Mississippi Democrat, together with fifty other senators as cosponsors. It received near unanimous approval from the Senate Foreign Relations Committee on May 17, with Senator Fulbright voting "present" and none of the Republican members voting against it. It differed from H.J. Res 542 in that it identified the emergency circumstances under which the president could commit troops, and it provided a thirty-day termination period for a U.S. military commitment without specific authorization, instead of 120 days as in the House version. However, the House bill would allow congressional termination of a military commitment at any time via passage of a concurrent resolution.

During the full Senate debate on S440, liberal Democrats voiced their concern that the bill was not restrictive enough. Senator Eagleton offered an amendment that would have broadened the scope of armed forces committed to include CIA or other civilian personnel because he believed "that presidential warmaking in the future will be conducted just through this loophole."[34] However, S440's floor manager, Democratic Senator Edmund S. Muskie of Maine, spoke against the amendment, and it was defeated on a 34–53 roll call vote.

Republican opponents of S440 were well aware that it had strong support in the Senate, given its near unanimous endorsement by the Foreign Relations Committee. Administration supporters were equally confident that President Nixon would veto S440 should it reach the White House. This knowledge probably influenced Senate Republican Minority Whip Robert P. Griffin of Michigan to withdraw his own amendment during the debate. His amendment would have established consulting procedures between the president and the Congress on questions concerning any commitment and for Congress to either approve the commitment or vote to cut off funds.[35]

A brickbat was tossed at S440 by Republican John G. Tower of Texas who proposed an amendment to change the bill's title to read: "A bill to make rules governing the use of the Armed Forces of the United States in the absence of a declaration of war by the Congress, and thereby reduce the United States of

America to the status of a second rate power."[36] Tower's proposal was ruled out of order and withdrawn. It was similar to Senator Griffin's withdrawn amendment in that it did not represent a strong or serious effort to block or modify the bill. Therefore, the only concerted Republican challenge was left to Barry Goldwater.

On July 18 Goldwater submitted a detailed list of twenty-five major problems with S440. Under number 25, the Conservative Republican noted that General George Washington "was harassed, second-guessed, and over-ruled with respect to his military plans and strategy throughout the War of Independence." Therefore, according to Goldwater, "the Founding Fathers realized that Congressional control of military functions had very nearly led to disaster during the Revolutionary War. For this reason, the use of the armed forces in the defense of American rights and freedoms was left with the President as Commander in Chief."[37]

The Senate's leading proponent and cosponsor of S440, Jacob Javits, countered Goldwater's commander in chief argument by noting that, "out of the crisis of World War II and the ensuing cold war, lawyers for the president had spun a spurious doctrine of 'inherent' Commander-in-Chief powers—broad enough to cover virtually every 'national security' contingency that could be thought of."[38] On July 20 Goldwater further buttressed his commander in chief argument by having printed in the *Record* 199 cases of U.S. military hostilities abroad without a declaration of war from 1798 to 1972, as opposed to the five declarations of war by the Congress during the same time period. The Arizona Republican then declared that he was "convinced" that "the President does have the warmaking power under the Constitution, that the Congress right to declare war means nothing except to declare." Furthermore, Goldwater stated to his Senate colleagues, "We can declare war every 5 minutes, but not one man will leave the shores of America until the President says so."[39]

Despite the additional support of the Senate's recognized authority on constitutional law, Democrat Sam J. Ervin, Jr., of North Carolina, the bill was passed by the Senate. Ervin would not support S440 because it said "expressly that the President of the United States cannot perform his constitutional duty and cannot exercise his constitutional power to protect his country against invasion for more than 30 days without the affirmative consent of Congress."[40]

An agreement reached by a House-Senate conference on October 4 set a sixty-day limit on any commitment of U.S. forces without a war declaration or specific congressional authorization. In addition, Senate conferees agreed on a general policy statement instead of the specific delineation of circumstances on which the president could act without congressional authority. On October 10 the Senate approved the conference report by a vote of 75–20 with twenty-six Republicans and forty-nine Democrats voting in the affirmative and fourteen Republicans and six Democrats voting against the report. House action on the conference report took place on October 12. An approving vote of 238–123 was recorded, with 163 Democrats and 75 Republicans supporting the compromise and 38 Democrats and 85 Republicans opposed. Thus, Republican voting opposition was clearly more evident in the House than in the Senate.[41]

NIXON VERSUS THE CONGRESS

In President Richard Nixon's veto message of October 24, 1973, returning House Joint Resolution 542—The War Powers Resolution—to the Congress without his approval, he declared that "the Founding Fathers understood the impossibility of foreseeing every contingency that might arise in this complex area. They acknowledged the need for flexibility in responding to changing circumstances. They recognized that foreign policy decisions must be made through close cooperation between the two branches and not through rigidly codified procedures."[42]

The president especially objected to the sixty-day limit on troop commitments abroad which were not authorized by the Congress while at the same time allowing the Congress "to eliminate certain authorities merely by the passage of a concurrent resolution." According to Nixon: "I believe that both these provisions are unconstitutional. The only way in which the constitutional powers of a branch of the Government can be altered is by amending the Constitution— and any attempt to make such alterations by legislation alone is clearly without force."[43]

Nixon was also "particularly disturbed"[44] that certain of the president's powers as commander in chief would be automatically terminated in sixty days unless the Congress authorized an extension. His veto defense of the commander in chief power was consistent with previous positions taken by Republican Senator Goldwater and Democrat Sam J. Ervin, Jr.

The president, however, did not object to all of the Joint Resolution's provisions. He referred to section 3's call "for consultations with the Congress before and during the involvement of the United States forces in hostilities" as a "constructive measure." He further stated that he would "welcome the establishment of a non-partisan commission on the constitutional roles of the Congress and the President in the conduct of foreign affairs."[45]

It was all to no avail. On November 7, 1973, the House of Representatives and the Senate voted to override the president's veto. It was the first successful override of a presidential veto in the 93rd Congress and in the House, which was required to vote first, it was a cliff-hanger. The 284–135 House vote was only four votes more than the two-thirds majority required to override a veto by the Constitution. The vote according to political party was as follows: 103 Republicans voted to sustain, 86 voted to override; 198 Democrats voted to override, 32 voted to sustain of which 23 were Southern Democrats. In the Senate, where the veto was expected to be overridden, the vote was 75–18, providing a 13 vote margin beyond the two-thirds requirement.[46]

The main immediate reason for the successful override in the House was the Watergate crisis that had enveloped the presidency. Only hours after the successful congressional override of the War Powers Resolution on November 7, Richard Nixon ended a televised speech on the energy crisis with a direct reference to the increasing demands that he resign over Watergate: "Tonight I would like to give my answer to those who have suggested that I resign. I have no intention whatever of walking away."[47] Representative William S. Mailliard of California, who led the Republican forces in the House seeking to sustain the president's veto, believed that several weeks prior to the override vote a veto could have been sustained, but that the Watergate crisis and other matters related to the scandal had contributed to a favorable override climate.[48]

While the White House was embattled over Watergate, lobbying efforts coordinated by Americans for Democratic Action (ADA) aimed their pro-resolution efforts at fifteen House liberals, many of whom believed the joint resolution gave the president too much power. The ADA and congressional supporters' efforts paid off: on the final House vote eight of the fifteen voted in favor of the override (seven Democrats, one Republican).[49]

After these immediate reasons for the override in the House, a broader analysis is necessary to assess Nixon's defeat by the Congress over passage of the War Powers Resolution. Certainly, the Vietnam War itself, which so poisoned executive-congressional relations during the late 1960s and into the 1970s, must be considered a major contributory reason. But any assessment of the causes of the conflict between president and Congress during the Vietnam War period must take into account two salient factors. First, the near unanimous congressional approval of the Tonkin Gulf Resolution in 1964, with its sweeping language of commitment, represented an historic foreign policy error by the legislative branch. Second, President Nixon's Cambodian incursion across a national frontier in 1970, without any consultation with the Congress, obviously widened the Vietnam War and greatly exacerbated the continuing feud over the war powers between president and Congress.

The War Powers Resolution must also be viewed as partially the product of a period of congressional reassertion and reform that roughly coincided with Richard Nixon's years in the White House. Congressional assertiveness not only encompassed the War Powers Resolution of 1973, but was, for instance, preceded by the Case Act in 1972 and followed by the Budget Act of 1974, which was a legislative effort to reassert congressional control over government spending and curb the presidential impoundment of funds. This period of congressional reassertion and reform had been long brewing, but its culmination during the Nixon Presidency and after was fueled especially by the notion that the presidency had become imperial, that is, gorged with power and indifferent toward the Congress.

The commander in chief power of the president remains at the center of the controversy over the war power between the executive and legislative branches. The president's power to conduct war was not in question at the Constitutional Convention of 1787. Numerous presidents have, in fact, committed the armed forces into hostile situations without declarations of war by the Congress. Indeed, the defense of the commander in chief power was a primary reason for Nixon's veto as stated in his message: "House Joint Resolution 542 would attempt to take away, by a mere legislative act, authorities which the President has properly exercised under the Constitution for almost 200 years."[50]

When viewed in an historical context, the War Powers Resolution (especially section 3 regarding consultation) represents an effort by the Congress to mandate by legislation what had been accomplished voluntarily beginning thirty years before through bipartisanship. Because bipartisanship is a process and not a policy, its utility in formulating various foreign policies, including the development of an alliance or a disarmament treaty is equally germane. Bipartisanship enhances trust between president and Congress. Conversely, the War Powers Resolution bespeaks of mistrust on the part of the Congress toward the president—a mistrust that was certainly understandable during the Vietnam War years, but may not serve the long-range interests of U.S. foreign policy formulation.

Richard Nixon has been at least partially vindicated in his conflict with the Congress over the War Powers Resolution. In 1983 the Supreme Court affirmed a lower court ruling that invalidated the legislative veto provisions in hundreds of laws.[51] Section 5(c) of the War Powers Resolution provides for a legislative veto by empowering the Congress, in the absence of a war declaration or statutory authorization, to force the removal of armed forces from hostilities abroad by concurrent resolution.

Yet, Nixon must bear at least part of the responsibility for bringing about a resolution he so strongly opposed. He did not sufficiently consult with the Congress, especially during a period when his own party was in the minority in both chambers. He did not sufficiently rally Republican representatives in the House during the struggle over the veto override—undoubtedly because of his own preoccupation with Watergate.

APPENDIX A: WAR POWERS RESOLUTION
PUBLIC LAW 93–148:87 STAT. 555 (H.J. RES. 542)

Source: *United States Statutes at Large* 87 (1973): 555–559.

JOINT RESOLUTION

Concerning the war powers of Congress and the President.

Resolved by the Senate and House of Representatives of the United States of America in Congress assembled,

SHORT TITLE

SECTION 1. This joint resolution may be cited as the "War Powers Resolution."

PURPOSE AND POLICY

SEC. 2. (a) It is the purpose of this joint resolution to fulfill the intent of the framers of the Constitution of the United States and insure that the collective judgment of both the Congress and the President will apply to the introduction of United States Armed Forces into hostilities, or into situations where imminent involvement in hostilities is clearly indicated by the circumstances, and to the continued use of such forces in hostilities or in such situations.

(b) Under article I, section 8, of the Constitution, it is specifically provided that the Congress shall have the power to make all laws necessary and proper for carrying into execution, not only its own powers but also all other powers vested by the Constitution in the Government of the United States, or in any department or officer thereof.

(c) The constitutional powers of the President as Commander-in-Chief to introduce United States Armed Forces into hostilities, or into situations where imminent involvement in hostilities is clearly indicated by the circumstances, are exercised only pursuant to (1) a declaration of war, (2) specific statutory authorization, or (3) a national emergency created by attack upon the United States, its territories or possessions, or its armed forces.

CONSULTATION

SEC. 3. The President in every possible instance shall consult with Congress before introducing United States Armed Forces into hostilities or into situations where imminent involvement in hostilities is clearly indicated by the circumstances, and after every such introduction shall consult regularly with the Congress until United States Armed Forces are no longer engaged in hostilities or have been removed from such situations.

REPORTING

SEC. 4. (a) In the absence of a declaration of war, in any case in which United States Armed Forces are introduced—

(1) into hostilities or into situations where imminent involvement in hostilities is clearly indicated by the circumstances;

(2) into the territory, airspace or waters of a foreign nation, while equipped for combat, except for deployments which relate solely to supply, replacement, repair, or training of such forces; or

(3) in numbers which substantially enlarge United States Armed Forces equipped for combat already located in a foreign nation; the President shall submit within 48 hours to the Speaker of the House of Representatives and to the President pro tempore of the Senate a report, in writing, setting forth—

(A) the circumstances necessitating the introduction of United States Armed Forces;

(B) the constitutional and legislative authority under which such introduction took place; and

(C) the estimated scope and duration of the hostilities or involvement.

(b) The President shall provide such other information as the Congress may request in the fulfillment of its constitutional responsibilities with respect to committing the Nation to war and to the use of United States Armed Forces abroad.

(c) Whenever United States Armed Forces are introduced into hostilities or into any situation described in subsection (a) of this section, the President shall, so long as such armed forces continue to be engaged in such hostilities or situation, report to the Congress periodically on the status of such hostilities or situation as well as on the scope and duration of such hostilities or situation, but in no event shall he report to the Congress less often than once every six months.

CONGRESSIONAL ACTION

SEC. 5. (a) Each report submitted pursuant to section 4(a) (1) shall be transmitted to the Speaker of the House of Representatives and to the President pro tempore of the Senate on the same calendar day. Each report so transmitted shall be referred to the Committee on Foreign Affairs of the House of Representatives and to the Committee on Foreign Relations of the Senate for appropriate action. If, when the report is transmitted, the Congress has adjourned sine die or has adjourned for any period in excess of three calendar days, the Speaker of the House of Representatives and the President pro tempore of the Senate, if they deem it advisable (or if petitioned by at least 30 percent of the membership of their respective Houses) shall jointly request the President to convene Congress in order that it may consider the report and take appropriate action pursuant to this section.

(b) Within sixty calendar days after a report is submitted or is required to be submitted pursuant to section 4(a)(1), whichever is earlier, the President shall terminate any use of United States Armed Forces with respect to which such report was submitted (or required to be submitted), unless the Congress (1) has Declared war or has enacted a specific authorization for such use of United States Armed Forces, (2) has extended by law such sixty-day period, or (3) is physically unable to meet as a result of an armed attack upon the United States. Such sixty-day period shall be extended for not more than an additional thirty days if the President determines and certifies to the Congress in writing that unavoidable military necessity respecting the safety of United States Armed Forces requires the continued use of such armed forces in the course of bringing about a prompt removal of such forces.

(c) Notwithstanding subsection (b), at any time that United States Armed Forces are engaged in hostilities outside the territory of the United States, its possessions and territories without a declaration of war or specific statutory authorization, such forces shall be removed by the President if the Congress so directs by concurrent resolution.

CONGRESSIONAL PRIORITY PROCEDURES FOR
JOINT RESOLUTION OR BILL

SEC. 6. (a) Any joint resolution or bill introduced pursuant to section 5(b) at least thirty calendar days before the expiration of the sixty-day period specified in such section shall be referred to the Committee on Foreign Affairs of the House of Representatives or the Committee on Foreign Relations of the Senate, as the case may be, and such committee shall report one such joint resolution or bill, together with its recommendations, not later than twenty-four calendar days before the expiration of the sixty-day period specified in such section, unless such House shall otherwise determine by the yeas and nays.

(b) Any joint resolution or bill so reported shall become the pending business of the House in question (in case of the Senate the time for debate shall be equally divided between the proponents and the opponents), and shall be voted on within three calendar days thereafter, unless such House shall otherwise determine by yeas and nays.

(c) Such a joint resolution or bill passed by one House shall be referred to the committee of the other House named in subsection (a) and shall be reported out not later than fourteen calendar days before the expiration of the sixty-day period specified in section 5(b). The joint resolution or bill so reported shall become the pending business of the House in question and shall be voted on within three calendar days after it has been reported, unless such House shall otherwise determine by yeas and nays.

(d) In the case of any disagreement between the two Houses of Congress with respect to a joint resolution or bill passed by both Houses, conferees shall be promptly appointed and the committee of conference shall make and file a report with respect to such resolution or bill not later than four calendar days before the expiration of the sixty-day period specified in section 5(b). In the event the conferees are unable to agree within 48 hours, they shall report back to their respective Houses in disagreement. Notwithstanding any rule in either House concerning the printing of conference reports in the *Record* or concerning any delay in the consideration of such reports, such report shall be acted on by both Houses not later than the expiration of such sixty-day period.

CONGRESSIONAL PRIORITY PROCEDURES FOR
CONCURRENT RESOLUTION

SEC. 7. (a) Any concurrent resolution introduced pursuant to section 5(c) shall be referred to the Committee on Foreign Affairs of the House of Representatives or the Committee on Foreign Relations of the Senate, as the case may be, and one such concurrent resolution shall be reported out by such committee together with its recommendations within fifteen calendar days, unless such House shall otherwise determine by the yeas and nays.

(b) Any concurrent resolution so reported shall become the pending business of the House in question (in the case of the Senate the time for debate shall be equally divided between the proponents and the opponents) and shall be voted on within three calendar days thereafter, unless such House shall otherwise determine by yeas and nays.

(c) Such a concurrent resolution passed by one House shall be referred to the committee of the other House named in subsection (a) and shall be reported out by such committee together with its recommendations within fifteen calendar days and shall thereupon become the pending business of such House and shall be voted upon within three calendar days, unless such House shall otherwise determine by yeas and nays.

(d) In the case of any disagreement between the two Houses of Congress with respect to a concurrent resolution passed by both Houses, conferees shall be promptly appointed and the committee of conference shall make and file a report with respect to such concurrent resolution within six calendar days after the legislation is referred to the committee of conference. Notwithstanding any rule in either House concerning the printing of conference reports in the *Record* or concerning any delay in the consideration of such reports, such report shall be acted on by both Houses not later than six calendar days after the conference report is filed. In the event the conferees are unable to agree within 48 hours, they shall report back to their respective Houses in disagreement.

INTERPRETATION OF JOINT RESOLUTION

SEC. 8 (a) Authority to introduce United States Armed Forces into hostilities or into situations wherein involvement in hostilities is clearly indicated by the circumstances shall not be inferred—

(1) from any provision of law (whether or not in effect before the date of the enactment of this joint resolution), including any provision contained in any appropriation Act, unless such provision specifically authorizes the introduction of United States Armed Forces into hostilities or into such situations and states that it is intended to constitute specific statutory authorization within the meaning of this joint resolution; or

(2) from any treaty heretofore or heretoafter ratified unless such treaty is implemented by legislation specifically authorizing the introduction of United States Armed Forces into hostilities or into such situations and stating that it is intended to constitute specific statutory authorization within the meaning of this joint resolution.

(b) Nothing in this joint resolution shall be construed to require any further specific statutory authorization to permit members of United States Armed Forces to participate jointly with members of the armed forces of one or more foreign countries in the headquarters operations of high-level military commands which were established prior to the date of enactment of this joint resolution and pursuant to the United Nations Charter or any treaty ratified by the United States prior to such date.

(c) For purposes of this joint resolution, the term "introduction of United

States Armed Forces'' includes the assignment of members of such armed forces to command, coordinate, participate in the movement of, or accompany the regular or irregular military forces of any foreign country or government when such military forces are engaged, or there exists an imminent threat that such forces will become engaged, in hostilities.

(d) Nothing in this joint resolution—

(1) is intended to alter the constitutional authority of the Congress or of the President, or the provisions of existing treaties; or

(2) shall be construed as granting any authority to the President with respect to the introduction of United States Armed Forces into hostilities or into situations wherein involvement in hostilities is clearly indicated by the circumstances which authority he would not have had in the absence of this joint resolution.

SEPARABILITY CLAUSE

SEC. 9. If any provision of this joint resolution or the application thereof to any person or circumstance is held invalid, the remainder of the joint resolution and the application of such provision to any other person or circumstance shall not be affected thereby.

EFFECTIVE DATE

SEC. 10. This joint resolution shall take effect on the date of its enactment.

APPENDIX B

Source: Richard Nixon, *Public Papers of the Presidents of the United States, 1973* (Washington, D.C.: U.S. Government Printing Office, 1975), pp. 893–895.

Veto of the War Powers Resolution

October 24, 1973

To the House of Representatives:

I hereby return without my approval House Joint Resolution 542—the War Powers Resolution. While I am in accord with the desire of the Congress to assert its proper role in the conduct of our foreign affairs, the restrictions which this resolution would impose upon the authority of the President are both unconstitutional and dangerous to the best interests of our Nation.

The proper roles of the Congress and the Executive in the conduct of foreign affairs have been debated since the founding of our country. Only recently, however, has there been a serious challenge to the wisdom of the Founding Fathers in choosing not to draw a precise and detailed line of demarcation between the foreign policy powers of the two branches.

The Founding Fathers understood the impossibility of foreseeing every contingency that might arise in this complex area. They acknowledged the need for flexibility in responding to changing circumstances. They recognized that foreign policy decisions must be made through close cooperation between the two branches and not through rigidly codified procedures.

These principles remain as valid today as they were when our Constitution was written. Yet House Joint Resolution 542 would violate those principles by defining the President's powers in ways which would strictly limit his constitutional authority.

CLEARLY UNCONSTITUTIONAL

House Joint Resolution 542 would attempt to take away, by a mere legislative act, authorities which the President has properly exercised under the Constitution for almost 200 years. One of its provisions would automatically cut off certain authorities after sixty days unless the Congress extended them. Another would allow the Congress to eliminate certain authorities merely by the passage of a concurrent resolution—an action which does not normally have the force of law, since it denies the President his constitutional role in approving legislation.

I believe that both these provisions are unconstitutional. The only way in which the constitutional powers of a branch of the Government can be altered is by amending the Constitution—and any attempt to make such alterations by legislation alone is clearly without force.

UNDERMINING OUR FOREIGN POLICY

While I firmly believe that a veto of House Joint Resolution 542 is warranted solely on constitutional grounds, I am also deeply disturbed by the practical consequences of this resolution. For it would seriously undermine this Nation's ability to act decisively and convincingly in times of international crisis. As a result, the confidence of our allies in our ability to assist them could be diminished and the respect of our adversaries for our deterrent posture could decline. A permanent and substantial element of unpredictability would be injected into the world's assessment of American behavior, further increasing the likelihood of miscalculation and war.

If this resolution had been in operation, America's effective response to a variety of challenges in recent years would have been vastly complicated or even made impossible. We may well have been unable to respond in the way we did during the Berlin crisis of 1961, the Cuban missile crisis of 1962, the Congo rescue operation in 1964, and the Jordanian crisis of 1970—to mention just a few examples. In addition, our recent actions to bring about a peaceful settlement of the hostilities in the Middle East would have been seriously impaired if this resolution had been in force.

While all the specific consequences of House Joint Resolution 542 cannot yet be predicted, it is clear that it would undercut the ability of the United States to act as an effective influence for peace. For example, the provision automatically cutting off certain authorities after 60 days unless they are extended by the Congress could work to prolong or intensify a crisis. Until the Congress suspended the deadline, there would be at least a chance of United States withdrawal and an adversary would be tempted therefore to postpone serious negotiations until the 60 days were up. Only after the Congress acted would there be a strong incentive for an adversary to negotiate. In addition, the very existence of a deadline could lead to an escalation of hostilities in order to achieve certain objectives before the 60 days expired.

The measure would jeopardize our role as a force for peace in other ways as well. It would, for example, strike from the President's hand a wide range of important peace-keeping tools by eliminating his ability to exercise quiet diplomacy backed by subtle shifts in our military deployments. It would also cast into doubt authorities which Presidents have used to undertake certain humanitarian relief missions in conflict areas, to protect fishing boats from seizure, to deal with ship or aircraft hijackings, and to respond to threats of attack. Not the least of the adverse consequences of this resolution would be the prohibition contained in section 8 against fulfilling our obligations under the NATO treaty as ratified by the Senate. Finally, since the bill is somewhat vague as to when the 60 day rule would apply, it could lead to extreme confusion and dangerous disagreements concerning the prerogatives of the two branches, seriously damaging our ability to respond to international crises.

FAILURE TO REQUIRE POSITIVE
CONGRESSIONAL ACTION

I am particularly disturbed by the fact that certain of the President's constitutional powers as Commander in Chief of the Armed Forces would terminate automatically under this resolution 60 days after they were invoked. No overt Congressional action would be required to cut off these powers—they would disappear automatically unless the Congress extended them. In effect, the Congress is here attempting to increase its policy-making role through a provision which requires it to take absolutely no action at all.

In my view, the proper way for the Congress to make known its will on such foreign policy questions is through a positive action, with full debate on the merits of the issue and with each member taking the responsibility of casting a yes or no vote after considering those merits. The authorization and appropriations process represents one of the ways in which such influence can be exercised. I do not, however, believe that the Congress can responsibly contribute its considered, collective judgment on such grave questions without full debate and without a yes or no vote. Yet this is precisely what the joint resolution would allow. It would give every future Congress the ability to handcuff every future President merely by doing nothing and sitting still. In my view, one cannot become a responsible partner unless one is prepared to take responsible action.

STRENGTHENING COOPERATION BETWEEN THE
CONGRESS AND THE EXECUTIVE BRANCHES

The responsible and effective exercise of the war powers requires the fullest cooperation between the Congress and the Executive and the prudent fulfillment by each branch of its constitutional responsibilities. House Joint Resolution 542 includes certain constructive measures which would foster this process by enhancing the flow of information from the executive branch to the Congress. Section 3, for example, calls for consultations with the Congress before and during the involvement of the United States forces in hostilities abroad. This provision is consistent with the desire of this Administration for regularized consultations with the Congress in an even wider range of circumstances.

I believe that full and cooperative participation in foreign policy matters by both the executive and the legislative branches could be enhanced by a careful and dispassionate study of their constitutional roles. Helpful proposals for such a study have already been made in the Congress. I would welcome the establishment of a non-partisan commission on the constitutional roles of the Congress and the President in the conduct of foreign affairs. This commission could make a thorough review of the principal constitutional issues in Executive-Congresssional relations, including the war powers, the international agreement powers, and the question of Executive privilege, and then submit its recommendations to the President and the Congress. The members of such a commission could be drawn from both parties—and could represent many perspectives including those of the Congress, the executive branch, the legal profession, and the academic community.

This Administration is dedicated to strengthening cooperation between the Congress and the President in the conduct of foreign affairs and to preserving the constitutional prerogatives of both branches of our Government. I know that the Congress shares that goal. A commission on the constitutional roles of the Congress and the President would provide a useful opportunity for both branches to work together toward that common objective.

                                                          Richard Nixon

NOTES

1. *RN: The Memoirs of Richard Nixon* (New York: Grosset & Dunlap, 1978), p. 889 (hereafter cited as *Memoirs*).

2. Max Farrand, ed., *The Records of the Federal Convention of 1787*, 4 vols. (New Haven: Yale University Press, 1937), 2, p. 318.

3. Ibid.; see footnote, p. 319.

4. Edward S. Corwin, *The President: Office and Powers, 1787–1957* (New York: New York University Press, 1957), p. 171.

5. See chronological list in *Congressional Record*, 93rd Cong., 1st Sess., 1973, 119, pt. 20:25066–25076.

6. Edward Conrad Smith, ed., *The Constitution of the United States With Case Summaries* (New York: Barnes & Noble, 1979), pp. 96–97.

7. Fred W. Friendly and Martha J. H. Elliott, *The Constitution: That Delicate Balance* (New York: Random House, 1984), pp. 266–281; Smith, *The Constitution*, p. 97.

8. *Cong. Rec.*, 119, pt. 20:25077.

9. Ibid., p. 25078.

10. Arthur M. Schlesinger, Jr., *The Imperial Presidency* (New York: Popular Library, 1974), p. 118.

11. See Briggs, "Congress and Collective Security: The Resolutions of 1943," *World Affairs* 132 (March 1970):343.

12. See Briggs, "Senator Vandenberg, Bipartisanship, and the Origin of United Nation's Article 51," *Mid-America: An Historical Review* 60 (October 1978):163; also see Briggs, "Kennedy and the Congress: The Nuclear Test Ban Treaty, 1963," in Harper, Paul, and Krieg, Joann P. (eds.), *John F. Kennedy: The Promise Revisited* (Westport, Conn.: Greenwood Press, 1988), pp. 35–55.

13. James E. Dougherty and Robert L. Pfaltzgraff, Jr., *American Foreign Policy: FDR to Reagan* (New York: Harper & Row, 1986), p. 227. For full study of Formosa Resolutions see "Congress and the Cold War: U.S.-China Policy, 1955," *The China Quarterly* 85 (March 1981): 80–95.

14. Neil Sheehan, Hedrick Smith, E. W. Kenworthy, and Fox Butterfield, *The Pentagon Papers* (New York: Bantam Books, 1971), p. 265.

15. Amos Yoder, *The Conduct of American Foreign Policy Since World War II* (New York: Pergamon Press, 1986), p. 95.

16. Robert A. Diamond, ed., *Origins and Development of Congress* (Washington, D.C.: Congressional Quarterly, 1976), p. 260.

17. *Pentagon Papers*, p. 511.

18. Nixon, *Memoirs*, p. 336.

19. See Nixon acceptance speech in Arthur M. Schlesinger, Jr., ed., *History of American Presidential Elections, 1789–1968*, 4 vols. (New York: McGraw-Hill, 1971), 4, pp. 3834–3835.

20. Henry T. Nash, *American Foreign Policy: Changing Perspectives on National Security* (Homewood, Ill.: Dorsey Press, 1978), p. 247.

21. Walter LaFeber, *America, Russia, and the Cold War 1945–1984* (New York: Knopf, 1985), p. 263.

22. Quote from title of study on Cambodian aspect of Vietnam War by William Shawcross, *Side-Show: Kissinger, Nixon and the Destruction of Cambodia* (New York: Pocket Books, 1974), p. iii.

23. James A. Nathan and James K. Oliver, *Foreign Policy Making and the American Political System* (Boston: Little, Brown, 1983), p. 102.

24. Letter from Elliot Richardson, Acting Secretary, Department of State, in *Cong. Rec.* 119, pt. 8:10421. U.N. Article 51 was included in the Charter at U.S. insistence. See Briggs, "Senator Vandenberg, Bipartisanship, and the Origin of United Nation's Article 51," pp. 163–169.

25. Cecil V. Crabb, Jr., and Pat M. Holt, *Invitation to Struggle: Congress, the President and Foreign Policy* (Washington, D.C.: Congressional Quarterly, 1980), p. 13.

26. Nelson W. Polsby and Aaron Wildavsky, *Presidential Elections: Strategies of American Electoral Politics* (New York: Scribner's, 1984), p. 179.

27. Nixon, *Memoirs*, p. 717.

28. Quoted in Yoder, *Conduct of American Foreign Policy*, p. 112.

29. Quoted in 1973 *Congressional Quarterly Almanac* (Washington, D.C.: Congressional Quarterly, 1974), p. 908.

30. *Cong. Rec.* 119, pt. 19:24664.

31. Ibid.

32. Ibid., p. 24663.

33. See 1973 *Quarterly Almanac*, pp. 910–911.

34. Quoted in ibid., p. 914.

35. Ibid.

36. Ibid.

37. *Cong. Rec.* 119, pt. 19:24533–24536.

38. Ibid., p. 24537.

39. Ibid., pp. 25066–25078.

40. Quoted in 1973 *Quarterly Almanac*, pp. 913–914.

41. See full text of War Powers Resolution in Appendix A; voting results in 1973 *Quarterly Almanac*, pp. 916–917.

42. See full text of Nixon's Veto of the War Powers Resolution in Appendix B.

43. Ibid.

44. Ibid.

45. Ibid.

46. Voting results in 1973 *Quarterly Almanac*, p. 905.

47. Nixon, *Memoirs*, p. 947.

48. 1973 *Quarterly Almanac*, p. 906.

49. Ibid.

50. See Appendix B.

51. *Immigration and Naturalization Service v. Chadha*, 103 S. Ct. 2764 (1983).

14

The War Powers Resolution: An Intersection of Law and Politics

NATHAN N. FIRESTONE

On November 7, 1973, in the midst of severe domestic and international crisis, the United States Congress voted to override President Nixon's veto of the War Powers Act. The vote in the House of Representatives was 284–135 to override and 75–18 in the Senate. Thus, the Congress apparently had finally decided to curtail the president's discretion to commit troops to danger zones without express congressional authorization, or to prevent such authorization from being expanded by the chief executive from a limited grant of authorization to the kinds of massive commitments that the United States had entered in Korea and Vietnam. To the *New York Times*, editorializing the following day, the vote signaled "a resurgence of Congressional independence after a long period of acquiescence to the Executive's accretion of power."[1] However, in seeming contradiction, the *Times* editorial also noted that

the war powers bill is not the revolutionary measure that Mr. Nixon and other critics have attempted to make it out to be. It does not in any way curtail the President's freedom, as Commander in Chief to respond to emergency situations. If anything, it gives the Chief Executive more discretionary authority than the framers of the Constitution intended in order to deal with modern contingencies that they could not have foreseen.[2]

Was the vote this insignificant? Or did enactment of the War Powers Act create "a dangerous whipsaw" emasculating our capability to conduct a "tough" foreign policy?[3] Was the War Powers Act nothing more than the product of a Congress, acting in anger and some petulance at the White House, passing a "paper tiger" act that was "ambiguous at best and maybe even unconstitutional," because "It [Congress] doesn't have the heart to impeach him or to

force his resignation, but it wants to warn and rebuke him, and so it did.''[4] To
Senator Thomas F. Eagleton, the War Powers Act represented a formalization
of Congress's surrender to executive power—''an unconstitutional delegation
of Congressional war powers.''[5] However, a conservative analyst of the warmaking authority and the separation of powers was equally confident that several
of the act's most fundamental provisions were ''flagrantly unconstitutional''—
obviously for different reasons than those suggested by Senator Eagleton.[6] Finally, to a former secretary of state, the purpose of the Resolution was not at
all ''to define or modify the constitutional powers of the President,'' but ''to
establish a procedure through which Congress and the President can exercise
their respective powers.''[7]

It is apparent that the War Powers Act was steeped in controversy when it
was being considered for passage, and now, fourteen and one-half years later,
the controversy about its effectiveness and constitutionality remains. This paper
examines some of the contending views of the War Powers Act that have been
argued and offers some concluding suggestions about the efficacy and possible
constitutionality of the Resolution. However, it is important to recognize, especially in the case of a measure such as this, that positions on constitutionality
and efficacy frequently are correlated to more general attitudes about foreign
policy. This is true in regard both to overall foreign policy objectives and to
views about the role of force in U.S. foreign policy.

It is also important to remind ourselves that the War Powers Act is, by its
very nature, unsatisfactory to those with very strongly held and clearly defined
views of the problem because it is a political compromise on two levels. On the
first level, its introduction, it represented a compromise between a more sharply
dovish proposal by New York Senator Charles Goodell in 1970 to force a
withdrawal from Vietnam by a congressional cutoff of funds and a continuation
of the president's conduct of the Vietnam War as he saw fit. ''As an alternative
to a funds cutoff, which not even the dovish Senate was willing to accept,
Senator Javits came up with the idea of defining the war powers of the President.''[8] That the generally hawkish Senator John Stennis of Mississippi, the
chairman of the Senate Armed Services Committee, had thrown his support
behind the proposal is virtually a *prima facie* case for the depth of the compromise.

On the second level of compromise—that of the substance of the act itself—
it is important to recall the kind of domestic and international crisis that had
seized the Nixon Administration and Congress. The presidency of Richard Nixon
had just entered the most dramatic phase of what many at that time had begun
to perceive as a terminal condition. The ''Saturday Night Massacre'' of October
1973 had destroyed all but some lingering shreds of legitimacy of the Nixon
Administration. An atmosphere of crisis surrounded Kissinger's efforts to pry
apart Egyptian and Israeli forces along the Suez Canal while the Soviet Union
threatened intervention. With this backdrop, Senate and House conferees fash-
ioned a bill that was offensive to some of its original supporters, who felt that

it was worse than nothing by legitimating the president's usurpation of power for "sixty-day wars." Supporters of the president, on the other hand, continued to maintain that the president's hands were now unacceptably tied by Congress. However, the majority of Congress clearly felt that it was important to send the president a strong message, even if the form was less than perfect.

Therefore, the passage of the War Powers Resolution and the substance of the law itself should be treated as an effort to use legal means to effect important political outcomes. To a very large degree, members of Congress viewed the War Powers Resolution within the broader context of what the United States' role in world affairs should be. This paper utilizes a simple typology that correlates general views of foreign policy with views of the War Powers Resolution, showing how attitudes toward the constitutionality and efficacy of the law are derived from, or at least are strongly associated with, perhaps even more basic questions. As the dean of Harvard's Kennedy School of Government has written, questions of warmaking are affected not only by constitutional provisions relating to who has the power to make war, but also to "sweeping considerations" such as basic political values, the prevailing political consensus "about the United States' role in international affairs in general; and the merits of the specific case in question."[9]

Students of U.S. foreign policy know how deeply the change in these basic political values has been over the past fifty years. This change has conditioned entirely new attitudes about the role of the United States in world affairs and about the appropriate constitutional and practical relationships between the president and Congress in the foreign affairs area.

THE GROWTH OF EXECUTIVE WARMAKING AND THE REASSERTION OF CONGRESSIONAL POWER

From 1940 to the late 1960s the imperatives of survival considerations seemed to dictate the growth of the national security state in the United States. The wrenching debate in 1940–41 over American assistance to Great Britain and the Soviet Union, and the question of ultimate American participation in the war, was conducted on procedural as well as substantive levels. The procedural arguments stressed how far down the road to war the nation was being led by President Roosevelt in his efforts to convoy supplies to Britain. "In the six months preceding Pearl Harbor, Franklin Roosevelt moved slowly but steadily toward war with Germany."[10] Among these steps were the American occupation of Iceland with four thousand marines and Roosevelt's authorization to the Navy to protect British convoys carrying desperately needed supplies to England.

Indeed, the period contained even an attack of questionable provocation against an American destroyer, reminiscent of the celebrated attacks by North Vietnamese boats in 1964 that precipitated the Gulf of Tonkin Resolution. With a German torpedo attack against the *Greer*, Roosevelt gave a radio address that implied, without so openly stating, "that American ships would shoot German submarines on sight.''[11] Although Roosevelt called the attack deliberate and an unprovoked act of aggression, ''subsequent reports revealed that the *Greer* had been following the U-boat for more than three hours and had been broadcasting its position to nearby British naval units.''[12]

Further activities by the Navy brought the country even closer to war, edging toward it rather than leaping in because of the still potent strength of isolationist legislators. Retrospectively, most students of the period are in agreement that had Roosevelt chosen to meet the issue frontally, assistance to the British might never have been accomplished. The consequences of such an outcome—a German victory and the entrenchment of Nazism—are so horrifying to contemplate that presidential encroachment on congressional warmaking prerogatives seemed to be an acceptable price to pay. Attacks against Roosevelt as a dictator could have little credibility when voiced by pro-Hitler isolationists such as Charles Lindbergh.

An attitude of executive superiority did, however, become entrenched among those who were to lead in the formation of national security policy. Central to this perspective was the belief that the president had a far better understanding of foreign policy than members of Congress. The consequence of exaggerated deference to congressional powers in the warmaking area was to deny the United States the power to take steps that were decidedly in its interests and those of free peoples everywhere.

In addition, and particularly in the earlier years of the Cold War, going through constitutional processes seemed to be excessively cumbersome and capable of boxing in an administration, desirous of flexibility in its use of power, into a more hardline position than conditions warranted. Thus, although a persistent argument in favor of locating the warmaking power in Congress was to insure public support for a war, in an era of McCarthyism, more responsible Cold Warriors feared that an intense public opinion calling for unconditional surrender might emerge from an extended debate over whether or not to go to war.

Such a consideration had great relevance to examining the ''lessons'' of the Korean War. Many academic analysts and foreign policy professionals saw limited war as an effective instrument for pursuing security objectives in the Cold War. Kennedy and Johnson Administration officials remembered with horror the disastrous decision in 1950 by the Truman Administration to acquiesce to General MacArthur's entreaties to expand the Korean War beyond its initial objective of restoring the status quo by pushing beyond the 38th parallel into North Korea. Had American operations been authorized by a declaration of war, it might well have been impossible for Truman to avoid using nuclear weapons and other all-out measures after China entered the war in November 1950.[13] It is ironic to note, then, that in the Korean case it was conservatives who led the opposition to this presidential assumption of warmaking prerogatives.

Perhaps the most influential and respected conservative critique of the Vietnam War argues that a winnable war was lost because, among other reasons, the government failed to mobilize the will of the American people by seeking a formal declaration of war that would have legitimated the war to the American people and to the rest of the world.[14]

As the war in Vietnam intensified, the debate over presidential warmaking powers now saw a reversal of position, with liberal critics arguing that the war represented an illegal assumption of presidential power and conservatives arguing that such power was necessary to the effective conduct of modern national security diplomacy. With the attack on Cambodia, the heat on both the substance of America's Vietnam policy and the apparent presidential usurpation of congressional war making prerogatives began to converge into the ultimate form of the War Powers Resolution that was finally passed over the president's veto in November 1973.

As has been suggested earlier, the law that was finally passed reflected compromise at two levels. First, it was a relatively moderate alternative to much harsher antiwar legislation suggested from 1969 on. Therefore, as repugnant as any congressional restraints on executive discretion in this area might have been to Cold Warriors, from the vantage point of a pragmatic supporter of gradual American disengagement from Vietnam, such legislation was to be preferred to resolutions calling for immediate withdrawal. In addition, as Graham T. Allison has written, "The War Powers Resolution did not leap full-blown from any single mind. Instead, Congress considered a number of alternative proposals of varying scope and intensity for restoring the constitutional balance between Congress and the presidency in warmaking."[15] When finally passed, the Resolution was closer to the "softer" House version than the "tough" bill proposed by Senate doves.

THE DEBATE OVER AMERICAN SECURITY POLICY

By 1973 the debate over Vietnam had broadened to a more general discussion of America's role in the world and, even more specifically, the place of force as an instrument of American security policy. Positions had been developed to the point where it was possible to define several distinct schools of thought about these issues.

The literature on this matter has produced an almost endless number of taxonomies describing different "schools." All of them have in common the organizing focus of perceptions of the Cold War and the component elements of such perceptions: beliefs about the Soviet threat, about North-South relations, and attitudes toward the general nature of world politics and the balance-of-power approach.[16] Based on such a focus of inquiry, American beliefs about foreign affairs seem to fit into three schools of thought: Cold War internationalists, post–Cold War internationalists, and radical critics.

Cold War Internationalists

The basic orientation of this school of thought is the struggle with the Soviet Union. *Cold War internationalists* perceive "a world of conflict in which the primary cleavages are those dividing the United States and its allies from the Soviet empire and in which most, if not all, of the salient issues and conflicts are closely linked to each other and to that fault line."[17] The Soviet Union is seen as an expansionist state with an unending appetite for global conquest—a mortal danger to the United States. The primary determinant of survival and prosperity in the international system is mastery of the principles and techniques of the balance of power. Indeed, Cold War internationalists diagnose as a central flaw in contemporary U.S. foreign policy "an imbalance in resolution and willingness to use power, if necessary to preserve vital national interests," compared to the tough-minded realism of Soviet thought and practice.[18]

Membership in this school includes conservatives ranging from the far right to the pragmatic, sophisticated realism of academic-practitioner types like Henry Kissinger and Zbigniew Brzezinski. Whatever differences members of this school share, they all seem to be united in the belief that military power remains an important tool of foreign policy. Until the collapse of the postwar foreign policy consensus, this school included not only the executive branch but also most members of Congress. With the beginnings of the antiwar movement, some liberals and certainly radical critics of U.S. foreign policy challenged it. During the Carter years, it was difficult to discern a single thread in American foreign policy because Brzezinski representing the Cold War internationalist approach and Vance, the secretary of state, appeared to fall into different schools.

Post–Cold War Internationalists

Vance and other liberal critics of U.S. foreign policy fit into a school that views the international system as being significantly different from that of the traditional balance-of-power approach defined in the Cold War internationalist school. The East-West axis can no longer be the primary focus of international politics.

At the center of their worldview is a series of closely related propositions concerning the international system, key actors, and America's proper role within it. The growing list of serious threats to a stable and just world order have created an international system of such complexity and interdependence as to render totally obsolete the premises that formed American foreign policy during the two decades following the end of World War II.[19]

The threat from the Soviet Union is perceived differently because the Soviet Union is viewed as a different kind of state. No longer can it be seen as marching captive puppets along a global chessboard. "Dangers arising from strategic/military issues remain real, but the roots of future conflict are to be located not merely in military imbalances—real or perceived—but also in problems arising from poverty, inequitable distribution of resources, unfulfilled demands for self-determination, regional antagonisms, population pressures, technology that outpaces the political means for controlling its consequences, and the like."[20]

This school of criticism of American foreign policy does not however, dismiss entirely the premises of the Cold War. The Soviet Union is still a hostile country that must be contained, but the Vietnam War has shown the limits of military capabilities. Constraints on the use of force had been established by the domestic and international environment in which the United States functioned.[21]

To the liberal members of this school, the primary lessons of the Vietnam War are not that the United States has *no* interests in the Third World, nor that military force is *never* an appropriate instrument of furthering the national interest. They are, rather, that the United States needs to be exceedingly careful about whom it supports and how that support is to be pursued. The resort to force should be employed only in a highly selective manner and under great restraints.[22]

Radical Critics

The sharpest divergence from the dominant assumptions of the pre-Vietnam years can be found in this school. Ole Holsti and James Rosenau, calling this school semi-isolationist, suggest that the distinction between this approach and the two preceding ones may be summarized through three propositions: First, that the Soviet Union does not have the "slightest intention" of destroying the United States and the other democracies; second, that the United States has limited capabilities for intervention in the Third World to influence it in positive or negative directions; and, third, that "the real threats to a just and humane social order in this country are largely to be found within its own borders rather than abroad."[23] A leading exponent of this school has written, *"The inescapable lesson common to both Vietnam and Watergate is that the ultimate trade-off is between internationalist foreign policies and the integrity of our constitution."*[24]

In constructing their taxonomy, Holsti and Rosenau dwell on the semi-isolationist's rejection of even a nonmilitary role in the Third World. While this is certainly so in some cases, it does not fit the views of politicians like McGovern and Jesse Jackson. Nor does it seem to be logically necessary to use such a point of divergence from the two other schools to create a meaningful distinction between this more radical approach and the others.

This approach would include the most liberal critics of U.S. foreign policy within Congress—a distinct minority—as well as those outside of government whose views depart more radically from conventional perspectives on the United States' role in world affairs.

Thus, these three views represent the current range of thinking about what kinds of threats the United States faces in the world and how America should respond to them. Since the War Powers Resolution of 1973 represented the most important institutional examination of the legal and practical means by which the United States could conduct itself in the national security area in the contemporary era of world politics, it can only be understood in relation to these more basic views.[25]

THE 1973 WAR POWERS RESOLUTION

The official name of the act is the War Powers Resolution. Its purpose, as given in Section 2(a), is to "insure that the collective judgment of both the Congress and the President will apply to the introduction of United States Armed Forces into hostilities, or into situations where imminent involvement in hostilities is clearly indicated by the circumstances, and to the continued use of such force in hostilities or in such situations."[26] The unstated purpose of the act, of course, is to insure that there be "No More Vietnams."

Stated in brief, the major provisions of the act can be summarized as follows (for the full text of the Resolution, see Appendix A in Chapter 13):

Section 2(c) states that, as policy, the president may introduce armed forces into situations where there are hostilities, or where hostilities are imminent, only pursuant to (1) a declaration of war; (2) specific statutory authorization by Congress; or (3) "a national emergency created by attack upon the United States, its territories or possessions, or its armed forces."[27]

Section 3 requires that "The President in every possible instance shall consult with Congress before introducing United States Armed Forces into hostilities or into situations where imminent involvement in hostilities is clearly indicated by the circumstances, and after every such introduction shall consult regularly with the Congress until United States Armed Forces are no longer engaged in hostilities or have been removed from such situations."[28]

Section 4 requires the president to report to Congress whenever United States armed forces are introduced in certain instances, within forty-eight hours after their deployment and periodically thereafter. These instances are

1. into hostilities or imminent hostilities
2. "into the territory, airspace or waters of a foreign nation, while equipped for combat, except for deployments which relate solely to supply, replacement, repair, or training of such forces; or
3. in numbers which substantially enlarge United States Armed Forces equipped for combat already located in a foreign nation."[29]

Section 5, which contains the heart of the Resolution, is also the one whose constitutionality seems to be most precarious because of several important issues. Section 5(b) compels the president "to terminate any use of United States Armed Forces" within sixty days after a report is submitted by the president to Congress, or should have been submitted under the provisions of §4(a)(1) unless Congress

1. has declared war or has enacted a specific authorization for such use of United States Armed Forces,
2. has extended by law such sixty-day period, or
3. is physically unable to meet as a result of an armed attack upon the United States.[30]

The president can extend the sixty-day period for thirty more days if he certifies "that unavoidable military necessity respecting the safety of United States Armed Forces requires the continued use of such armed forces in the course of bringing about a prompt removal of such forces."[31]

The constitutionality of 5(b) depends on the Court's rendering of judgment on the issue of whether this provision impinges "upon the President's exercise of the inherent war-making powers he possesses by being vested with the executive power of the federal government and his designation as Commander-in-Chief."[32]

In his veto message, President Nixon claimed that the War Powers Act was unconstitutional because of the above-stated reason and also because 5(c) of the act allowed the Congress to compel the removal of American forces engaged in hostilities without a declaration of war or specific statutory authorization through the device of a concurrent resolution. However, such a device contains a legislative veto, which was ruled unconstitutional by the Supreme Court in 1983.[33]

At the moment of the Senate's override of the Nixon veto, Senator Tower expressed "the hope that the constitutionality of the measure . . . will be challenged at the earliest possible opportunity."[34] To this date, this has not happened, and questions of constitutionality remain one of the major issues surrounding the act. To a large degree, we can identify three distinct positions on the issue of constitutionality that conform roughly to the three views of the United States' role in world affairs discussed in the preceding section.

THE DEBATE OVER THE CONSTITUTIONALITY OF THE WAR POWERS RESOLUTION

Discussion of the current distribution of war powers between the executive and legislative branches must take into account several factors. First, it is increasingly more difficult to differentiate between warmaking and foreign policy-making, especially where relatively small amounts of force (and even paramilitary operations) are involved. The power of the president to commit force can give him the power to conduct a particular kind of foreign policy. Therefore, constraining the president's power to commit force in certain situations can be viewed as an illegitimate restraint on his ability to conduct foreign policy.[35] As has been often noted, the allocation of foreign powers between president and Congress is unclear, with the Constitution described in a memorable statement as "an invitation to struggle for the privilege of directing American foreign policy."[36]

Second, we must ask if it is meaningful and relevant to try to ascertain the intent of the Framers in regard to distributing war powers between the executive and legislative branches. Several basic elements regarding the current conduct of foreign affairs and the structure of the contemporary international system have changed profoundly since the Constitution was ratified. The existence of nuclear weapons, the need for rapid response, the virtual end of declared wars, and the seeming constancy of threats to the national interest and perhaps to national survival suggest conditions that require a greater grant of authority to the executive branch to insure speed of response and secrecy.[37] Ironically, critics of expanded war powers make "original intent" arguments to show that our Founding Fathers knew what they were doing in circumscribing the president's warmaking powers. To these critics, recent excesses point out, more than anything else could, how wise the Framers of the Constitution were.

Broadly, views on the constitutionality question can be divided into three schools of thought: a generally conservative view corresponding to the Cold War internationalist position, which sees the law as constitutional because it takes lawful power from the executive; a mainstream moderate-liberal view corresponding to the post–Cold War internationalist perspective, which sees the War Powers Resolution as a necessary, constitutionally sound, and potentially effective approach to the problem of excessive executive authority; and a liberal-radical view, corresponding to some features of the radical school, which sees the law as unconstitutional because it delegates Congress's warmaking powers to the president, enabling him to fight sixty- to ninety-day wars without a declaration of war.[38]

Position One: The War Powers Resolution as an Unconstitutional Limitation on Executive Authority

This view was articulated very effectively, if not ultimately successfully, by Senator Barry Goldwater during Senate floor debate over passage of the original Senate version of the bill, S.440, in the summer of 1973. Stripped of the trimmings, the conservative argument rests on two reeds. First, as commander in chief, the president is charged with supreme control and direction of the armed forces. To Goldwater, the Founding Fathers recognized that "the nation cannot be safe unless there is a single Commander-in-Chief with an unrestricted discretion to resist foreign dangers wherever and whenever they may exist."[39] In addition, argued Goldwater:

Constitutional authorities throughout our history have been almost unanimous in concluding that the President is vested with an independent control and direction over the military forces in any situation where he believes there is a threat to our country or its freedoms. The notion that the President is subject to the policy directives of Congress has been rejected by leading jurists time and again. It is only during the last decade or so, after the going got tough in Vietnam, that constitutional revisionists began changing their minds.[40]

To conservative supporters of an expansive presidential role in the commitment of force, practice and usage comprise an important part of the argument. During this debate, in order to reinforce his argument, Goldwater had inserted into the *Congressional Record* a chronological listing of 199 instances in which American forces had been committed without a declaration of war.[41] Robert Turner has also noted that "One hundred and eighty years of practice also reinforces the conclusion that there is nothing sacred about a formal declaration of war. Indeed, during our history, the instrument has been seldom used, and even when used has had little or no influence on the actual decision to use force."[42] Louis Henkin has also conceded that, although the constitutional foundations and limitations of such power are in dispute, "by repeated exercise without successful opposition, Presidents have established their authority to send troops abroad probably beyond effective range."[43] Another critic of excessive presidential power, Thomas Franck, also noted the force of the longstanding practice, calling these military actions "common-law wars."[44]

The other major support on which the argument rests is the notion that the president does have very expansive powers in the foreign affairs area and that the power to commit forces is a significant aspect of that authority. Goldwater's legislative assistant, Terry Emerson, wrote approvingly of the *Curtiss-Wright* doctrine as being very much alive in 1971. Argued Emerson:[45]

Whenever the President, as the primary author for foreign policy and the exclusive Commander-in-Chief of United States forces determines there is a future danger to the ultimate preservation of the United States and its citizens which is highly probable arising either as a direct or indirect result of a present crisis, he may commit United States forces on his own authority in any way he deems fit for the purpose of defending the future of this country and its two hundred and ten million citizens.[46]

Therefore, basic to this argument is the conviction that the president has inherent foreign affairs powers that cannot be limited by Congress.

Position Two: The War Powers Resolution as Constitutional

Both this approach and the subsequent one begin with the premise that executive assertion of warmaking authority is illegal. The foundation of this argument is the intent of the Framers and close reading of the text of the Constitution itself. This school of thought maintains that the delegates to the 1787 Convention wanted to keep the power of war and peace in the hands of the legislature.

As a matter of textual analysis, the Constitution could not be clearer regarding allocation of war powers: Congress is given the power to declare war, grant letters of marque and reprisal, raise support and regulate the armed forces, organize and arm the militia, and exercise control over all "needful" military arsenals and encampments. The President, on the other hand, is simply named Commander-in-Chief, and given the power to commission officers. As Commander-in-Chief, his authority extends to the day-to-day conduct of wars authorized or declared by Congress; in Hamilton's words, he is the "first General and Admiral," but has no power to initiate wars or unilaterally to call up the armed forces. Thus the plain language of the Constitution clearly vest the bulk of the war power in Congress, while limiting the President to the conduct of wars once approved.[47]

The authors of this article cite two major reasons for giving the legislature warmaking authority: the Framers were wary of giving too much power to the executive, given the reason for the American Revolution; and the United States, as a young and weak nation, had a strong interest in maintaining its neutrality and "Congress would be less likely to get the country involved in wars than the President, who might be tempted to enter conflicts for self-aggrandizement."[48]

Therefore, the broad authority in this area that emerged, especially in the post–World War II era, was conditioned primarily by political considerations but not by constitutional ones. In Senate floor debate, Senator Muskie asserted that the Constitution was not "in the slightest degree ambiguous" about the war power. To Muskie, the Founding Fathers conferred on Congress simply the power to decide "whether or not, and under what circumstances, the United States would make war upon another sovereign nation."[49] However, it seems important to a moderate-liberal perspective—the post–Cold War international-ists—that there be some flexibility and some presidential authority. In line with the overall view of foreign affairs held by this school, the United States may find itself in circumstances in which the president's ability to respond is not constrained excessively. Unlike the other two schools, what is being sought here is constitutional authority for a middle road—one in which the president has some leeway to commit force on his own—but not too much!

Cyrus Vance, Carter's secretary of state and an advocate of this view, develops the idea of power-sharing between the branches: "The roles of Congress and the President in foreign and military affairs do not fit neatly into the classic concept of the separation of legislative and executive powers. Instead, the area is one of shared and overlapping responsibilities as each branch participates in both the formulation and implementation of policy."[50]

Given these assumptions about the warmaking powers of the executive, the War Powers Resolution is simply seen "as a procedure by which Congress can express its institutional judgment on the question."[51] The War Powers Resolution does not introduce any constitutional changes, rather, it "sought only to create a procedural mechanism to effectuate the constitutional scheme."[52]

This is an important theme because it becomes the basis for legitimating sec-tions 5(b) and 5(c). That troops must be withdrawn after sixty days in the event of congressional silence would be clearly unconstitutional were this a power that the executive enjoyed initially. However, if one denies that the executive has such powers and that the sections under discussion are simply means for Congress to express itself authoritatively about a function in which it, *at the very least*, ought to have a substantial share of decision-making authority, then no constitutional problem ensues. An interesting argument along this line suggests that the "fixed powers" approach to presidential power taken in *Curtiss-Wright* and other cases has given way to a "fluctuating powers" approach developed by Justice Robert Jackson in his famous concurring opinion in *Youngstown Sheet and Tube*, "and formally adopted by Justice William Rehnquist in *Dames and Moore v. Regan*. Under the fluctuating powers approach, the scope of the president's power is a function of the concurrence or nonconcurrence of the Congress; once Congress acts, its negative provides the 'rule of the case.' "[53] Therefore, for Congress to veto the president's dispatch of troops to a hostile zone indicates "that in Congress' judgment the President lacked authority for his actions or that Congress is asserting its inherent authority to terminate hostilities."[54]

In an extremely interesting pre-*Chadha* analysis, one of the supporters of the War Powers Resolution admits doubts about the constitutionality of 5(b) and almost fatal doubts about 5(c) [the legislative veto].[55] Since the *Chadha* decision, the constitutionality of that provision seems to be even more precarious. Nevertheless, there are a number of arguments that *Chadha* is inapplicable to the War Powers Resolution because this case does not involve "the delegation of broad, discretionary lawmaking authority to the executive branch, coupled with congressional control over the administration of such laws by means of legislative veto."[56] However, these constitutional concerns are substantial reasons for amending the War Powers Resolution in such a way as to prevent presidential action from the beginning, rather than trying to stop it after it has already begun.[57]

The War Powers Resolution as Unconstitutional Delegation of Warmaking Authority from Congress to the Executive

The most radical critique of the War Powers Resolution is one that has been developed most fully by Senator Eagleton. The argument is a simple but compelling one. Eagleton said:

The bill in its present form is worse than no bill at all. It fails to address directly the question of just what authority the president has to engage our forces in hostilities without the approval of Congress. It is of questionable constitutionality in that it creates a 60-to–90 day period of Presidentially declared war, in derogation of the war powers conferred by the founders on Congress. And it creates a legal base for the continuing claims of virtually untrammeled Presidential authority to take the Nation to war without prior congressional declaration.[58]

Continued Eagleton:

I must reluctantly conclude that in the absence of an operative and effective definition of Presidential authority the effect of this bill would be to permit the President to nullify Congress' obligation to declare war before we commit forces. Whether or not the mechanism included in this bill to stop the President after the fact is more efficient than present remedies available to us, we cannot delegate our responsibility to authorize offensive war before it begins.[59]

At an earlier stage in the process, the debate on the Senate version in the summer of 1973, Senator James Abourezk expressed similarly strong reservations, arguing that the bill "simply abandons the constitutional requirement that no war be entered into without prior congressional declaration." Abourezk reminded the Senate that the Framers "feared that rulers tended to make war for reasons of honor, pique and pride. They sought to make war difficult to enter, because the genius of a democracy was that it was peaceful and peaceloving."[60] Of course, Eagleton and Abourezk stressed the practical aspect of the argument as well, with both fearing that once executive wars had begun they would be extremely difficult to stop even if Congress had its War Powers Resolution.

Is Eagleton's argument a persuasive one? The answer to this question depends on how strictly we choose to interpret Congress's warmaking powers and how severely we believe the executive should be limited in his ability to use discretionary force in any but the clearest examples of self-defense. From a perspective that is willing to admit some blurring of executive and legislative warmaking functions even in areas other than strict self-defense, this would not constitute a delegation but rather a recognition of a virtually irreversible condition. Indeed, a natural conclusion from this perspective is that the War Powers Resolution is simply an effort to ameliorate excesses. In other words, the present act is about as far as Congress was willing to go fourteen years ago—at a time when congressional tolerance of executive discretion was at the lowest point of the century. Therefore, to accept no act in the hope of getting a good one seems to be too ideological a response. Of course, in regard to this law, questions of constitutionality and politics are inextricably intertwined.

THE WAR POWERS RESOLUTION IN PRACTICE: COMMENTS AND CRITICISMS

Since the passage of the War Powers Resolution in 1973, the reporting requirements of the act have been met in ten instances. But there have also been several instances in which they have not been fulfilled when they apparently should have been. From the perspective of those who wish to limit the president's ability to initiate hostilities independently of congressional participation, this record constitutes "a fundamental flaw in the Resolution's procedural framework."[61] According to Michael Glennon:

The vagueness of the reporting requirement . . . has led to the Resolution's virtual unraveling. Although the Executive's record here is clearly at odds with the Resolution's spirit, there is an argument to be made that presidential reports have complied with its letter. The reason is that there is in fact not one reporting requirement set forth in the Resolution, but three. Only one—that required by section 4(a)(1)—triggers the sixty-day time limit; those required by sections 4(a)(2) and 4(a)(3) are merely informational (although in the original House version they too triggered the time limitations). The problem arises in that the three situations overlap: facts that would require a report under section 4(a)(1) might also require a report under one of the two succeeding paragraphs, and the Resolution contains no requirement that the President specify which of the three reports he is submitting.[62]

Thus, under the so-called triggering clause, only the situations that require section 4(a)(1) reports—the commitment of United States armed forces to hostilities or imminent hostilities—trigger the Resolution's automatic termination provisions.[63] Only such a report can start the sixty- (or potentially ninety-) day clock, which compels a withdrawal of American forces in the absence of specific congressional action. The provision has been cited in this manner only once— by President Ford at the time of the *Mayaguez* incident in 1975. In that case, which involved brief, intense fighting in which thirty-eight Marines were killed, the president only "took note" of section 4(a)(1) without acknowledging that he was required to report under this provision. Michael Ratner and David Cole write:

This is the closest any President has come to submitting a §4(a)(1) report. That the "taking note of" language, however, was a deliberate avoidance of the triggering requirement can no longer be doubted. After he left office, President Ford stated that he "never admitted that the WPR was applicable" to instances where he had committed United States armed forces. He further believed that the Resolution was not constitutionally binding on the President. *The President and Political Leadership*, in 2 Virginia Papers on the Presidency 28 (K. Thompson, ed., 1980).[64]

Perhaps the most egregious example of the cavalier treatment given this provision by the executive was that provided by the situation in Lebanon in the late summer of 1983. In that case, the Reagan Administration found itself in a confrontation with varying forces in Lebanon and, ultimately, with Syria. The administration sought to check Syrian influence in Lebanon through coercive diplomacy. By the use of air power and naval gunfire, it sought to guide the development of Lebanon in a pro-American direction. After two Marines were killed and fourteen wounded on August 29, 1983, and after two more American deaths and constant shelling over the next few weeks, the president still resisted reporting the Marine presence to trigger the time limit set by the Resolution. Finally, on September 28, 1983, Congress passed legislation that declared that sections 4(a)(1) and 5(b)(2) had become operative as of August 29, the date of the death of the first two Marines.[65] However, in order to pass this legislation, a compromise with the White House was required which authorized the Marine presence for eighteen months—an insignificant restriction given the objectives of the administration. "By the time the Lebanon issue arose in Congress, United States involvement was a foregone conclusion, and the only real debates concerned how long, not *whether* to authorize continued United States presence."[66]

Because of this apparent loophole, presidents are able to appear to be in compliance with the Resolution, while Congress, quite clearly contrary to the intent of the drafters, is compelled to pass a resolution to extract a noncomplying president's report under the only "teeth" part of the Resolution—section 4(a)(1). Given the president's veto power, ultimately a two-thirds vote of each house of Congress is required to compel a presidential report—unless Congress and the

White House negotiate a different result as they did in the Lebanon case. It is difficult to imagine that such was the intent of the authors of the act.

Another area of difficulty concerns compliance with section 3, which requires the president "in every possible instance" to consult with Congress *before* introducing U.S. armed forces into situations that fall under the coverage of the act. Former Secretary of State Cyrus Vance, recalling the unfortunate Iranian hostage rescue mission of 1980 that precipitated his resignation, writes that "there was no prior consultation with members of Congress concerning the planned rescue attempt. There were those in the Administration who favored consulting congressional leaders in accordance with Section 3 of the War Powers Resolution before our units were set in motion. However, concerns for secrecy prevailed."[67]

Similarly, in the case of the Grenada operation, the executive made the decision unilaterally without consultation with Congress. Only on the evening before the invasion did the president notify leaders of Congress that the invasion would begin the next morning.[68] Regarding the air strike against Libya in 1986, President Reagan informed congressional leaders only after the planes were in the air nearing their targets.[69]

Although it is understandable why presidents would want minimal interference from Congress, the fact that they have apparently perceived the consultation requirement as a discretionary one is troublesome to supporters of a meaningful resolution.[70] In current practice, the consulting requirement leaves "the application of this provision to the vagaries of political circumstance and presidential creativity. The decisions of whether and to what extent consultation is required are made by the President . . . [which] may mean nothing more than a preview of tomorrow's news for a selected few."[71]

In spite of these problems, some have argued that the Resolution has been effective in restraining presidential adventurism in foreign affairs. The author of the House version, the late Representative Clement Zablocki, claimed that

the Resolution has served to restore the balance in the rights and responsibilities of the Congress and the President in the decision to commit troops. The executive branch cannot merely run roughshod over the Congress and must factor likely Congressional insistence or the Resolution's implementation in its foreign policy formulation, particularly with respect to options involving military action. The resolution is therefore a meaningful brake on military adventurism and poorly planned military actions without serving as a handcuff on *any* decision to commit troops.[72]

Such an argument seems to have little substance when considered in the light of President Reagan's refusal to employ the consulting or reporting provisions of the War Powers Resolution in the most recent Persian Gulf situation in the summer of 1987. At the same time, it seems to be inaccurate to assert that the Resolution is virtually irrelevant. While the record of presidential compliance is a poor one, the War Powers Resolution has introduced a significant variable into the process.

Certainly, conservative critics of the law have reached different conclusions about its impact, aside from whatever constitutional reservations they have. Considering the case of Central America, Boston University President John Silber sees the War Powers Resolution as having "deprive[d] the president of the authority to back his diplomacy with a military action short of declared war."[73] In a generally hostile world, military issues have become political, and the "president must now consider not the efficacy of his actions, but the reaction of Congress to them."[74]

On the tactical level, conservative critics of the law have argued that, assuming the implementation of the section 4 "triggering clause," the need for the president to get congressional authorization beyond the sixty- (or ninety-) day period can have mischievous effects in several ways. First, it "might encourage a president to escalate a conflict unnecessarily with accompanying increased loss of life and property on all sides—in order to try to achieve a quick victory."[75]

Another concern is the "Mendes-France syndrome." Upon becoming the French premier in June 1954, Pierre Mendès-France announced that he would resign if he had not concluded a peace treaty by July 20. Knowing of these constraints, the adversary is obviously given an immense diplomatic advantage. There is little doubt that an antagonist, confronting an American position constrained by the need to withdraw forces in the near future, has gained a significant bargaining advantage. "In such a situation, the president might conclude that it was necessary to make major concessions and sacrifice substantial U.S. interests in order to negotiate a quick truce and avoid the risk of having his commander-in-chief powers withdrawn and losing everything to the enemy."[76]

In addition to weakening the United States in specific confrontational situations, Turner argues that the overall effect of the Resolution is deleterious to the process of foreign policy-making. The Resolution "pit[s] the political branches against each other . . . resoundingly and before the entire world—with predictably damaging consequences."[77] He also shares Silber's concern that the president will be undermined in his efforts to stabilize Central America. He writes:

In El Salvador, where President Reagan is valiantly trying to dissuade Moscow and Havana from underwriting the overthrow of a popularly elected government, the prospects for peace are being jeopardized by the War Powers Resolution. Virtually every time the president speaks or acts firmly to deter the communists, his congressional critics cite the War Powers Resolution and tell the world—occasionally in language reminiscent of the old Ludlow Amendment—'He can't do that!' "[78]

During the debate on the Senate floor, Senator Goldwater, a leader of the opposition to the proposed law, opened the discussion by offering twenty-five "problems" associated with the Senate version of the bill (see also Chapter 13 of the present volume). The first of these difficulties was the argument that passage of the bill would prevent "shows of force" and other such demonstrations of American power and resolve. He said:

I might inject that the show of force has done more to keep peace in the history of the world than the actual deployment of arms. Great Britain, with her mastery of the seas and her willingness to use her fleet, kept peace, a comfortable peace, for nearly 200 years. On the occasions when the United States has been forced into a show of force, we have prevented hostilities on at least five occasions since World War II.[79]

To conservatives, then, the practical effects of the War Powers Resolution go to the heart of the American ability to pursue a policy of projection of its power. Crucial to an assertive balance-of-power type of foreign policy is the nation's ability to communicate to potential adversaries both the actual strength of the nation and its resolve to use force in appropriate situations. Thus, while decrying growing imbalances in military capabilities in favor of the Soviet bloc, Cold War internationalists "are concerned about what they diagnose as an imbalance in resolution and willingness to use power, if necessary."[80] In terms of power politics, the combination of capability and resolve creates prestige. The leading exponent of the postwar power politics school, Hans Morgenthau, has written: "A policy of prestige attains its very triumph when it gives the nation pursuing it such a reputation for power as to enable it to forego the actual employment of the instrument of power."[81]

He further states:

The individual members of a national society, protected as they are in their existence and social position by an integrated system of social institutions and rules of conduct, can afford to indulge in the competition for prestige as a kind of harmless social game. But nations, which as members of the international society must in the main rely on their own power for the protection of their existence and power position, can hardly neglect the effect that a gain or loss of prestige will have upon their power position on the international scene.[82]

From this perspective, the War Powers Resolution does not simply create impediments to quick and effective responses and jeopardize the American negotiating posture in specific situations. Far worse, it is dramatic evidence and announcement to the world of the collapse of America's will to do what is necessary to safeguard its interests.

RECOMMENDATIONS FOR CHANGE

Amidst all the debate and controversy, it is clear that the War Powers Resolution is offensive to Cold War internationalists because of its very existence, but disappointing in varying degrees to those who had hoped to curtail executive discretion in the employment of armed forces. Therefore, conservatives want no law or an emasculated one. The post–Cold War internationalists and radicals have advanced a number of recommendations for improving the War Powers Resolution's capabilities for dealing with presidential deployment of force. These recommendations range from minimalist to centrist to maximalist.

Minimalist Recommendations

The key to this position is the perception that, at the very least, the president's obligation should be to consult meaningfully with representative members of Congress *before* and *during* military operations that fall under the provisions of the Resolution. Former Secretary of State Vance has written "the goal that the President and Congress should form a 'collective judgment' about the wisdom of such actions has not been realized."[83] Representative Zablocki had also accepted the need for creating structures "to establish orderly consultation under section 3."[84] One analyst explains the reasons for the executive's "perfunctory" consultations as resulting from the failure to specify the meaning of consultations, as well as a fear by congressional leaders of "being mistakenly seen by the public as somehow critical of a military initiative."[85]

Vance offered two specific recommendations for improving the consultation process.[86] First, he would define statutorily what is meant by consultation. "The definition would make clear that what is required is the timely sharing of information and views among the President and the congressional leadership concerning a proposed deployment."[87]

Second, Vance proposes a method by which presidents would be unable to evade the need for consultation by designating military operations as "humanitarian rescue or evacuation operations rather than as the introduction of troops into potentially 'hostile' situations."[88] Not only should the consultation requirement be invoked in situations covered under section 4(a)(1) as reportable events,[89] but also the list should add a requirement for the president to "consult before and report after introducing United States forces 'into any situation in which there is armed conflict.' "[90]

Although a tighter definition of what is to be consulted about, and with whom the consultations would take place, could only improve the Resolution, ultimately recommendations to sharpen this section are unlikely to fashion a strong law without additional measures. However, it is important to note that this position flows logically from the more conservative (or moderate) wing of the post–Cold War internationalist position, which does not want a law that restricts the executive to too large a degree. As such, these minimalist recommendations fit this moderate critique of U.S. foreign policy quite naturally. As a cynical observer of the act has commented, however: "Thus, the true function of the War Powers Act: it allows jittery members of Congress to avoid responsibility for risky military actions, while at the same time avoiding responsibility for the consequences of *not* taking action."[91]

Centrist Recommendations

Into this category fall those recommendations for adding real "teeth" to the War Powers Resolution. Central to this position is the following argument:

The primary focus of the War Powers Resolution should be shifted away from limitations on presidential action and aimed directly upon the affirmative obligations of Congress. This could be accomplished through the adoption of a precise and relatively automatic system for reviewing deployments arising under the War Powers Resolution. The invasion of Grenada and its aftermath suggest two such devices: (1) creation of a trigger device that requires an immediate decision by Congress, through joint resolution, of whether section 4(a)(1) has been activated; and (2) upon a determination that section 4(a)(1) has been activated, a requirement that Congress immediately convene hearings for a prompt determination on the constitutionality of the presidential action.[92]

Presidents have been able to avoid the requirements of the act by reporting under the broad provisions of section 4 rather than under the triggering provision of section 4(a)(1). Enabling the Congress to determine the existence of such a requirement helps, but not too much. As we have already noted, passage of such a resolution compels compromise with the administration, as was the case in the passage of the Lebanon War Powers Resolution, or a bruising struggle that would probably require the necessity to overide a certain presidential veto.[93]

Once 4(a)(1) has been activated, however, the automatic termination provisions of 5(b)(2) become enforceable—the heart of the War Powers Resolution. Without such an automatic triggering mechanism, however, the heart remains cut off, until the passage of a "bypass" amendment to bring it into play.

Another recommendation is one that can fall into either a centrist or maximalist category, depending on the procedures developed for implementing it. This recommendation is to amend the Resolution to set forth a definition of hostilities.

In the absence of such a definition, officials of the executive branch and members of Congress engaged in a running argument whether United States military activities in Lebanon constituted "hostilities." When ten marines died in a twenty-day period after having been fired upon regularly by hostile forces, it seemed utterly disingenuous to claim, as the Reagan administration did, that the hostilities test was not met. Nonetheless, the term is not self-defining, and because the Resolution provides no guidance as to its meaning, a gradual escalation of hostilities can generate serious confusion as to the date on which the time limit is triggered. Similarly, there is no clear indication in the Resolution whether a variety of different activities are intended to fall within the "hostilities" test, such as exposure to minefields, missile attack, chemical or biological agents, or neutron rays. If Congress is serious about removing uncertainty and closing the door to semantic circumvention by the executive branch, it must define the term "hostilities."[94]

As befits recommendations that are designated centrist, these are proposals that seek neither too little nor too much. These recommendations go beyond consultation by seeking an almost automatic reporting requirement that would trigger Congress's role in approving the commitment of force after sixty to ninety days. In this case, these proposals reflect not only the letter but also the spirit of the law that was passed in 1973. That law, while seeking to limit presidential adventurism, was a compromise between tougher and gentler restrictions on the president. Ultimately, presidents could commit troops and pursue an assertive policy when they felt it necessary to do so. The only restraints on their actions provided by the act occurred either when military operations were projected to last longer than sixty days (certainly not the case in Libya or Grenada), or, when presidents did not have the political clout to extract congressional approval. Thus, such proposals seem to fit squarely into the assumptions underlying the post–Cold War internationalist school.

Maximalist Recommendations

Both maximalist and centrist recommendations recognize that a fundamental objection to the War Powers Resolution is its inability to restrain meaningfully a president's decision to commit troops or other means of force, thereby creating a *fait accompli* that could render the sixty- or ninety-day termination clause meaningless.

The most articulate exponent of this position is former Senator Thomas Eagleton, who saw the War Powers Resolution as an essentially flawed action because of its failure to establish a system of prior restraint against the president's warmaking powers.[95] To Eagleton, the fatal flaw in the 1973 bill was its adoption of the essential features of the House of Representatives version of the bill as a product of the Conference Committee's efforts, rather than the Senate's version. In the Senate version, with the exception of a few clearly enumerated, clearly defensive actions that required immediate responses, the president could not respond unilaterally. These exceptions were as follows:

First, the President could repel an armed attack upon the United States, its territories and possessions; he could take necessary and appropriate retaliatory action in the event of such an attack; and he could act to forestall the direct and imminent threat of such an attack.

Second, he could respond to an attack on American forces legally deployed abroad.

And, third, under specified conditions the President could rescue American citizens abroad to provide for their immediate evacuation from a danger zone.

Each of these exceptions is a defensive action.[96]

However, what had emerged from the Conference Committee was a completely different version because these defensive limitations on the president's authority were now contained in subsection 2(c) of the bill—"Purpose and Policy" section, "a section usually reserved for broad statements which are used for interpretive purposes in resolving questions relating to other sections."[97] To Eagleton, the intent of the conferees was now clear:

They were explicitly divorcing the interpretive definition of the President's emergency authority in the "Purpose and Policy" section from the legally binding portions of the bill. The authority language was not only not legally binding, but now even its value as a statement of policy was questionable.[98]

During debate on the Senate floor, Eagleton stressed that the present bill was even worse than no bill at all because it legitimated presidential action by an unlawful congressional delegation of its warmaking authority to the president.[99] Moreover, from a practical perspective:

We must recognize the incredible powers of persuasion the President has at his command at all times, and especially during periods of crisis. The Senate bill dealt with this reality by establishing clear signposts of authority—signposts which could be readily understood by the American people.

But this bill avoids the difficult task of establishing signposts by rendering even the limited definition of Presidential emergency authority contained in section 2(c) legally meaningless. The House bill—the original Zablocki bill—completely avoided any definition of such Presidential authority, and it would appear that the conference report represents a victory—a complete, total unvarnished victory—for that approach to war powers legislation.[100]

Therefore, in announcing his intention to vote against the bill, Eagleton stressed that the key to effective war powers legislation was to participate in the decision-making process before the troops are committed, when perhaps "a rational, calm decision conceivably could be made on the floor of Congress."[101] To Eagleton, it was far better that the bill be defeated and an effort be made to pass an acceptable and workable one, "than to enact into law a measure that will come back to haunt us for generations to come."[102] Thus, Eagleton's approach might be termed maximalist in the sense that he wishes to go very far in preventing executive discretionary use of force and is, in fact, quite radical in its conviction that the present bill is virtually beyond repair.[103]

Another approach that might be termed maximalist in the sense of process rather than substance is one that calls for the federal court system to intervene in restraining executive action. A more modest proposal like this was coupled with the Eagleton suggestion calling for an enumeration of circumstances in which presidential use of force is authorized.[104] However, to assure the efficacy of such a device, it should not stand alone but contain in the resolution the establishment of the "justiciability of an action to test the constitutionality and ultra vires of a presidential use of force."[105] Such a resolution could contain stipulations regarding standing and remedies providing

that no court in the United States shall decline, on grounds that it is a nonjusticiable or political question, to make a determination of the merits, giving effect to the Constitution of the United States and to this resolution, in any case in which a claim of ultra vires is asserted against the President as Commander in Chief by Congress or an appropriate congressional committee, in an action arising out of the introduction by the President of the armed forces into hostilities.[106]

Franck's recommendations appeared about four years after the passage of the War Powers Resolution, when noncompliance was still confined to the much less assertive presidency of the immediate post–Vietnam era.[107] There is little doubt that President Reagan has outgrown the "Vietnam Syndrome" and would be prepared to use force where he felt it was politically acceptable and possible within a legal framework that was mightily expandable. It is within this context that we should view the argument of Michael Ratner and David Cole, who conclude that only if the War Powers Resolution is "given the force of law" can the constitutional imbalance be redressed, since "recent presidents have been as reluctant to honor the War Powers Resolution as earlier presidents had been to follow the war powers clause."[108] Citing the Reagan Administration as a particularly egregious violator because of its failure to file 4(a)(1) ["hostilities" or "imminent hostilities"] reports in three cases where they were clearly warranted (El Salvador, Grenada, and Lebanon), they conclude that President Reagan has clearly demonstrated "(1) the continued refusal of the Executive to report under Section 4(a)(1); (2) the refusal to acknowledge that the Executive is bound by the Resolution; and (3) the Executive's refusal to be bound by legislation signed pursuant to the Resolution."[109]

Given this condition of presidential insouciance regarding congressional restrictions on his warmaking powers, and given the ineffectiveness of congressional actions in compelling compliance from the executive, the authors conclude that the only answer is judicial enforcement—"a court order that the President file a section 4(a)(1) report."[110] Such was the kind of action brought in *Crockett v. Reagan*, which sought "a declaratory judgment that the Resolution's sixty-day cut-off provision had been triggered, and/or injunctive relief directing that the United States Armed Forces be withdrawn from El Salvador."[111] The case was dismissed, not on the broad political question claim that it would interfere with presidential discretion in foreign affairs, but on the narrower ground that determination of the facts needed for the judgment "would require resolution of disputed questions of fact beyond judicial competence. In essence, it found the case too close to call.[112]

It is in this line of reasoning that Ratner and Cole see hope, notwithstanding their displeasure at the *Crockett* result. For the decision did not hold that "the appropriate judicial response under a War Powers Resolution claim where no report had been filed would be to require the filing of a report."[113] This was a much more plausible remedy than that sought in many of the cases litigated during the Vietnam War, since "Courts were reluctant to declare a war illegal or to order a cessation of hostilities."[114]

They note also that the Crockett decision seemed to follow the line of many of the later Vietnam War cases in narrowing the political question doctrine, even in the foreign affairs area, by showing a willingness to decide in the abstract "without taking the final step required for meaningful judicial action in each particular instance."[115]

Another scholar suggested that while there was "little that Congress can do in any mandatory constitutional sense, to overcome the political question impediment," there were two legislative steps that could be helpful.[116] First, the

War Powers Resolution could be amended "to set forth the opinion of Congress that disputes concerning violation could be adjudicated by the Courts."[117] Another step would be for Congress to remove by statute any potential standing problem by amending the Resolution in such a way as to create expressly a cause of action for its violation.[118]

Both of these kinds of suggestions reflect a more radical critique of U.S. foreign policy in the following ways. The Eagleton proposals would create an effective congressional restraint by compelling congressional participation in armed forces commitment decisions in all but the most carefully defined self-defense circumstances. Therefore, they certainly go beyond the relatively moderate, compromising spirit of the 1973 act.

The proposals for judicial intervention are radical in a different way. By calling for the judicial branch to be the arbiter, advocates of these steps are really asking for a fundamental redefinition of the separation of powers in the foreign affairs area. The foreseeable consequence of this call is a drastic change in the ability of the executive to use force as an instrument of diplomacy. Therefore, if future courts show their willingness to reach such decisions, then the changes in this area can be immense, and truly radical.

CONCLUSION

Has the War Powers Resolution been successful? Is it desirable? Is it constitutional? In considering these questions, this paper has sought to discover the point of intersection between legal and political analysis of the Resolution. Although the constitutional issues in particular can be approached from a reasonably objective perspective, there is also a substantial subjective component for evaluating the law. The essence of the subjectivity is the view one has of the basic nature of international politics and the role of the United States in the world.

Since the Vietnam War, enormous changes have taken place in the way Americans think about world politics. The most important of these has been the attack on the basic premises of the traditional balance-of-power model. Emergent theories charged that the old model was both analytically and normatively deficient. The proper focus of analysis was cooperation as well as conflict, economic and environmental as well as "power as force" issues, and the North-South debate as well as the traditional Cold War between the Soviets and Americans. To this school, interdependence was as much a matter of realism as conflict, and as worthy of the attention of the analyst and the orientation of the policymaker.

While the balance-of-power school continues to view international politics as a struggle for power, those in the interdependence school address themselves more to the limits of power. Therefore, in considering appropriate American responses to this new world, we can detect considerable divergence between the schools and, of course, divergence within each of the schools as well.

To those who analyze world politics through the lenses of power politics, U.S. foreign policy is determined by geostrategic imperatives. To this school, power is an indispensable instrument of foreign policy, and any domestic determinants that are seen as detracting from a state's power are viewed with great wariness. Indeed, the entire democratic enterprise can be seen as the obstacle to constructing a rational, power-based foreign policy. It stands to reason then, that in this school, the War Powers Resolution is viewed as unwise because of the obstacles it places in the path of the executive's construction of foreign policy. It is seen as dangerous to the national interest because of the signals of vacillation and weakness that it sends to adversaries. And it is seen as unconstitutional because the ability to conduct an effective power-based foreign policy is regarded as an inherent right of the state, since the state's international environment is such a dangerous one.

Within the opposing school, there are two variants on these issues. One, occupied by more centrist liberals, sees a mixture of power politics and interdependence in today's world. Vietnam should have taught us that not all problems are amenable to military solution, that the United States does not have the capability to be the "policeman of the world," and that it is not necessarily in the national interest for the United States of 1987 to be guided by the principles of a 1950s Cold War approach. Therefore, presidential power must be limited because of the dangers of overextending ourselves and because of the problems of trying to fight an unpopular war. From this perspective, the War Powers Resolution is a reasonable response to this issue. It is seen neither as unduly limiting nor as unconstitutional. To a large extent, it can be seen as being closely associated with a much more moderate foreign policy that does not abandon entirely the precepts of the Cold War. Therefore, the recommendations for change that emanate from this school tend to focus more on consultation than on actual blocking of the executive's ability to make war on his own.

On the other hand, there is a more radical variant within the complex interdependence school that views the United States as imperialist and dangerous, that sees the great problems of world politics as emanating from anticolonialism and the desire to redress economic and social injustice on the part of Third World peoples. From the perspective of this school, allowing the executive discretion in warmaking is like putting a weapon into the hands of a criminal. American behavior in Central America, Vietnam, and other parts of the world has stamped it indelibly as a dangerous state. Meaningful war powers restraint are, therefore, imperative in modifying this behavior.

Ultimately, the most telling point about the War Powers Resolution might be that the more pragmatic elements of the balance-of-power approach find that they can live with the War Powers Act because it does not impinge too severely on the United States' ability to conduct its business in the world. If this is true, then the War Powers Resolution has, to this date, really had little more than a symbolic impact on the process of U.S. foreign policy-making, argue radical critics of the law.

At the present time, the foreign policy debate in America is dominated by the traditional Cold War approach of the Cold War internationalists and the modified Cold War views of the post–Cold War internationalists. As much as they dislike the act, conservatives realize that its repeal is not possible. Moreover, practically speaking, it has not created unassailable obstacles to presidential discretion in the use of force. They have found they can live with it.

Although post–Cold War internationalists are disappointed with the Resolution's inability to do more to compel the president to report and consult, they are not likely to press for more vigorous enforcement of these provisions unless they feel they have to. They also find that they can live with the act because it reinforces their contention that foreign policy power must be shared between the branches of government. The War Powers Resolution has created a somewhat different framework for decision making than existed from the time of Korea through the most intense days of the Cold War. Although this contribution is largely symbolic, it cannot be ignored.

At some point, however, this *modus vivendi* with the law, which both dominant foreign policy schools have achieved, will be threatened by events. When that occurs, presidential noncompliance will compel sharp political and legal challenges to the executive, inviting a similar response from that office. Only at that time will the real consequences of the War Powers Resolution be known.

NOTES

1. *New York Times*, November 8, 1973, p. 46.

2. Ibid.

3. John A. Silber, "Presidential Handcuffs," *The New Republic*, February 18, 1985, p. 14.

4. *New York Times*, November 9, 1973, column by James Reston, p. 41.

5. *War and Presidential Power: A Chronicle of Congressional Surrender* (New York: Liveright, 1974), p. 221.

6. Robert F. Turner, *The War Powers Resolution: Its Implementation in Theory and Practice* (Philadelphia: Foreign Policy Research Institute, Philadelphia Policy Papers, 1983), p. 107.

7. Cyrus R. Vance, "Striking the Balance: Congress and the President under the War Powers Resolution," 133 *U. Pa. L. Rev.* 85 (1984).

8. *New York Times*, November 11, 1973, p. 4E.

9. Graham T. Allison, "Making War: The President and Congress," 40 *Law and Contemp. Probs.* 87 (1976).

10. Robert A. Divine, "Roosevelt the Isolationist," in Thomas G. Patterson, ed., *Major Problems in American Foreign Policy*, Vol. II: *Since 1914* (Lexington, Mass.: Heath, 1984), p. 183.

11. Ibid.

12. Ibid.

13. Secretary of Defense McNamara was quoted as saying that "the ability to go to war without the necessity of arousing the public ire" was an important contribution of

the Vietnam War. See Harry G. Summers, Jr., *On Strategy: A Critical Analysis of the Vietnam War* (New York: Dell, 1984), p. 42.

14. Summers, *On Strategy*, pp. 40–41.

15. Allison, "Making War," p. 96.

16. One of the best describes a three-way classification scheme to categorize American attitudes on foreign affairs: Cold War internationalism, post–Cold War internationalism, and semi-isolationism. I am heavily indebted to this study in shaping my own framework, which is identical in describing the first two schools but differs in its discussion of a radical critique of American foreign policy. See Ole R. Holsti and James N. Rosenau, *American Leadership in World Affairs* (Boston: Allen & Unwin, 1984), pp. 108–133.

17. Ole R. Holsti and James N. Rosenau, "A Leadership Divided: The Foreign Policy Beliefs of American Leaders, 1976–1980," in Charles W. Kegley, Jr., and Eugene R. Wittkopf, eds., *Perspectives on American Foreign Policy* (New York: St. Martin's Press, 1983), p. 198.

18. Ibid., p. 200.

19. Ibid.

20. Ibid., p. 201.

21. For further development of this perspective in the Carter years, see James A. Nathan and James K. Oliver, *United States Foreign Policy and World Order*, 2nd ed. (Boston: Little, Brown, 1981), pp. 412–422.

22. For an extensive exposition of this view, see *The Lessons of Vietnam: Hearing before the Subcommittee on Asian and Pacific Affairs of the Committee on Foreign Affairs, House of Representatives*, 99th Cong., 1st Sess., 20–28 (1985), Statement of George Ball.

23. Holsti and Rosenau, "A Leadership Divided," pp. 205–206.

24. Earl Ravenal, quoted in ibid., p. 206.

25. However, Holsti and Rosenau point out that both the Cold War internationalists and post–Cold War internationalists are "constitutional pragmatists" in preferring strong executives when one of their own occupies the White House and strong Congresses when the opposite situation exists. While this is true, when the constitutional discussion is confined to questions regarding the use of force, the positions attain greater consistency. Holsti and Rosenau, "A Leadership Divided," p. 121.

26. 50 U.S.C. sect. 1541 (a) (1982).

27. Ibid., sect. 1541 (c).

28. Ibid., sect. 1542.

29. Ibid., sect. 1543 (a).

30. Ibid., sect. 1544 (5) (b).

31. Ibid.

32. Vance, "Striking the Balance," pp. 84, 85.

33. *Immigration and Naturalization Service v. Chadha*, 462 U.S. 919, 103 S.Ct. 2764, 77 L. Ed. 2d 317 (1983). Generally, discussion of the legislative veto issue is beyond the scope of this paper.

34. 119 *Cong. Rec.* 36198 (1973).

35. Louis Fisher has argued that the sweeping pronouncements about executive power in Justice Sutherland's *Curtiss-Wright* opinion should be viewed in the context of Sutherland's views of America's role in world affairs. He had served earlier on the Senate Foreign Relations Committee, where he was a "forceful exponent of the use of American power abroad." See Fisher's *President and Congress* (New York: Free Press, 1972), p. 65.

36. Edward S. Corwin, *The President: Office and Powers, 1787–1957* (New York: New York University Press, 1957), p. 200.

37. However, Abraham D. Sofaer, currently legal adviser to the State Department, has argued that in the foreign affairs area "many practices and doctrines commonly assumed to be of relatively recent origin are rooted in the early precedents." *War, Foreign Affairs and Constitutional Power* (Cambridge, Mass.: Ballinger, 1976), p. 127.

38. The fact that Senator Eagleton was one of the sharpest critics of the law in its formative and early years shows the limitations of this framework in enabling the analyst to draw a tight correlation between a position on the foreign policy spectrum and position in regard to the constitutionality of the act. Based on an impressionistic evaluation of his views, Eagleton seems to belong to the post–Cold War Internationalist rather than the radical school.

39. 119 *Cong. Rec.* 25057 (1973).

40. Ibid., p. 25056.

41. Ibid., p. 25066–25076.

42. Turner, *The War Powers Resolution*, p. 30.

43. Henkin, *Foreign Affairs and the Constitution* (New York: W.W. Norton, 1972), p. 101.

44. Thomas Franck, "After the Fall: The New Procedural Framework for Congressional Control over the War Power," 71 *A.J.I.L.* 609 (1977).

45. 119 *Cong. Rec.* 25060 (1973).

46. Ibid., 25062.

47. Michael Ratner and David Cole, "The Force of Law: Judicial Enforcement of the War Powers Resolution" 17 *Loy. L. A. L. Rev.* 719, 720 (1984).

48. Ibid.

49. 119 *Cong. Rec.* 33551 (1973).

50. Vance, "Striking the Balance," p. 84.

51. Ibid., p. 85.

52. Ratner and Cole, "The Force of Law," p. 736.

53. Michael J. Glennon, "The War Powers Resolution: Sad Record, Dismal Promise," 17 *Loy. L. A. L. Rev.* 661 (1984).

54. Vance, "The Force of Law," p. 85.

55. Franck, "After the Fall," p. 633. See also Glennon, "The War Power Resolution," p. 663.

56. Vance, "The Force of Law," p. 86.

57. Franck, "After the Fall," p. 639.

58. 119 *Cong. Rec.* 33556 (1973).

59. Ibid.

60. Ibid., 25053.

61. Glennon, "The War Powers Resolution," p. 666.

62. Ibid., p. 665.

63. Ibid.

64. Ratner and Cole, "The Force of Law," p. 738.

65. Ibid., p. 743. This seems to be a case in point of Thomas Franck's observation that "To whatever extent the President has made an effort to comply with aspects of the War Powers Resolution, he has also taken care to disabuse Congress of any notion that he was carrying out a legal obligation." See Franck, "After the Fall," p. 621.

66. Ratner and Cole, "The Force of Law," p. 747.

67. Vance, "Striking the Balance," p. 89.

68. Ellen C. Collier, *The War Powers Resolution: A Decade of Experience*, Congressional Research Service, Report No. 84–22 F, February 6, 1984, CRS–29.

69. *Time* 130, no. 1, July 6, 1987, p. 38.

70. In a particularly biting analysis, Timothy Noah, *Newsweek's* congressional correspondent, argues that "the consultation requirement has given Congress frequent opportunity, in times of crisis, to complain that the orderly process of government has been subverted." *The New Republic* 197, no. 1, July 6, 1987, p. 11.

71. Allan Ides, "Congress, Constitutional Responsibility and the War Power," 17 *Loy. L. A. L. Rev.* 627 (1984).

72. Clement J. Zablocki, "War Powers Resolution: Its Past Record and Future Promise," 17 *Loy. L. A. L. Rev.* 597 (1984).

73. Silber, "Presidential Handcuffs," p. 15.

74. Ibid.

75. Turner, *The War Powers Resolution*, p. 110.

76. Ibid., p. 111.

77. Ibid., p. 129.

78. Ibid., p. 131.

79. 119 *Cong. Rec.* 24532 (1973).

80. Holsti and Rosenau, *American Leadership in World Affairs*, p. 113.

81. Hans J. Morgenthau, *Politics Among Nations*, 5th ed. rev. (New York: Knopf, 1978), p. 87.

82. Ibid., p. 85.

83. Vance, "Striking the Balance," p. 90.

84. Zablocki, "War Powers Resolution," p. 598.

85. Glennon, "The War Powers Resolution," p. 665.

86. In developing this argument, Vance was quite persuasive in recalling from his own experience how much the decision-making process was enhanced by the addition of "experienced outsiders who owed no special deference to the President." See Vance, "Striking the Balance," p. 91.

87. Ibid., p. 92.

88. Ibid.

89. The originator of this recommendation suggests consultation "at least 24 hours prior to any decision to commit forces" under the circumstances called for in S4 (a) (1). See Franck, "After the Fall," p. 639.

90. Vance, "Striking the Balance," p. 93.

91. Noah, *The New Republic*.

92. Ides, "Congress," p. 640.

93. To Representative Zablocki, passage of the Lebanon War Powers Resolution was a vindication of the act's ability to constrain executive action. See Zablocki, "War Power Resolution," p. 595. However, to a critical scholar, the Lebanon Resolution was not only a weak compromise, but also one that established the unfortunate precedent of compelling Congress to act affirmatively to trigger the Resolution. Wrote Glennon: "As a result of Representative Zablocki's efforts to 'invoke' the War Powers Resolution, a measure that was intended to be self-invoking, Congress now found itself, upon the invasion of Grenada, precisely where it would have been in the absence of the Resolution: attempting to enact a statutory time limitation" (Glennon, "The War Powers Resolution," p. 669).

94. Glennon, "The War Powers Resolution," pp. 664, 665.

95. *War Powers Resolution: Hearings on a Review of the Operation and Effectiveness of the War Powers Resolution before the Committee on Foreign Relations, United States Senate*, 95th Cong., 1st Sess. pp. 4–5 (1977). Statement of Thomas F. Eagleton, United States Senate, Missouri.

96. Ibid., p. 4.

97. Eagleton, *War and Presidential Power*, pp. 202, 203.

98. Ibid., p. 203.

99. 119 *Cong. Rec.* 33555–33556 (1973).

100. Ibid., 33556.

101. Ibid., 33557.

102. Ibid.

103. Eagleton's amendment in 1977 was along these strong lines—to restore the original Senate version. *Hearings*, 95th Cong., 1st Sess., p. 2.

104. Franck, "After the Fall," p. 639.

105. Ibid., p. 640.

106. Ibid.

107. Franck (ibid., p. 641) expressed optimism that presidents would abide by what he termed as a "general understanding" on the proper allocation of war powers between the branches.

108. Ratner and Cole, "The Force of Law," p. 715.

109. Ibid., p. 744.

110. Ratner and Cole, "The Force of Law," p. 759.

111. 558 F. Supp. 893 (D.D.C. 1982), 720 F.2d 1355 (D.C. Cir. 1983).

112. Ratner and Cole, "The Force of Law," p. 763.

113. Ibid., p. 764.

114. Ibid., p. 757.

115. Ibid., p. 765.

116. Michael J. Glennon, "The War Powers Resolution Ten Years Later: More Politics than Law," 78 *A.J.I.L.* 579 (1984).

117. Ibid., p. 580.

118. Ibid.

Discussant: Harold H. Koh

It's a pleasure to join this panel and especially to return to Hofstra, where my father taught political science almost two decades ago. While sitting where my father once sat and listening to our two main papers, I was reminded of a famous saying by one of our greatest living American philosophers, a man much revered in these parts, the legendary Lawrence "Yogi" Berra. During his career, Yogi issued many famous "Berra-isms"—for example, "ya can't think and hit at the same time" and "it's tough to be in two places at once, especially without a car." But as I considered Professors Briggs' and Firestone's accounts of the birth of the War Powers Resolution in 1973 in light of recent headlines, I kept thinking of what may have been Yogi's most famous pronouncement, namely, "It's *déjà vu* all over again."

The papers we have just heard remind us that the debate over the war powers—in traveling from the Tonkin Gulf in August 1964 to the Persian Gulf in November 1987—has essentially come full circle. As Professor Briggs recounted, twenty-three years ago, American ships conducting covert operations in the Tonkin Gulf were attacked. They responded, allegedly in self-defense, which led President Johnson to ask Congress for a joint resolution of support (the Tonkin Gulf Resolution), which enabled him to escalate the Vietnam War. That foreign policy disaster led in 1973 to the passage over President Nixon's veto of the War Powers Resolution, which imposed consultation and reporting requirements and a sixty-day time limit on the president's ability to commit troops overseas without express congressional authorization.

Well, fourteen years later, it's *déjà vu* all over again. This time, we have ships in the Persian Gulf, convoying reflagged Kuwaiti tankers. To head off an Iranian attack on our ships, which would almost certainly lead the president to ask Congress for another joint resolution of support, the Senate has passed the Byrd-Warner Resolution, a bill that would impose a sixty-day reporting require-ment on the president and that contemplates a future resolution that may impose a time limit on the president's ability to commit troops overseas without express congressional authorization. In other words, fourteen years after the War Powers Resolution was first passed, Congress is considering reenacting a variant of it in order to *enforce* the War Powers Resolution.

To me, the fact that fourteen years of debate have brought us from the Tonkin Gulf only as far as the Persian Gulf strongly suggests that the War Powers Resolution has failed Congress as a device to check presidential warmaking. Professor Briggs has summarized the history of the Resolution, and what its sponsors hoped to accomplish. Professor Firestone has described some of the subsequent practice under the Resolution and the debate over its constitutionality. But what I missed in both of their papers was a broader, institutional explanation of *why* the War Powers Resolution has failed to accomplish its intended goals.

In the time available, let me suggest an answer to that question by identifying four problems that have undercut the effectiveness of the War Powers Resolution. For the sake of convenience, let me call these the problem of the last war, the legislative drafting problem, the judicial abstention problem, and the problem of political will.

THE PROBLEM OF THE LAST WAR

First, as so often happens, Congress drafted the War Powers Act to stop the last war. Before the Korean War, Americans knew only overt declared wars of the kind that we fought in World War II, where visible military forces openly engaged in identifiable patterns of attack and counterattack. But as the two papers remind us, Vietnam introduced us to a new type of war: the overt but undeclared, creeping war—an escalating conflict that starts and builds before anyone is fully aware. And it was precisely to stop this kind of creeping war—to ensure no more Vietnams—that Congress passed the War Powers Resolution in the first place.

But what Congress did not address in 1973 were two new types of military action that have come to dominate the 1980s. The first are short-term U.S. military strikes whose duration can be measured in days or hours rather than weeks—whether retaliatory strikes, like the U.S. attack last month on the Iranian oil platforms in the Persian Gulf, or acts in anticipatory self-defense, like the U.S. bombing raid on Qaddafi's headquarters last April, or humanitarian rescue attempts, like President Ford's rescue of the *Mayaguez*, President Carter's unsuccessful attempt to rescue the American hostages in Iran, or what President Reagan claimed was the rationale for sending U.S. troops to Grenada. In short, the War Powers Resolution's time limits—which were designed to stop the president from introducing armed forces into hostilities for more than sixty days—have had no effect on short-term military actions. To the contrary, those time limits have acted as a de facto blank check for the president to take such short-term actions, as long as he consults in advance with a few key congressmen and sends some kind of report to the Hill within two days.

The second, new type of warfare which the 93rd Congress did not anticipate was the covert undeclared war, where paramilitary activities are conducted against foreign governments, not by U.S. "armed forces," who are expressly subject to the War Powers Resolution, but by nonmilitary intelligence operatives, or private armies acting under CIA supervision and comprised of people like Eugene Hasenfus. Although Senator Eagleton tried to amend the War Powers Resolution to reach such cases, his efforts failed. Instead, Congress chose to regulate this kind of activity not under the War Powers Resolution, but under the intelligence oversight laws, which, as the Iran/Contra affair has recently revealed, the executive branch has been able to bend or circumvent all too easily. Whether the War Powers Resolution has been overtaken by events, or whether it has actually channeled executive action toward these new, unregulated forms of warfare, the point should be clear: the act's provisions simply were not designed to address the kind of warfare that dominates this day and age.

THE LEGISLATIVE DRAFTING PROBLEM

A second reason why the War Powers Resolution has failed—one that law professors love to point out—is that it was poorly drafted in the first place. Professor Firestone's paper mentions some of these drafting loopholes, but let me quickly highlight three. First, section 3's consultation requirements are weak, requiring the president to consult ''in every possible instance,'' but then allowing the president to decide what that term means. Second, the Resolution requires the president to consult ''Congress'' before he sends troops abroad, but it does not specify how many congressmen must be consulted or how far in advance. In the Libyan case, for example, that consultation did not occur until the planes were already in the air. Third and most glaring, only one of the three types of presidential report permitted by the act, a so-called hostilities report under section 4(a)(1), expressly triggers the Resolution's automatic sixty-day clock. This means that the president can report to Congress that he has committed troops abroad without also accepting the obligation to remove those troops in sixty days.

We can debate exactly why these drafting errors occurred. Perhaps the best explanation is that some of these procedural provisions were substantially watered down in conference in a futile effort to avoid a presidential veto. But what should be clear is that their net effect has been to make the War Powers Resolution *nonself-executing*. Rather than putting the pressure where it should be—on the president to start thinking about removing armed forces sixty days after he has committed them to a hostile situation—the War Powers Resolution has instead put pressure on *Congress* to declare that U.S. forces are in fact ''in hostilities'' just to start the sixty-day clock running. The ironic result is that, even though Congress designed the War Powers Resolution to stop the last war—creeping wars like Vietnam—in recent years, the Resolution's drafting flaws have destroyed its effectiveness in preventing creeping escalation of precisely this type in both Lebanon and the Persian Gulf.

THE JUDICIAL ABSTENTION PROBLEM

A third, and often overlooked, reason why the War Powers Resolution has failed is that its story has been a tale of not just of two branches—the president and Congress—but of three. The president has ''gotten away'' with apparent violations of the Resolution in part because the courts have either refused to hear challenges to his conduct—citing doctrines such as congressional standing, the political question doctrine, lack of a private right of action, equitable discretion, ripeness, and mootness—or because the courts have heard those challenges and have ruled for the president on the merits.

Let me cite just two examples. In the 1983 case of *Crockett v. Reagan*, some congressman sought a declaratory judgment that the president should remove U.S. armed forces from El Salvador because the War Powers Resolution's sixty-day cutoff provision had been triggered. The District Court held, and the Court of Appeals affirmed, that the question of whether the War Powers Resolution required the president to submit a report was a political question that a court could not decide. By contrast, in the legislative veto case, the 1983 decision in *Immigration and Naturalization Service v. Chadha*, the Supreme Court rejected Congress's claim that the president's challenge to the constitutionality of the legislative veto raised a political question. The Court then went on to strike down the legislative veto, by implication invalidating the legislative veto provision [section 5(c)] in the War Powers Resolution, one of the only provisions of the act that has any real teeth.

I should note that both issues—the justiciability and the constitutionality of the War Powers Resolution—are currently before the U.S. District Court for the District of Columbia in *Lowry v. Reagan*, a suit brought against the president's Persian Gulf policy by more than 111 congressmen. But notice that if the president wins on either of these issues—if the courts either refuse to hear this challenge or hear the challenge and rule in the president's favor—the president's Persian Gulf policy can continue. So in a real sense, the courts have been not just a bystander, but an accomplice in the president's continuing domination of the warmaking power.

THE PROBLEM OF POLITICAL WILL

If drafting errors have rendered the War Powers Resolution nonself-enforcing, and if the courts have refused to enforce it, the final question becomes why hasn't Congress enforced it on the president directly? This raises the fourth and last problem: Congress cannot enforce the War Powers Resolution directly on the president, without an extraordinary exercise of political will. The Supreme Court's decision striking down the legislative veto denies any legal effect to simple or concurrent resolutions—that is, resolutions passed by one or both houses of Congress but not presented to the president for his signature or veto. This means that Congress has only two options if it wants directly to challenge a president's actions—either to disapprove the president's action by joint resolution or to cut off appropriations for a particular foreign campaign—but in either case, it must be prepared to override the president's veto by a two-thirds vote.

Why hasn't Congress been able to muster this political will? There are three reasons: first, if Congress must muster a two-thirds vote in both houses, it takes only thirty-four senators to stop Congress from enforcing the War Powers Resolution, and it is a crippled president indeed who cannot muster at least thirty-four votes for something he really wants. Even in his current weakened state, for example, President Reagan was able to get forty-two votes for the confirmation of Judge Bork, and he has been consistently able to secure the forty-one votes necessary to sustain filibusters against a variety of recent resolutions that have sought to trigger the War Powers Resolution. Second, individual congresspersons have all too often confused procedure with substance and applauded rather than challenged the president when he has violated the War Powers Act's procedural terms in pursuit of substantive policies that they favor (as happened, for example, with the Grenada invasion or the recent U.S. air strikes on Libya and the Iranian oil platforms). Third and finally, even when Congress has forced the president to the bargaining table on war powers issues, as it did over Lebanon in 1984, the president has been able to negotiate for joint resolutions that extend the War Powers Resolution's time deadlines well beyond sixty days (in the case of Lebanon, eighteen months) without ever articulating what precise policy our military presence is designed to further.

POLICY PRESCRIPTIONS

Given these four diagnoses, how should Congress redraft the War Powers Resolution so that it can play its intended checking function? Let me suggest that each of the first three problems I've identified suggests its own solution. The problem of the last war suggests that Congress should redraft the Resolution expressly to address short-term military strikes and covert undeclared wars. As my retired colleague Charles Black once pointed out, it is a peculiar War Powers Act that defines how many months U.S. troops may stay abroad, but says nothing about the only question that really matters: namely, under what circumstances does Congress believe that the president should not commit troops abroad for even ten minutes? The drafting problem suggests that Congress should tighten currently vague provisions in the act to include more detailed definitions of the terms *armed forces, hostilities, consult, Congress,* and *in every possible instance.* To alleviate the judicial abstention problem, Congress may wish to amend the Resolution to insert a congressional standing provision of the type it placed in the Gramm-Rudman budget-balancing bill, which Congressman Michael L. Synar invoked to bring his successful challenge to that legislation, a statutory cause of action to challenge violations of the Resolution, or a sense-of-Congress resolution that violations of the act are justiciable.

Let me close by saying that the fourth and last problem, that of political will, is far less susceptible to solution by legal tinkering. To solve this problem, let me suggest that Congress heed the advice of another famous, but more mysterious, American philosopher who has been mentioned elsewhere during this conference, in connection not with Vietnam, but with Watergate: namely, the informant "Deep Throat," from Bob Woodward and Carl Bernstein's book and the movie, *All the President's Men*. If you recall, in the movie there is a scene where Bob Woodward meets Deep Throat in an underground parking garage and begs him for a lead—any lead—that will give him a break in his Watergate investigation. And Deep Throat, standing in the shadows smoking, tells Woodward, "Follow the money, follow the money."

So how can Congress reassert its authority over warmaking after fourteen years of failure? In a nutshell, "follow the money." Whether in the Tonkin Gulf or the Persian Gulf, presidential warmaking costs money. We all recognize that under the appropriations clause of the Constitution, it is Congress, not the president, who holds the power of the purse. Following the example of the 1970 Cooper-Church Amendment, the 1973 Eagleton Amendment regarding Cambodia and Laos, the 1983 Cranston-Eagleton-Stennis amendments to the War Powers Resolution, and, more recently, the Boland Amendment and Senator Nunn's amendments to the Department of Defense Authorization Act related to presidential ABM Reinterpretation, Congress could now amend the War Powers Resolution to declare that "no funds made available under any law may be obligated or expended for any presidential use of force not authorized by Congress under an amended War Powers Resolution." In conclusion, let me suggest that only by "following the money," and tying its future authorizations of warmaking to spending and appropriations, can Congress hope effectively to exercise its political will to stop "*déjà vu* from happening all over again."

Thank you.

Discussant: Burt Neuborne

Thank you. I, too, am very pleased to be back at Hofstra again. I spent a delightful summer in 1959 here studying economics and political science. As Harold Koh knows, it is impossible for anybody to mention Yogi Berra in my presence without precipitating another attempt at a story. The eminent philosopher encapsulated the problem that we are going to be dealing with today quite well at his retirement party. When he was leaving active service, somebody asked him how baseball could be improved. Yogi thought for a while and said, ''One of the ways that baseball could be improved is by getting rid of all those close plays at first base by moving the base a foot further from homeplate.'' It may well be, that all the drafting and all the activity that attempt to deal with the reality of executive warmaking in the modern world will simply finally come down to moving first base around a lot, but the problems just don't go away.

I found the papers today quite helpful. Both share understandable tendencies to view the war powers issue, or War Powers Resolution, as a political issue, an isolated political issue of allocating specific power to perform a particular function between the two political branches. Let me take a crack at attempting to place the war power issue in a slightly broader context, in the general context of separation of powers that underlies the structure of American government. The bicentennial year is not a bad time to go back to basics in our system and to remember that the fragmentation of power that is inherent in separation of powers is probably the greatest protection we have. The people who drafted the Constitution thought that we could do without a Bill of Rights. They didn't think we could do without the safeguard the separation of powers brings to the system. When you are thinking about separation of powers, it's almost necessary to take a trip back to seventh grade civics because we seem to forget so often about the extraordinary and majestic simplicity of the Founders' initial wisdom. Governmental power is divisible into three kinds of power. Now at the margins, they blend into each other, and it is not always easy to say which is what. But, at the core, governmental power is divisible into three different kinds of power— the enunication of new rules, the enforcement of existing rules, and the resolution and disputes about applying rules to facts. If you think about it for a moment, that is exactly the structure they set up:

- Article I, the Congress, the legislature, with the power to make rules, with the power to enunciate law.
- Article II, the executive branch, with the power to carry out laws that are in effect and to enforce them.
- Article III, the judiciary branch, with the power to resolve disputes about the application of laws to specific facts.

There are at least three different theories about the allocation of power within that structure. Let's take a look at them for a moment. The war power, for example, is a very neat, and I think interesting, example of how the Founders placed that very simple notion into the context of reality. There was debate at the convention about what to do about the war powers. The compromise that arose was the compromise that arose in virtually every other area of the convention as well. The legislative branch was given the power to make the rules to create the new state of affairs to declare the war. The executive branch was given the responsibility of carrying out the affairs of making the war, of executing the decisions of the legislative branch.

One of the great problems that we see in the twentieth century is the degree to which we departed from that very simple structure. One of the dramatic questions we have to ask ourselves is whether, as part of the price of living in a terribly complicated twentieth-century world, we will have to throw that structure overboard. What we see slowly evolving is the erosion of the congressional power to have much of the say at all, in what goes on in the use of military force, in the context of U.S. foreign policy. Instead, the power both to enunciate the policy and to carry it out is now de facto vested in the executive. The fear concerns the possible merger of those two powers, which we have tried so hard to keep apart almost everywhere else in our structure. Only rarely in the American governmental structure, do we find the power to make the rules, and the power to enforce them, vested in the same structure. The reason is that placing those two powers in the same institution would be a fundamental violation of the principle of the separation of powers. One of the checking functions of the separation of powers is to attempt to force the division of the responsibility.

Now, there are two theories on which responsibility can be divided: (1) you can divide it functionally, or (2) you can divide it prophylactically. Functionally, we try to rate the various powers of government to the agency that will do it best. It is an efficiency mechanism, and when you think about how the government is structured, there is an obvious functional, comparative advantage to do certain things. If you are laying down new ground rules for society, you want those ground rules to reflect consensus and compromise. You want a large representative body to be the body that enunciates those new rules. That is why Congress is given that responsibility: it is functionally superior in terms of enunciating the democratic will. When you want somebody to carry out those rules, however, you want someone who can act quickly and vigorously. That is why you give the power to the executive branch headed by a single actor capable of quick decisive action. When you want somebody to resolve disputes about those issues, you give the power to an insulated branch like the courts which are capable of reflective and unbiased activity. Functional separation of powers would call for these various governmental responsibilities to be given to the organ that does it best.

Then, there is a second theory that goes right along with it: the prophylactic separation of powers or negative separation of powers. Negative separation of powers says that you never let two of the three powers get into the same hands. You never allow the power to make the law get into the hands of the same people who have the power to carry it out. You never let the power to resolve disputes get into the hands of the people who are supposed to be carrying it out.

Well, obviously, there could be a war between functional separation and prophylactic separation. Occasionally, a functional design will allocate power among the branches in a way that creates risks for a prophylactic standpoint. That is exactly what we have seen over the years with the use of military force, as an aspect of foreign policy. We have seen a very powerful argument that says that the president needs a functional plan with a capacity both to make foreign policy and to carry it out through military action without inteference from anyone. He has to act quickly, decisively, and without the inefficiencies of democratic control, but that has led to precisely the kind of problems that Professor Koh has described to you: the merger within the same political branch within the executive, of the power to make the rules, and the power to carry them out, which is a flat violation of the traditional notions of prophylactic separation of powers. The huge risk in our society, at present is that the executive branch can embroil us in a war without the input of the democratic branches, which are given the traditional power to decide when the status quo should be changed. The War Powers Resolution was an attempt to cut the gordian knot. It was an attempt at a compromise, and as all the speakers have pointed out today, it was a very sloppy compromise. It was a compromise that was forged in the midst of powerful, political passions; it was forged with one eye on the Vietnam War in a set of hastily put-together drafting sessions, which only too painfully, fourteen years later, show the difficulty of drafting resolutions on the fly. The theory of the War Powers Resolution is an attempt to say, "Look, we know in a modern world a president has to have some flexibility." We want to give the president a substantial amount of capability, of muscle behind American foreign policy. No one, not even the radical critique, wants to freeze American foreign policy in a mold where it won't be credible. So, the need for some flexibility is recognized, but at the same time there has to be some check on the president; no president should be able to do whatever he wants.

The War Powers Resolution was an attempt to find a middle ground, and the middle ground was the following position: Look, Mr. President, tell us when you do it, if you're going to be committing troops in a situation in which hostilities are a reasonable likelihood; tell us that you are doing it, and then if it is genuinely a situation in which military hostilities are a likelihood, you have sixty days in order to explain to us and assemble the materials that we need to persuade us as a nation that your policy is correct. We then ask if the people will support it. You can even have an extra thirty days, if you insist.

So you have given the president ninety days to persuade Congress that the commitment of troops is a good idea under circumstances in which there will be imminent hostility. Many argue that that goes too far in giving the president power; Professor Koh has also pointed out that it doesn't deal with covert activities. Nor does it deal with short-term wars. But it does, at least, deal with Korea, with Vietnam, and with the extended military conflicts that drain this country both emotionally and physically. It is an attempt to assure that a democratic consensus will lie behind any executive adventure that risks large-scale loss of American lives. That's the core of the bill; it's not an attempt to paralyze the president. If the president needs to get in and out somewhere very quickly, the bill permits it. What the bill prevents is what took place in Vietnam. The Gulf of Tonkin Resolution was a lie. It was tricked out of an unsuspecting Congress by a series of, at best, misleading assertions by the executive. It was then used as a blank check for thousands and thousands of lives to be lost, based on a single flimsy piece of evidence, which itself was repealed in 1970.

When we return to the functional aspects, again let us remember that the War Powers Resolution attempts not only to solve the prophylactic situation by assuring that some power is kept in Congress to check executive adventure, but also to provide an enormous functional advantage. It is inconceivable why the current administration has refused to use the War Powers Act to assemble a genuine democratic consensus on policy in the Persian Gulf. If the president goes to Congress and explains why it is necessary to have those troops there, Congress will authorize it, and then we will have a policy that has the full support of the American people, instead of risking the exact same divisions that so weakened us in Vietnam. If we, as a people, are going to conduct military adventures, let them be united military adventures that have the support of the democratic strength of the nation. The War Powers Resolution, imperfect as it is, is an attempt to enforce that. It is a tragedy that the Resolution is not being enforced; it is a tragedy that we are not learning from the mistakes of the Johnson and the Nixon era to use this as a mechanism for building democratic support for foreign policy.

Professor Koh listed four reasons why it is not being enforced; I will cut them down to one: the judiciary's failure to perform the separation of powers role. It is the role of the courts to enforce the War Powers Resolution. Everybody knows that the president is in violation of it; everybody knows that the law requires the president to do something in connection with the Persian Gulf policy; and the courts simply have failed to fulfill their responsibilities. Until they do so, no piece of legislation is going to be able to solve the problem. We have the solution within our grasp if only separation of powers will work as the Founders hoped that it would.

HOFSTRA CULTURAL CENTER

RICHARD NIXON

SIXTH ANNUAL
PRESIDENTIAL
CONFERENCE

A Retrospective on His Presidency

NOVEMBER 19-21, 1987

**HOFSTRA
UNIVERSITY**

HEMPSTEAD, NEW YORK 11550

332

RICHARD NIXON:

A Retrospective on His Presidency

NOVEMBER 19-21, 1987

JAMES M. SHUART	*President*
LEON FRIEDMAN	*Conference Co-Director* *Hofstra University School of Law*
WILLIAM F. LEVANTROSSER	*Conference Co-Director* *Department of Political Science*
NATALIE DATLOF	*Conference Coordinator*
ALEXEJ UGRINSKY	*Conference Coordinator*

Hofstra University Richard Nixon Conference Committee: Faculty and Administration Members

MAYER BARASH
Sociology/Anthropology
SEYMOUR BENSTOCK
Music
DAVID J. CHIU
Asian Studies
MICHAEL DE LUISE
Public Relations
MICHAEL D'INNOCENZO
History
ROBERT L. DOUGLAS
Law
BERNARD J. FIRESTONE
Political Science
ANDREW J. GRANT
Grant Development
JAMES E. HICKEY, JR.
Law
RONALD JANSSEN
English

IRA KAPLAN
Psychology
HAROLD A. KLEIN
Research in Development
JAMES J. KOLB
University College for
Continuing Education
ROBERT J. KUHNE
School of Business
HAROLD LAZARUS
School of Business
HARVEY LEVIN
Economics
LINDA LONGMIRE
Political Science
JOSEPH R. MACALUSO
Student Activities
THOMAS PARSONS
Computer Science

SONDRA RUBENSTEIN
Communication Arts
ROBERT E. SALFI
Computer Science
SHASHI K. SHAH
School of Business
RONALD H. SILVERMAN
Law
MARION E. PONSFORD
English
KETTY SETTON
Political Science
ROBERT SOBEL
History
LYNN TURGEON
Economics
JOHN E. ULLMANN
School of Business

Hofstra Cultural Center Richard Nixon Conference Assistants

PATRICIA BARTO
Conference Assistant
KAREN CASTRO
Conference Assistant

CONRAD DAVIES
Graduate Assistant
ABDUL MACAN MARKAR
Graduate Assistant
DIANE PATERSON
Conference Assistant

MICHAEL QUATTRUCCI
Conference Assistant
TARA STAHMAN
Conference Assistant

Hofstra University Richard Nixon Conference Committee: Student Members

TAMMY ALBERT
CAROL ANGRISANI
PAMELA ANTHONY
ANGELA SUE BELLUCCI
LANE BORON
DARREN BOSIK
FELICIA BROWN

SAMIR P. BULSARA
MARIA CASTRO
CAROLYN CHIARELLA
LAWRENCE D'AMICO
SANDRA DONNELLY
LISA DUCKETT
SANDRA DUBE

ANITA ELLIS
ELIZABETH ENCK
STACY FELLMAN
ALAN FISHKIN
DAVID FOX
JONATHON FURR
JENNIFER FUSCO

(continued)

DIRECTORS' MESSAGE

Perhaps no other political figure has occupied such a prominent position on the American political scene for so long a period as Richard Nixon has in the post-World War II era. Perhaps no other person in politics has demonstrated such perseverance and durability as the former president. More significantly, no other political figure has generated such strong public reactions, both positive and negative, as President Nixon. There has rarely been a period in American history in which the people have felt so intimately involved as participants in the political events of the time and identified themselves as closely either in favor of or against a President. Americans still have retained those identifications and allegiances. The events of the Nixon administration are not distant historical episodes to most Americans but personal occurrences.

The major events of the Nixon Presidency continue to generate controversy. To this day, intense debates and disputes are sparked by discussions of Watergate, the impeachment proceedings, the nominations of Haynesworth and Carswell, the impoundment of appropriated funds, the War Powers Act, the invasion of Cambodia and the ending of the Vietnam War, and the Middle East crisis and the oil embargo. Less controversial subjects but of equal or greater historical importance to the Nixon Presidency would include the opening to China, the establishment of revenue sharing, the beginnings of detente, the passage of the basic environmental protection laws, welfare reform proposals, and such important initiatives as going off the gold standard and instituting wage and price controls.

Hofstra's Sixth Annual Presidential Conference follows in the tradition of our prior conferences in assembling a group of former government officials involved in the subjects under consideration as well as leading scholars and journalists. Panels have been organized to focus on the key accomplishments of the Nixon years as well as those matters which generated the greatest controversy. Participants in these events will review their experiences from the perspective of the thirteen years since the Nixon administration ended. We have attempted to provide a variety of viewpoints so that whatever preliminary judgments are made will reflect a balanced array of evidence.

We urge you to visit the Richard Nixon Presidential Conference Exhibition in the David Filderman Gallery on the 9th floor of the Joan and Donald E. Axinn Library. The Exhibition includes memorabilia on loan from the National Archives and a large selection of books on President Nixon. Many are from the private collection of Paulette and Robert J. Greene of Rockville Centre, New York. They have graciously donated their collection to Hofstra University. Mr. and Mrs. F. Jarvis Page of Garden City, New York have lent campaign material to the Exhibition and have donated Nixon campaign posters to the University as well. The Exhibition has been arranged by the staff of the David Filderman Gallery of the library.

A program of this magnitude does not materialize without substantial assistance, and many thanks are due to those who have helped make this conference possible. A special thanks goes to the scholars who submitted papers and to the notables who agreed to participate in the various conference forums. Thanks also to the Hofstra Faculty Committee who read and helped to choose papers for the conference.

We are especially grateful to Frank G. Zarb, the Chairman of the Hofstra University Board of Trustees, who was an active participant in the planning and organization of the proceedings and whose good sense played a key role in the development of the program. We are also thankful to James Hastings and his staff at the National Archives who was very helpful in supplying information and material.

Finally, our sincere thanks are extended to members of the Hofstra community with whom we have worked so closely over the last several months: Mike DeLuise, Jim Merritt, Wendy Vahey, Marge Regan, Anne Rubino, M.F. Klerk, Donna Testa, Harold A. Klein and the Hofstra Cultural Center student assistants, a group of extraordinarily talented, resourceful and hard-working young men and women, all students here at Hofstra University. They include: Patricia Barto, Karen Castro, Conrad Davies, Abdul Macan Makar, Diane Paterson, Michael Quattrucci and Tara Stahman. A special word of thanks is extended to the Cultural Center's staff, Athelene A. Collins, Marilyn Seidman, Jessica Richter and Laura Tringone, whose dedication to the daily tasks contributed to the overall success of the conference.

The Hofstra Cultural Center's co-directors, Natalie Datlof and Alexej Ugrinsky, have worked tirelessly to build on the legacy of the late Professor Joseph G. Astman, who founded the Center eleven years ago, and this conference is a tribute to their efforts, as well as to those of the staff that serves them and the University so well.

We welcome our guests and we hope our three days together will be enjoyable, intellectually rewarding and historically significant.

Leon Friedman
Conference Co-Director
Hofstra University School of Law

William F. Levantrosser
Conference Co-Director
Department of Political Science

Thursday, November 19, 1987

8:00 a.m. - 8:00 p.m.	Registration Multi-Purpose Room, North Campus

9:30 a.m. **John Cranford Adams** **Playhouse, South Campus**	Opening Ceremonies
Greetings	***James M. Shuart,*** President Hofstra University
	Frank G. Zarb, Chair Hofstra University Board of Trustees
Introductions	***William F. Levantrosser*** Conference Co-Director Department of Political Science
	Leon Friedman Conference Co-Director Hofstra University School of Law
Addresses	PERSPECTIVES ON RICHARD NIXON
	Elliot L. Richardson Milbank, Tweed, Hadley & McCloy Washington, DC
	Hugh Sidey Contributing Editor Time Magazine Washington, DC
	Stephen E. Ambrose Alumni Distinguished Professor of History University of New Orleans

For Conference Exhibit Schedules see page 25
For Dining Facilities see page 27

11:00 a.m.	CONCURRENT PANELS
Panel Ia **Student Center Theater** **North Campus**	REORGANIZATION OF THE EXECUTIVE BRANCH

Moderator: *James P. Pfiffner*
Department of Public Affairs
George Mason University

"The Implementation of Cabinet Government During the
Nixon Administration"
Shirley Anne Warshaw
Department of Political Science
Gettysburg College

"The Nixon Administration and the Federal Bureaucracy in Retrospect"
Bert A. Rockman
Department of Political Science
Research Professor, University Center for International Studies
University of Pittsburgh
and
Joel D. Aberbach
Department of Political Science
Director, Program for the Study of American Institutions, Politics, and Policy
Institute for Social Science Research
University of California—Los Angeles

Discussants: *Roy L. Ash*
Los Angeles, CA

H. R. Haldeman
Santa Barbara, CA

Arnold A. Saltzman
Chairman
Vista Resources, Inc.
New York, NY

Panel Ib
John Cranford Adams
Playhouse, South Campus

SOCIAL WELFARE POLICIES

Moderator: *James E. Hickey, Jr.*
Hofstra University School of Law

"Outflanking the Liberals on Welfare"
Joan Hoff-Wilson
Department of History
Indiana University
Executive Secretary
Organization of American Historians

"Legislative Success and Failure: Social Welfare Policy of the
Nixon Administration"
Carl Lieberman
Department of Political Science
University of Akron

(continued)

Panel Ib
John Cranford Adams
Playhouse, South Campus

SOCIAL WELFARE POLICIES   (continued)

Discussants: ***John Ehrlichman***
Santa Fe, NM

Robert H. Finch
Fleming, Anderson, McClung & Finch
Pasadena, CA

Elliot L. Richardson
Milbank, Tweed, Hadley & McCloy
Washington, DC

Panel Ic
Dining Rooms ABC
North Campus

ENVIRONMENTAL POLICY

Moderator: ***William R. Ginsberg***
Rivkin, Radler, Dunne & Bayh
Distinguished Professor of Environmental Law
Hofstra University School of Law

"The Nixon Environmental Record: A Mixed Picture"
Charles Warren
Berle, Kass & Case
New York, NY

Discussants: ***Barry Commoner***
Center for Biology of Natural Systems
Queens College–CUNY
Scientific Advisor to the New York State Legislative Commission
on Science and Technology

David Sive
Sive, Paget & Riesel
New York, NY
Board Member, National Resources
Defense Council (NRDC)

John C. Whitaker
Vice President of Public Affairs
Union Camp Corporation
Washington, DC

12:45 p.m.

Lunch–See page 27 for Dining Facilities

2:00 p.m.

Plenary Session
John Cranford Adams
Playhouse, South Campus

THE OPENING TO CHINA

Introduction: *Frank G. Zarb*, Chair
Hofstra Universty Board of Trustees

Address: *The Honorable Han Xu*
Ambassador of the People's Republic of China in the United States

Moderator: *Robert C. Vogt*, Dean
Hofstra College of Liberal Arts and Sciences

"The Asian Balance and Sino-American Rapprochement
During the Nixon Administration"
Robert G. Sutter
Senior Specialist
Congressional Research Service
Library of Congress
Washington, DC

Discussants: *Jerome A. Cohen*
Paul, Weiss, Rifkind, Wharton & Garrison
New York, NY

Kenneth Lieberthal
Director
Center for Chinese Studies
University of Michigan—Ann Arbor

C.L. Sulzberger
Author and Former Journalist
Paris, France
Author of
The World and Richard Nixon, (1987)

4:00 p.m.

CONCURRENT PANELS

Panel IIa
Student Center Theater
North Campus

THE FOREIGN POLICY PROCESS

Moderator: *Bernard J. Firestone*
Department of Political Science
Hofstra University

"The Nixon Doctrine as History and Portent"
Earl C. Ravenal
Distinguished Research Professor of International Affairs
School of Foreign Service
Georgetown University

"Richard Nixon as Diplomat-in-Chief"
Elmer Plischke
Professor Emeritus, University of Maryland
Adjunct Scholar, American Enterprise Institute for Public Policy Research

(continued)

Panel IIa   THE FOREIGN POLICY PROCESS (continued)

Student Center Theater   "Continuities and Contradictions in the Nixon Foreign Policy"
North Campus   ***Kenneth W. Thompson***
                                Director, White Burkett Miller Center of Public Affairs
                                University of Virginia

                                Discussants: ***Lloyd S. Etheredge***
                                                Director, Graduate Studies
                                                International Relations Program
                                                Yale University

                                                Roger Morris
                                                Sant Fe, NM

                                                C. L. Sulzberger
                                                Author and Former Journalist
                                                Paris, France
                                                Author of
                                                The World and Richard Nixon, (1987)

Panel IIb   POLITICS AND THE GOVERNMENTAL PROCESS
John Cranford Adams
Playhouse, South Campus   Moderator: ***Monroe H. Freedman***
                                            Hofstra University School of Law

                                "Information, Dissent and Political Power:
                                The Paradoxes of the Nixon Administration"
                                Alan F. Westin
                                Department of Political Science
                                Columbia University

                                "Richard Nixon and the Politicization of Justice"
                                Michael A. Genovese
                                Department of Political Science
                                Loyola Marymount University
                                Los Angeles, CA

                                Discussants: ***Charles W. Colson***
                                                Chairman of the Board
                                                Prison Fellowship Ministries
                                                Washington, DC

                                                Egil Krogh
                                                Culp, Dwyer, Guterson & Grader
                                                Seattle, WA

                                                John Shattuck
                                                Vice President, Government, Community and
                                                Public Affairs, Harvard University
                                                Lecturer, Harvard Law School

6:00 - 7:30 p.m.   Dinner–See page 27 for Dining Facilities

8:00 p.m.
Plenary Session

Presiding

James M. Shuart, President
Hofstra University

Moderator:

Sanford Hammer
Provost & Dean of Faculties
Hofstra University

Introduction

The Honorable Han Xu
Ambassador of the People's Republic of China to the United States

Address

Henry A. Kissinger

Henry Alfred Kissinger was sworn in on September 22, 1973, as the 56th Secretary of State, a position he held until January 20, 1977. He also served as Assistant to the President for National Security Affairs from January 20, 1969, until November 3, 1975.

At present Dr. Kissinger is Chairman of Kissinger Associates, Inc., an international consulting firm. Dr. Kissinger is also a member of the President's Foreign Intelligence Advisory Board, a Counselor to the Chase Manhattan Bank and a member of its International Advisory Committee, a member of the Commission on Integrated Long-Term Strategy of the National Security Council and Defense Department, and an Honorary Governor of the Foreign Policy Association.

Among the awards Dr. Kissinger has received have been the Nobel Peace Prize in 1973; the Presidential Medal of Freedom, this nation's highest civilian award, in 1977; and the Medal of Liberty in 1986.

Henry A. Kissinger received the B.A. degree summa cum laude at Harvard College in 1950, and the M.A. and Ph.D. degrees at Harvard University in 1952 and 1954.

8:00 a.m. - 5:00 p.m.	**Registration** **Multi-Purpose Room, North Campus**

9:00 a.m.   CONCURRENT PANELS

Panel IIIa   DEFENSE POLICY AND MILITARY MANPOWER
Student Center Theater
North Campus   Moderator: *Morris Honick*
                                   Chief, Historical Section
                                   Command Historian
                                   Supreme Headquarters Allied
                                   Powers Europe, (SHAPE)
                                   Brussels, Belgium

                   "Defense Policy During the Nixon Administration"
                   Lawrence J. Korb
                   Dean, Graduate School of Public and International Affairs
                   University of Pittsburgh
                   Adjunct Scholar, American Enterprise Institute for Public Policy Research

                   "The Making of the All-Volunteer Armed Force"
                   Martin Anderson
                   Senior Fellow
                   The Hoover Institution
                   Stanford University

                   Discussants: *Martin Binkin*
                                     Senior Fellow
                                   Foreign Policy Studies
                                   The Brookings Institution

                                   Adam Yarmolinsky
                                   Provost and Vice Chancellor for Academic Affairs
                                   University of Maryland, Baltimore County

Panel IIIb   ECONOMIC AND MONETARY POLICY
Dining Rooms ABC
North Campus   Moderator: *Lynn Turgeon*
                                     Department of Economics
                                     Hofstra University

                   "Market Integration Policies During the Nixon Presidency"
                   M. Mark Amen
                   International Studies
                   University of South Florida/Tampa

(continued)

Panel IIIb
Dining Rooms ABC
North Campus

ECONOMIC AND MONETARY POLICY (continued)

"President Nixon's Political Business Cycle"
Ann Mari May
Department of Economics
University of Nebraska–Lincoln
and
Robert R. Keller
Chair, Department of Economics
Colorado State University

"Nixon's Economic Policy Toward Minorities"
Maurice H. Stans
Pasadena, CA

Discussants: *Robert Lekachman*
Distinguished Professor of Economics
Lehman College and
The Graduate Center/CUNY

Herbert Stein
Senior Fellow
American Enterprise Institute for
Public Policy Research

Forum IIIc
John Cranford Adams
Playhouse, South Campus

THE PROTEST MOVEMENT

Moderator: *Ronald H. Silverman*
Peter S. Kalikow Distinguished Professor of Real Estate Law
Hofstra University School of Law

Discussants: *Sam W. Brown, Jr.*
Centennial Partners, Ltd.
Denver, CO

David Dellinger
Peacham, VT

David J. Garrow
Department of Political Science
The City College/CUNY

Sanford Gottlieb
Senior Analyst
Center for Defense Information

Tom Hayden
California State Assemblyman
Santa Monica, CA

Egil Krogh
Culp, Dwyer, Guterson & Grader
Seattle, WA

High School Colloquium
9:00-10:30 a.m.
See page 24

10:45 a.m. - 12:15 p.m.   CONCURRENT PANELS

Panel IVa   WATERGATE RE-EXAMINED
John Cranford Adams
Playhouse, South Campus   Moderator: ***John DeWitt Gregory***
          Vice Dean and Sidney and Walter Siben
          Distinguished Professor of Family Law
          Hofstra University School of Law

"Watergate and the Nixon Presidency: A Comparative Ideological Analysis"
David R. Simon
Department of Criminal Justice Administration and Sociology
San Diego State University—Calexico

"Nixon's Dismissal of Special Prosecutor Cox:
The Constitutionality and Legality of an Exercise of
Presidential Removal Power"
Nancy Kassop
Department of Political Science
State University of New York/College at New Paltz

Discussants: ***Stanley I. Kutler***
          E. Gordon Fox Professor of American Institutions
          University of Wisconsin—Madison

          J. Anthony Lukas
          New York, NY

          Rev. Jeb Stuart Magruder
          Executive Minister
          First Community Church
          Columbus, OH

          Earl J. Silbert
          Schwalb, Donnenfeld, Bray & Silbert
          Washington, DC

Panel IVb   THE MIDDLE EAST AND ENERGY POLICY
Student Center Theater
North Campus   Moderator: ***Sondra Rubenstein***
          Department of Communication Arts
          Hofstra University

"Oil and/or the Olive Branch: The Nixon Administration's
Choices in Its Middle East Policies"
Gideon Doron
Visiting Professor of Political Science
New York University and
Tel Aviv University
Ramat Aviv, Israel

Discussants: ***Alfred L. Atherton***
          Harkness Fellowships
          of the Commonwealth Fund
          Washington, DC

(continued)

Panel IVb
Student Center Theater
North Campus

THE MIDDLE EAST AND ENERGY POLICY (continued)

Hermann Frederick Eilts
Director, Center for International Relations
Boston University

Jo-Ann Hart
Department of Political Science
Brown University

Dale R. Tahtinen
Director, International Program
Cray Research
Washington, DC

12:30 - 1:15 p.m.   Lunch: See page 27 for Dining Facilities

1:15 - 2:30 p.m.

Plenary Session
John Cranford Adams
Playhouse, South Campus

NIXON BIOGRAPHERS

Moderator: Louis W. Koenig
Professor Emeritus
New York University and
Visiting Distinguished Professor
Long Island University/C.W. Post Center

Discussants: *Stephen E. Ambrose*
Alumni Distinguished Professor of History
University of New Orleans
Author of
Nixon: The Education of a Politician, (1987)

Roger Morris
Sante Fe, NM
Author of
Richard Milhous Nixon: To the
Threshold of Power, 1913-1960, (Summer 1988)

Herbert S. Parmet
Distinguished Professor of History
Queensborough Community College and
The Graduate Center/CUNY
Author of
The Age of Nixon, (1988/1989)

Raymond K. Price, Jr.
President
The Economic Club of New York
New York, NY
Author of
With Nixon, (1977)

345

2:45 p.m.   CONCURRENT PANELS

Panel Va   THE WAR POWERS RESOLUTION
John Cranford Adams
Playhouse, South Campus   Moderator: *Linda Longmire*
                                              Teaching Fellow, New College
                                              Hofstra University

                                   "Nixon versus the Congress: The War Powers Act, 1973"
                                   Philip J. Briggs
                                   Department of Political Science
                                   East Stroudsburg University

                                   "The War Powers Resolution: An Intersection of Law and Politics"
                                   Nathan N. Firestone
                                   Department of Political Science
                                   Point Park College

                                   Discussants: *Harold H. Koh*
                                                Yale Law Schol

                                                Burt Neuborne
                                                New York University School of Law

                                                General Brent Scowcroft, USA (Ret.)
                                                Kissinger Associates
                                                Washington, DC

                                                Stephen J. Solarz
                                                Member, U.S. House of Representatives
                                                New York

Panel Vb   THE NEW FEDERALISM AND REVENUE SHARING
Dining Rooms ABC
North Campus   Moderator: *Andrew J. Grant*
                                              Director, Grants Development
                                              Hofstra University

                                   "Nixon's General Revenue-Sharing and American Federalism"
                                   David Caputo, Dean
                                   School of Humanities, Social Sciences and Education
                                   Purdue University

(continued)

Panel Vb
Dining Rooms ABC
North Campus

THE NEW FEDERALISM AND REVENUE SHARING (continued)

Discussants: *John Ehrlichman*
Santa Fe, NM

Richard P. Nathan
Professor of Public and International Affairs
Woodrow Wilson School of Public and International Affairs
Princeton University

Paul H. O'Neill
Director
Chairman of the Board and
Chief Executive Officer
ALCOA
Pittsburgh, PA

Forum Vc
Student Center Theater
North Campus

THE SILENT MAJORITY: SUPPORT FOR THE PRESIDENT

Moderator: *Eric J. Schmertz*
Dean and Edward F. Carlough
Distinguished Professor of Labor Law
Hofstra University School of Law

Discussants: *Henry C. Cashen II*
Dickstein, Shapiro & Morin
Washington, DC

Charles W. Colson
Chairman of the Board
Prison Fellowship Ministries
Washington, DC

Col. John A. Dramesi U.S.A.F. (Ret.)
Blackwood, NJ

Donald F. Rodgers
Special Coordinator for Seniors
Office of the Secretary of Labor
Washington, DC

Philip K. Straw
Honors Program
University of Maryland/College Park

4:15 p.m.	CONCURRENT PANELS

Panel VIa
John Cranford Adams
Playhouse, South Campus

DETENTE AND THE SOVIET UNION

Moderator: ***Frederic A. Bergerson***
Department of Political Science
Whittier College

"The Rise and Stall of Detente, 1969-1974"
Robert D. Schulzinger
Department of History
University of Colorado

Discussants: ***The Honorable Aleksandr M. Belonogov***
Permanent Representative of the USSR to the United Nations

Dimitri Simes
Senior Associate and Director
Project on U.S.-Soviet Relations
Carnegie Endowment for International Peace

Hedrick Smith
Washington Correspondent
The New York Times

Helmut Sonnenfeldt
Guest Scholar
The Brookings Institution

Panel VIb
Student Center Theater
North Campus

ELECTION CAMPAIGNING

Moderator ***Michael D'Innocenzo***
Department of History
Hofstra University

"Campaign Finance and the Nixon Presidency: End of an Era"
Joel M. Gora
Brooklyn Law School

"Richard Nixon: The Southern Strategy and the 1968 Presidential Election"
Glen Moore
Department of History
Auburn University

Discussants: ***David M. Dorsen***
Sachs, Greenebaum & Tayler
Washington, DC

Thomas W. Evans
Mudge, Rose, Guthrie, Alexander & Ferdon
New York, NY

John Herbers
The Council of the Humanities
Princeton University

John Kessel
Department of Political Science
Ohio State University

Maurice H. Stans
Pasadena, CA

7:00 p.m.	Joan and Donald E. Axinn Library, South Campus
Exhibits	***Richard Nixon*** Book, Manuscript, Photograph and Memorabilia Exhibit David Filderman Gallery, Ninth Floor
	Mother and Child: The Art of Henry Moore Art Exhibit Hofstra Cultural Center, Tenth Floor
	Reception
8:00 p.m.	RICHARD NIXON PRESIDENTIAL CONFERENCE BANQUET
	Dining Room, Student Center, North Campus
Presiding	***James M. Shuart*** President Hofstra University
Introductions	***Leon Friedman*** Conference Co-Director Hofstra University School of Law
	William F. Levantrosser Conference Co-Director Department of Political Science
Introduction of Banquet Speaker	***James M. Shuart***
Banquet Address	***Tom Wicker*** Political Columnist, "In the Nation," *The New York Times* New York, NY

8:00 a.m. - 2:00 p.m.	Registration Multi-Purpose Room, North Campus
8:00 a.m.	Complimentary Continental Breakfast Multi-Purpose Room, North Campus

9:00 a.m. CONCURRENT PANELS

Panel VIIa THE ENDING OF THE VIETNAM WAR
John Cranford Adams
Playhouse, South Campus

Moderator: **Richard Sobel**
  Department of Political Science
  University of Connecticut

"Military and Political Considerations Leading to the End of the Vietnam War"
William M. Hammond
Historian
U.S. Army Center of Military History
Washington, DC

"Secret Commitments in President Nixon's Foreign Policy: The National
Security Council and Nixon's Letters to South Vietnam's
President Nguyen Van Thieu"
Nguyen Tien Hung
Department of Economics
Howard University
and
Jerrold L. Schecter
Chairman
Schecter Communications Corp.
Washington, DC

Discussants: **Frances FitzGerald**
  New York, NY

  Guenter Lewy
  Washington, DC

  Robert Miller
  Vice President
  National Defense University
  Washington, DC

Panel VIIb
Dining Rooms ABC
North Campus

SEPARATION OF POWERS: ISSUES AND PROBLEMS

Moderator: ***Linda K. Champlin***
Maurice A. Deane Distinguished
Professor of Constitutional Law
Hofstra University School of Law

"United States v. Nixon Re-Examined: The Supreme Court's
Self-Imposed 'Duty' to Come to Judgment on the Question of
Presidential Confidentiality"
Howard Ball
Dean and Professor of Political Science
College of Social and Behavioral Science
University of Utah

Discussants: ***Robert L. Keuch***
Executive Director & General Counsel
Judicial Inquiry and Review Board
Commonwealth of Pennsylvania
Harrisburg, PA

Arthur Kinoy
Rutgers University School of Law
Newark, NJ

Phillip Lacovara
Hughes, Hubbard & Reed
Washington, DC

Panel VIIc
Student Center Theater
North Campus

APPOINTMENTS TO THE SUPREME COURT

Moderator: ***Bernard E. Jacob***
Hofstra University School of Law

"The Supreme Court Under Siege: The Battle over Nixon's Nominees"
Joseph Calluori
Michael Kennedy, P.C.
New York, NY

Discussants: ***Birch Bayh***
Rivkin, Radler, Dunne & Bayh
Washington, DC

John P. MacKenzie
The New York Times
New York, NY

James McClellan
President
Center for Judicial Studies
Cumberland, VA

11:00 a.m. - 1:00 p.m.   CONCURRENT PANELS

Panel VIIIa   IMPEACHMENT PROCEEDINGS
John Cranford Adams
Playhouse, South Campus   Moderator: *Leon Friedman*
                                                     Hofstra University School of Law

                                          "The Nixon Impeachment and Abuse of Presidential Power"
                                          Dagmar S. Hamilton
                                          Associate Dean, Lyndon B. Johnson
                                          School of Public Affairs
                                          University of Texas — Austin

                                          "Normal Legislative Coalitions and Impeachment"
                                          Terry Sullivan
                                          Department of Government
                                          University of Texas—Austin

                                          Discussants: *John Doar*
                                                       New York, NY

                                                       Elizabeth Holtzman
                                                       District Attorney—Kings County
                                                       Brooklyn, NY

                                                       Judge Charles E. Wiggins
                                                       United States Court of Appeals
                                                       Ninth Circuit
                                                       Reno, NV

Panel VIIIb   CIVIL RIGHTS POLICY
Student Center Theater
North Campus   Moderator: *John E. Stergis*
                                                     President
                                                     Student Government Association
                                                     Hofstra University

                                          "Richard M. Nixon, Southern Strategies and Desegregation of Public Schools"
                                          Al L. King
                                          Austin, TX

                                          "The Incoherence of the Civil Rights Policy in the Nixon Administration"
                                          Hugh D. Graham
                                          Department of History
                                          University of Maryland—Baltimore County

                                          Discussants: *Robert H. Finch*
                                                       Fleming, Anderson, McClung & Finch
                                                       Pasadena, CA

                                                       Sallyanne F. Payton
                                                       University of Michigan School of Law
                                                       Anne Arbor, MI

                                                       Roger Wilkins
                                                       Senior Fellow
                                                       Institute for Policy Studies and
                                                       Robinson Professor of History
                                                       George Mason University

Panel VIIIc
Dining Rooms ABC
North Campus

RESEARCHING THE NIXON PRESIDENCY:
DOCUMENTS AND EVIDENCE

Moderator: *Joseph Dmobowski*
Librarian
Whittier College

"Status of the Nixon Presidential Materials"
James J. Hastings
Acting Director
Nixon Presidential Materials Project
National Archives and Records Administration
Washington, DC

Discussants: *Joan Hoff-Wilson*
Department of History
Indiana University
Executive Secretary
Oganization of American Historians

Harry P. Jeffrey
Department of History
Director, Richard Nixon Oral History Project
California State University—Fullerton

Harry J. Middleton
Director
Lyndon B. Johnson Library
Austin, TX

Mark Weiss
Visiting Professor
Doctoral Program in Speech and Hearing Sciences
The Graduate Center/CUNY

1:00 - 2:00 p.m.   Lunch—See page 27 for Dining Facilities

2:00 p.m.

Plenary Session
John Cranford Adams
Playhouse, South Campus

SECRECY, THE GOVERNMENT AND THE MEDIA

Moderator: *Victor Navasky*
Editor
The Nation
New York, NY

"Secrecy and Democracy: The Unresolved Legacy of the Pentagon Papers"
John Kincaid
Director of Research
Advisory Commission on Intergovernmental Relations
Washington, DC

"President Nixon's Conception of Executive Privilege: Defining the
Scope and Limits of Governmental Secrecy"
Mark J. Rozell
Department of Political Science
Mary Washington College

Discussants: *Tom Brokaw*
NBC News
New York, NY

Howard Simons
Curator, Nieman Fellowships Program
Harvard University

Gerald L. Warren
Editor
The San Diego Union

Ronald L. Ziegler
President
National Association of Truck Stop Operators
Alexandria, VA

4:00 p.m.

Plenary Session
John Cranford Adams
Playhouse, South Campus

THE EVOLUTION OF THE NIXON LEGACY

Moderator: *Fred I. Greenstein*
          Professor of Politics and Director
          Program in Leadership Studies
          Woodrow Wilson School of Public
          and International Affairs
          Princeton University

"Richard Nixon Reconsidered: The Conservative as Liberal?"
Barry D. Riccio
Department of History
University of Illinois at Urbana–Champaign

"Richard Nixon and the Idea of Rehabilitation"
Sherri Cavan
Department of Sociology
San Francisco State University

Discussants: *John Ehrlichman*
          Santa Fe, NM

          H.R. Haldeman
          Santa Barbara, CA

          Robert H. Finch
          Fleming, Anderson, McClung & Finch
          Pasadena, CA

          Arthur M. Schlesinger, Jr.
          Albert Schweitzer Professor of the Humanities
          The Graduate Center/CUNY

          C.L. Sulzberger
          Author and Former Journalist
          Paris, France
          Author of
          The World and Richard Nixon, (1987)

6:00 p.m.
Dining Rooms ABC
North Campus

Reception

HIGH SCHOOL COLLOQUIUM

Friday, November 20, 1987
9:00 - 10:30 a.m.—Hofstra USA

**Presiding and
Welcoming Remarks**

James M. Shuart
President, Hofstra University

Introductions

William F. Levantrosser
Conference Co-Director
Department of Political Science

Speakers

Stephen E. Ambrose
Alumni Distinguished Professor of History
University of New Orleans
Author of
Nixon: The Education of a Politician, (1987)

Robert H. Finch
Fleming, Anderson, McClung & Finch
Pasadena, CA

H. R. Haldeman
Santa Barbara, CA

Questions/Answers

High School Colloquium Committee

Mark Dion, Vice President for Student Services
David J. Obedzinski, Assistant Dean of Student Services
Edward Carp, Special Assistant for Promotions
Maria Castro, Promotion Assistant
Pam Anthony, Promotion Assistant
Michael DeLuise, Director, Public Relations

PARTICIPATING SCHOOLS

East Islip High School Islip Terrace, NY	John F. Kennedy High School Bellmore, NY	Shoreham-Wading River High School Shoreham, NY
Farmingdale High School Farmingdale, NY	Mepham High School Bellmore, NY	Smithtown High School East Saint James, NY
Harborfields High School Greenlawn, NY	Merrick Avenue Junior High School Merrick, NY	Great Neck South High School Great Neck, NY
Hauppauge High School Hauppauge, NY	North Valley Stream High School Franklin Square, NY	South Side High School Rockville Centre, NY
Holy Child High School Westbury, NY	Saint Agnes High school Rockville Centre, NY	The Wheatley School Old Westbury, NY
John Glenn High School East Northport, NY	Saint Hugh of Lincoln School Huntington Station, NY	Woodmere Academy Woodmere, NY

Index

About the Editors and Contributors

MARTIN ANDERSON is a senior fellow of the Hoover Institution at Stanford University and was previously associate professor of business at the Graduate School of Business of Columbia University. He served in the White House as a special assistant to President Nixon and as President Reagan's domestic and economic policy adviser. He is the author of *The Federal Bulldozer*, *Welfare*, *The Military Draft*, *Conscription, Registration and the Draft*, and *Revolution*.

ALFRED L. ATHERTON, a retired Foreign Service officer, served as deputy assistant secretary (1970–74) and assistant secretary of state for Near Eastern and South Asian affairs (1974–78), as ambassador-at-large for Middle East Negotiations (1978–79), and as ambassador to Egypt (1979–83). Since retiring in 1985, he has been a foundation program director, a visiting professor of international relations at Hamilton College and Mount Holyoke College, and a writer and speaker on Middle East topics.

ALEKSANDR M. BELONOGOV was a Russian diplomat, ambassador, and permanent representative of the former USSR to the United Nations (1986–90). In the years of the Nixon Administration, he was in charge of the U.S.-USSR relations in the Policy Planning Department of the USSR Ministry of Foreign Affairs, helping in preparations for Soviet-American summits. He is the author and co-author of a number of publications on Soviet-American relations and U.S. foreign policy-making.

MARTIN BINKIN is a senior fellow in the Foreign Policy Studies program at the Brookings Institution and formerly taught at the American University and the United States Naval Academy. He has written extensively about defense manpower issues, including *America's Volunteer Military: Progress and Prospects*.

PHILIP J. BRIGGS is professor and chairperson of the Department of Political Science at East Stroudsburg University in Pennsylvania. He has lectured widely on U.S. foreign policy formulation before civic and academic audiences and is executive director of the Research Committee on Armed Forces and the Society of the International Political Science Association. He is the author of *Making American Foreign Policy: President-Congress Relations from the Second World War to Vietnam*.

JEROME A. COHEN is a law professor at New York University and counsel to the law firm of Paul, Weiss, Rifkind, Wharton & Garrison. He previously was a member of the faculty at Harvard Law School and the University of California (Berkeley). He is the author of many books and articles on Chinese law.

GIDEON DORON is an associate professor and chairman of both the Political Science Department and the Public Policy Graduate Programme at Tel-Aviv University. He previously held appointments at the University of Rochester, New York University, SUNY-Binghamton, and other American and Israeli universities. His research efforts have concentrated in the area of political-economy, public policy, politics in the Middle East and Israel, electoral behavior, and intelligence. He is the author of *The Smoking Paradox, To Decide and to Implement, Games in Israeli Politics* and many other books and articles.

HERMANN FREDERICK EILTS is distinguished university professor of international relations and chairman of the Department of International Relations at Boston University. He was previously U.S. ambassador to Saudi Arabia and later to Egypt.

LLOYD S. ETHEREDGE is visiting professor of political science at the University of Toronto and, formerly, was a member of the faculty at MIT, Yale, and the University of California at Berkeley and other institutions. He has written extensively about the effects of personality on foreign policy and the processes of learning in international politics. His books include *A World of Men: The Private Sources of American Foreign Policy* and *Can Governments Learn? American Foreign Policy and Central American Revolutions*.

NATHAN N. FIRESTONE is professor of government and international studies at Point Park College in Pittsburgh, Pennsylvania. He also teaches at the University of Pittsburgh. He is a member of the Pennsylvania Bar and has been a practicing attorney.

FRANCES FITZGERALD is the author of *Fire in the Lake: The Vietnamese and the Americans in Vietnam*. She spent a total of two years in Vietnam during the war reporting for *The Atlantic, The New Yorker*, and other publications. She has written two other books, including, *America Revised*, on the reinterpretation of American history in U.S. school textbooks. She is a frequent contributor to *The New Yorker* magazine.

LEON FRIEDMAN is the Joseph Kushner Professor of Civil Liberties Law at the Hofstra University Law School. He is the author or editor of many books on politics and law including *The Justices of the United States Supreme Court, 1789–1990*. As an ACLU lawyer, he handled a number of law suits against members of the Nixon Administration.

WILLIAM M. HAMMOND is a senior historian with the United States Army's Center of Military History in Washington, D.C. He has lectured and published widely on the subject of the military and the news media and is the author of a well-known two-volume history of military relations with the press during the Vietnam War. The first of those volumes, covering 1962–68, was published in 1989; the second, examining the years 1968–73, is in publication.

JO-ANNE HART is assistant professor of political science and research associate at the Center for Foreign Policy Development at Brown University. Her area of expertise is American policy in the Middle East. She is the author of a forth-coming case study on the war against Iraq and has published several articles on international relations of the Middle East.

NGUYEN TIEN HUNG is a professor of economics at Howard University. He served as special assistant to President Nguyen Van Thieu and also as a cabinet minister during the last years of the Republic of South Vietnam. Just before the fall of Saigon he was sent to Washington to seek additional U.S. help, taking with him copies of the letters from Nixon and Ford to Thieu that are included in his book *The Palace File* (1986). Professor Hung has written articles for the *Washington Post*, the *New York Times*, the *International Herald Tribune*, and several professional journals, and he is the author of *The Economic Development of Socialist Vietnam, 1955–1980* and *Agriculture and Rural Development in the Congo*.

HENRY A. KISSINGER served as Secretary of State and National Security adviser in the Nixon Administration. Among his awards has been the Nobel Peace Prize (1973), the Presidential Medal of Freedom (1977), and the Medal of Liberty (1986). At present, Dr. Kissinger is chairman of Kissinger Associates, Inc., an international consulting firm.

HAROLD H. KOH is a professor at Yale Law School where he teaches international law and the Constitution and foreign affairs. Before coming to Yale, he practiced law in Washington, D.C., in private practice and at the Department of Justice. Professor Koh has written numerous articles on international, foreign relations, and constitutional law and is the author of *The National Security Constitution: Sharing Power after the Iran-Contra Affair* (1990).

LAWRENCE J. KORB is director of the Center for Public Policy Education and senior fellow in the Foreign Policy Studies Program at the Brookings Institution. He received his M.A. from St. John's University and his Ph.D. from the State University of New York at Albany. He is the author of over one hundred books, monographs, and articles on national security issues. His most recent book is *The 1990 Defense Budget* (with William W. Kaufman) (1989).

WILLIAM F. LEVANTROSSER is professor emeritus of Political Science at Hofstra University. He is the author of *Congress and the Citizen-Soldier* and editor of *Harry S. Truman: The Man from Independence* (Greenwood Press, 1986). Levantrosser has also published numerous articles on national security issues, including "Tonkin Gulf Revisited," in *Lyndon Baines Johnson and the Uses of Power*, edited by Bernard J. Firestone and Robert C. Vogt (Greenwood Press, 1988).

GUENTER LEWY is professor emeritus at the University of Massachusetts at Amherst. He is the author of *America in Vietnam* and has published many other books and articles.

ROBERT H. MILLER is a retired Foreign Service officer and formerly served as ambassador to Malaysia and to Côte d'Ivoire, and as vice president of the National Defense University in Washington. He is the author of *The United States and Vietnam, 1787–1941*, and of several articles on Vietnam and Southeast Asia.

ROGER MORRIS is the author of *Richard Milhous Nixon: The Rise of an American Politician* (1990), winner of the Silver Medal of the National Book Award. A former senior member of the National Security Council Staff under both Presidents Johnson and Nixon, he teaches political science at the University of New Mexico. He also hosts a public affairs program on PBS and lectures on American politics and history.

BURT NEUBORNE is professor of law at the New York University School of Law and was educated at Cornell University and Harvard Law School. His published works include *Political and Civil Rights in the United States*, vols. 1 (1976) and 2 (1979) (co-author), and numerous chapters and articles on constitutional law.

ELMER PLISCHKE is professor emeritus at the University of Maryland (College Park). He has published twenty-eight books and monographs and dozens of articles in professional and literary journals, largely in the field of foreign relations, including *Conduct of American Diplomacy*, and *Foreign Relations: Analysis of Its Anatomy*.

EARL C. RAVENAL is distinguished research professor of international affairs at the Georgetown University School of Foreign Service. He is a former official in the Office of the Secretary of Defense and has been a fellow of the Cato Institute and the Woodrow Wilson International Center for Scholars. He is author of eleven books on foreign and military policy and over 170 articles and papers.

JERROLD L. SCHECTER is an independent author and journalist. He was diplomatic editor of *Time* magazine and covered Kissinger's negotiations with North Vietnam in the 1970s. He served as associate White House press secretary and spokesman for the National Security Council (1977–80). He is co-author, with Nguyen Tien Hung, of *The Palace File* (1986).

ROBERT D. SCHULZINGER is professor of history at the University of Colorado, Boulder. He is a specialist in recent U.S. foreign relations and politics. His most recent books include *Henry Kissinger: Doctor of Diplomacy* and *Present Tense: The United States since 1945*.

HEDRICK SMITH is a fellow and editor in residence at the Foreign Policy Institute of Johns Hopkins University in Washington, D.C. As a correspondent for the *New York Times*, he won a Pulitzer Prize. He is the author of several major books on Russia and American politics. He is well known as a television commentator on "Washington Week in Review" and is the creator of major public television documentaries.

HELMUT SONNENFELDT is a guest scholar at the Brookings Institution in Washington, D.C. He served as counselor of the Department of State from 1974 to 1977. He has published articles on various foreign policy matters in *Foreign Affairs*, *Washington Quarterly*, the *NATO Review*, and several newspapers and other publications.

ROBERT G. SUTTER is chief of the Foreign Affairs and National Defense Division and a senior specialist in International Policy with the Congressional Research Service. He received a Ph.D. in history and East Asian languages from Harvard University. He teaches regularly at Washington area universities and has published several books and articles dealing with contemporary China and Japan.

DALE R. TAHTINEN is vice president for governmental relations and secretary to the Board of Control, Michigan Technological University in Houghton. He was educated at the University of Maryland, receiving his doctoral degree in 1974. He has published over twenty-five books and major articles on international economic issues and national security.

KENNETH W. THOMPSON is J. Wilson Newman professor of government and foreign affairs at the University of Virginia. He was formerly a member of the faculties of the University of Chicago, Columbia University, and the University of California at Berkeley. He is the author of twenty books, including *Political Realism and the Crisis of World Politics* and *Churchill's Worldview*.

HAN XU served as Chinese ambassador to the United States and is at present president of the Chinese People's Association for Friendship with Foreign Countries (CPAFFC).

ADAM YARMOLINSKY is provost and vice president for academic affairs at the University of Maryland in Baltimore County. He served in the Kennedy, Johnson and Carter administrations in the Pentagon, the White House, and the Arms Control and Disarmament Agency. His publications include *The Military Establishment, Paradoxes of Power*, and *Race and Schooling in the City*.

Hofstra University's
Cultural and Intercultural Studies
Coordinating Editor, Alexej Ugrinsky

José Ortega y Gasset: Proceedings of the *Espectador universal* International
Interdisciplinary Conference
(Editor: Nora de Marval-McNair)

George Orwell
(Editors: Courtney T. Wemyss and Alexej Ugrinsky)

John F. Kennedy: The Promise Revisited
(Editors: Paul Harper and Joann P. Krieg)

Lyndon Baines Johnson and the Uses of Power
(Editors: Bernard J. Firestone and Robert C. Vogt)

Eighteenth-Century Women and the Arts
(Editors: Frederick M. Keener and Susan E. Lorsch)

Suburbia Re-examined
(Editor: Barbara M. Kelly)

James Joyce and His Contemporaries
(Editors: Diana A. Ben-Merre and Maureen Murphy)

The World of George Sand
(Editors: Natalie Datlof, Jeanne Fuchs, and David A. Powell)

Richard M. Nixon: Politician, President, Administrator
(Editors: Leon Friedman and William F. Levantrosser)

Watergate and Afterward: The Legacy of Richard M. Nixon
Editors: Leon Friedman and William F. Levantrosser)

Immigration and Ethnicity: American Society—"Melting Pot" or "Salad Bowl"?
(Editors: Michael D'Innocenzo and Josef P. Sirefman)

Johann Sebastian: A Tercentenary Celebration
(Editor: Seymour L. Benstock)